55 stanford alley
Brannan + Townsend
near 2nd

Frieght Door

to George Lithograph

Pieces to Patty Flynn -
↓

Marji Herron

11:00 Tues

# THE SIERRA CLUB
# ADVENTURE TRAVEL GUIDES

SUSANNA MARGOLIS

# ADVENTURING IN THE PACIFIC

*The Sierra Club Travel Guide to the Islands of Polynesia, Melanesia, and Micronesia*

Sierra Club Books • San Francisco

*For Jan Tiura, who, with Joe, captained
my first Pacific voyage, in gratitude and in friendship*

The Sierra Club, founded in 1892 by John Muir, has devoted itself to the study and protection of the earth's scenic and ecological resources—mountains, wetlands, woodlands, wild shores and rivers, deserts and plains. The publishing program of the Sierra Club offers books to the public as a nonprofit educational service in the hope that they may enlarge the public's understanding of the Club's basic concerns. The point of view expressed in each book, however, does not necessarily represent that of the Club. The Sierra Club has some sixty chapters coast to coast, in Canada, Hawaii, and Alaska. For information about how you may participate in its programs to preserve wilderness and the quality of life, please address inquiries to Sierra Club, 730 Polk Street, San Francisco, CA 94109.

**Library of Congress Cataloging-in-Publication Data**

Margolis, Susanna.
    Adventuring in the Pacific.

    Bibliography: p.
    Includes index.
    1. Oceania—Description and travel—1981-
Guide-books. I. Title.
DU15.M37    1988      919´.04        87-23558
ISBN 0-87156-780-6 (pbk.)

Production by **Eileen Max**

Cover design by **Bonnie Smetts**

Book design by **Drake Jordan**

Illustrations by **Hilda Chen**

Printed in the United States of America

10 9 8 7 6 5 4 3 2 1

# CONTENTS

# ACKNOWLEDGMENTS

In travel around the Pacific totaling many, many months, visiting scores of islands, logging perhaps a hundred thousand kilometers in planes and boats, and who knows how many more on foot, the author received help from hundreds of people. Many remain nameless, but many others who offered assistance, advice, information, or companionship must be acknowledged—a poor form of thanks, but just about all an author can give.

First and unquestionably foremost, I am grateful to Jim Cohee, senior editor of Sierra Club Books and progenitor of this book—and of the adventures I was able to enjoy in researching it.

Particular thanks are also due to those people in the travel industry who struggled with schedules of Byzantine complexity, with demanding itineraries, and with the vagaries of on-again, off-again Pacific carriers to get me where I wanted to go: Carole Phillips of New York's Certified Travel Consultants, a tenacious expert; the cool and exceedingly competent Flora Tschong of Air New Zealand in Papeete; the cheerily unflappable Denise Hubble of Qantas' Auckland office; Air Niugini's Sylvia Seccombe in Sydney; Kathy Harvey in Saipan. It does seem that the world's travel industry has a special pipeline into a reservoir of extremely intelligent, terrifically effective, unfailingly delightful women employees.

To those officials, hotelkeepers, contract workers, traveling salesmen, pilots, boat skippers, beachcombers, and companions of the route who smoothed the way, told stories, drank beer with me, and often became my friends, I offer my thanks and my affection—island by island:

In French Polynesia, I am grateful to OPATTI's Manuel Terai, to Pierre Florentin, Edouard Malakai, Susan Viets, Elaine and Greg Claytor of the Hotel Oa Oa, Jean and Glorine Toi, and Henriette Richmond.

My thanks to Chris Wong of the Cook Islands Tourist Authority, to Conservation Officer Teariki Rongo, and to Dora Harrington of the Rapae Cottage Motel on Aitutaki.

In Tonga, I owe special debts to the inimitable Patricia Ledyard Matheson, the indomitable Seletute Falevai, Christiane Schlottman, and to Gail Evenari and the crew of the *Hokule'a*.

In Western Samoa, I am grateful to Kalati Poai for the time he spent and the knowledge and spirit he imparted, to Lui A. J. Bell for his expertise and his insight, and to the extraordinary Vaasili Tevaga Moelagi Jackson for being Moelagi. Special thanks to Ruth Robinson, now of New York, for her reminiscences about her childhood home.

My thanks in American Samoa to Minnie Mann and Kalilimoku Hunt of the Office of Tourism and to Bob Blauvelt, TV engineer, guide, sharer of music.

To Malakai B. Gucake and Allyson Ah Tong of the Fiji Visitors Bureau, I offer my thanks. I am also grateful to Mike Eng of the U.S. Peace Corps, to Inder Singh, my above-ground guide, and to John Anthony, my superb underwater guide—as well as to Denis Beckmann and all the guys at Sea Sports Ltd.

In New Caledonia, I am grateful to Othis Maanoi, "Titice," and to the gentlemen of La Rotonde, and in Vanuatu, I owe thanks to the staff of the Nautilus Dive Shop.

In the Solomon Islands, I am grateful to Duane Beard, Carol Kimble, and all the Peace Corps volunteers who were my *wantok*; to Phillip Wanga of the Guadalcanal Travel Service; and to Dorothy Prince, manager of the wonderful Aruligo bookshop.

For help and companionship in Papua New Guinea, that most extraordinary country, I owe extraordinary thanks to Emmanuel Balamus in Sydney and to David Choulai of Pacific Expeditions in Moresby.

My thanks to Dirk Ballendorf of the Micronesian Area Research Center and to Bob Rogers of the Guam Commission on Self-Determination, met in Palau but based in Guam, and to Kevin Rogers, for his hospitality.

In the Northern Marianas, I am grateful to Kent Harvey as well as to Kathy, to Eddie Cabrera of SPIA, to Masahiko Tsuchimoto, Cisco Uludong, and America's last high commissioner, Janet McCoy.

Thanks in Palau to Ed Rampell of New York, and in the Federated States of Micronesia, thanks to John Buchun and James Lakan, two very thoughtful tourism officials, to Silvester Alfonso, to all the crew of the Ghost Fleet Dive Shop, and to Jonathan Polisar, "One-Eyed Jack," expert arranger.

Finally, in the Marshall Islands, my thanks to Rick Bush of the Community Action Agency, to government minister Tony DeBrum, and to Howard Graves of the Associated Press for an illuminating and enjoyable conversation one slow and lazy Sunday morning.

New York, 1987

# Note on Names

Many island names have changed over time, as possession or ruler-ship of the island has passed from power to power, and particularly in today's climate of "returning" to native names. For the most part, these changes are described in the text—i.e., islands that had no group name in the 15th century but were later named New Hebrides on European charts are present-day Vanuatu.

"New Guinea," in the body of the book, refers to the large island which is today politically divided into Irian Jaya in the west and Papua New Guinea in the east; "New Guinea" is thus a geographical label, "Papua New Guinea" a political reality.

# THE PACIFIC ISLANDS

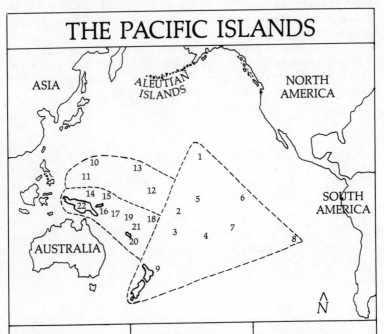

ASIA

ALEUTIAN ISLANDS

NORTH AMERICA

SOUTH AMERICA

AUSTRALIA

N

## POLYNESIA
1. Hawaiian Islands
2. Samoan Islands
   (Western Samoa &
   American Samoa)
3. Kingdom of Tonga
4. Southern Cook Islands
5. Northern Cook Islands
6. Marquesas
7. Society Islands
8. Easter Island
9. New Zealand

## MICRONESIA
10. Mariana Islands
11. Caroline Islands
12. Gilbert Islands
13. Marshall Islands

## MELANESIA
14. Admiralty Islands
15. New Ireland
16. New Britain
17. Solomon Islands
18. Fiji
19. Vanuatu
20. New Caledonia
21. Loyalty Islands
22. New Guinea

# DISCOVERING
# THE PACIFIC

Paradise is subjective. Ask half a dozen people their notion of paradise and you will get six different answers—maybe twelve. Places to be, people to be with, states of mind, the successful conclusion to a series of events, the absence of particular annoyances—all of these and more qualify as paradise to different people at different times in their lives.

One place, however, has long loomed—in the Western imagination, at least—as the ultimate paradise, universally longed for, so that you have only to say the words South Sea island and the image appears in the mind's eye: a small and very distant island set in the middle of a serene blue ocean and ringed by white-sand beaches. Palm trees stride these beaches, and their green fronds sway in the breezes made fragrant by extravagantly colored and perfumed flowers. An island lush in its interior, where clear streams and waterfalls tumble down a hillside carpeted in green, where all you have to do is reach up your arm and fruits tumble into your hand. An island whose inhabitants live in innocence and harmony—healthy, beautiful, untroubled. A place whose very existence constitutes an important message for the world, a refuge for the defeated, a haven for dreamers.

There never was and is not now such a place. Although the description holds true for many islands in the Pacific, it is not the whole truth. Not that the whole truth will destroy the hold these islands continue to have on the imagination. Travel agents confirm what psychologists have studied: almost any outbreak of dreadful world news is quickly followed by a flurry of inquiries about travel in the Pacific. There seems no end to the human need for this elusive paradise.

The image was first planted in the minds of Westerners when the men who had sailed with Wallis and Cook and Bougainville returned home to Europe with their stories of islands of exotic beauty, whose inhabitants were free of envy and greed, whose women had no notion of Western morals and engaged in love as their "chief occupation." Cook himself knew there was more to it than this. He observed a human sacrifice, studied the often rigid social structure of these islands, and well knew that the inhabitants were as capable as anyone else of hating one another and even fighting with one another.

Nevertheless, there was *something* here—perhaps a sense of freedom, or maybe just the feeling that an individual could manage life better on a small, limited island—that seemed to answer a strong yearning in Western, Christian civilization. Whatever it was the bearers of that civilization were looking for when they came to the Pacific, they almost completely destroyed it when they got here. Even that doesn't stop people coming.

## TRAVEL TO THE PACIFIC

Oceania, to use the traditional term, can claim many "lasts." It was probably the last place on earth to be occupied by humans. It was the last "discovered" by the rest of the world, although people living there were quite aware of it. It was the last place on earth that was colonized, and it is among the last to emerge into self-governing independence. It is also one of the last places to develop tourism— access to itself, facilities for those who arrive.

As a destination, the Pacific almost defeats the traveler with its vastness. Its geography is daunting. It daunted the Allied commanders in World War II, and it daunted the Americans back home who went racing to their maps to find Saipan or Truk, only to be confronted, if they could find them at all, by tiny specks floating in an enormous sea. The diversity very nearly matches the size of the place—diversity of landscape, cultures, ways of life. About the only absolute you can count on here is that every piece of land in Oceania is an island, and all the inhabitants of Oceania are islanders. Simple as that sounds, it is the key to everything. It is what makes this place and these people different from us, and it is what makes them different from one another.

Travel here often means moving a great distance to arrive on an island that can be crossed from side to side in a few steps. It can mean complex arrangements for enjoying the simplest kind of life. Contrasts abound. The climate of Oceania is unfailingly gentle— except when it suddenly turns unremittingly fierce. The physical beauty of these islands is enchanting—except where people have shown indifference to the beauty in favor of something else. The Pacific idyll isn't really Eden at all. On an island, physical limits are absolute. You have to find or create other things to get beyond those limits. The traveler will learn, if he explores it, what this has meant in the past, and what it means today.

Travel in Oceania is fun. An easygoing informality is the rule; meeting people is not only easy, it is a way of life, making this an excellent destination for solo travelers. The Pacific has long been known for the "colorful characters" it has produced or attracted. You can still find such characters. They might be among the expatriates (expats, as they are everywhere called) of every stripe who people these islands—contract workers, missionaries, aid-givers, service volunteers, entrepreneurs, beachcombers, remittance men. They might be among your fellow travelers—packaged tourists and resort holidayers, drifters backpacking their way around the world watching every penny, traveling salesmen, yachties, even conventioneers. They might, of course, be among the islanders you meet.

The sights of Oceania are certainly exotic and always interesting. Things to do here range from rugged hikes and exciting underwater dives to absolutely nothing at all, a favorite pastime that is usually carried out in the shade. Travelers who are not used to this form of recreation grow used to it; it is one of the lessons of travel in the Pacific.

# THE PACIFIC TRAVELER

In its vastness, Oceania has long been divided into three areas. Seen at various times as racial or cultural or linguistic or political descriptors, these distinctions are at best a handy way to get some grasp of the variegated hugeness of the Pacific. Polynesia, Melanesia, Micronesia—many islands, black islands, small islands. The groupings aren't exact and they may not say a lot, but they help. They provide the organizing principle of this book, which attempts to explore the particularity of each area and to guide the traveler to the best ways of experiencing it—island by island.

The book is written for a hypothetical Pacific traveler, an adventure traveler, about whom some assumptions are made. This traveler is independent and doesn't want to be packaged. He is not devoted to the idea of poverty as a virtue, but he eschews the kind of costly transnational luxury that is the same in Nome and Nairobi, except for the temperature outside. He wants to explore beyond the beaches and shops and restaurants that cater primarily to tourists, and he is willing to put some effort behind this desire. He'll spend time to plan carefully, but he won't plan for every moment of time; he'll

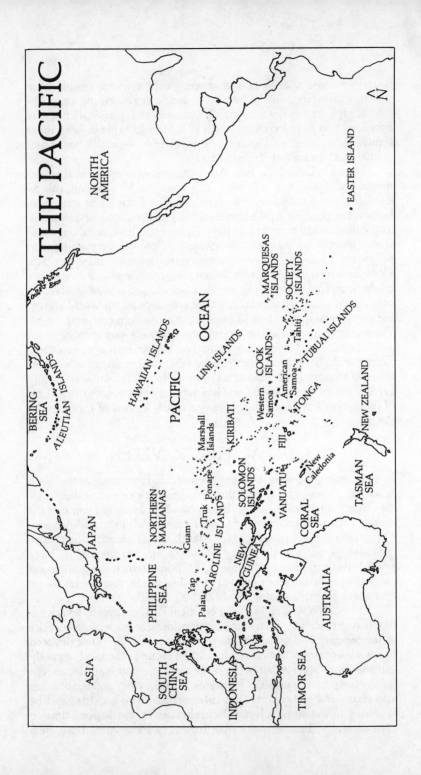

leave room for adventure to *happen*. He won't settle for the lowest common denominator of information given. He likes to venture off the beaten track.

Chances are he doesn't have unlimited time or unlimited funds, so this book is for the air traveler, and it guides him to selected islands. For each destination, the book locates the island nation, describes its makeup, terrain, and climate, introduces its flora and fauna, tells the history of its people. Once the scene has thus been set, the book suggests where and how to travel. It won't tell you the same sort of thing for every destination, because every destination is different, but in all cases, the book tries to demonstrate how the traveler can experience what is unique or irresistible about the place. The experiencing part is up to the traveler.

This hypothetical Pacific traveler follows an itinerary, a looping route around Oceania. He starts from the west coast of the U.S. and flies directly to Tahiti in French Polynesia. He then travels around Polynesia and works his way westward to Melanesia, starting at Fiji, the crossroads of Oceania. From Fiji, he swings more or less northwestward through Melanesia to the westernmost point on his route, Papua New Guinea. There, he at last turns east, island-hopping his way across Micronesia to return to the U.S. at Honolulu.

In all, he visits 15 island nations, each of which may contain numerous island groups, in which the traveler might visit any number of separate islands. In each destination, the traveler flies into a gateway island, usually the location of the island nation's capital. The gateway is to be explored, but it also serves as the traveler's resource center—for travel information and planning as well as for supplies and for solutions to the occasional problems that travelers are heir to. From here, the traveler connects to the out-islands (or outliers) beyond the gateway and explores these islands.

The route is aimed at covering at least one instance of all the major distinguishing features of Pacific travel, the features of terrain and climate and history and natural history and culture that make it the Pacific—high island, atoll, reef, bush, lagoon, ancient history, colonial history, World War II history, village, sophisticated city, culture, crafts, politics, the variety of flora and fauna you can get to know here (excluding sharks, direct acquaintance with which is not encouraged), and the diverse but universally gracious peoples of the Pacific.

Where you go and how long you travel depends, as always, on how much time and money you have to spend, as well as on your inclinations. To follow in the exact footsteps of the Pacific traveler of this book requires four to five months—minimum. Most of the expense is airfare, and the bulk of airfare expense is the international passage, although interisland travel can also be costly. Given a specific time limit and budget, you can look to this book for help in choosing where you want to travel and what you want to experience. No specific prices for facilities are given here; both the facilities and the prices tend to change—as do currency exchange rates. But Oceania offers a range of prices, and, in most places, most budgets can be accommodated. Finding the right hotel or the best restaurant is part of the work of travel—and part of the fun of the travel experience.

In the 13th century, the Persian poet Sa'di wrote: "Of journeying, the benefits are many; the freshness it brings to the heart, the seeing and hearing of marvelous things, the delight of beholding cities, the meeting of unknown friends. . . ." Substitute "islands" for "cities" and that pretty much says what travel in the Pacific is like. That alone may be about as close to paradise as you can get.

## The Pacific Traveler's Route

**Polynesia**
French Polynesia
Cook Islands
Western Samoa
American Samoa
Tonga

**Melanesia**
Fiji
New Caledonia
Vanuatu
Solomon Islands
Papua New Guinea

**Micronesia**
Guam
Northern Marianas
Palau
Federated States of Micronesia:
    Yap, Truk, Ponape
Marshall Islands

# CHAPTER 1

# SEA AND LAND

Here from this mountain shore, headland beyond
stormy headland plunging like dolphins
through the blue seasmoke
Into pale sea—look west at the hill of water: it is half
the planet: this dome, this half-globe, this bulging
Eyeball of water, arched over to Asia,
Australia and white Antarctica: those are the eyelids
that never close; this is the staring unsleeping
Eye of the earth. . . .
—Robinson Jeffers, *The Eye*, 1941

The Pacific Ocean is the largest single geographic feature on planet Earth. With a total area of 166 million square kilometers, it occupies more than one-third of the globe. North to south from the Bering Strait to Antarctica is a distance of 15,761 kilometers. East to west along the wide stretch from Mindanao in the Philippines to the Panama Canal, the Pacific measures 17,220 kilometers. If you were to take the entire land surface of the globe and set it down on the surface of the Pacific Ocean, the remaining fringe of water would equal in area the combined land masses of the U.S. and Australia.

In the north, the Pacific is very nearly landlocked; the Bering Strait leading to the Arctic Ocean is only 64 kilometers wide and in some places has a depth of less than 55 meters. The Pacific is linked to the Indian Ocean south of Tasmania and via the sea passages of New Guinea and Indonesia—the Torres Strait leading to the Arafura Sea leading to the Timor Sea and flowing west into the Indian Ocean. In the narrow Drake Passage between the Antarctic Peninsula and Cape Horn at the bottom of South America, the Pacific just barely mingles its waters with those of the Atlantic.

It's an unfair meeting. The Pacific's waters add up to about 750 cubic kilometers, twice as much as the Atlantic holds and nearly half of all the water on earth. The ocean's average depth is 4267 meters; its greatest depth, reached near Guam, is 11,033 meters, the deepest point on earth.

These waters flow in currents, affected by and more and less followed by prevailing winds. Starting from the "doldrums," the low-pressure region of intertropical convergence along the equator, the currents create circuits moving from east to west, both north of the equator as the north equatorial current and south of the equator as the south equatorial current. These broad currents, both several hundred kilometers wide, start off warm at the equator. They are pushed by the tradewinds, the southeast trades south of the equator, the northeast trades north of the equator. As the trades drive these currents further from the equator, they reach the region of high-pressure and subtropical convergences—the so-called horse latitudes at about 30 degrees north and south—where they begin to pick up cooler temperatures as the westerlies push them eastward. At the easternmost limit of the ocean basin, they again swing toward the equator, "completing" the circuit. In the process of making the circuit, the currents have brought warmer waters to cooler regions, and they return to the equator with cooler waters for the tropics.

Across this vast expanse of Pacific Ocean, in the path of its currents, washed by its tides, caressed and sometimes mauled by its winds, are more than 27,000 islands. Their range is astonishing. Some are mere clods of earth; others are thousands of kilometers square. Some are lushly vegetated and rich in resources; others are spare and inimical. Some support vital communities of flora, fauna, and humans; others—most—are home only to coconuts and land snails, if to them. In all, the islands of the Pacific compose a total land area of some 1.6 million square kilometers, scattered like afterthoughts across the wide, deep sea. Together, sea and land constitute what is virtually an aquatic continent—Oceania.

# THE GEOLOGY OF THE PACIFIC

Two hundred million years ago, all of what we today call the continents constituted a single giant landmass, Pangaea, "all the earth," that stretched from north of the equator to the south pole. About 180 million years ago, an equatorial ocean formed, cutting Pangaea into a northern portion, Laurasia, and a southern part, Gondwanaland. This ocean, the Tethys Sea, included what are today the Mediterranean, the Indian Ocean, and the western Pacific and may have extended as far to the east as present-day Central America and the Caribbean. Fifteen million years later, molten magma from the earth's interior caused a north-to-south split down Laurasia and Gondwanaland. As the continents rifted apart, the Atlantic and Indian oceans formed. The continents continued to move, eventually bordering a huge ocean delineated to the east of their movement—the Pacific.

The ocean's subsequent history is explained by plate tectonic theory, which holds that the earth's surface comprises a mosaic of constantly moving plates. Of the six major plates, only one does not contain a sizeable portion of a continent; instead, it underlies virtually all of the Pacific Ocean. This Pacific Plate is produced at the East Pacific Rise, a mound some 16 kilometers wide rising above the sea floor in a north-to-south crescent that parallels the west coast of South America. The plate "ends" where it subducts—or plunges under—various lighter-weight continental plates: the Alaskan portion of the North American Plate to the north, the Philippine and Australian plates to the west and southwest. Where the Pacific Plate has bent to begin its descent into the mantle below these continental plates, deep oceanic trenches have formed. The Pacific is thus bounded to the north by the Aleutian Trench, running west to east. The Kurile, Japan, Bonin, and Mariana trenches, all more or less north-to-south in orientation, form the ocean's northwestern and western borders. All of these trenches are some 3000 meters below the ocean floor, and they average nearly 5000 kilometers in length. To the southwest, the Pacific is bounded by the Tonga-Kermadec Trench, more than 10,000 meters deep.

The subduction that formed these trenches was not a gentle process. Heavier oceanic plate tends to resist the forced bending into the mantle below. It heaves and jumps, and the pressures this movement releases cause earthquakes that shake the crust around the trench. The lighter continental plate is jolted by these earthquakes; fractures are creased into its edge, and volcanoes form parallel to the trench. If you follow a line upward through the trenches formed by Pacific Plate subduction, you are on the Pacific Ring of Fire, a chain of volcanic activity that has formed arcs of islands along the Ring and that is still active today.

Indeed, all of this plate movement is ongoing. New crust continually erupts from the East Pacific Rise, creeps northwestward, sinking as it goes, and is subducted at the Mariana or Kurile or Aleutian Trench. Recent high-technology studies have confirmed that the crust around the East Pacific Rise is young, whereas samples collected from the ocean floor near the Aleutian Trench are roughly 150 million years old—and have traveled quite a distance since they were born. Other researches, some carried out in the submersible *Alvin*, the craft that explored the *Titanic*, have found extraordinary colonies of exotic animals along the East Pacific Rise and just west of the Mariana Trench—giant gastropods, anemones, mollusks, crabs, shrimps, and the like—animals dependent on volcanic hydrogen sulfide. These researches, delving as deep as 3600 meters, have attempted to track the little-understood eruptions going on in these areas: a tearing apart of the sea floor that causes volcanic activity and hot spring eruptions—fields of geysers populated by these strange, outsized creatures.

Northwestward is the general direction of the Pacific Plate's midocean rise; the situation in the southern Pacific is a little more complicated. Here, the Pacific Plate must do battle with the eastern edge of the Australian Plate. At the Tonga-Kermadec Trench, the Pacific Plate dives to oblivion under the Australian, but further north and west, just under the Solomon Islands, it is the Australian Plate that slides to destruction while the Pacific remains intact. At the bight where these two processes converge are numerous jostling plate fragments.

Trenches, troughs, rises, seamounts, ridges, basins, and mountain peaks: all of these lie under the surface of the Pacific, formed by collisions, slides, subsidence, and erosion—the forces that formed, and continue to form, the islands of the Pacific.

## FORMING ISLANDS AND REEFS

Assume a more or less stable environment, one untouched by the geologic upheavals or worldwide changes of climate and temperature that have in fact occurred over the past several million years. Now let us create an island.

It starts with a hole or vent in the oceanic crust, perhaps along a crack or rift. Through this vent, molten lava reaches the surface of the ocean floor. It flows quickly, easily, spreading wide before solidifying—very different from the volcanic action that creates continents—and a lot of it is required to raise a submarine volcano. But eventually, as the eruption continues, the volcano emerges above the surface of ocean. A new island has formed. (If the eruption stops before reaching the ocean surface, that is either an island-in-the-making or a submerged seamount. About 10,000 such have been identified.)

Because of the type of lava that has formed it, this volcano-island will probably have a gradual slope, although it may be a peaked slope. If the slope remains peaked, age will render it more angular. But if the magma beneath the summit cools and contracts, the peak may collapse inward to form a caldera. Whichever happens, the weight of the new island is loading a lot of tonnage on the molten layer beneath the earth's crust. Eventually, when the eruption has eased, the ocean floor supporting the island begins to settle into this molten mantle, and the island subsides.

At the same time, waves and wind are advancing against the new island, cutting off portions of its slope, which fall into the sea like so much debris. The eroded slope is now a series of cliffs, while the churning action of the waves pulverizes the fallen debris into boulders, then pebbles, then sand that waves and wind may in turn sweep to other portions of the island. Eventually, this process of erosion levels the cliffs and the top of the island, a process known as planation. (If subsidence continues to the point that the island is beyond the reach of wave action, and only the flattened top remains, that is called a guyot. Oceanographers have identified about two hundred of these submerged former islands, some as deep as 2000 meters.)

The new island blocks not only the prevailing currents, causing the eroding force of the waves, but the prevailing winds as well. The intense heating that results causes updrafts, clouds, rain. The rain cuts rivulets down the slopes as it falls to the sea; the rivulets become streams. These streams are debris-carriers down the submerged slopes of the leeward side of the island, the side toward which the wind is blowing and the side that is therefore sheltered from it; they are hurtling cascades down the cliff faces of the windward side of the island.

Gradually, the island is dissected into valleys separated by ridges. As the island's subsidence continues, bays are formed where the valleys meet the sea; most of the debris discharged down the valleys settles within the bays, and the heads of the valleys may fill in to form deltas. With the streams cutting deeper into dense lava, plants begin to grow, covering the slopes and halting further erosion. Meanwhile, in the bays where debris is trapped, coral reefs begin to appear.

That corals are animal and not plants was first put forth by the 18th-century French naturalist Peyssonnel. His theory was so thoroughly dismissed that he had to find another line of work. Today, it is understood that the diverse corals in tropical waters belong to a very ancient phylum, the coelenterates ("hollow-guts"), and that they represent an extremely successful organism, one that lives in a complex but perfect harmony of physiochemical reactions to plants and minerals.

Corals may be divided into soft corals, those that produce flexible skeletons of organic materials, and hard corals, which secrete skeletons that are mostly minerals. Of the hard corals, one category occurs in deep, dark, frigid waters and does not produce reefs. The others, the reef-builders, thrive in waters warmer than 20 degrees Celsius. Fresh water or extremely high temperatures will kill these corals, however, as they have virtually no ability to regulate their body fluids or to prevent overheating.

A coral polyp is a tube-shaped creature; one end is attached to a solid support, while the free end is a single opening through which materials proceed to and from the central body cavity, the hollow gut. The oral disc around this opening has numerous small tentacles; both disc and tentacles are covered with cilia that beat toward or away from the mouth opening as needed. Each tentacle is equipped with stinging cells called nematocysts that harpoon drifting plankton—all reef-building corals are carnivorous—which is then entangled by a secreted mucus and swept into the digestive cavity.

(Among the stimuli that may put the nematocysts in the firing position are swimmers.)

Coral larvae must often overcome numerous obstacles—predatory zooplankton, currents and winds that may sweep them into the open ocean, freshwater currents—before they grow old enough, a matter of a few days, to settle to the sea bed and find a suitable solid foundation to which they can become attached.

Corals attaching themselves to the edges of debris in the bay of our new island create enough of a reef to rise toward the surface of the water, thus lessening the effect of waves on the shoreline and slowing the formation of cliffs on the island. This spurs further growth. With less wave erosion, the waters clear, and the corals can colonize a wider area. Finally, the reef goes all around the island—a fringing reef, broken only where there is considerable freshwater run-off or where delta-headed bays have too much silt.

As the island continues to subside, it seems to recede from the ever-growing reef. The water between reef and shoreline gets deeper, becoming a lagoon, an enclosed body of water that traps coralline sand now carried across the top of the reef by waves. It is now the reef itself that the waves are fighting; cliffs are no longer formed on the island as the sea spends its energy beating against this reef, now called a barrier reef.

If the process continues—the reef growing, the island subsiding—the island eventually sinks beneath the surface of the water; only the encircling reef remains to mark its life and death. The upper plateau of the encircling reef continues to trap sand and coral rubble, however, until another kind of island is created—the coral atoll. It was Charles Darwin, in *Coral Reefs*, who first suggested the relationships between reef forms. Darwin theorized that you could estimate the age of an atoll and the depth of its subsidence by the distance between the "top" of the coral rock and the dense lava on which the original corals had settled. Such measurements have now been achieved through drilling; they show coral rock extending more than a kilometer beneath the surface, yielding an age of some 43 million years of emergence, erosion, and subsidence.

"An island," Joseph Conrad wrote, "is but the tip of a mountain." The Pacific traveler who finds himself on the low, flat, sandy surface of an atoll is really atop a great height, at the summit of a long process of history.

# ISLAND TYPES

Scientists draw subtle distinctions among island types, but four basic types describe the destinations of the Pacific traveler—simply put, two kinds of high islands and two kinds of low islands.

The two kinds of high islands are continental and volcanic. The large islands of Melanesia may be said to be *continental* islands, formed of continental materials, perhaps as a result of a collision and subduction cycle that caused them to break off from larger, very ancient continents. Such islands have rugged interiors, precipitous valleys, and twisting rivers. Many are rich in mineral deposits, and their rugged topography has tended to isolate human communities from one another. The *high volcanic* islands also contain numerous kinds of environment, although they typically lack mineral resources. Erosion has produced gentle windward slopes, while the leeward can be cliffbound. They are often encircled by fringing reefs. Tahiti and Rarotonga in Polynesia, and Ponape in Micronesia, are examples of high volcanic islands visited in this book.

Of the low islands, there are atolls and raised coral atolls. *Atolls* can vary in size—from tiny islets a few meters above sea level at high tide to Kwajalein in the Marshall Islands of Micronesia, the world's largest atoll with the world's largest lagoon, 1350 square kilometers. Indeed, the Marshall Islands consist almost exclusively of atolls. Where an atoll's lagoon has disappeared partially or completely, so that the border is elevated above the surrounding sea, a *raised coral island* is the result. Here, thin layers of soil cover the successive elevations of limestone left by old coral reef. Peleliu in Micronesia and most of the Cook Islands of Polynesia are such islands.

These labels are convenient, and because geography and topography play such a large role in history, an understanding of island types is important. But for every island that can be neatly categorized, there is another that defies easy labeling—islands of mixed type, islands in the making, islands in the unmaking. In this respect, one of the most interesting island destinations for the Pacific traveler is Truk, in the Carolines of Micronesia. Truk has been described as an almost-atoll, and some eight different combinations of atolls and reef formations have been defined in it. The central island, with its volcanic basalt formation, appears to be still subsiding. The outer-island groups resemble the pure atolls of the Marshalls. The huge lagoon is encircled by one of the largest barrier reefs in the world; within it are numerous half-submerged mountain peaks. Truk thus seems to encompass almost all phases of Pacific island formation, save the continental.

# PACIFIC FLORA AND FAUNA

For flora and fauna, an island is not necessarily the best place to land. Plants and animals can become literally marooned, unable to go home or to move onward because of currents, winds, weather. They may not find the essentials that have sustained their species in the past; studies in island biogeography confirm that species are more prone to extinction on islands than on continents, where the variety of resources is greater and accessibility to those resources less difficult.

On the other hand, the little worlds that islands represent, each an environment unto itself, may give rise to species found nowhere else, or may so change arriving species that they turn into rare variants of the original. There are birds on Pacific islands that have forgotten how to fly—in their case, the environment is easy enough and free enough of the predators that plagued them in their original habitats that all they have to do is scratch their way across the surface of the land to find the pickings they need for survival.

The biotic communities of Oceania are as varied as the island topographies and weather conditions that determine the environments of those communities. What the traveler can look for in each environment he visits is treated in following chapters by destination. Of the Pacific as a whole, certain generalizations clarify our understanding of the natural histories of the islands.

Like the people of Oceania, Pacific biota came from the west. This Indo-Pacific biota, as it is called, seems to have emerged between 50 and 25 million years ago, in the epochs geologists call the Eocene and Miocene. The theory is that earlier biota, from the Tethyan period, somehow disappeared some 100 million years ago or so, in a worldwide extinction process associated with a rise in sea level. The Miocene and Eocene biota that replaced the Tethyan in fact shares many characteristics with Eocene and Miocene fossils found in what are today France and Austria; in any event, it is this biota that is today characterized as Indo-Pacific.

Simple drift seems to have been responsible for the eastward movement of biota—from Southeast Asia and New Guinea across the islands of the Pacific. Winds and currents carried with them a variety of plants and animals, and those best equipped to jump wide stretches of water survived to make their homes on Oceania's islands and reefs. The deep sea between the eastern Pacific—the Line Islands, Hawaii—and the west coast of the Americas proved too big a jump for most; indeed, the flora and fauna of these eastern islands of Oceania show commonalities with those of the Americas, suggesting a westward dispersal in this part of the Pacific.

But the major dispersal of biota *was* eastward, and it grew tougher the further east it went, giving rise to one of the important generalized facts of Pacific biogeography—eastward attenuation. That is, there is a downward diversity gradient from west to east in the Pacific, a gradual reduction in the number of species. This is true for birds, insects, ferns, higher plants, sea grasses, marine algae, corals, marine mollusks, even fish. There is also a gradual elimination of animals and plants, with some major groups simply dropping out of the picture in the east. The result is a progressively more disharmonic biota as you move eastward across the Pacific, with species and genera occurring in disjointed patches and not in logical patterns.

This eastward attenuation is complicated by the fact that both marine and terrestrial biota develop differently according to different island type. High islands tend to have more numerous and more diverse flora and fauna than low islands. This makes sense when you put the geological histories of high islands into ecological terms; "younger" than low islands, with evolution still proceeding, the high islands localize the processes of speciation and extinction. Atolls, ephemeral structures highly vulnerable to constant change and to destructive forces, exhibit only limited biota. The trend extends to marine life as well.

Despite being poor in the *number* of forms of life—nothing to do with the lushness or extravagant beauty of many of the forms— the Pacific does have a recognizable island biota and significant areas of endemism. A host of marine organisms is endemic to the islands of Oceania; a few genera of higher plants and several of ferns are restricted to this part of the world; several genera of birds, certain insects, and four entire families of land snail are either found only here or show their greatest development in these islands.

There are patterns to this endemism. Among birds, the highest proportions of endemism are in Papua New Guinea, Fiji, and Samoa. Among flowering plants, there seems to be a distinct break east of a line running down the Solomons, Tonga, and Samoa. Among insects, southeastern Polynesia exhibits endemic species. Southeastern Polynesia is also a hotbed of endemism for terrestrial and marine mollusks and for land snails. Another fact about endemism is that the percentage of it is lower among marine organisms than among land organisms. The difference is quantitative, not qualitative, for marine life ranges over vast distances, while the populations *on* an island may be barricaded from one another over a distance measurable in meters.

The Pacific traveler will note these generalizations about Pacific biota as he wends his way, first westward to the center and sometime source of Oceania's life, then eastward across progressively sparser islands. Yet the major impression he is likely to have of these islands is one of tropical lushness. The birds and flowers and fish he does see will appear to him exotic, often brilliant. The land animals he will come into greatest contact with will be those introduced by humans for food or work; the most dangerous creature in all of the Pacific may be the malarial mosquito—on land, anyway.

The lushness comes home to the traveler in other ways—perhaps while trying to walk a track that was certainly there yesterday but has now been completely obscured by sudden growth in the wake of last night's rain. Or perhaps in a sudden realization that the world is unfairly imbalanced in its resources—that while Africa, only a couple of continents away, has become a fatal arena of drought, all you have to do when you're hungry out here is pluck a fruit from a tree or throw a line into a lagoon. It isn't exactly true; there are islands in the Pacific that cannot support any population, and others that do not support the populations they have. But the impression of lushness persists—in the air heavy with moisture and smelling of excess, in the brilliantly colored corals waving their cilia in perfectly clear water, in the simultaneously delicate and ostentatious petals of the ubiquitous hibiscus, many-colored and as fragrant as perfume.

# CHAPTER 2

# THE COMING OF THE ISLANDERS

Where-do-the-Pacific-islanders-come-from? was for a long time a popular parlor game, spawning both serious theory and fanciful myth. There were partisans of the Lost Continent origin and partisans of the outer-space origin, even a few romantics who put the Lost Tribes of Israel into world-circling canoes and sent them on their weary way to the Pacific.

Less farfetched but almost equally unlikely in the light of considerable modern scholarship is the South-American-origin or sweet potato theory. Widely cultivated and eaten virtually all across the Pacific, the sweet potato has been shown conclusively to be of South American origin. Since the seeds can neither float safely that distance nor be carried that way by birds, which do not migrate in that direction, there was long a controversy whether the Indians of the tropical Americas brought the sweet potato to the South Seas or vice versa.

Thor Heyerdahl's 1947 voyage from Peru to the Tuamotus of Polynesia in the raft *Kon Tiki* was intended to prove that South American
inhabitants *could have* drifted west to settle those islands. What it
*did* prove was that Thor Heyerdahl could drift west and then write
an exciting book about the adventure.

Historians have produced a formidable body of evidence to show
that the South-American-origin theory is untenable. Even on Easter
Island, separated from present-day Chile by "only" a little over 3000
kilometers, there is neither linguistic evidence of South American
contact nor any tangible artifact of South American influence. Indeed, the best known artifacts of that island, the famous stone statues, have been shown to be typically Polynesian—figurative but not
realistic, stylized, balancing form, mass, and the material from which
they are made. As for the sweet potato, how it reached Polynesia
and spread across the Pacific remains a mystery, but it is probable
that the Pacific islanders, some of the greatest voyagers of history,
had some temporary contact with South America or its inhabitants,
picked up the sweet potato habit, and carried the plant with them
on their wanderings.

Those wanderings represent one of the great migrations of world
history, a process lasting several millennia and spreading human
habitation over the entire vastness of the world's greatest ocean.

# HOW AND WHEN THEY CAME

Among the many "lasts" to which the Pacific region can lay claim
is that it was one of the last to be investigated by scientists in any
serious or deliberate way. Today, however, the researches of archaeologists, linguists, anthropologists, botanists, and others representing a range of disciplines have produced a story of far grander
drama and romance than ever emerged from the early wishful guessing of the proponents of this or that theory of origin.

These researches complement one another to conclude that
Southeast Asia was the ancient homeland of Pacific island populations. *Homo erectus* first arrived there some two million years ago,
and modern man, *homo sapiens*, appeared perhaps sixty thousand
years ago. Traces of the lives of these hunters and gatherers are found
throughout what is today Indonesia. That they had a need or desire
to venture beyond their own shores is proven by events.

Perhaps as early as fifty thousand years ago, some of these
hunters and gatherers began to move south and east. In that era of
lower sea levels, the water spaces between Indonesia and New Guinea,
and from there to present-day Australia, were much narrower than
they are today. Even so, there were at least 70 kilometers of open

water for these immigrants to cross; how they did so—whether by some form of canoe, by raft, on logs, even swimming part of the way—is not known, nor do we know what they brought with them. It is likely that they came in small numbers, at long intervals, and perhaps as a result of crisis. Anthropologists tell us that these first migrants, dark-skinned, short of stature, with frizzy hair, were the direct ancestors of modern Australoids—the aborigines of Australia, the Highlands people of Papua New Guinea, and the Negritos still living in the rugged interiors of the Philippines and Malaysia. Locked in by difficult terrain, requiring large land areas to support their hunting and gathering way of life, these ancient peoples did not venture much further for thousands of years, but by about 8000 B.C., their descendants had migrated from New Guinea to its nearby islands and the Solomons, and over the next couple of thousand years they reached as far as present-day New Caledonia and Vanuatu. The people we today call Melanesians are their descendants—once you add in mixtures with and absorptions by and of numerous other races and cultures.

Somewhere around the time the "last" of Melanesia was being settled—that is, roughly 5000 years ago—a second migration of people from Southeast Asia was getting underway. These people were of a different racial stock, a composite of Mongoloid and white often referred to as Indonesian or proto-Malay. More important, they were speakers of related languages of the Austronesian family, different from the languages of the first migrants, which are today classified, for want of perfect understanding, as Papuan. By reconstructing proto-Austronesian vocabulary, linguists have determined that these peoples made pottery, sailed in seagoing outrigger canoes, and were adept at a variety of fishing techniques as well as at the neolithic arts of crop cultivation and animal husbandry. These were brown-skinned, broad-faced, black-haired folk who would take themselves, their skills, and their languages westward through the Indian Ocean as far as Madagascar and would press down into insular Southeast Asia, where they absorbed most of their predecessors, adding to the hybrid nature of their racial stock and culture. Eventually, they moved eastward from here, across virtually all of the Pacific Ocean.

When they first struck out into the Pacific, they scouted and settled the northern coast of New Guinea and other islands of Melanesia, possibly introducing the settlers there to their neolithic technologies. Later, other groups went directly from Southeast Asia to the western archipelagoes of Micronesia—Palau, Yap, the Marianas Chain. Still later, another movement northward from eastern Melanesia settled the eastern islands of Micronesia.

At first, all these migrations may have been undertaken by small family groups; then they perhaps became well-organized expeditions for the express purpose of colonization. In any event, at some point in this long and probably very complicated process, some of these people began to venture beyond the island outposts of Melanesia. The islands of the Pacific became stepping stones to these wanderers, whose navigational expertise developed over the centuries through journeys that were extended lap by lap over some 13,000 kilometers.

That there was an identifiable cultural tradition behind many of these wanderings is evidenced by the trail of a particular pottery with stamped and incised surface designs. This pottery, called Lapita after the site in New Caledonia where it was first excavated, appears in the archaeological record all across Melanesia and as far afield as Samoa and Tonga—but not in Micronesia. It has been defined as a specialization within an Austronesian adaptation, and its dispersal around Melanesia and to the east was probably dependent on a complex network of exchange carried out in two-way voyaging. Often associated with Lapita finds are pieces of obsidian that served as tools and possibly as the tooth-edged implements for decorating the pottery. Since this mineral was quarried only in a few sites identified in the Bismarck Archipelago, New Britain, and the Louisiade Archipelago—all off New Guinea—the trail it traces does more than define a geographic route. As archaeologist Roger Green has put it, "You can't really have people importing obsidian for 700 years over a thousand miles without crediting them as being very skillful navigators and sailors."

The Lapita trail traces cultures with navigational skills and an agricultural system based almost entirely on tubers and fruits—taro, yams, breadfruit, bananas, coconuts, and sago palms. About 3500 years ago, Lapita makers arrived in Fiji from island Melanesia, bringing with them their pottery skills—and the pig. From Fiji, the Lapita seafarers ranged onward, penetrating Polynesia with settlements at Tonga and Samoa. It was here, in the so-called cradle of Polynesia, that the inhabitants of Tonga and Samoa developed the linguistic and cultural attributes that today are characterized as Polynesian. Centuries later, perhaps a thousand years before the birth of Christ, the early Polynesians set out on their own voyages, eventually reaching every habitable island in the vast triangle created by Hawaii, New Zealand, and Easter Island. Some went as far east as the Americas, where they may have picked up the sweet potato before back-migrating to the South Seas. Others back-migrated into Melanesia or northwest into Micronesia.

Some of these back-migrations continued into recent history—so too many forward migrations. Newer Asian settlers have included Indians, Malaysians, and Japanese. Pacific islanders are on the move from small islands to big ones, from villages to towns, from areas of subsistence farming to areas with opportunities for modern jobs, from the insular Pacific to the Pacific rim. They fly, they sail, and occasionally they still drift. The mixing of cultures and ethnic strains also continues, while overseas influences pour into the islands from such Pacific powers as Australia, New Zealand, the U.S., Japan, even South America. Perhaps today's airborne "migrations" of islanders will produce new cultures just as the early migrations did, a new Pacific melting pot that adds to the pluralism which emerged from the wanderings of millennia ago.

# TRADITIONAL SOCIETIES

The convenient regional labels—Melanesian, Micronesian, Polynesian—are just that. None of them really captures a single or uniform cultural definition. It is possible to distinguish ethnic, cultural, and linguistic norms for Polynesia, but the word Melanesia absolutely defies definition except as a useful term for a geographic region, while our understanding of Micronesia is still so meager that that term also describes a place on the map more than it defines a civilization.

The language situation alone is a muddle. It is true that all Micronesian languages, all Polynesian languages, and the newer languages of Melanesia belong to the Austronesian family. Yet the total number of languages spoken in Melanesia is conservatively estimated at 1200—including the more ancient Papuan languages, a catchall for anything not Austronesian. In Micronesia, people from west and east are mutually unintelligible. The languages of the west seem to form a subgrouping with very ancient roots—remember that the first settlers here probably came directly from Southeast Asia. In the eastern islands of Micronesia, the languages seem to have a common origin in eastern Melanesia, but linguists are still not certain whether some major variants here are distinct languages or dialects; in any event, a Trukese and a Marshallese cannot communicate with one another in their native tongues. Only Polynesia, the most recently settled island region, can lay claim to some homogeneity in its nearly 30 separate languages—a Cook Islander and a Tahitian can each make out what the other is saying, and each finds the other's language fairly easy to learn.

The cultures formed in these regions differ virtually from island to island, shaped by geography, environment, and particular historical events. A Pacific islander thinks of himself as a Tongan or Yapese and understands in that a particular cultural identity. It is a misconception at best to think that, once settled on an island, the early migrants assumed a fixed culture that did not change until contact with Europeans. It is equally misguided to suppose a linear cultural development from west to east, as if the people who settled Melanesia became Melanesians and then traveled eastward where they became Polynesians. In fact, with the striking exception of the Highlands of Papua New Guinea (and the aborigines of Australia), no culture remained unchanged or unchanging on these islands. Change came from many sources—a changing environment, outside pressures, war, economics, human passion.

The different histories and cultures of the Pacific are treated in this book by destination, but a few generalized findings may help clarify the traveler's understanding of this vast and variegated area.

Melanesia is the largest of the three regions, with 95 percent of the land and more than 70 percent of the population of the Pacific islands. It is also the least healthy region of the Pacific, with malaria a particular scourge. And it is an anthropologist's paradise, preserving much of traditional culture and social organization. However, anthropologists looking for generalizations soon grow frustrated; they can note at best that some culture traits occur with greater frequency in some areas than in others, but that's about as far as most are prepared to go. Among these "frequent" culture traits are a preoccupation with trade, diligence in farming and gardening, kinship ramifications, and deep-seated fears, perhaps fostered by the difficult environment of these islands, that find release in magic and warfare.

Traditional societies here tended to be more egalitarian than in Polynesia or Micronesia, at least for men, with Big Man status achieved by effort and force of personality. Pigs and small portable valuables were the main forms of wealth, and these were exchanged along elaborate networks; important ceremonial importance accrued to the transactions along these networks. More than anywhere in the Pacific, Melanesia proclaims the inferior status of women. More than anywhere else, its traditional society has been obsessed with magic and sorcery, inextricably linked with religion. Warfare was common, often accompanied by head-hunting and cannibalism. At the same time, artistic creativity reached a zenith of lavishness and elaborate skill in Melanesia—and still does.

Micronesia, a long necklace of islands across the northern Pacific, has traditionally fostered societies in which status was ascribed at birth and matrilineal institutions dominated. *The* matrilineal institution was the clan, and *the* arena of clan power was the holding of land—still a major cultural attribute across Micronesia today, an ongoing system of social security. (The exception is Yap, where land was held by patrilineages, and the land itself held rank.) Society was divided into rigid class distinctions; paramount chieftaincies often developed into highly centralized political regimes that spread to numerous other islands. The primacy of navigation and the authority of the navigator, who was imbued with magical powers, developed in these extended political organizations, which often effected their governance by sailing expeditions to exact tribute or to collect needed resources. Warfare was endemic here as throughout the Pacific.

Traditional Polynesian society was at first all rigidly stratified, a basically religious system in which the chiefs held *mana*, power for accomplishment, and in which bilateral descent and primogeniture determined social life. Some Polynesian societies grew more open as resources and population dwindled; at that point, military and political skill rather than religious authority became the determinant of power. This power consisted in decision-making authority that in some cases created a class of serfs, although in most of Polynesia, all people had rights to land. Nevertheless, chiefly power was so enormous as to require a rigid separation from commoners, a separation defined by rites of avoidance or *tabu*. Warfare was virtually universal between rival chiefs in Polynesia.

Such was the variety and such the commonality of the societies of Oceania when a new group of aliens, this time from the east, made contact with the islands of the Pacific.

# CHAPTER 3

# CONTACT

History records that on September 25, 1513, Vasco Núñez de Balboa crossed the Isthmus of Panama and became the first European to look upon the Pacific Ocean. Poetry records inaccurately that it was "stout Cortez," but gives an idea of what it must have been like "when with eagle eyes / He star'd at the Pacific—and all his men / Look'd at each other with a wild surmise— / Silent, upon a peak in Darien."

Rarely has an ocean been more misnamed. Pacific it is not, neither in its origin, nor in the waves beaten by swimmers and high-ridden by surfers off California's coast, nor in the human history it has seen. There are enough corpses and battle wagons on the floor of this ocean to belie its name a million times over. A disproportionate amount of the tragedy the Pacific has seen has occurred during the short amount of time—not quite five centuries—of European contact.

For reasons of economics, power politics, godliness, and sheer adventure, the Europeans (and later the Japanese and Americans) sought to change the cultures and lives of the Pacific islanders. To an extraordinary extent, they succeeded. What is perhaps more extraordinary is the extent to which they failed, the extent to which "the Pacific" maintains its separateness, a cultural resilience, something distinctively pre-contact about itself. The success, however, is well described, in the lightest of tones, by Henry Adams, in a letter to Henry Cabot Lodge dated August 4, 1891. "The South Seas," Adams wrote, "swarm with laughable satires on everything civilized, and especially on every known standard of morality. They flourished in outrageous defiance of every known moral, economical, social and sanitary law, until morality and economy were taught them, and then they went, promptly and unanimously to the devil. Nine in every ten perished of virtue, among all the islands and races, little and big; and they go on perishing with an unanimity quite conclusive. I do not undertake to draw a moral from their euthanasia. Only the wise draw morals, and I am one of the foolish. . . ."

Yet in recent years, Europeans have indeed begun to draw a moral from the story of their contact with the Pacific islands. Particularly in the postwar period, with the end of colonialism and the emergence of island self-government, Europeans in or concerned with the Pacific have gone through a highly self-critical appraisal of their past role, and of the role they should now play in Oceania. No longer certain of the legitimacy of their presence here, Europeans—Westerners, more accurately—also question the legitimacy of their attitudes toward and actions in the Pacific region. In some cases, it is fair to say, some do so with a fatuousness as bad as and perhaps not dissimilar from the ethnocentric arrogance displayed by their predecessors.

Part of the adventure of Pacific travel is to be present at a moment of transition in the lives of these islands, to visit places that are on the edge of a dilemma in great part not of their own making— the clash of cultures, the assumption of new political realities, the passing of one way of life and the attempts to define clearly what is to replace it. Against this background, there are Westerners who assign blame for every aspect of the dilemma on European contact, past and present. Many want to roll back the very facts of contact, not to mention its effects. That is clearly not possible. History isn't easily erased, as the recent example of Cambodia makes clear. Many other Europeans are horrified by what they see as a Western commercial conspiracy that has duped the Pacific islanders into a pernicious consumerism. There are Englishmen in Fiji at this moment writing editorials that denounce the coming of commercial television on the grounds that it is bad for the islanders. Perhaps it *is* bad for the islanders, whatever that means, but are the peoples of the Pacific so easily duped? There are Europeans whose battle cry is Pacific racial purity; in Hawaii, they complain, there is not a single "pure" Hawaiian left, and that must not happen, these Westerners argue, in the rest of the Pacific. Perhaps they have forgotten that the Pacific islanders have never been a "pure" race, any more than any of the rest of us. And perhaps they have also forgotten that the last time in this century the idea of racial purity gained credence, the result was mass murder.

It is fair to ask if this Western self-criticism is not in itself a new form of Western arrogance. When Europeans rail against Western influence but set themselves up as the watchdogs against it, is this not perhaps another breed of neocolonialism? Perhaps what we really miss is the untrammeled, untroubled Pacific island life of our imagination, and maybe we still want these islands to be refuges, for ourselves, of the purity and innocence our societies lack. But to demand that the islanders hold in trust for us the values we fear we have lost and want them to have may prove to be just as manipulative and harmful as we now believe the actions of well-intentioned missionaries and colonial administrators once were.

In any event, the course of Western contact with the islands of the Pacific has never run smooth. It is a story best understood in waves: explorers in search of a southern continent; whalers and traders in search of resources and markets; missionaries in search of converts; planters and merchants in search of wealth; administrators in search of empire; and, finally, soldiers and sailors in search of battlefields. Accompanying almost all these waves of searchers were adventurers, would-be kings, beachcombers, remittance men, and wanderers. They were looking for paradise.

# THE ERA OF EUROPEAN DISCOVERY

Think of this era in three neat stages: the Spanish and Portuguese period of the 16th century, the Dutch 17th century, and the English— or English and French—period in the 18th century. By this time, the voyages of the English captain James Cook had "discovered" so much that, as a Frenchman put it, his successors were left with little to do but admire.

As everyone remembers from the fourth grade, the Portuguese had established themselves in the East Indies by the beginning of the 16th century. Their navigators had achieved a laborious route around the Cape of Good Hope, up the east coast of Africa, and east across the Indian Ocean to Indonesia—the edge of the insular Pacific. Spain was eager to challenge Portugal's hold on this trade; she also wanted to find the unseen Terra Australia Incognita, the supposed southern landmass that presumably balanced out the northern landforms. Spain sent Magellan westward on the expedition that would become the first circumnavigation of the globe. Yet so huge was the Pacific that Magellan sailed almost the entire way across it without hitting an island, until he reached Guam and the Marianas in 1521, when history records the first fight—and fatalities—in Pacific-European relations. Magellan pushed on to the Philippines, where he was killed by natives. Forty years later, however, Spain took possession of the Philippines and established a trans-Pacific trade route from Manila to Acapulco, the goods to be transported overland from there to the Caribbean before being shipped to Spain.

From their separate bases, Portuguese and Spanish explorers dominated Pacific discovery for the rest of the century. Both sighted and claimed New Guinea. Spaniard Álvaro de Mendaña de Neira discovered the Solomon Islands in the late 1560s and, in 1595, the Marquesas, first of the Polynesian islands to be sighted by Europeans. When Mendaña died en route, his pilot, Pedro Fernandez de Quirós, took over. Obsessed with finding the southern continent and new souls for conversion to Christianity, Quirós traveled through the Tuamotu Archipelago of Polynesia and discovered the New Hebrides—present-day Vanuatu—which he wrongly identified as the southern continent. Quirós' pilot, Luis Vaez de Torres, heading for Manila, passed through the strait that now bears his name, thus demonstrating that New Guinea was an island and not a northern projection of the still-elusive southern continent.

By 1602, the torch of discovery had passed to the Dutch, whose United East India Company monopolized trade in the Indies. As businesslike as their Latin predecessors had been visionary, the Dutch explored the south coast of New Guinea and mapped northern and western Australia, still unaware that it was the fabled continent. These were exploratory voyages only, grudgingly funded by the company. With similar reluctance, the company gave trading permission to an independent merchant, Isaac Le Maire, provided he did not trespass on their routes. Le Maire's son, Jacob, and the navigator William Schouten set sail from Holland in 1615, going around the southernmost point of South America, named Cape Horn after Schouten's birthplace, then sailing across the Pacific, discovering some more of the Tuamotus and some islands of Tonga. Twenty-five years later, the Dutch governor-general in the Indies, Anthony Van Diemen, sent out another mission to find the southern continent. The captain, Abel Tasman, sailed around the southern coast of Australia in 1642, discovering Tasmania, New Zealand, Tonga, and parts of Fiji. He was the first European to enter the Pacific from the west, and his voyages between 1642 and 1644 contributed a great deal of knowledge about the Pacific and were considered a complete flop by the company. Company policy, as expressed in a report from the directors, was that new discoveries should be "continued still unknown and never explored, so as not to tell foreigners the way to the Company's overthrow." Nevertheless, one more Dutchman, the independent Admiral Jacob Roggeveen, set out in 1722 and managed to discover Easter Island, yet more of the Tuamotus, and the Samoas.

For the next several years, European exploration of the Pacific was confined to armchairs in European drawing rooms and meetings in European geographic societies, but the scholarly disputations may have succeeded in shaping the style of the real exploration that was soon to commence—a far more scientific effort than heretofore. To be sure, the accomplished English buccaneer, William Dampier, following the precedent of Sir Francis Drake, had made three circumnavigations between 1699 and 1711 and learned a lot about the New Guinea coast and the Manila-Acapulco route. But exploration was not Dampier's aim, as it very much was for three Englishmen and a Frenchman who would undertake both serious and important Pacific exploration beginning in 1764.

First, English commodore John Byron, ignoring his orders to find the northwest passage to the East, sailed through Polynesia to the Marianas. Along the way, he discovered several northern Tuamotus—obviously situated on everyone's favorite Pacific route—and islands in the Cooks and Tokelaus.

Next came Samuel Wallis and Philip Carteret, sent on a joint Admiralty expedition to search for the southern continent. Parted during a storm, Wallis went on to discover Tahiti while Carteret made several discoveries in Melanesia—and at least eliminated from consideration certain areas where the southern continent was not.

The French, down on their prestige and eager to bolster the national honor, instructed Louis Antoine de Bougainville to circumnavigate. Bougainville's extraordinary voyage took him from Tahiti to Samoa to the New Hebrides and the Great Barrier Reef. He then sailed northeast through the Louisiade Archipelago off New Guinea, past many of the outliers of New Guinea, including the island that bears his name, and homeward via Java and the Indian Ocean.

Extraordinary Bougainville's voyage certain was; indeed, all these voyages of European discovery represent feats of endurance and skill, and many added considerably to knowledge of the Pacific—and certainly to European interest in the Pacific. Yet for sheer accomplishment, they are eclipsed by the voyages of that most extraordinary man, Captain James Cook.

The son of a Yorkshire laborer, Cook worked as a farmer's boy and grocer's assistant before going to sea in the coal trade. He joined the navy at the age of 27 and was soon recognized as an outstanding navigator and hydrographer. What was less evident to the Admiralty but is obvious today were his talents as an anthropologist, naturalist, and dispassionate observer and recorder of his observations. In the openness of his mind, in his curiosity and wide vision, Cook was a true explorer, and his three voyages constitute one of the most remarkable careers of any explorer, anywhere, anytime.

In his first voyage in the *Endeavor*, 1768–71, Cook explored the Society Islands and surveyed the coasts of New Zealand and Australia. His second voyage, 1772–75, was a circumnavigation in which he came close to Antarctica, discovered Niue, New Caledonia, and Norfolk Island, and charted new islands in the Tuamotus, the Cooks, and the Marquesas. Cook's third voyage, 1776–79, took him along the American northwest coast and Alaska in search of the northwest passage; it also took him to Hawaii, where this remarkable man was killed by natives at beautiful Kealekekua Bay.

The era of discovery had shown the islanders of the Pacific the value of iron and other Western goods. It had shown the Europeans a part of the world that would inflame their imaginations, giving rise both to the "noble savage" philosophy and to interest in the political, economic, and religious potential of the islands. Among the news brought home by European sailors were stories of the ease of sexual contact; the mixing of islander and European blood had begun, and venereal disease had arrived in the Pacific.

# THE NINETEENTH CENTURY: THE SACRED AND THE PROFANE

The century began with little European political presence in the Pacific and ended with a great deal. Britain *did* acquire Australia in 1788, but it was as a penal colony, a place for outcasts, not as an outpost of empire. France as usual expended her energies keeping a wary eye on Britain. Spain had South America to worry about; the Dutch had Indonesia; and Germany, still split into separate states, had no cohesive policy toward the Pacific. Yet all of these nations, as well as the United States, would be drawn ever more deeply into Pacific affairs as the century progressed, and as each sought to protect, with political and sometimes military actions, the interests established in the region by their businessmen and missionaries.

## The Transient Outsiders

In the explorers' wake, beachcombers, sealers, whalers, and traders were usually the first Europeans to arrive in the islands—mostly in the islands of Polynesia and Micronesia, as Melanesia's environment and natives were considered inhospitable. Missionaries usually followed once a beachhead was established; they typically sought to keep their distance from their "profane" fellow Westerners, and the feeling was mutual.

The beachcombers often came *with* the explorers, and later with the traders and whalers. They were survivors of shipwrecks or sailors who had jumped ship or fugitives from penal colonies or from scandal at home—or plain adventurers. They tended to start families on the islands, to learn the language, and to serve as advisers to the chiefs and as intermediaries with later European arrivals. Some became influential or famous or both. William Mariner was detained in Tonga from 1806 to 1810 and has left a famous account of it, *Tonga Islands*, actually written by one John Martin. Melville jumped ship in the Marquesas and described his adventures in *Typee* and *Omoo*. James O'Connell was a famous beachcomber on Ponape in the heyday years of the 1820s and 1830s.

The first trading that propelled Westerners into the Pacific was the seal and fur trade between North America and China in the 1790s. A salt pork trade grew up between Tahiti and Sydney at about the same time. Sandalwood—highly valued in China—was discovered in Polynesia and Melanesia in the early 1800s and sparked an enormous and brutal trade, bringing violence and bad relations almost everywhere. Fiji and the Marquesas, in Polynesia, and all of southern Melanesia were affected. When the sandalwood had been depleted, the traders latched onto *bêche de mer*, or trepang—a sea cucumber or slug also highly prized in China. Where traders went, services for traders—and for their sailors and ships—soon appeared, often with deleterious impact on the islands and the islanders.

By the late 1700s, Oceania had become a paradise for whalers, and the whaling trade reached its peak in the 1850s, dominated by Americans from Nantucket and New Bedford. The ports of call that grew in response to the whaling industry became notorious throughout the Pacific. These ports restored and resupplied the whaling vessels and offered every variety of restorative and refreshment to the whalers, who typically traded liquor, guns, hardware, and textiles to get what they wanted. Disease, violence, alcoholism, and firearms all took a heavy toll on island populations.

Perhaps more widespread and certainly less depopulating than the whaling industry was the copra industry, launched in 1856 in Western Samoa by the German firm of Johann Cesar Godeffroy & Sons. The large European demand for tropical vegetable oils gave rise to the trade, which has touched the lives of more Pacific islanders than any other Western *economic* activity. Still today, as the Pacific traveler will see everywhere, copra is a way of life in these islands— growing the trees; harvesting the nuts; drying the coconut meat; loading, shipping, and unloading the copra; processing the oil. Because copra production requires only coconut trees and sunshine, it could take place, as it does, all over the Pacific; small traders as well as great mercantile firms like Godeffroy—and later Burns Philp, Carpenters, and the like—could participate, traveling in small boats throughout an island chain, trading cash and goods for cottage-industry copra. Copra has therefore been a natural product for the Pacific islands and a major income earner, as it still is, for island inhabitants. Copra also brought planters, and planters brought black-birders, but first it is necessary to speak of Pacific missionaries.

## The Christian Missionaries

The missionary influence was certainly as great as that wrought by economic activities and probably brought more radical consequences to island culture and society; whether these consequences are seen as disruptive or beneficial depends on point of view. The first missionaries were the 17th-century Spanish, whose priests established the pattern of converting the paramount chiefs first, and letting the common folk follow suit. The first mission–cum–military garrison, on Guam, also established another pattern that would be repeated elsewhere: when some natives resisted the presence of the priests and killed a few, the soldiers retaliated ruthlessly, and the colonial government grew larger and stronger in response to the "threat."

The first Protestant mission arrived in Tahiti in 1797, on the ship *Duff,* sent by the London Missionary Society. The *Duff* missionaries, backed by Britain's Colonial Office and the fervor of Victorian evangelicalism, also followed a trickle-down conversion policy that proved highly successful.

LMS missions spread wide in Polynesia, but other Protestants followed, and spheres of influence soon were formed and no-trespass rules agreed to. The Wesleyans were at work in Tonga, Fiji, and the Loyalty Islands of present-day New Caledonia; these last two missions represented the first incursions into Melanesia, always the last place to be penetrated by Westerners. The Boston-based American Board of Commissioners for Foreign Missions—the so-called Boston Mission—began to get into the act in 1820 in Hawaii but soon spread to the eastern Carolines, the Marshalls, and the Gilberts. The Mormons, among the most interesting and successful missionaries in the Pacific (see Chapter 4, Travel in Oceania), arrived in Polynesia in 1844.

Catholic France, unhappy about growing Protestant and therefore British influence, made a successful move into Polynesia in 1834, in the remote Mangareva Islands where they were unopposed and unwatched. Their missions soon spread to Tahiti, the Marquesas, New Caledonia, Fiji, and the Samoas. The Catholics, of course, did not play by the no-trespass rules agreed to among Protestants.

By the 1860s, there were missionaries—either Westerners or converted islanders—at work virtually throughout the Pacific. The Protestants, with little financial support from home, worked to create indigenous churches, and the European missionaries soon became part of island life. Their work, however, included the preaching not only of Christian theology but of their own British or New England work ethics and behavior. Island women were clothed from head to toe in Mother Hubbards; islanders were told it was the will of God that they live in Western-style houses. It was certainly not the will of God, they were told, to engage in the sexual practices their former cultures approved, nor to drink rum or smoke tobacco. Many have wondered how these missionaries, having alighted in paradise, could be so concerned with hell.

Catholic missionaries made little effort to create indigenous churches; rather, they promoted French language and culture along with Catholic dogma. They were clearly agents of French imperialism as well as ministers of God.

Between Catholics and Protestants, French and English, little love was lost, and the feeling filtered down among their converts, resulting in a number of religious wars in the islands. Yet to both sets of missionaries may be attributed the orthographies of the hitherto unwritten islands of the Pacific, as well as the beginnings of medical care and education.

## The Planters and Blackbirders

By the latter half of the 19th century, there was a new kind of commercial pioneer in the islands—the planter. He did not come for quick wealth or quick refreshment on his way to wealth, nor did he care about the islanders' immortal souls. He wanted land, and he intended to develop it, work it for profit, and live on it. In the late 1800s, planters from Australia and New Zealand established plantations for copra, sugar, coffee, cacao, vanilla, fruit, cotton, and rubber. Rubber was limited to New Guinea, and the cotton boom ended when the American Civil War ended and Europe could again trade easily with the American South.

Pacific planters usually obtained their land by making a deal with the local chief, often in good faith, often not, with results felt to this day; there is hardly a Pacific island nation that allows foreigners to own land, although they may lease it. When it came to laborers, the planters complained they could not find good workers among Polynesians and Micronesians. They looked further afield—to India, in the case of Fiji, but mostly to Melanesia, which became the main target for the hideous practice of blackbirding.

Theoretically, blackbirding was a system of indentured labor. Islanders indentured themselves to a planter for a stated amount of time in exchange for food and board, a small wage, and a bonus for the return home. In practice, islanders were as often as not shanghaied aboard blackbirding ships, and the expected rewards did not materialize. Many people—recruiters and greedy island chiefs as well—grew rich on this quasi-slave trade, and many blackbirded islanders never saw their homes again. The colonial powers, moving closer to a partition of the Pacific and prodded by some planters and most missionaries, finally put an end to blackbirding in the late 1800s and early 1900s.

# THE PARTITIONING OF THE PACIFIC

French territorial ambitions were the tinder that kindled the flames of Pacific colonial partition. Deciding that the Marquesas and Tahiti could serve as valuable ports along the sailing route that might result if the Panama Canal were built, France in 1842 declared sovereignty in the Marquesas and a protectorate over Tahiti. They spread out to New Caledonia in 1853, using it first as a penal colony, then as a rich source of nickel. The other islands of French Polynesia came under the tricolor in the later years of the century, firmly establishing France as a colonial power in the Pacific.

The British colonists of Australia and New Zealand were fairly hysterical about the spread of French power and asked for the mother country to take action. Indeed, since 1840, they had been urging Britain to annex every clod of earth and every reef in the Pacific, but the British were reluctant to extend themselves so widely and perhaps thinly. Nevertheless, the British finally gave in to the importunings of planters on Fiji and annexed it in 1874. With the precedent set, the Australians began agitating for a British solution to German influence in New Guinea, just a quick sail from their north coast, and in the Bismarck Archipelago nearby. The British reluctantly claimed the southeast of New Guinea—Germany had the northeast and the Dutch were still in charge in the west—and the boundary was solidified in 1885. Britain went on to declare protectorates over the Cooks, the Gilberts, and several other atolls as well as the Solomon Islands.

Meanwhile, German influence continued to expand in the northern Pacific, also as a result of pressure from German traders on those islands. Germany bought most of Micronesia from the Spanish after the Spanish-American War in 1899, while the U.S., a new entrant in the political game here, acquired the Philippines and Guam. The U.S. also used Pago Pago, on Samoa, as a coaling station, but the islands were claimed as well by Germany and Britain. In 1899, Britain renounced its claim, the U.S. took formal possession of what would become American Samoa, and Germany got the lion's share, Western Samoa. In return for renouncing her claims, Britain obtained the undisputed rights to Tonga, Niue, and the Solomons. In 1900, Britain turned over Niue and the Cooks to New Zealand and signed a treaty of semiindependence for Tonga.

Only the New Hebrides were left unclaimed, so in 1906, Britain and France, which both had naval commissions there, established a condominium government over the archipelago. This awkward arrangement would eventually result in one of the most tragic independence efforts in postwar Pacific history. Also in 1906, Britain turned over the administration of Papua, its part of New Guinea, to Australia.

Thus, by 1906, the process begun in Guam in 1668 was completed, and the power that had started the process, Spain, was out of the picture. South of the equator, the Pacific was pretty much a "British lake," or a British–Australian–New Zealand lake, with the glaring exceptions of French Polynesia and New Caledonia. Germany, the Netherlands, and the United States were the other owners of the islands of Oceania.

# WORLD WAR I

In terms of shots fired, World War I barely touched the Pacific. Most islanders saw it as a European folly, and life went on as it was: the white man was in charge, planters grew rich and powerful, missionaries continued to look for souls in need of saving, and the peoples of Oceania, growing increasingly dependent on Western imports, joined the world economic order.

The major consequence of the war was Germany's ouster from the Pacific and Japan's entry. German possessions in Micronesia were occupied by the Japanese at the outbreak of the war; their holdings south of the equator moved into the British sphere. The League of Nations formalized these realities as mandates after the war.

North of the equator, only Guam remained an isolated U.S. outpost. Everything else was subject to Japanese colonial policy, which had the very clear aim of "Japanizing" the islands. Japanese settlers eventually outnumbered native Micronesians two to one; the islands were developed economically for the benefit of the home country; Japanese language and culture were taught universally; and only Japanese could access the islands. There was little contact between Japanese Micronesia and the rest of the Pacific, and few people noticed when, in the 1930s, the Japanese began to fortify the islands.

Elsewhere, in the British lake to the south, planters sat on their verandahs and colonial administrators went to their clubs. Native depopulation ceased, and in a few places the trend was actually reversed. Some strides were made in health care, and a new worldwide awareness of indigenous cultures found its way into the hearts and minds of a very few colonial administrations. Education was still the province of the missionaries, but cricket—by Jove!—was played almost everywhere.

# WORLD WAR II

The Japanese attack on the American fleet at Pearl Harbor on December 7, 1941, ranks as one of the most decisive events of Pacific history. The fighting in the "Pacific theater," as the general staff called it, primarily affected Micronesia and Melanesia, many of whose islands were devastated. Polynesia was the least hurt; the wartime role of many of its islands was to play host to Allied soldiers. Yet throughout Oceania, this sudden, hurtling shove into the modern world of technological warfare would bring as many intangible as tangible changes—with important repercussions.

The attack on Pearl Harbor had caught the Americans unaware and unprepared. The disaster for the Allies that began there continued for the next several months as the Japanese advanced throughout the Pacific. The Americans were attempting to regroup after the destruction of Pearl Harbor; Australian and New Zealand troops, veterans of the fighting in North Africa, were steaming homeward. The Japanese took Guam, Nauru, and the Gilberts, thus placing all of Micronesia, for the first time in history, under a single ruler. Bataan fell, then Corregidor, and MacArthur fled by night to the shaky safety of Australia. "I shall return," the general declared in answer to being ordered to leave the Philippines, at a time when it was not entirely clear—especially to Australia's military chiefs—that Australia wasn't about to fall too.

Now the Japanese invaded New Guinea, but their advance by sea to the capital at Port Moresby was halted in the Battle of the Coral Sea, the first naval engagement in history in which all the fighting was done by carrier-based planes. A month later, in June 1942, the Japanese suffered their first major naval defeat in the Battle of Midway. The tide was turning, and a month later, the Japanese overland advance in New Guinea was stopped along the Kokoda

Trail, at great cost to themselves and to the Allied troops, mostly Australians, and the islanders who opposed them. The rest of Melanesia saw little ground combat, but Nouméa in New Caledonia became U.S. headquarters in the Pacific, and the islands of the New Hebrides became American bases, staging areas for the eventual recapture of Micronesia and invasion of Japan. This meant the presence of thousands of U.S. service personnel, the magical efficiency of the navy's construction battalion—the beloved Seabees, and the introduction of all sorts of technological wizardry that seemed to drop from the sky or come up from the sea in cargo planes and ships.

The strategy as the Allies eventually formed it was a pincer movement, a two-pronged offensive. Admiral Nimitz and the navy would move westward against Japanese positions while MacArthur's ground forces advanced northwestward from New Guinea. They would meet in a joint action against the Philippines and then fight northward to Japan itself. This counteroffensive began on Guadalcanal; success there, combined with the success in New Guinea, enabled the Allies to continue their advance, turning seized islands into air and supply bases and leapfrogging many of the more heavily fortified Japanese islands—isolating them in the rear and blockading them by air and sea.

The strategy of course worked, but at a great cost to Micronesia in particular. The American invasion began at Tarawa in 1943, then moved on to the bombardment of the Marshalls and the Japanese fleet in the Truk Lagoon. The Allies then bypassed most of central Micronesia, bombing and blockading islands with Japanese garrisons, to head for Guam and the northern Marianas in the summer of 1944. It was from Tinian in the Northern Marianas that the atomic bomb attacks on Hiroshima and Nagasaki were eventually launched.

In Polynesia, supply bases were established on Tonga, Tahiti, the Samoas, and the Cooks, and many islanders suffered from shortages of imports—a condition endemic to the war in the Pacific. But the now-rusted guns that guarded the sea passes to the islands of Polynesia never had to be fired; the enemy was stopped in time.

The war left the islands of Micronesia and Papua New Guinea devastated—their infrastructure destroyed, their economies in chaos. Of the six colonial powers left after the war, one, the U.S., replaced Japan in much of Micronesia, which became a "strategic trust" mandated by the United Nations to U.S. authority. One other tangible and still visible side effect of the war in the Pacific was the work of the Seabees. Almost every airport the Pacific traveler passes through is or started out as a Seabee-built airstrip, and many of the support structures of today's harbors were also built by the construction battalion—not to mention the Quonset huts and other structures still used as hospitals, schools, and government offices.

But other changes wrought by the war were less tangible and more far-reaching in their impact. Islanders had lost confidence in their white masters, many of whom they had seen defeated or in flight. The arrival of thousands of American service personnel had shown many islanders a more egalitarian form of islander-Westerner interaction than they had ever seen before. Particularly in Melanesia, the sight of American blacks working alongside American whites (although not, at that time, fighting alongside them) and in charge of the marvels of advanced technology was something of a revelation. Add to this the worldwide restlessness felt by dependent peoples, and you have fertile ground for change. Once it started, it moved pretty fast.

# THE POSTWAR PERIOD

Two movements may be said to characterize Pacific history in the postwar period. One is decolonization. Independence movements were organized or reorganized shortly after the end of the war, and Pacific sovereignties started coming into being in the 1960s; the process is not yet complete. The second postwar trend is regionalism. It is less clearly defined or definable than the trend toward self-government, but it may prove equally important to the Pacific future.

At the end of the war, there were but six colonial powers left in the Pacific. An indication of the level of embarrassment inherent in that distinction is that they now began to call themselves metropolitan powers. In 1947, at the invitation of Australia and New Zealand, the six metropolitan powers met in Nouméa to form the South Pacific Commission. Its aim was to advise metropolitan administrations in such matters as economic development, social welfare, health, and education; it kept strictly away from political and military issues.

In 1950, the SPC sponsored the first South Pacific Conference, composed of delegates from all the Pacific islands who were asked to advise the commission. Toothless as the SPC charter sounds, the South Pacific Conference, which has continued to meet, took on an unforeseen importance as a forum in which representatives of countries from all over the Pacific could meet face to face. In 1962, when Western Samoa became the first Pacific nation to achieve political independence, it took a seat alongside the metropolitan powers in the SPC.

Since then, decolonization has changed the face of the SPC several times over, although it has long been a troubled organization, tainted by its metropolitan origins and still apolitical. But numerous other regional organizations have since been formed. The South Pacific Forum, created in 1971, convenes the heads of government of all the Pacific nations and deals very openly and vocally with such "regional" issues as decolonization, nuclear testing, transit of nuclear vessels, and the deployment of nuclear weapons. The forum's executive arm, SPEC, the South Pacific Bureau for Economic Cooperation, formed in 1972, promotes regional economic projects in areas of trade, investment, shipping, air services, telecommunications, marketing, and aid. The University of the South Pacific, the Pacific Conference of Churches, the Festival of Pacific Arts, a variety of women's organizations, and professional associations are also organized on a regional basis.

The decolonization that began in Western Samoa in 1962 quickly spread—to Nauru in 1968, Fiji and Tonga in 1970, Papua New Guinea in 1975, the Solomon Islands and Tuvalu in 1978, Kiribati in 1979, Vanuatu in 1980. In 1987, the Trust Territory of the Pacific Islands, the U.S.-administered Micronesian islands under U.N. mandate, was formally ended; the arcane history of the TTPI is covered in the introduction to Part IV, Adventuring in Micronesia, but those new island nations are today self-governing "in free association" with the U.S., an unusual political situation similar to that existing between the Cook Islands and New Zealand.

France remains a colonial power in the Pacific, although the Paris government has run into trouble with independence movements in New Caledonia; any change in the status quo there would surely affect French Polynesia as well.

Likewise, American Samoa and Guam remain U.S. territories, and while a commission is now studying the future political status of Guam, the status of American Samoa remains unchanged and so far unchanging.

It is indeed possible that these two postwar trends—regionalism and decolonization—may converge. Many of the new nations remain heavily dependent on their former colonial powers, who maintain "presences" in the Pacific through grants in aid and the infrastructures required to dispense such aid. Meanwhile, the Pacific has become an arena for great-power confrontation, just as it was in the 19th century, only now the great powers are the U.S. and the USSR. Playing one side against the other—over fishing rights, nuclear power, and aid—has had both beneficial and deleterious effects on islands acting alone. Regional alliances, concerted efforts by a group of island nations linked by commonality of interest if nothing else, may prove more effective. Meanwhile, ethnic and nationalistic pride in identity work sometimes for and sometimes against the emerging notion of "Pacificness."

Many islanders now speak of a new kind of pan-Pacific person, an individual who may eventually feel himself a Pacific islander first and a Tongan or Trukese second. In the great rim powers of

Australia and New Zealand, there are indications that today's generation sees itself as a Pacific people, not as an offshoot of Britain or
Europe. Many of the current and potential Pacific nation leaders have
spent a good deal of time outside their home islands and have returned to them. They may be the children of two different ethnic
categories and may be married to someone of an ethnic category
different from their own. Thus, by both background and tempera-
ment, such people are multicultural in a unique way—pluralistic but
completely Pacific.

Island leaders also speak of a "Pacific way" of doing things—a
common heritage of peaceful human relations, consensus decision-
making, an unrushed pace of life in which social values outweigh
materialistic considerations. The contention is not perhaps historically accurate, but then neither is the notion of the "land of the free."
Both are rather models to work toward, and the Pacific way seems
a good guideline for leading the Pacific peoples into the future. Also,
it is theirs.

# PROBLEMS, REALPOLITIK, AND THE PACIFIC DILEMMA

Applying the Pacific way to the realities of the late 20th century has
not always proven easy. The problems faced by the new nations of
the Pacific are formidable. How to define oneself as a nation? What
role to take on the world stage, and how to execute that role? These
and other questions are daily being answered in response to numerous important issues.

In the world arena, one of the issues is nuclear—the drive toward
a "nuclear-free Pacific." Certainly, a world free of nuclear destructive capability is universally desired, but in the Pacific, people have
had some direct experience of that destructive capability. The first
nuclear weapons were launched from Micronesia, which also saw
12 years of testing by the U.S. military after the war, with disastrous
results for many islanders and for the area's environment; the French
government continues to carry out nuclear tests—underwater only,
since 1974—in French Polynesia at the Mururoa Atoll.

The presence of nuclear-powered or nuclear-armed ships in the
region has also become an arena for the nuclear issue and a battlefield
of the U.S.-USSR cold war. Several island nations, along with New
Zealand, have denied port access to U.S. ships on the grounds that
they *might be* nuclear; U.S. policy is that that information is not
available, while the Soviet Union is estimated to have thirty nuclear
submarines in its Pacific fleet. The prohibitions against U.S. ships
have frequently been applauded on the world stage as David-vs.-
Goliath moves that draw important attention to the nuclear issue.

Such gestures are frequently answered by aid reductions, while those ports that welcome the U.S. vessels are rewarded with more assistance. In this game of *realpolitik,* issues and special interests are frequently confused and confounded.

Another issue that has been a superpower tug-of-war in the Pacific is that of fishing rights. When, in 1985, Kiribati signed an agreement with the USSR, allowing fishing in its waters in exchange for a $1.6 million fee, the U.S. added a new level of concern to its wariness about the growing Soviet presence in the Pacific. In the past, the U.S. tuna industry had been adamantly opposed to any payments for access to large areas of Pacific waters. But the Soviet move spurred the U.S. government to join with 16 other Pacific nations in a regional agreement, sponsored by the South Pacific Forum, to channel millions in technical aid—now called license fees—to the region in exchange for fishing rights. The agreement was approved in 1987.

Another economic reality with which the Pacific nations must grapple is the mixture of subsistence and cash economies. The issue becomes more intractable as Pacific populations stabilize and even begin to increase. The capacity of many islands—particularly atolls— to support these populations is limited; both island economies and island ecosystems are being strained. Thus, the Pacific way comes smack up against the 20th-century phenomenon of economic development vs. environmental integrity.

Moreover, urbanization is a growing trend, placing an even greater burden on ecosystems. Local and regional efforts to provide incentives for remaining rural have thus far had little impact.

Only a few of Oceania's nations—Papua New Guinea, New Caledonia, and perhaps Fiji—can look to natural resources on land for future economic growth. For the most part, these islands have limited cash crops—copra, mostly—and those they have are fragile, vulnerable to destruction from cyclones, drought, or plant infestation. The regional fishing agreement will, it is hoped, encourage the growth of indigenous commercial fishing operations, for exploitation of the seas seems a major avenue down which many Pacific nations can break the aid dependency that still links them to their former colonial administrators.

Another avenue is tourism. Developed only since the 1960s, when direct commercial jet traffic put these islands within reach of Pacific rim countries, the Pacific may be the last unspoiled tourist mecca on earth. But "unspoiled" is a relative term; its definition is very much in the eyes of the beholder. In fact, the beginning of tourism here was—and in many cases still is—controlled by the metropolitan country or, increasingly, by the main tourist sources: Australia, New Zealand, Japan, the U.S. The travel organizations of these countries set out originally to meet the needs of their own, usually affluent, travel market. They defined, promoted, and controlled the tourist flow, typically funneling it to those destinations where the organizations had subsidiary tourist companies. In many cases, this has meant luxury hotels of international standards and every sort of facility to meet expectations for a "tropical island holiday." The result has usually been foreign ownership, leakage of foreign exchange earnings, and little cconomic benefit for the island destination.

In the face of this, many Pacific nations are rethinking their tourism programs. At the same time, the individual-country approach to marketing and promotion may be giving way to pooling of resources. It is the Pacific dilemma in microcosm. First of all, is tourism wanted? What kind of tourism—what kind of tourist? How does a nation keep the economic benefits home? A number of island governments are moving toward a "cultural tourism"—less sea-and-sun holiday, more exotic-interest. How is that to be marketed? How is it to be served? In marketing and serving tourism, does an island risk destroying the very attractions that are the lure of tourism? If you advertise an unspoiled paradise, and people flock to it, might they not spoil the paradise? And if you don't, have you lost an important opportunity?

These are among the new realities of contact with the Western world. If they seem less harsh than those of the past several centuries, they are, for the inhabitants of these islands, and perhaps for the rest of the world as well, no less far-ranging in their implications. How the realities are dealt with will be an interesting story—and an important one.

# CHAPTER 4
# TRAVEL IN OCEANIA

## THE SEASONS OF TRAVEL

It is in the northern winter that most people think of tropical travel. That is summer below the equator—very hot, often rainy, with the possibility of hurricanes. Cruising yachts head for Australia or New Zealand or hole up in some Polynesian port to wait it out till April 15, the traditional end of the hurricane season, before raising sail again.

North of the equator, it's the opposite. Summer, with its chance of hurricanes, *starts* in April. Winter, December to March, is cooler and drier.

If you are planning a long and varied trip, you might try to plan it to stay one step ahead of the rain and one step behind the fierce heat—or vice versa. But the fact is, on a long and varied trip, you are bound to fry and get drenched at some time or other, somewhere or other. It is part of the Pacific experience. These islands are always warm and humid; the waters offshore rarely are cooler than 20 degrees Celsius. The longer you travel here, the thinner your blood becomes. You learn to dress coolly, to wear a hat, to linger in the shade. Rain is warm and refreshing, reducing the weight of the air, at least for the moment. And while no one would advise that a traveler pray for a hurricane, finding oneself on a small Pacific island during a cyclone whose worst effect is that it cuts off the electricity, forcing the population to drink as much beer as possible before it gets warm, is not such a dreadful experience at all.

Trying to describe the climate of a region of the Pacific is almost silly. The distances within a region may be vast and the conditions quite different from place to place. Nor does weather always obey the schedules devised for it. But here are a few generalities:

## The South Pacific: Polynesia, Melanesia

Summer: December to March
Temperatures of about 25–27 degrees Celsius
Abundant, frequent rainfall

Winter: April to November
Temperatures of about 22–25 degrees Celsius
Cooler, drier, with southeast tradewinds

## The North Pacific: Micronesia

Summer: April to November
Temperatures of about 26–27 degrees Celsius
Abundant, frequent rainfall—especially in the Carolines

Winter: December to March
Temperatures of about 24–27 degrees Celsius
Cooler, drier with northeast tradewinds

## All Over

The closer you are to the equator, the hotter it is.

On high islands, the windward side is wetter than the leeward; it catches the trades head-on.

There is hardly any twilight, and there are few spectacular sunsets in the Pacific. The sun drops suddenly, and you're in darkness. You may catch a "Pacific sunset" in Micronesia, but it will be a fast one.

In recent years, the weather of the tropical Pacific has been shown to have far-reaching impact on the global weather system. Pacific conditions in general, and sea surface temperature in particular, have been linked to events at higher latitudes—specifically to El Niño, the Pacific Warm Event with its widespread and long-lasting destructive implications. Scientists have identified El Niño as an extreme anomaly of the Southern Oscillation, the east-west circulation evidenced by large-scale exchanges of mass between the Indian Ocean and the Pacific.

In January 1985, a project known as TOGA—Tropical Ocean Global Atmosphere—was initiated with the sponsorship of the American National Weather Service. Its aim is to synthesize observational studies and modeling programs to provide new insights into the weather interaction between the tropics and midlatitudes. It is hoped that this understanding will enable scientists to explain and even predict some of the phenomena caused by tropical weather. Along island coasts at various locations all over the Pacific, the traveler may see the TOGA tide stations, established as far east as Chile, as far west as Hong Kong, with plans to spread into the Indian Ocean as well. The stations monitor the ocean to track changes in sea level. The data is transmitted in real-time via satellite to a station in Virginia and disseminated from there to users. In 1985 alone, TOGA enabled meteorologists and seismologists to detect the *tsunami*, or tidal wave, that resulted from the Mexican earthquake and another from a Valparaiso earthquake. Both were small enough that no warnings had to be issued, but the system proved its worth precisely for that reason: it detected *small* disruptions. Because earthquakes typically disrupt local power supplies and communications, word of the quake often doesn't get out to those who might be most affected by a resulting tsunami. The TOGA project, providing real-time data, may now make it possible to warn populations in the path of a tidal wave; eventually, it may make it possible to predict another El Niño and to act in advance to protect against it.

# REQUIREMENTS FOR TRAVEL

North Americans and most Europeans will not need visas for any of the nations visited in this book *except* Papua New Guinea. (If you plan to take advantage of being in this part of the world to visit Australia, you need an Australian visa.) PNG visas may be obtained on arrival, or check with the PNG Embassy in Washington, DC, or Air Niugini offices (see Chapter 15, Papua New Guinea).

A passport is of course required, except for U.S. citizens in American Samoa, Guam, and the countries in free association with the U.S., but proper identification is required there, and the best form of ID is the passport.

What *is* required, virtually everywhere in the Pacific, is an onward ticket—i.e., proof that you are not staying.

Most Pacific countries have restrictions on imports of fresh fruit or flowers, meat, live animals and plants, and artifacts that might serve as home to unwanted pests. On arrival in a number of these countries, your airplane will be fumigated before any passengers can disembark. The spray, though harmless to humans, is not terrifically pleasant; keep a bandana handy for covering your face.

# TRAVEL TO AND AROUND THE PACIFIC

Air transport accounts for more than 90 percent of all travel to and around the Pacific. There are three groups of trans-Pacific routes. One links the west coast of North America to Hawaii and from there traverses the Pacific. Another, the Asian route, typically comes through Micronesia and Japan to Southeast Asia and goes southwest to Melanesia, Australia, and New Zealand. The third route, the so-called Great Circle, connects North and Central America to New Zealand and Australia via French Polynesia or Fiji. Eastbound, this route generally goes through Japan to both U.S. coasts; westbound, it goes to Japan and Southeast Asia. Its main purpose is to link the major countries of the Pacific rim; it therefore overflies most Pacific island destinations.

The major hubs of international travel are Guam, Nadi in Fiji, Pago Pago in American Samoa, Nouméa in New Caledonia, Papeete in Tahiti, and Port Moresby in Papua New Guinea. Feeder flights radiate outward from these hubs to connect all of the Pacific, often in a crazy patchwork of routes, depending on where you want to go when and whether or not there is a flight there. A few other destinations—Apia, in Western Samoa, and Tonga—have been on-again, off-again extensions on some international flights.

"On-again, off-again" is an apt description of much of Pacific air travel. The number of international airlines flying here is not constant. Neither is the number of regional airlines or of small, domestic, so-called third-level airlines. Neither are the routes or schedules these airlines fly. U.S. deregulation, increased competition, price fluctuations, Chapter 11s, employee lawsuits, and the mercurial changes in world currency rates have all played a part in the seesaw nature of air travel to and around the Pacific.

Just about every Pacific traveler's favorite Pacific airline, even if they've never flown it, is Air Nauru. The Republic of Nauru, just under the equator, is a 21-square-kilometer pile of high-grade phosphate derived from the guano of millions of birds who have nested here for millions of years. It has the highest per capita annual income in the world and very little else—*except* an international airline. Air Nauru theoretically connects Southeast Asia, Hong Kong, and Japan with Micronesia, Melanesia, Polynesia, and Australia and New Zealand through Nauru's own very central location. That's the catch: you must fly through and usually stop overnight in Nauru itself. The other catch is that Air Nauru's routes are particularly on-again, off-again. But the airline is building plush offices everywhere, and its brochures are the slickest in the Pacific. The concept, linking north Pacific to south, is an excellent one.

Interisland connections in the Pacific are on regional and/or third-level airlines. The regionals, South Pacific International Airlines, for one—SPIA, as it is known—link island nation to island nation but also link different islands within a nation or group. Third-level airlines typically fly only from island to island within their own countries.

Scheduling can be the *bête noire* of long-distance, multi-destination Pacific travel. Suppose your flight from Tonga to Western Samoa leaves a week from tomorrow, a Tuesday. Here it is Monday and you're just dying to hop over to the outliers—a few days in the Vava'u Group, a few in the Ha'apai Group. The flights are heavily booked, but you manage to find a seat on the leg to Vava'u with a standby on the continuation to Ha'apai a few days later. In the meantime, you had better book a return from Vava'u to meet the Tuesday flight to Apia, Western Samoa—you can't miss that. Then it turns out that you *can* get on the flight to Ha'apai, *if* the flight that day has reason to put down in Vava'u to pick you up, and you can certainly get a confirmed seat on the flight returning from Ha'apai to Tonga on Tuesday, although it won't give you much time to connect with your flight to Apia, and if it should be late. . . . The permutations are endless. If it is frustrating for the traveler, think how difficult it is for the airlines staffer who must juggle the boardings and disembarkations and accompanying luggage distributions and possibly pilot changes of a single plane ride through numerous stops—and who must often do all this via static-ridden radio. It is also worth mentioning that the author, in millions of miles of Pacific air travel covering many, many places and totaling many, many months, was never unable to get to or away from a destination—even when a typhoon on one occasion and an airline bankruptcy on another brought some disruption to the schedule.

*The essential, inviolable, cardinal rule about air travel in the Pacific can be summed up in three words: Reconfirm. Reconfirm. Reconfirm.* This is the very first thing every Pacific traveler should do on arrival at his destination—not only for gateway-to-gateway travel, but for island-to-island travel within an individual country. It *must* be done within 72 hours before your next flight is due to depart, but the safe rule of thumb is to do it as soon as possible—at the airport, from your hotel by telephone, by making the airline office your first stop and by standing there while the reconfirmation is effected, often by radio transmission. If you don't reconfirm your flight, you will lose it. (Unhappily, in some places, you might lose it even if you do.) Also, if you miss a flight through no fault of your own—if the flight is cancelled because of a typhoon, for example—and if you must then rereserve that one flight, be sure to reconfirm *all* succeeding flights as well. Some airlines have a policy that if one flight is missed, you are then obviously going to miss everything else with which you're connecting.

Another important aspect of air travel is the requirement to arrive early for a flight. In most cases, you are asked to be there at least 45 minutes in advance; if this seems crazy for a 30-minute flight, remember that check-in procedures are not automated and tend to go slowly, as do luggage and freight loading. You will likely find yourself waiting in a lot of airports. The refreshment stand may or may not be open; the shop, if there is one, is quickly exhausted. Bring a book, but don't fall into too much of a reverie—announcements are not made often and are sometimes inaudible if they are made, unless you're standing right there, so keep a sharp eye for something happening, and if you're not sure if that's *your* flight loading, ask.

If these caveats and imperatives sound laborious, in practice they're easy. It all quickly becomes habit, and the truth is, it's fun. Indeed, air travel in the Pacific is fun for a variety of reasons. Airports and airlines are small, friendly. Dealing with them is like taking a step back in time, and for travelers accustomed to the manic slickness of Kennedy, Heathrow, Hong Kong, and the like, it is charming.

The traveler will grow to love the small planes—Britten-Norman Islanders or Twin Otters—that take him from island to island within an island group. Out-island airports are often sheds on grassy fields. You and your luggage are weighed together; the luggage, at least, must not exceed ten kilos, but then, if some passengers are underweight, or if there are only a few passengers, others can be overweight. The pace is slow, the interisland flight often low enough that you can see well down through the clear water or watch the people on islands you overfly. On short flights with few passengers, there may be only a single pilot—often a New Zealand Kiwi or an Aussie in Bermuda shorts, knee socks, and shirt with epaulets—and you might get the chance to sit copilot. The noise of the engine makes conversation impossible, so you can concentrate on looking around, and the up-front view of instrument panel, the puffs of clouds at eye level, and the short, narrow strip as you come in for a landing really let you know you're flying.

Although this book is written primarily for the air traveler, a few words about sea travel are in order. Holiday cruise ships do ply the Pacific from ports in Honolulu, American Samoa, Fiji, Tahiti, New Zealand, and Australia. Freighter travel is virtually nonexistent, as the big trans-Pacific ships do not take passengers. Freight vessels between American Samoa, Western Samoa, and Tonga may take passengers along that route only.

Within an individual island nation, travel by sea is certainly possible, although these interisland vessels—often freighters bringing commodities and picking up copra—rarely have set schedules and are low on comfort. If you have the time, or for a short interisland trip even if you don't, the experience is worth it. Head down to the harbor, hang around, ask around—if there's a boat going and it has room, you're aboard.

Virtually everywhere the traveler goes in the Pacific, he will see yachts—and yachties, as they are universally called. They cruise the southern Pacific from mid-April to about November, the northern Pacific from about June to October. They are "out" for years at a time. The author's favorite was a Californian who had gone to Taiwan to buy his yacht and was heading home from there; at the time of the meeting, he was in Pago Pago, and he had been sailing for ten years. Contrary to the hoary perception, yachties are not, by any stretch of the imagination, all blazer-wearing plutocrats; most are not wealthy at all. Many are young single people or couples who have put all their savings into an "adventure" before they put down roots. Some are families with children whom they educate by correspondence courses. Most, it seems, are retired couples. For all of them, this is, as one put it, "the way we want to live, and there's nothing particularly brave or extraordinary about it."

That there is a yachtie community is undeniable. They communicate by radio, know one another by yacht name and specifications, meet in much-frequented ports, remeet year after year, help one another when there's trouble. The amount of actual sailing they do in a single year may come to fewer than a hundred days; the rest of the time, they're exploring an out-of-the-way island the rest of us cannot get to, or they're in port. There, they're eager for hot showers, fresh fruit and vegetables, mail, and phone calls to family, friends, and, it seems, the banker in charge of their cash management accounts. Some islands—and some facilities on those islands— are particularly friendly to yachties and become hang-outs for this worldwide crowd with its world-roving experience. You'll hear them complaining about some particularly tough harbormaster—there are heavy restrictions and financial requirements for cruising yachts in many island nations—or applauding a particularly nice one. They are a distinctly friendly crowd to fall in with, and they are admirable for living their passion. One yachtie told a visitor that she and her husband had "no house to go home to, no insurance on the boat (it's prohibitively expensive), no savings to fall back on. If anything happens to our yacht, we're in trouble. But I wouldn't give this up for anything."

Skilled, experienced sailors traveling in the Pacific often sign on as crew for a leg or two of some yacht's journey. If you have time, you may want to hitch a ride to some island or other, or you may get an invitation to do so. Be sure you're a good sailor; no one is going to turn around for a seasick landlubber.

There is one other form of Pacific travel that requires mention— the bicycle. Obviously, you cannot get from island to island with this means of transportation, but on many islands, in many parts of the Pacific, it is a good way to get around. A few U.S. adventure travel outfitters have begun running cycle tours to Polynesia and even to Papua New Guinea (mountain bikes there, to be sure), so the bicycle as a piece of Pacific luggage is not as farfetched as all that. That, of course, is the problem: it is a piece of luggage that must be thought about and dealt with at every destination. Most airlines consider a bicycle luggage; some require that it be packed; a few charge for the privilege of having it transported, although the charge is minimal—the same is true on boats and ferries. Fold-up bikes are recommended. Keep in mind also that bike rentals are available on many of the Polynesian islands, though not elsewhere. In any event, bringing a bicycle to the Pacific is possible, but think hard about doing so.

# HEALTH

The Pacific is in general a most healthy travel destination. The air and sea—with a very few exceptions—are free of pollution. The weather is agreeable, to say the least. Fresh fruit and bright sun are packed with vitamins. The humidity does wonderful things to a person's skin; one reason it is so hard to guess the age of Pacific islanders is that even the very old have smooth, clear, healthy-looking skin.

There are, however, a few hazards to be aware of and one big one—malaria—to take precautions against.

The first potential hazard is the sun. Islanders stay out of it, but in Australia, where the predominantly white-skinned population has a reputation for sports fanaticism, the world's highest per capita incidence of skin cancer is achieved—a result, it is believed, of overexposure to the fierce tropical sun.

Old-time expats warn newcomers—white and black—simply to stay in the shade between the hours of 11 A.M. and 2 P.M. In any event, you should at all times wear or have with you a brimmed hat, a shirt, sunglasses, and PABA-based sunscreen—especially if you go out on the water, where you cannot find natural protection. Ease into it; when you first arrive in the Pacific, limit your initial exposure to the sun, increasing it gradually. Keep your pores open by drinking plenty of liquid. If a tan is your goal, get it sensibly. You *will* tan in the tropics whether you try to or not, so it makes sense to exercise caution.

There are a lot of insects on these lush islands, and if you tend to be vulnerable to these pests (for malaria precautions, see below, "Malaria"), there are a few things you can do. First, before your trip, start taking vitamin B-1. Doctors say they don't know why, but B-1 seems to build up a resistance to being bitten; check with your physician as to dosage. Once you have arrived, keep in mind that perfumes, hair sprays, and other scents may attract bugs. So does brightly colored or flower-patterned fabric; stick to tan, white, or green. Don't go barefoot, a good precaution to follow in general in the Pacific. Use an insect repellent and keep it near your bed at night. You might also want to carry a mosquito coil; many hotels and guesthouses throughout the Pacific supply these as a matter of course in every room.

Lice are occasionally a problem in some areas—particularly those where you see people picking them out of one another's hair as a sign of affection. Most trading stores and pharmacies have remedies, in the unlikely event that you pick up lice.

Nonmalarial mosquitoes transmit dengue fever, a disease often associated with the tropical Pacific, although its occurrence is rare. Dengue is not fatal (except occasionally to infants), but it is no fun. The symptoms are the fever, headache, pain in the joints, nausea, sore throat. Call a doctor if you think you have it; he can relieve the symptoms somewhat, although the cure is to stay in bed and let it run its course—a matter of from a few days to two weeks.

Another potential hazard, which sounds funny but can have deadly serious results, is falling coconuts. When one of these weighty items comes hurtling down with increasing speed from 30 feet up, it can have a major impact on whatever it hits. Coconut beaning can be fatal; it has happened to tourists fulfilling their South Seas fantasies on quiet beaches and cycling along past coconut groves minding their own business. Even if what's hit isn't your head, a blow or graze from a falling coconut can cause serious and painful injury. Watch out.

Bites, burns, and cuts have a tendency to turn septic in the tropics and should be cleaned, treated with an antiseptic and/or antibiotic, and covered at once. Coral cuts should be vigorously washed to completely remove the calcareous bits, then treated with hydrogen peroxide (alcohol if you don't have this and whisky if you don't have rubbing alcohol) and an antibiotic ointment.

People with weak stomachs may suffer the usual, varied traveler's tummy ailments, but these are usually not serious and are easily treated. If you're that kind of traveler, you already know what to do about such discomforts.

## Malaria

Vanuatu, the Solomon Islands, and Papua New Guinea are all malaria-infested areas, and travelers are advised to take precautions. What precautions to take, however, is the sixty-four-dollar question. Within those countries, malaria prophylaxis is one of the major topics of conversation among travelers. There is a standing joke among Peace Corps volunteers in the Solomons about Washington's monthly bulletins offering new recommendations for malaria prevention and cancelling last month's advisory. Many PCVs contract the disease anyway. Expats in these countries tend to take no preventive at all; they wait until they feel sick and then take Fansidar, as there is no known cure for malaria. Almost all these expats *do* get malaria, once a year, year after year after year.

The female anopheles mosquito is the culprit, so trying not to get bitten by one is obviously a good idea. Use repellent, cover your body, sleep under a net; dusk to dawn is major feeding time for the anopheles.

You must start taking antimalarials at least a week before entering a malaria-infested area and must continue taking it for six weeks after you have left the last infested area you're in. To find out which prophylaxis to use, in what dosage, and how often, Americans should phone the Center for Disease Control in Atlanta, Georgia (tel. (404) 329-3311), or the local Public Health Service.

As of this writing, the recommended prophylaxis was chloraquin once a week, supplemented by Fansidar if you plan to be in malarial areas for more than three weeks or if fever occurs. (In some areas, a chloraquin-resistant strain of mosquito has developed. Ask CDC about this.) These and other antimalarials—Maloprim, Amodiaquine, Paludrine—are available in pharmacies and at clinics and hospitals in all the malarial areas. By that time, however, you should have been on the stuff for a week, so you should arrange a supply beforehand—either from home or from another Pacific destination. Most hospitals in most countries of the Pacific do supply these important drugs, even though they are not malarial areas.

Antimalarials can cause side effects, and almost none of them is recommended for pregnant women or infants. If you *are* taking Fansidar, the most common side effects are nausea, headache, liver upsets, and rashes. A more serious potential side effect is bone marrow disease.

The malaria disease, if it comes, may often be confused with the flu or common cold. If you feel ill, have aches and pains, and are showing a slight temperature, you *may be* in the first stages of malaria, before the classic symptoms appear. Those classic symptoms are a feeling of intense cold accompanied by marked shivering and lasting for perhaps two hours, followed by high fever, nausea, a feeling of dryness, and possibly delirium, followed by profuse sweating. Similar attacks can occur at intervals of from 48 to 72 hours unless the patient is treated.

The bottom line on malaria is this: take an antimalarial, and at the first sign of an ill feeling, call a doctor—even if you left the malarial area weeks ago.

## Inoculations

No inoculations are required for travel in the Pacific, but a few are a good idea—especially if you might go to out-of-the-way destinations, as indeed you might. Check how up-to-date you are on tetanus, typhoid, polio, and diphtheria prevention; if you need booster shots, now is a good time to get them, even though none of these diseases is prevalent in the Pacific. There have been cholera outbreaks in Truk, in the Federated States of Micronesia. The area has been declared safe, but if you are worried, get a cholera shot. If you think you may be really roughing it, infectious hepatitis is a possible danger; gamma globulin shots are recommended in that case.

## Medical Kit

Most of the health problems you will encounter in the Pacific, if any, are pretty much the same sort of thing you encounter at home—the occasional cut, bite, headache, stuffed nose. Take along some basics—as well as any special medications you use regularly. Here is a recommended list; if you run out, almost everything on the list can be resupplied on the gateway islands and on many of the outliers visited in this book:

Antibiotic ointment (Bacitracin, Polysporin, or equivalent)
Antihistamine
Antiseptic spray
Painkiller
Band-Aids
Antifungal
PABA sunscreen
Insect repellent
Nosedrops

If you think you might need them, pack an antidiarrheal and something for motion sickness.

As a matter of course, the traveler should carry some medical identification—a card with your Social Security number and stating blood type, allergies, chronic or special health problems, eyeglass prescription, a name and number to contact in case of emergency. (Medic Alert Foundation sells identification necklaces and bracelets embossed with this information. The necklace or bracelet also shows a telephone number through which medical personnel can access your complete medical history. A good idea if you are unable to speak for yourself. Medic Alert, P.O. Box 1009, Turlock, CA 95381–9986; tel. [800] 344–3226.)

# WHAT TO BRING

Even if you are traveling far and wide in the Pacific—perhaps *especially* if you are traveling far and wide—you need bring very little with you. Everything should fit into a carry-on suitcase or knapsack, with room to spare for your purchases—until you can get to a post office and mail them off. Buy a straw or *tapa* basket or, in Papua New Guinea, a string *bilum* to serve as your day bag. A small padlock on the suitcase or knapsack zipper opener is not a bad idea for travel anywhere.

As with travel anywhere, pack clothing and accessories that can serve multiple purposes.

## Clothing

A hot part of the world, where rain is to be expected, and where religious and social mores and a persistent informality dictate fashion: these are the principles that determine what the Pacific traveler will wear. For both men and women, the essentials are T-shirts and/or cotton shirts—at least one with long sleeves, loose-fitting cotton slacks, a light jacket—water-resistant to double as rain gear, a pair of running shoes, a pair of sandals, a bathing suit, and, obviously, underwear.

Shorts are fine for men but are very rarely appropriate for women. Some European women—and a few island women—have taken to wearing shorts along the streets of various Pacific capitals, but they are offending people when they do so, and this book strongly recommends against it. Skirts, sundresses, and *pareus* are cooler and just as comfortable anyway. Men also will appreciate the comfort of the pareu or lavalava (sarong-type skirt), and this tends to be an early purchase for every Pacific traveler. It serves as skirt, dress, beach wrap, and more and is variously knotted around the waist, neck, shoulder, or across the bust.

Washable cotton is definitely the fabric of choice for everything you wear; synthetics can be hot and sticky.

Dressing up is easy in the Pacific. For women, changing from running shoes to sandals will do it; for men, a clean or cleanish shirt is tantamount to evening wear (plus pants, of course). If you see a man with a tie in the Pacific, he is invariably a Mormon missionary—with a short-sleeved white shirt, short hair, a bicycle, and a skilled lay-up shot in basketball to complete the image. Some island men may wear ties to church on Sunday. In Western Samoa, where the Sunday color is white, many men wear white lavalavas, white shirts, white ties, and white coats; the effect is stunning.

The best way to pack for a Pacific journey is to start with old clothes, then ditch them on the way, replacing them with the tee-shirts that make such good souvenirs and with pareus, slacks, and sundresses of island design. You might wait for the islands to buy your sandals as well—rubber thong sandals are universal here. The running shoes you bring will serve you for hiking, reef-walking (scuba booties are also excellent), and sightseeing on foot.

## Toiletries

In addition to your medical kit (see above), you will also of course require toiletries. Toothpaste, toothbrush, shampoo, deodorant, shaving gear, nail clipper, comb and brush, and—for women—tampons or napkins, makeup, skin creams and scents if you use them: all these are available in the gateway islands and on many of the outliers. There is no need to worry about running out. Coconut creams, coconut soaps, and scents hinting of tropical flower fragrances are, in fact, among the nicer souvenirs of Pacific travel.

## Accessories

Perhaps the most useful item for Pacific packing is a set of plastic bags—readily available in the islands if you run out. Use them both to organize things and to keep them dry.

Bring plenty of film; it tends to be expensive in the Pacific, and not every type is universally available. Carry both film and camera in the lead bags easily obtainable at camera stores in the U.S. (and in many Pacific capitals)—protection against airport X-ray monitors.

A waterproof watch with an alarm is a good idea, as is a pen knife with lots of functions, including a corkscrew. Bring a sewing kit, sink plug, and pocket flashlight for emergencies; bring a compass for hiking and for fun. If you are bringing any plug-in appliances, you will need a converter—unless the appliance is good for dual voltages, as many are—and a plug adaptor to accommodate the variety of sockets.

Mask, snorkel, and fins can be cumbersome to pack, and such equipment is readily available—to buy, rent, or borrow—almost everywhere in the Pacific. If you are attached to your own, and if there is room, bring it. The same is true of diving regulator and buoyancy control device. If you intend to dive absolutely everywhere, by all means pack your own gear. But if diving is only to be an ancillary activity to this journey, you may be better off renting equipment, despite the cost.

Identification—passport, driver's license, C-card (diver's certification), youth hostel card, medical history—and such items as airline tickets, travelers' checks, and money should of course be carried carefully. Some travelers keep such valuables in money belts or special cases worn around the neck. Keeping them close—in a wallet that goes where you go—is probably just as good. Make two sets of photocopies of all ID and of the record of your travelers' checks numbers; entrust one set to a friend or family member at home, and keep the second separate in your luggage.

Notebooks, address book, writing implements should be kept in plastic bags. If you are traveling with a portable computer, keep the disks in antistatic mailers and don't let the hardware go through airport X-rays; hold the machine out for manual inspection.

Reading matter is not easy to come by in the Pacific. The bigger capitals have bookstores with good selections, but the bigger capitals are few in number. The standard, meager offering consists of supermarket romances, one or two of the older glitzy trash novels, and—if you're lucky, a classic or two (now is the time to reread them) and some of the Pacific books of James Michener. The great danger is that you will soon exhaust this scanty library, and, since books tend to weigh a lot and take up a lot of space, you don't want to bring an entire supply from home. Fortunately, swapping is prevalent among Pacific travelers; yachties, in particular, will be delighted to have something "new, from home," so save your best-sellers for them. Where there are luxury resorts, even if you're not staying there, check out their hotel shops, which frequently sell books, or their hotel libraries, where you may be able to swap. When you *do* find a cornucopia of good reading, buy as many as you think you can carry—two to three paperbacks—and choose big, long epics.

By all means, bring a clip-on book light and extra batteries.

Here is a recap of useful accessories:

Plastic bags
Film and film bags
Camera
Alarm watch
Penknife
Sewing kit
Sink plug
Flashlight
Compass
Plug adaptor and convertor (if needed)
Dive gear
Identification documents and copies
Notebook
Address book
Clip-on book light and batteries

# MONEY

The Pacific traveler deals in numerous currencies throughout Polynesia and Melanesia, in U.S. dollars almost everywhere in Micronesia. Carry travelers' checks of course; those issued by the large international financial corporations can all be replaced if lost—even though you may have to phone Australia and wait for a while. In this respect, American Express has numerous offices and agencies throughout the Pacific and promises fairly fast reissue.

It is a good idea to keep handy some amount of U.S. and Australian cash; as international currencies, these can be useful if you get stuck—if you arrive someplace in the middle of the night, for example, and cannot change money at the airport.

In general, apart from coins or bills you want to keep as souvenirs, you should be sure to change all local currency *before* you leave that country. Keep enough for the ride to the airport, airport tax—if there is one—and a cold drink or snack while you wait for the plane, and leave yourself enough time at the airport to change the currency back to dollars or, preferably, into the currency of your next location. *Be sure to check the opening hours of the airport banking office.* Some currencies—of Western Samoa and the Solomons, for instance—are completely useless outside their home countries; if you do not exchange them there, you will simply lose the value of the money.

If you have not managed to obtain currency before arriving in a destination, you can usually do so at the airport on arrival. Of course, always try to change money at banks rather than in hotels or from "dealers."

The large international credit cards—American Express, Visa, MasterCard—are in wide use throughout the capitals and larger gateway towns of the Pacific, everywhere travelers are likely to go. On the outliers, however, you will need cash for everything, so be sure to have plenty with you. However, many outliers accessible by plane also have small banking offices, so you will be able to change more travelers' checks there.

Tipping is *really* not the custom in the Pacific and can be embarrassing to both tipper and tippee if tried. In Americanized Micronesia, tipping is more or less expected on super-Americanized Guam, but it is seldom expected elsewhere.

Nor is bargaining a custom in the Pacific; even in the open-air markets, the price quoted is the price you're expected to pay. On the other hand, the sales tax is unknown.

It is difficult to put a price tag on Pacific travel. Prices change, and currency values change; what cost $25 a day last year costs $40 a day this year and may cost $20 a day next year despite rising prices. After the huge expense of airfare, how much you spend will depend on where and for how long you are traveling. In almost every country in this book, it is possible to find a range of accommodation and eating places—from low-budget to luxury with stops in between. The exceptions are the French territories of French Polynesia and New Caledonia, where even budget living is not particularly cheap and where the in-between points are few.

The money issue has more to do with defining the range than with absolute cost. What is considered top of the line in Tonga is very different from top of the line in Fiji, with a corresponding price differential. This means that if you have set yourself a budget that you consider moderate, sticking to it may put you in bathroom-down-the-hall lodgings in some places and in full-service pool-and-bar hostelries in others. But with few exceptions, almost any budget *can* be adhered to.

# COMMUNICATIONS

Mail *everything* airmail; surface mail is not just slow, it's unreliable. Postal service is excellent throughout the Pacific, although, strangely enough, mail from sophisticated Fiji has frequently been unreliable.

The USPS facilities in Micronesia remind traveling Americans how dirt cheap our postal service is compared to much of the rest of the world.

*Getting* mail in the Pacific is a different matter. Of course, every Pacific nation has a General Delivery/Poste Restante facility (mail to the central post office, capital city), but such mail may often be lumped together and stashed someplace out of the way. If you are an American Express customer—and if you have their credit card or travelers' checks, you are a customer—you can collect mail from their offices and agencies around the Pacific. As of this writing, there were AmEx offices in French Polynesia, Tonga, Western Samoa, American Samoa, Fiji (two: one in Suva, one in Nadi), New Caledonia, Papua New Guinea, and Guam. For an up-to-date list, go to an American Express travel office and ask for the latest directory; it lists the complete addresses of the offices in these locations. Sometimes, the American Express agency is a small one "in care of" another travel organization.

Whichever method you use for receiving mail, if any, tell your correspondents to write your name out in full and to print it clearly. For mail from the U.S., count on at least two weeks for delivery. In fact, the USPS can get the mail to almost any Pacific capital in a few days, although they recommend eight days as a working formula. Once the mail arrives, however, it may take some time to find its way to its final destination and to be properly sorted—island time.

If you hope to receive mail in Fiji, tell your correspondents to address it to Fiji Islands; otherwise, for some reason, it tends to go to Fuji in Japan.

Where there is telephone service in the Pacific, it is almost always possible to arrange an international call. International phone communication is easiest and most efficient in the gateway capitals, however, where the traveler's best bet is to make the call from the post office.

# ACCOMMODATIONS

The "guesthouse," in a variety of forms and under a variety of names, is to be found almost everywhere in the Pacific. It's a little like a European pension or bed-and-breakfast and a little like staying with friends, and it's also something else entirely. These are inexpensive to moderate-priced establishments that may or may not offer meals, electricity, or private bath. They are an excellent bet for the traveler; typically owned and managed by native islanders, they offer a good opportunity for getting to know the hosts and for picking their brains about places to go and things to do.

Of course, the Pacific boasts its luxury resorts. Like luxury resorts everywhere, they are just that: like luxury resorts everywhere. No condemnation intended, as such places are certainly comfortable and can be most pleasant to spend time in—if you have the tariff. As a steady diet, however, they do little to enhance the traveler's acquaintance with the islands of Oceania.

The range of hotels downward from luxury are also like hotels everywhere—the more you pay, the more you get in terms of location, conveniences, comforts. It's worth remembering that, in the Pacific, hot water isn't always all that necessary for a refreshing shower. If you have brought a book light, neither is electricity.

In some areas—especially French Polynesia—you may be able to arrange homestays, *logement chez l'habitant,* where you literally live with the family in their home. It's not terribly different from some guesthouse arrangements.

Off the beaten track, you may want to stay in villages where there are no traveler's facilities. In Micronesia in particular, very few of the outliers have hotels at all. Many, however, have council resthouses, places where traveling officials are put up. Except for these establishments, accommodations in hotelless towns and villages will likely be at the invitation of a family—often arranged for you beforehand by the tourism office or government officials. While you are probably not expected to pay for this, it is certainly the custom to express your appreciation in some way. Cash is one way; ask your arranger what would be appropriate. Gifts are another way. In some places—Fiji, for example—there is a strict etiquette about this; a Fijian village chief expects an offering of the root from which *kava,* the ritual drink, is made. Elsewhere, cloth, T-shirts, running shoes, food, and numerous other items available in the gateway markets and shops are all acceptable. Again, check before you head out to the villages or outliers, and be sure to bring the stuff with you.

# FOOD

No one comes to the Pacific for a gourmet feast. The excepted areas, not surprisingly, are the French territories, where you can eat very well indeed. Island food runs to tubers—taro, yam, manioc, sweet potato—and to coconuts, other fresh fruit, lagoon fish. Add rice for Micronesia, where it is the staple.

Fish is eaten both raw and cooked. In the southern Pacific, raw fish has a variety of names but is almost everywhere prepared by being marinated in coconut milk and a variety of condiments. In Micronesia, where the Japanese were firmly in control until World War II, it is *sashimi.* In either case, it's delicious.

Island feasts are prepared in earth ovens, called by a variety of names throughout the Pacific. Cooking method and what is cooked also differ from place to place, but basically you start by digging a pit. Wood or coconut husks are burned in it, and stones are then placed on top of the fire. The food is wrapped in leaves—usually banana, then placed in courses on the hot stones. Fish and meat go first; vegetables are on top. It is all covered with more leaves and more stones and sometimes with sand and is left to cook for several hours.

An awful lot of island food is marinated in or covered with coconut oil, coconut cream, or coconut meat, which is also a universal snack. All this eating of coconut is one reason so many Pacific islanders take on such thick proportions. Unhappily, Pacific coconut is perfectly delicious, as are papaya (pawpaw to the Aussies), banana, and just about every other fruit available.

One of the dreadful ironies of the Pacific is to see islanders eating canned fish from Japan. Either their lagoon has been overfished or they lack the time or inclination for fishing, but it does seem bizarre that fish must be imported to this aquatic continent.

Another canned favorite is corned beef, sometimes called *pisupo* because the first canned good imported to the islands was pea soup. Junk food is plentiful in Micronesia, where feeding it to infants has resulted in cases of malnutrition and blindness.

Most of the Pacific capitals—and some other towns as well—have Chinese and Japanese restaurants. A few major tourist centers, even outside the French territories, have restaurants with French or even Italian menus. Most hotel and restaurant food is more or less fish, meat, French fries (i.e., "chips," where the British colonized), and cooked vegetables. Undistinguished, "continental style," perfectly fine, occasionally very tasty.

Some islanders drink kava, made from the dried root of the pepper plant, or its equivalent. It is nonalcoholic but definitely tranquilizing and in some places can be unbelievably potent. Islanders also drink beer—those who drink—and Pacific beers are excellent. Wine comes mostly from Australia and New Zealand, as does whisky. Duty-free ports are the best places to buy these.

In parts of Melanesia and Micronesia, many islanders chew betel—the unripe nut, wrapped in the leaf, sprinkled with lime. It has a slight narcotic effect and turns the saliva—and eventually the mouth and teeth—a bright, distinctive red.

Many hotels put electric water kettles, tea bags, instant coffee, sugar, and creamer in every room. Serious coffee drinkers will appreciate the French territories of Polynesia and New Caledonia, and they will love Papua New Guinea, where the coffee is superb.

# MEASUREMENTS AND TIME

All the measurements in this book are metric. To convert square kilometers to square miles, multiply by 0.386. To turn kilometers to miles, multiply by 0.6214. To turn meters to feet, multiply by 3.2808.

Multiply Celsius temperatures by 1.8 and add 32 to get the Fahrenheit equivalent.

The toughest thing about time in the Pacific, even for old Pacific hands, is the International Dateline. This is an imaginary line down the 180th meridian of longitude, except that it turns east at Tuvalu to avoid cutting Fiji in half. For the Pacific traveler of this book, that also puts Tonga on the "far" side of the dateline—i.e., west of it.

To the east of the dateline, the calendar date is one day earlier than to the west. East = Earlier, if that helps you remember. Another favorite mnemonic is "If it's Sunday in Samoa, it's Monday in Melbourne." What it all means is that if you travel west across the dateline, you arrive on the next day, even after a two-hour flight. But as everyone says, don't worry, you get it all back eventually.

There is another fact about time in the Pacific that every traveler must master—island time. It is sometimes called "coconut time"— that is, when the coconut is ripe, it will fall. Except at sporting events, no one moves very fast here. In the heat and languid air, it would be foolish to do so. There are no seasons per se that chart a cycle; there is wetter or drier, trades or calms. A cultural dimension is also at work. Traditional society in all areas of the Pacific was communal; the community provided a safety net, so that you were confident of being taken care. In many of these societies, it was considered foolish or worse to make a commitment, lest circumstances beyond your control force you to violate the commitment. Personal needs therefore are viewed here from a different perspective; appointments are iffy. There is no point whatever in working up a fury against a waiter who moves with what the traveler may come to call the Pacific shuffle. There is no sense in being angry if someone with whom you had a firm appointment fails to show up; take a walk— he'll find you. The best thing to do about island time is to adjust to it and, except for getting to airports early enough, live it.

# INFORMATION

The capital city of every gateway island in this book has a tourism office. These are sponsored by government departments and ministries of varied coloration—economic development, resources, tourism. They also vary as to efficiency and effectiveness, from well-staffed reception centers with slick brochures to small, homey holes in the wall. They should be the traveler's first stop—after reconfirming onward flights.

Your first visit will be a fishing expedition—what should I see, where should I go, do you have maps, and if I want to do this, what's the best way. After you have given some time and thought to your sojourn, helped, it is hoped, by the guidance of this book, ask the tourism office for help in arrangements.

But the tourism office is by no means the only source of information and assistance. The Pacific is notable for a kind of tourism where almost anything can be *arranged.* Hotel and guesthouse keepers are prime arrangers. Waiters, barmen, and hotel staff are also extremely useful. Everywhere in the Pacific, you can find someone who can find someone who can arrange virtually whatever it is you want. This is a travel tip that cannot be overemphasized—live by it.

For topographic maps, you want what is usually called the Lands & Surveys office. It is typically located in the government offices area, and going there is always an interesting experience. For other maps and city plans, start by asking at your hotel, then try bookstores, and airlines.

Airlines offices are indeed important centers of travel information. In most areas of the Pacific, you can book your lodgings at the same time you book your flights. In the Cook Islands, in fact, you must have a hotel booking on arrival. As a result, airlines offices keep up-to-date lists of available accommodations. In addition, many local airlines staff people, accustomed to dealing with travelers, can provide excellent advice about things to do on their island.

Bookstores often sell works about the island or island nation that are not obtainable elsewhere. Many of these may not be immediately applicable to your travel in the islands—histories, novels, myths, and folk tales—but will certainly enhance your being here. Bookstores may also offer specialist maps—walking tour maps, for instance.

Finally, the people you meet can be a superb source of information—not just the islanders, but other travelers as well. Someone who has come from the place you're en route to can be a real find, although the traveler may justifiably become tired of the endless refrain about the place "you *have* to go to."

## MAPS AND GUIDES

Maps of the entire Pacific are necessarily so huge in size and small in scale that they both are unwieldy to use and provide little detail. They do, however, give you an idea of the vastness of the region, and some, with topographical detail, show the submarine features of the ocean you are traveling across. Most major cartographers—

Bartholomew, for one—produce Pacific-area maps, and they can be purchased at good map stores in the U.S.

A full collection of separate maps for all the island nations visited in this book will likely be hard to come by in the U.S., but such maps are almost always available in the island nations themselves, both topographical maps and travel or tourist maps.

Specialist guidebooks are also best purchased on-site: guides to bird life, animal life, varied fauna, and the all-important marine life of the Pacific. Histories and travel guides to most islands are also available in local bookstores or at local tourist offices.

# NEWS OF THE WORLD

Many travelers delight in being out of touch when they're abroad. Others hold news-seeking travelers in contempt, contending that knowing what's going on in the world detracts somehow from the traveler's ability to connect with the lands he is traveling through. This book assumes, however, that news junkies are not cured of their addiction the moment they board a plane. For such people, especially Americans used to reading at least one local and perhaps two "national" papers a day before settling in for ninety minutes of television news, the Pacific can cause painful withdrawal symptoms.

Local newspapers throughout the Pacific are fascinating for the insights they give into local culture and politics, not to mention the schedules they give of imminent events that may attract the traveler. Some carry a few wire-service items, but for the most part, they are distinctly local.

The *International Herald Tribune* is a rare, rare treat in the nations visited in this book, but Australian and New Zealand papers are frequently available—especially where tourists from those countries abound. The Asian editions of *Time* and *Newsweek* are also often to be found in major tourism and/or business capitals.

Three Pacific magazines are of interest, although these have a regional focus and are not geared to other world news. The granddaddy of them all is *Pacific Islands Monthly*, known affectionately as *PIM*, founded in 1930 by R. W. Robson in Sydney, where it is still published today. *Pacific Magazine* is a Hawaii-based publication featuring bulletins and briefs from all over the islands. *Islands Business*, which calls itself "The News Magazine of the South Pacific," is published in Suva, Fiji, and offers an interesting regional viewpoint.

A good companion for the news-junkie traveler is a portable, battery-run shortwave radio. What you receive depends on where you are and when you tune in, but you can count on hearing news from somewhere just about every day, and the radio can also be great fun. The BBC World Service, despite its high reputation, tends to offer skimpy headline news and to spend a lot of time on features like "How to Garden with Mulch." Voice of America is of course unabashed propaganda for overseas audiences, and it certainly sounds it. Its news and features are about on a level with Radio Moscow's English-language service—peace and light and everything wonderful. The best news and most interesting broadcasting by far come from Down Under's ABC, the Australian Broadcasting Corporation, and the Armed Forces Network of the U.S. The latter features a number of programs from National Public Radio, and it broadcasts U.S. professional sports—baseball, football, basketball, etc.

A shortwave of course also tunes you in to local news and music, and you often pick up such things as a concert from Manila or the odd Muslim religious hour. It makes for interesting listening.

In American Samoa, you can see Cable News Network on TV, via satellite.

# SHOPPING

The best piece of shopping advice the author knows is that if you see something you want, buy it. The idea that you can get it later, or you might find something better somewhere else, or there's no point carrying it around is a fast, effective route to regret. You may not find anything like it ever again, and you only have to carry it as far as the post office where you can mail it home—unless the shop does that for you.

T-shirts are great souvenirs; consider buying one per destination. Back home, you could find yourself the first kid on the block with a chest that advertises Hinano Beer or the Stone Money of Yap. Other island clothing also makes a good purchase—pareus, silk-screened or hand-painted fabrics, loose and languid island styles. Rubber or plastic thong sandals are worn universally and sold universally; other styles of sandal are also available.

Stamps are also excellent souvenirs. The Pacific is a philatelist's paradise, and many Pacific governments have established philately centers as a way to attract foreign currency. Even the noncollector, however, will find these stamps beautiful.

Shell jewelry is everywhere. Pearls are sold in French Polynesia. Some islands are known for jewelry beaded from stones, glass, and seeds. Serious jewelry buyers should check out duty-free shopping centers, where gold, silver, and precious-gem items are offered.

The duty-free centers in general feature appliances and clothing, jewelry, luggage, perfumes, and accessories from abroad. For Americans used to discount emporiums, there are no real bargains on appliances or electronics—unless you are reading this at a time of trade war with Japan. The other items, and particularly designer labels, may be somewhat cheaper than at home.

Crafts and handicrafts—the arts of the Pacific—are the main shopping attraction. Keep in mind that many places, in an attempt to appeal to the tourist market and especially the cruise market, have begun to produce "Pacific" items that really do not belong to their own tradition. You can find tikis, for example—wood or stone images of gods or ancestors—in places where there is absolutely no tradition of making tikis. If this doesn't bother you, and you like the tiki, buy it by all means, but the traveler should at least be aware of the kinds of crafts authentically native to each destination. This book provides that guidance, by destination.

Be aware also that some items traditionally used in making island crafts are prohibited entry into the U.S. or are forbidden to be taken from the islands themselves. Tortoise shell and whales' teeth items, for example, can be seized by U.S. Customs officials because both the sea turtle and the marine mammal are considered endangered or threatened species. Papua New Guinea has declared the bird of paradise—and its feathers—a restricted item.

Most island nations have handicraft centers on the gateway island where crafts from the outliers are sold at reasonable and protected prices. Look also in the Women's Cooperative shops, church group shops, and local markets. The goods sold in luxury hotels or at airport shops may have been homogenized and their prices inflated for the tourist crowd, but not always.

Among the crafts practiced with great skill and creativity in the Pacific are weaving, woodcarving, basket making, mat-weaving, and creating masks and tapa. Tapa (*siapo* in Samoa, *masi* in Fiji), made from the bark of the paper mulberry, continues to have great importance to traditional Polynesian culture. It is often "dress wear," reserved for ceremonies and rituals and used as a sign of rank or wealth. The traveler can see it being made in Western Samoa and Tonga in particular—and should try to do so. The bark of the mulberry stalk is stripped and the inner bark scraped and beaten with a mallet. Then the strips are moistened and smoothed, first by being drawn across a plank, then with a shell. The stretched strip is folded and the water is pressed out of it; then it is folded and pressed again and again. Once a bundle of folded strips is ready, it is beaten with a four-sided wooden beater to form it into a single cloth of a particular size and thickness. When dry, the tapa is printed and overpainted, usually in red and black; the tapa designs once served as cultural signatures of communities or extended families. Tapa is today used widely for items sold to tourists—place mats, briefcases and handbags, a variety of accessories.

Papua New Guinea is something of an exception to the general run of crafts in the Pacific—as it is to almost everything. If Melanesia in general seems a particularly creative artistic area, PNG remains today a world center of primitive art. Authentic old pieces are hard to come by and, justifiably, extremely expensive when available, but the contemporary art of PNG, and particularly along the Sepik, is often quite exceptional. If you are saving your pennies for one supreme purchase, PNG is probably the place.

A final note about shopping concerns places to shop. Virtually every island in the Pacific has an open-air public market to which people come to sell and buy a variety of food and wares. As for commercial stores, they vary in size and style from island to island. Everywhere in the Pacific, however, the traveler finds the "general trading store," the direct descendant of the 19th-century trading station started by the great mercantile houses. Those great firms—Burns Philp (often called BP and once known as "Bloody Pirate"), W. R. Carpenter, Morris Hedstrom, and Godeffroy & Sons—are still represented today throughout the Pacific, both in plush hypermarkets and in some capitals and in darkened, ramshackle structures on the out-islands. On almost every Polynesian island—except in the Cooks—the local trading store is known as "the Chinaman's"—*chez le Chinois*, in French—and is efficiently run by immigrants or the children of immigrants from this nation of merchants. The general trading store is a combination grocery–hardware–package store–clothing emporium–candy store–tobacco shop–stationery and all-round supplier of anything an interisland vessel can carry. It is also, very often, the center of town.

# ADVENTURES IN THE PACIFIC

The adventure of travel in the Pacific does not reside in museums and cathedrals, although both are to be found here. If you want to spend weeks climbing wilderness mountains, this is not the place, although there are mountains to be climbed here. (And PNG is again an exception, possessing wilderness so dense it may never have been penetrated, as well as mountain trails, whitewater rivers, etc.) The Pacific adventure consists in smaller pleasures, less dramatic activities—except, perhaps, underwater—and in the travel itself.

## Land Adventures

The higher islands offer hiking that is in some places a moderate walk and in others a desperate slog. There is fine walking everywhere in the Pacific, especially on the outliers, where motor traffic ranges from none to very little. Tracks crisscross most islands, the highways of intervillage communication.

## On, Under, and Beside the Water

There is almost no limit to water activities in the Pacific. To swim, travel in any direction on the island; one thing you can be sure of is that you will come to water. Lagoon water is limpidly calm and delightfully warm; sea swimming can be rugged on the leeward side of an island—it doesn't hurt to ask someone if the water looks rough and you're not sure about it.

Snorkel anywhere. For scuba, you are best advised to go with a reputable dive operator. The islands of the Pacific, not surprisingly, have an abundance of these. Many offer certification courses, mostly PADI (Professional Association of Dive Instructors) or, in the French territories, CMAS (Confédération Mondiale des Activités Subaquatiques). Both certifications are acceptable worldwide; the CMAS certification is called the *brevet élémentaire.* Snorkelers are almost always welcome on dive trips; it's a good way for the snorkeler to get out from the shore and see some new waters, but if the dive destination is to a particularly deep site, it may not be worth it.

You can ride in all sorts of boats in the Pacific, but the one sort you shouldn't miss is the outrigger canoe. See if you can hitch a ride with some fishermen heading out to the open sea, although you might want to watch them before you decide to go along. It is a thrill to see these islanders bobbing up and down in their puny little craft, waiting for the right wave, until they shoot the pass from lagoon to ocean. Try paddling an outrigger yourself; it's more difficult than it looks, tending to go in circles when you apply paddling techniques perfected on New England ponds.

Lagoon fishing is mostly spearfishing, but the traveler can arrange line-fishing trips both in the lagoon and in the deep sea. Hope that you will find a communal fish drive, with a circle of villagers holding the net in the lagoon while others, often in canoes, "beat" the fish toward them.

Island tides, by the way, typically have a limited rise and fall due to the islands' location in the deep waters of midocean, far from continental coastline and the continental shelf. High and low tides tend to occur at about the same time each day because solar oscillation is greater here than lunar.

That every Pacific island is ringed by exquisite beaches is so much applesauce, but it is true that you can find beaches here that are beautiful, unspoiled, and completely empty of anyone but yourself—especially on the out-islands.

## Entertainment, Events, Nightlife

Forms of entertainment differ from country to country, between gateway and outliers, from day to day. There are movie houses in many Pacific capitals; the movies shown run to decade-old teen horror flicks, and the schedules are erratic. To a great extent, movie theaters have been beaten out by video, which is everywhere in the Pacific. Someone in some village will have a player, and the whole village will show up to watch the movie; they seem to stand on one another's shoulders twenty deep outside the hut or house. Video rental shops are almost everywhere; Westerners for some reason find their occurrence incongruous.

Many hotels, especially in Polynesia, run "island nights" once a week—parties with native feast food and performances of native dancing. These run the gamut from dreadful, Hollywoodized floor shows to congenial gatherings where the dancing is authentic and very exciting. Hotel bars, local watering holes, and clubs and discos in the gateway capitals are also good places for spending an evening.

All island nations have their national days or important holidays or festivals of one sort or another. If you're the kind of person who likes to plan a trip around festivals, check with the tourism boards of the islands you intend to visit. Otherwise, if you luck into a festival or national celebration, enjoy it. Former British colonies typically celebrate the queen's birthday on June 14; the French territories celebrate Bastille Day a month later; American Samoa and Guam celebrate the Fourth of July. The two great pan-Pacific celebrations are the South Pacific Festival of the Arts, held every four years (1988, 1992, 1996, etc.) in a different location, and the South Pacific Games, held every three years (1987, 1990, etc.).

Some island cultural centers will occasionally put on special performances of theater, dance, or music. Ask about this at the tourism office or your hotel. If the Raun Raun Theater is in residence when you are in Papua New Guinea, by all means try to see a performance.

One of the great forms of entertainment in the Pacific—with no disrespect intended—is churchgoing. Services are well attended, the worshippers are fervent, and the singing is absolutely fantastic. Denominations include Roman Catholic, "basic" Protestant, and the so-called new religions: Mormon, Jehovah's Witness, Pentecostal, and, on Saturday, Seventh-Day Adventist. Several Baha'i centers are scattered through the Pacific. Weeknights, if you hear some terrific singing down the street, that is probably choir practice; drop in, or drop down on the ground outside and listen.

Among all of these new religions, a special word about the Mormons is in order. This unusual denomination, based in the state of Utah in the U.S., has achieved enormous success in the Pacific, particularly in Polynesia, which is referred to by the church organization as "Mormonia." That the Mormons should have made such efforts among the brown-skinned peoples of the Pacific is striking in light of Mormon resistance, until very recent history, to the admission of any blacks into the church clergy in America.

The Church of Jesus Christ of Latter-Day Saints, the official name of the Mormon Church, first set foot in the Pacific on Tubuai, south of Tahiti, in 1844. The idea for the mission was approved personally by Joseph Smith, whose experience of receiving a visitation of angels in the spring of 1820 had started the Mormon church. Early missionary efforts received but meager support from the home church in Utah, and the missionaries—known as elders—were called home in 1852. In 1873, bonds were restored with the Reorganized Church, and, in 1892, the Mormon Church of Utah recognized the Pacific missions.

Since then, Mormon practice has spread to Samoa, Tonga, Fiji, the Cook Islands, New Caledonia, Vanuatu, the Solomon Islands, and the Gilberts. Micronesia has been a particularly active area for Mormon missionary work in recent years. Now, all over the Pacific, the traveler will see the distinctive cream-colored churches and outbuildings of the Mormon center or centers on an island, always with a basketball court. The outbuildings are often elementary and high schools, and many islanders of the Mormon faith go on to Brigham Young University in Hawaii under scholarship.

Equally telltale are the young Mormon missionaries—white shirted, the men with ties, short haired, with unfailingly good manners, riding their bikes down the roads of outliers throughout the Pacific. These young elders spend two years on missionary assignment, often at a great remove from towns or cities, often the only Westerner for miles around. Many show an exceptional ability to learn the local language.

There are cynics who say that the great success of the Mormons is directly attributable to the schooling offered, that once the children have finished high school, Mormon fervor ends. But old Pacific hands rebut that contention; the Mormons, they say, from very early on showed a tolerance of traditional ways that was unusual among missionaries—and surprising, given the perspective most people have of the Mormon Church in the U.S. Yet it is true that the first missionaries did not tithe the islanders, they did respond quickly to the Polynesian love of singing by translating hymns into the local language, and they began their efforts of persuasion by working in homes on domestic issues close to the core of daily life and far from the wider spiritual issues. Whatever the reasons for Mormon success in the Pacific, the fact of it cannot be denied—as the traveler will see.

In villages and towns across Oceania, the church is *the* community center and the focus of most social life. Dances for young people, socials for young and old, picnics, meetings, and study groups are all held regularly and provide what entertainment there is on the island. If you are lucky enough to find yourself on an island when a religious conference is being held, you may well be in for days of island-style Christianity—with round-the-clock dance and music performances and marathon eating.

One caveat about nightlife on many out-islands: Friday night is the traditional night for letting it all hang out, and beer, even if theoretically prohibited in some places, is everywhere. On Saturday nights, villagers are preparing for church the next day, so the evening tends to be calm and controlled. But Friday night, with work ended and the weekend ahead, can be rowdy.

## The Pacific Night Sky

Pacific stargazing is an event, an entertainment, and a kind of nightlife all in one. What everyone wants to see is Crux, the Southern Cross, visible the year round in the southern Pacific and in the spring months north of the equator to about 20 degrees latitude.

The Southern Cross consists of five stars. Draw a connecting line down and another across, and you have a cross; without the imaginary lines, the constellation looks like a diamond. It is in the Milky Way, near the south celestial pole, around which the Cross seems to move in a circle throughout the night. Since the south celestial pole is always above south in the sky, being able to recognize the Cross means you can use it as a compass. The ancient Pacific navigators did just that.

Where you find the Cross depends on your latitude, the time of year, and the time of the night. There are, however, two pointer stars, Alpha Centauri and Beta Centauri. The further south you go in the Pacific, the more "overhead" is the Cross in relation to the south pole until, at the pole, the axis of the Cross points directly overhead. It could thus be used to determine latitude as well as direction.

In the north Pacific, where the Cross is way down in the spring sky almost everywhere this book travels, the expert navigators of the Caroline Islands still use it to mark five different steering points as it moves across the sky; at its zenith, the third position, it points south.

The Southern Cross appears on the national flags of Western Samoa, Papua New Guinea, Australia, and New Zealand.

The rest of the Pacific night sky is also splendid. The traveler might want to buy a sky chart before leaving home; try your nearest planetarium or inquire at the American Museum of Natural History in New York.

# ON AN ECOLOGICAL NOTE

Before the era of contact, Pacific islanders lived in harmony with their natural environment—and perforce submitted meekly to natural disasters. A lot has changed since then: the cash economy, war, urbanization, and development have all taken their toll on the health of these often lush and always beautiful island environments. Like most of us, the peoples of the Pacific have only recently come to an awareness of the environment's fragility and of the far-reaching implications, both economic and psychological or spiritual, that environmental destruction can bring. The traveler, as a guest here, has a particular responsibility to be scrupulous in his attention to ecological concerns.

The concerns cover every aspect of the environment. Start with the water. Its tropical blue color comes from the way minute particles suspended in the water—or molecules of the water itself—scatter the sunlight. You'll describe it variously as azure, aquamarine, lapis lazuli, but no word can do justice to the extraordinary clarity of the water, through which you can see down to the life below the surface. Both the health and beauty of the water have been adversely affected by development and particularly tourism development in almost every Pacific nation. Accidental oil spills and, in some places, pollution by industrial wastes haven't helped.

Beneath the surface of the water, out of the sunlight, are the coral reefs, very fragile, easily disturbed, highly productive. In addition to protecting the islands from rough seas, reef life—fish, clams, crabs, squid, oysters, and other organisms—provides much of the protein requirement of islander diets. Yet nearly half of all Pacific countries report reef damage from illegal dynamiting and chemical poisoning—new methods of fishing, and almost all Pacific countries report problems of reef pollution. Siltation, land erosion, dredging on land, and actual construction activities on the reefs themselves have also caused destruction. The traveler should keep in mind certain cautions. When reef-walking, step carefully so as not to break any coral—it has taken a long time to grow. If you pick up any rocks to look underneath, return them to their original position so that the organisms living on the underside are not killed. And never, never break off a piece of reef for a souvenir.

The forests of the Pacific islands prevent erosion, ensure water supplies, and offer a potential economic resource. Yet all over they are being cut down, burned, or destroyed for development. The loss of forest trees means the loss of local sources of food, traditional medicines, and building materials. It wreaks havoc with water supply. The erosion that results leads to myriad disasters—a decline in soil fertility, disruption of weather patterns, increases in storm and cyclone damage. Be careful in Pacific forests: don't think that just because the climate is humid, fires can't start. They can.

Another important aspect of the Pacific environment is the mangrove swamp. These forests and associated wetlands are nurseries of nature, providing habitats to innumerable forms of life. The mangrove tree is one of the few woody plants that can tolerate a saltwater environment; its roots have adapted to growing in the shallow oxygenated layers of mud, avoiding the deeper layers of hydrogen sulphide. Cable roots anchor the tree downward, and aerial roots reach upward. The leaf canopy of mangrove trees provides shade and prevents evaporation of the sediments that house numerous mud-dwelling organisms. Birds rest in these trees and feed on the swamp's ample food supplies. Fish and shellfish feed here, spawn here, and the young "get their feet wet" here. Yet perhaps the most important feature of the mangrove forest is its land-building function. Growing naturally along sheltered shores associated with estuaries and lagoons, the trees and shrubs accumulate sediments silted down the river systems and grow seaward. Although this changes the shape of a seacoast—often dramatically—it also controls floods, prevents wave damage, and helps maintain good water quality. Oil spills and thoughtless development have proven extremely damaging to the mangrove environment.

Of the three kinds of Pacific soil—continental, volcanic, and coral—all are subject to erosion. Overuse has robbed these soils of their nutrients in many places, as has fire—a traditional method of clearing. Salinization occurs on many low-lying islands or across eroded land during storms or if seawater enters the groundwater during a drought. Urbanization has often happened willy-nilly, without careful land use planning, so that good growing areas have been taken over for urban development. Pesticides and chemical fertilizers have also often been used excessively, further depleting the soil.

Conservation movements are a growth industry in the Pacific, although, in the depressed economies of most of the region, conservation officers have their work cut out for them. Many conservation efforts are pan-Pacific, fostered by such regional organizations as the South Pacific Commission and the University of the South Pacific. The commission has formed a Regional Environmental Program aimed at raising conservation consciousness, particularly among the young. One of the program's posters speaks of the Pacific way applied to conservation, inextricably linked to island traditions—a national park or reserve, for example, is equated with a tabu area. The Pacific way, the poster says, is "to rediscover a way of living which will enable us to enjoy our life and in which we constantly improve ourselves and our island life. . . . The most important thing to do is to show respect for our islands in our everyday life. This means looking after our soils, our forests, our reefs. Most importantly, it means caring for each other, working together to achieve a better island life and being of one mind with our people."

## CHAPTER 5

# THE LITERARY PACIFIC

There is, one knows not what sweet mystery about this sea, whose gently awful stirrings seem to speak of some hidden soul beneath; like those fabled undulations of the Ephesian sod over the buried Evangelist St. John. And meet it is, that over these sea-pastures, wide-rolling watery prairies and Potters' Fields of all four continents, the waves should rise and fall, and ebb and flow unceasingly; for here, millions of mixed shades and shadows, drowned dreams, somnambulisms, reveries; all that we call lives and souls, lie dreaming, dreaming, still; tossing like slumberers in their beds; the ever-rolling waves but made so by their restlessness.

To any meditative Magian rover, this serene Pacific, once beheld, must ever after be the sea of his adoption. It rolls the mid-most waters of the world, the Indian Ocean and Atlantic being but its arms. The same waves wash the moles of the new-built Californian towns, but yesterday planted by the recentest race of men, and lave the faded but still gorgeous skirts of Asiatic lands, older than Abraham; while all between float milky-ways of coral isles, and low-lying, endless, unknown Archipelagoes, and impenetrable Japans. Thus this mysterious, divine Pacific zones the world's whole bulk about; makes all coasts one bay to it; seems the tide-beating heart of earth. Lifted by those eternal swells, you needs must own the seductive god, bowing your head to Pan.

Not every writer inspired by the Pacific is as great as Herman Melville, musing here as Ahab finds fresh waters in which to search for Moby Dick, but that an awful lot of writers have been inspired by the ocean and its islands is undeniable.

# THE CLASSICS AND NEAR-CLASSICS

Melville himself, having jumped ship in the Marquesas, and later serving time in a Tahitian jail, wrote about the experiences in two classics, *Typee* and *Omoo*. Both mix fact with a little fancy; both have the author's deadly keen observations and his storytelling power; both rail against the ruination of Polynesian culture from its contact with Western civilization.

Jack London was entranced by *Typee*, as were many before and after him, and made a pilgrimage to Nuku Hiva to follow in his hero's footsteps. He was bitterly disappointed by the journey, as he writes in his vivid account of the year-long, somewhat plagued *Cruise of the Snark* through Polynesia and as far as the Solomon Islands. More can be found in London's collected *South Sea Tales*, one story of which, about the Tahitian pearl buyer Emile Levy, resulted in a lawsuit for which London paid dearly.

Robert Louis Stevenson, who spent the last years of his life in Samoa, has left numerous essays and short stories. These are collected in *Island Nights' Entertainment* and *In the South Seas*.

Somerset Maugham traveled in the Pacific in 1916–17, primarily to do research for the novel *The Moon and Sixpence*, based on the life of Paul Gauguin. Maugham also wrote six stories, collected in *The Trembling of a Leaf*. Among these excellent stories are "Red," which Maugham considered one of his best, and "Rain," the highly successful story about Sadie Thompson that made Maugham even more famous—and much more wealthy.

Two books of less literary worth than these but of great importance for their influence and the longevity of their appeal are *The Marriage of Loti* and that mainstay of high seas novels, *Mutiny on the Bounty*. *The Marriage of Loti* is the largely autobiographical account of the love affair between Louis Marie Julien Viaud—Pierre Loti—and the Polynesian woman Rarahu. Loti came to Tahiti as a midshipman in the French Navy; he later became a friend of Queen Pomare IV, and that friendship is also described in this work, said to have influenced Paul Gauguin to come to Tahiti. *Mutiny on the Bounty*, by the Americans James Norman Hall and Charles Nordhoff, influenced Hollywood to come to Tahiti—again and again and again. There is a *Bounty* trilogy—*Mutiny on the Bounty*, about the mutiny; *Men Against the Sea*, about Captain Bligh's open-sea voyage to Timor; and *Pitcairn Island*, finishing the story of Fletcher Christian and the mutineers. Published in 1934, *Mutiny* is a classic of seagoing adventure.

Not just novelists but poets too were drawn to the Pacific. Rupert Brooke traveled in the South Seas, particularly Samoa and

Tahiti, in 1913–14. In Tahiti, he fell in love with a Tahitian woman, Taata, whom he called Mamua in the three great poems inspired by the love affair: "The Great Lover," "Retrospect," and "Tiare Tahiti."

And not just novelists and poets but artists too—most famous among them, Paul Gauguin. Apart from the paintings, Gauguin left his *Intimate Journals*, first published in French as *Avant et Après* in 1918 and including 28 drawings. The journals provide a vivid portrait of both Polynesia and Gauguin himself—a unique personality, witty, spirited, relentlessly at war with hypocrisy.

One of the very best writers about the Pacific was an unlettered Australian whose works are easily criticized as unpolished and even unskilled. They are never, however, unbelievable, for Louis Becke wrote of events and a way of life he knew at first hand—the heyday of Pacific trade and adventure in the 19th century, when Oceania was thick with rogues and a kind of Wild West lawlessness prevailed. The "dashed good yarns" a Sydney editor asked Becke to write tell of traders at their island stations, of sailors, drunken captains, buccaneers, and beachcombers. He writes about one of the most famous villains of the Pacific, Bully Hayes, with whom Becke served as supercargo, the business agent aboard a trading vessel. Becke evokes the life of this era perhaps more vividly than any other writer, and he places his readers in these Pacific settings with great immediacy. Some of the best of his stories have been collected in *South Sea Supercargo*; look also for *By Reef and Palm*, *The Ebbing of the Tide*, *Pacific Tales*, and *Rodman the Boatsteerer*.

James Michener was a fan of Becke, and Michener's Pacific writings reach their zenith in the first of them, the classic *Tales of the South Pacific*. The tales, from which the Broadway musical *South Pacific* was born, focus on what World War II did to the islands, and what the islands did to the men and women brought here to carry out the war. *Return to Paradise*, published in 1950, is a collection of essays and short stories. Michener also collaborated with A. Grove Day in the writing of *Rascals in Paradise*, accounts of three centuries of Pacific characters.

A. Grove Day is an important name in the literature of the Pacific. A professor at the University of Hawaii, Day has specialized in collecting and interpreting this literature. In turn, the University of Hawaii has specialized in publishing such literature, particularly in its Pacific Classics series.

There are many other fine books and stories inspired by the Pacific—look for works by Eugene Burdick and Robert Dean Frisbie, to name but two, but books *about* the Pacific are often as interesting as the tales spun in or enhanced by a fiction writer's imagination.

# HISTORIES AND OBSERVATIONS

The classic firsthand accounts of Pacific travel and adventure are Captain James Cook's logbooks, *The Voyages of the Endeavor*; William Mariner's account of his involuntary sojourn in Tonga 1806–10, published as *Tonga Islands: William Mariner's Account*, by John Martin; the above-named accounts by Melville, London, and Gauguin; records of the London Missionary Society, published as *A Missionary Voyage to the Southern Pacific Ocean*; and Louise Michel's *Memoires*, about her seven-year deportation to New Caledonia and her life and work with the natives there.

Other expats, adventurers, sojourners, and of course scientists have added greatly to knowledge and understanding of the Pacific. Perhaps the classic anthropological history of the region is Douglas L. Oliver's *The Pacific Islands*. Although originally published in 1951—revised since—the author's vision is so comprehensive and compassionate and his writing so lucid that the book remains extremely valuable. Margaret Mead's *Coming of Age in Samoa*, despite the controversy, and *Growing Up in New Guinea* also represent important milestones in the West's understanding of the Pacific—and of itself.

Of books by expatriates, among the most charming are Patricia Ledyard Matheson's *Friendly Isles, A Tale of Tonga*, and *'Utulei: My Tongan Home*. Ledyard has also written a history, *The Tongan Past*. The author is a native San Franciscan who first went to Tonga after the war and never left.

An excellent and very readable history of Tahiti is David Howarth's *Tahiti: A Paradise Lost*. For a helpfully clarifying if highly dramatic history of World War II fighting in the Pacific, see William Manchester's *Goodbye, Darkness*.

A superb book about Micronesia is Kenneth Brower's *Song for Satawal*—natural history, human history, and travel.

Alan Moorehead's *The Fatal Impact*, subtitled *An Account of the Invasion of the South Pacific 1767–1840*, is a brilliant work about what happened when "civilization," with perhaps the best of intentions, made contact with the waters and lands of the Pacific. If you read only one book about the Pacific before traveling there, this should be the one.

For scholarly and popular works about the Pacific, covering anthropology, botany, entomology, geography, geology, icthyology, malacology, and zoology, the best source is the Bishop Museum Press, P. O. Box 19000-A, Honolulu, Hawaii 96817, tel. (808) 847-3511. University of Hawaii Press, 535 Ward Avenue, Honolulu, also offers an excellent list. In libraries, look under "Pacific," "Oceania," and region and island names.

# PACIFIC LITERATURE

Until the 1960s, Pacific "literature" was expressed in dance, integrating music and movement to illustrate a story, and through the oral tradition of myths, fables, and genealogies. Many local narratives based on oral sources have long been collected and written down, in particular by researchers sponsored by the Universities of Papua New Guinea and the South Pacific, the Australian National University, and the Micronesian Area Research Center of the University of Guam.

The first works of fiction by Pacific writers date to the early 1960s, and fiction as a Pacific literary form gained force with the establishment of the University of PNG in 1966 and the University of the South Pacific in 1968. If we can speak of an emerging Pacific literature, it is being born out of the progressive dissolution of the oral tradition and the accompanying fragmentation of a traditional worldview. What fuels this literature are diverse cultural traditions, the effects of colonialism on those traditions, the introduction of English or French as a lingua franca and of literacy, and the ferment of independence movements.

Some of the most active voices in Pacific creativity today come from Hawaii, Australia, and New Zealand. Although these literatures share common motifs with the rest of the Pacific, they more properly "belong" to their own ethnically diverse nations.

There is some indigenous Pacific literature in French, coming from French Polynesia, New Caledonia, and Vanuatu, but this literature, mostly drama and poetry, forms a proportionately small part of Pacific literature. At the same time, Micronesia and its University of Guam have thus far contributed little to Pacific literature.

Papua New Guinea, by contrast, has produced a great deal in a short time. Literary expression here has centered at the university and has been given circulation and stimulus through numerous indigenous literary magazines. Indeed, supported by the Institute of Papua New Guinea Studies and the National Cultural Council, creative expression in all forms is very much alive in PNG. The name to conjure with here is Ulli Beier, a writer and a significant catalyst to the literary activity of this extraordinary place.

But perhaps the best known of contemporary Pacific writers come from the Commonwealth countries—English-speaking Polynesia, the Solomons, Nauru, and Vanuatu. The writers here may be said to share an oral culture, a colonial experience, and a Western education communicated through a single language, English. Not surprisingly, an underlying theme of much of the literature produced in this region is an indictment of Western values and an extolling of the virtues of the Pacific way. Mitigating against a single ideology or region-wide, uniform movement are nationalistic tendencies and, to be sure, the individuality that is at the core of any writer's talent and imagination.

At the center of Pacific literature is the Samoan Albert Wendt, whose ability to synthesize island fable and feeling with Western literary structure is nothing short of remarkable. Wendt succeeds across a wide range of writing—story, novel, satire, autobiography—and his influence on other writers in the region continues to be profound. *Leaves of the Banyan Tree, Sons for the Return Home,* and *Pouliuli* are Wendt's well-known novels; *Flying-Fox in a Freedom Tree* is a collection of short stories.

The Tongan Epeli Hau'ofa has written a hilarious satire in *Tales of the Tikongs,* short pieces set on the island of Tiko, a fictional island group that is immediately recognizable to the Pacific traveler. Hau'ofa sends up islanders and island life—like the "traditional thatched house that was traditionally small, traditionally dark, and traditionally damp, a traditionally appropriate abode"—as well as foreign aid-bringers, do-gooders, and know-betterers—like Mr. Higginbotham, who took to drink when "events to which he was morally unaccustomed piled up." Read Hau'ofa's book after you have been traveling in the Pacific for a while; it will crack you up.

There are numerous other novelists, short fiction writers, poets, and playwrights who form today's Pacific literature, and there are numerous anthologies of Pacific literature that give the reader a basic sampling of this emerging phenomenon. Many of these works are hard to come by in the U.S. except in large library collections—the New York Public Library, for one. Many are published by the University of the South Pacific, the University of Papua New Guinea, and by publishers based in Australia and New Zealand. Fortunately for the traveler, indigenous works are available throughout the Pacific, and reading them en route adds immeasurably to the adventure of Pacific travel. The best places for bookstores are Fiji, both the commercial center of Suva and the bookstore of the University of the South Pacific; Papeete and Nouméa; Port Moresby in PNG (the university bookstore); and Honiara, home of the exceptional Aruligo Book Center—but check out local bookstores everywhere.

# PART
# II

# ADVENTURING
# IN POLYNESIA

FRENCH POLYNESIA
THE COOK ISLANDS
WESTERN SAMOA
AMERICAN SAMOA
TONGA

The many islands of Polynesia represent the last place on earth to be settled. Sailing, drifting, or swept eastward from Southeast Asia or from islands in the western Pacific, the ancestors of the Polynesians came last of all to the archipelagoes contained within the so-called Polynesian triangle: from Hawaii in the north to New Zealand in the southwest and east as far as Easter Island.

These were also among the last islands to be "discovered" by Europeans—in what is known as the English period of Pacific exploration (really English and French) of the 18th century. Perhaps timing had something to do with the impact Polynesia would have on the Western imagination; in any event, in the hearts and minds of the inhabitants of gray, cool northern Europe, where the air was beginning to smell of industrial smoke and moral restrictiveness, the accounts of the voyages of Wallis, Bougainville, and Cook struck a resounding chord. Even today, the nations of Polynesia include the most fabled of romantic island dreams, the hoped-for paradises people think of when they think of "the South Seas"—Tahiti, whose siren song of beauty, plenty, and graciousness lured Fletcher Christian and the other *Bounty* mutineers to their intriguing doom; the Marquesas, where Gauguin finally came to rest, and in whose Typee Valley Herman Melville found an exquisite paradise from which he longed to escape; Samoa, described by that most romantic of poets, Rupert Brooke, as "sheer beauty, so pure it is difficult to breathe in it."

The European love affair with Polynesia has left scars, both visible and recondite. All too widely, current realities have obscured or effaced the very things that made these islands so famous in the West in the first place. The traveler who is looking for a paradise of secluded beaches where he can wear little and do less will have to look very hard, travel quite far, and expend a fair amount of energy to find what he has come for, although, except for the scanty clothing, frowned upon in pious Polynesia, it can be found.

The 20th century has had a long reach in this vast area—hardly an out-island lacks a VCR. Tourism plays a major role in many places, though not all. While Tahiti has certainly become an institutionalized "tropical holiday paradise," most of the other island nations have either failed to achieve that status or have chosen not to. It is also a fact that both Micronesia's Guam and Melanesia's Fiji get more foreign *arrivals* than Polynesia, even if many are transient.

Yet tourism, along with fishing and the exploitation of the seas, holds a potential for economic growth that must be exploited as the subsistence economy stagnates. It is a situation that presents local governments with some hard decisions. How to keep or regain traditional values when one of its anchors—subsistence living—is passing from the scene? How to combine the best of precontact with the facts of contact? How to recapture the paradise that the Europeans, wanting a taste of it, devoured? How to be a small island in the 20th century? And how to do it all in the pride of independence that must often be tempered by the realities of dependence on greater powers and of interdependence with regional neighbors?

The answers vary, for the traveler no less than for the islanders most profoundly affected. In French Polynesia, the traveler can see the impact of tourism development gone rampant, creating, on the world's most beautiful islands, carbon copies of Waikiki or Hilton Head or Miami Beach. In American Samoa, he can see the impact of foreign aid gone rampant, effacing a traditional culture and replacing it with absolutely nothing at all. Yet right next door, in Western Samoa, the traveler can explore a traditional culture that is very much alive. In the Cook Islands and Tonga, the traveler will note a seeming absence of turmoil—or stimulation. Looking harder, he notes the absence of many islanders, and the long lines at the exit visa office—another Pacific migration underway.

These observations alone make Polynesia a fascinating experience for the traveler. So does the undeniable beauty of these islands. So does the fact that, over time and distance and across many dif-

ferences, the distinctively Polynesian culture colors every minute of
the travel experience.

## DISTANCES AND DIFFERENCES

The most Polynesian city in the world today is Auckland, New
Zealand. Yet in both New Zealand and Hawaii, decidedly non-Poly-
nesian populations and cultures prevail, and these island chains cannot properly be said to be part of Polynesia. Excluding these two
points of the Polynesian triangle still leaves an area of some 39 million
square kilometers, from west of the International Dateline and the
Kermadec/South Fiji Ridge at Tuvalu to Easter Island beyond the
East Pacific Ridge, and from just north of the 10th parallel to just
below the Tropic of Capricorn. Within this vast area, hundreds of
islands of varying size compose a total land area of 8260 square
kilometers.

Look at the map. Virtually every clod of earth east of the 180th
meridian is Polynesia—save the Line Islands, which have historically
been heavily influenced by Polynesian culture. Moreover, the distances between clods are enormous. So are the differences, from nation to nation, even from island to island.

Some of the differences are immediately obvious to the traveler
and derive from recent colonial history. There are Frenchified Polynesia, Americanized Polynesia, and New Zealandized Polynesia
where the population out-Englishes the English. These legacies determine which side of the road cars drive on, where the beer comes
from, which lingua franca the traveler can rely on.

More fundamentally, island types vary, from the jagged heights
of the Society Islands to verdant, amiable Samoa to the low, reef-
ringed atolls of Tonga. Climates vary; because Polynesia encom-
passes so extended an area, latitude, elevation, and the prevailing
winds all affect the weather of a particular moment in a particular
place. Political entities vary, from independent parliamentary democracies to independent kingdoms to territories and possessions and
spheres of influence. France, New Zealand, and the United States
are deeply involved in Polynesia, which also includes the Kingdom
of Tonga, the one Pacific nation that never came under foreign
rule—at least officially.

Even the makeup of the tourist and expatriate population varies. If Melanesia is filled with Australians and New Zealanders—
and the French of New Caledonia—and Micronesia is stocked with
Japanese tourists and American contract workers, Polynesia's expats and tourists are harder to categorize. The watering holes favored by *palagis*, foreigners, in the capitals of Polynesia tend to

have a more international clientele than elsewhere in the Pacific.

The traveler will find that the style—and the costs—of travel differ greatly among these five island nations. In French Polynesia, even basic necessities don't come cheap; in Tonga, even the height of luxury is affordable, though the definition of luxury is also different. The traveler will everywhere be treated to the basic Polynesian dish of raw fish marinated in coconut cream, though it will have different names and slight variations in taste from island to island. Equally pervasive is *pisupo*.

# THE POLYNESIANS

The unifying essence in the midst of all this diversity is the Polynesian people (and the pisupo). Robert Louis Stevenson called them "God's best, at least God's sweetest work." The traveler will not dispute the statement. Despite linguistic distinctions and variations in social patterns, there is a single overriding Polynesian culture shared by all Polynesian people.

There are today about half a million Polynesians scattered over their numerous islands. Only Western Samoa, Tonga, and Tahiti—at 1042 square kilometers, the largest island by far of Polynesia—can claim populations of over 100,000. Archaeological evidence is fairly conclusive that today's Polynesians are descended from the Lapita pottery makers who reached Fiji around 3500 B.C. and were themselves the descendants of original Southeast Asian migrants via the Melanesian Chain. It was from Fiji, starting in around 3000 B.C., that the Lapita seafarers struck out to settle, over the course of centuries, the Polynesian triangle.

Their first stops were Tonga and Samoa, together regarded as the cradle of Polynesia. In these island groups, over a period of perhaps a thousand years, distinctively Polynesian linguistic and cultural characteristics were developed. From here, voyagers went first to the Marquesas. From the Marquesas, some moved southwest to the Society Islands, while others struck out south and east along the Tuamotu Archipelago as far as Easter Island. From the Society Islands, meanwhile, other seafarers also moved in opposing directions, some heading down to New Zealand, others up the Line Islands to Hawaii. Perhaps somewhat later, similar split-direction voyages were carried out from the Marquesas. There are also Polynesian influences of long standing in parts of Melanesia and Micronesia, so it seems clear that Polynesian voyagers pushed and pulled in various directions. Indeed, it is not unlikely that some reached the shores of South America and then moved back westward; as travelers only, they left no lasting influence, but may have taken with them the problematic sweet potato.

Indeed, what the voyagers picked up, and what they lost, during their centuries of migration is still fertile territory for researches in a variety of disciplines—history, archaeology, ethnography, linguistics, botany. What is known is that, on the relatively lush islands they settled, the first Polynesians were both farmers and fishermen. They cultivated taro, yams, sweet potato, bananas. They worked the bark of the paper mulberry tree into tapa mats, aprons, shawls. They fished the streams and lagoons, and in their outrigger canoes braved the passes of reefs to search for tuna and bonito in the open sea.

Within a highly collectivist social structure, there was nevertheless a measure of flexibility. Group kinship could be claimed through either the paternal or maternal line, and superior skill afforded mobility within the group. Such a system was probably a necessary concession to land scarcity; choice of affiliation enabled the society to balance available land and population density. In Huahine and Raiatea in the Society Islands, the traveler today can see the remains of *maraes*, the open-air structures of terrace and uprights that gave concrete form to these groupings of kinship, profession, even household—each begun with its source stone from the first marae of the original grouping.

But rank did exist. Within each grouping—or ramage, as the anthropologists call it—preference was given to the firstborn, particularly to the firstborn son. The firstborn in turn founded his own branch of the ramage, so that succeeding generations continually expanded the grouping. The highest-ranking member of the ramage, the *arii* or *ariki* or *alii*, held a certain amount of authority and commanded a certain amount of deference by dint of possessing a major share of mana, the probably supernatural power of accomplishment which the deities held to a superlative degree, but which could also be lodged within an object or was the source of skill in an individual. Though junior members of a ramage, the commoners, had land rights and could advance in rank through evidence of mana, ariis, having inherited mana, in general had to be separated from commoners. Their domains, and even objects they touched, held such power as to be dangerous to ordinary individuals and thus had to be avoided—they were tabu. On some islands, notably Tonga and Tahiti, these concepts of mana and tabu became so institutionalized that contact between those of high rank and low was virtually nil, while chiefly personages became almost immobilized. In more open societies, such as Samoa, genealogical and achieved statuses were equally important; Samoan leaders, the *matai*, were and continue to be selected by their kinsmen on the basis of ability, achievement, or political alliance. The theory is that the more open societies of ancient Polynesia evolved on islands where population and resources were dwindling; stability here depended more on military or political effectiveness—status rivalry and warfare between chiefs was almost universal and virtually constant—than on religious clout. Nevertheless, in Polynesia today, rank counts.

To the early explorers, what was most wonderful about the islands of Polynesia was the hospitality of the people. This was expressed most dramatically in the sexual freedom that prevailed, to the delight of Western sailors, whalers, and traders, and to the horror, or so they said, of Western missionaries.

The hospitality was deeply rooted in Polynesian social structure. It *was* Polynesian social structure. To a Westerner, a culture in which private property was an unknown concept, all necessities obviously belonged to all, and necessities were pretty much all anyone bothered to work for must have looked very hospitable indeed. The early Western traders were able to exploit this. For natives trying to set up as traders, however, it spelled disaster. Since an islander had to give, not sell, whatever a member of his kinship group might ask for, the trader's stores were quickly depleted, with little profit to show for it. Polynesians have now learned how to be storekeepers—and store customers—but Polynesian hospitality persists.

## ARTS AND CRAFTS

In the traditional culture, where steady work ensured the necessities of life and a collectivist society guaranteed them, there was time for expending creative energy in religious, political, genealogical, and behavioral elaborations. This was reflected in the arts and crafts of the island groups, and it is in the arts and crafts of the islands that such cultural vestiges persist today. Tapa, for example, remains important throughout Polynesia today, although tapa designs are no longer necessarily the cultural signature of a kinship group. Yet there is hardly an important occasion in Tonga that does not merit the presentation of tapa, or at which the traditional pandanus-weave mats, the ta'ovalas, are not worn. *Kava* bowls are still elaborately made, often for sale to tourists who will turn them into salad bowls, but the kava ceremony of Samoa still proceeds according to elaborate ritual, although you can also buy a cup of kava in the market in Apia. Tourists can also buy the "fly whisks" that are the badge of office of talking chiefs in Samoa, but the talking chiefs still use them when they hold forth in their meetings. Indeed, Western Samoa, whose advanced openness made it an exception among the societies of ancient Polynesia, showed such resilience that today it affords the traveler his best look at what *remains* of traditional Polynesia.

Many of the arts of Polynesia were lost under the fatal impact of European settlement and Christian missionary work. Religious stone and wood carvings exist now in museums and, as mass-produced tikis, in tourist shops. Breastplates of wood, tied by coconut fibers and decorated with shark's teeth and doghair, and the spears, axes, and clubs meant to pierce or destroy them, are no longer needed or made. Also gone are the elaborate headdresses of feathers, shell, ivory—the top of the head was the sacred part of the body throughout Polynesia.

Feeling of form characterized these arts—the performing arts as well as the plastic arts—and it continues to do so today. The traveler may buy baskets in Tonga, kava bowls in Samoa, carvings in Tahiti and the Cooks, but it is the dance, the one art you cannot wrap up and take home with you, that should not be missed.

Dance was one of the most important art forms of traditional society—the visual embodiment of poetry, story, ritual. Especially in Tonga, the Cook Islands, and Samoa, the traveler today can see some of the extraordinary dancing still being learned and vigorously performed almost whenever an occasion can be thought up for an excuse. Of course, the dancing varies from island group to island group, and it takes a good deal of experience and knowledge to "read" the dancing. But little expertise is needed to recognize the spirit—by turns aggressive, graceful, sensuous, funny, earthy, and always very much alive—of the traditional Polynesian societies virtually effaced by Western influence.

# THE TRAVELER IN POLYNESIA

The hypothetical Pacific traveler of this book visits five island nations of Polynesia and some twenty separate islands. International airport to international airport, the flights from Tahiti to the Cooks to the Samoas to Tonga cover more than 3000 kilometers; interisland flights add several hundred kilometers more. Distance is a key to Polynesia.

In fact, the distances within Polynesia are a major obstacle to travel here. The trips from island nation to island nation, and sometimes from gateway to outliers, can be so time consuming and costly that the traveler with the usual limits on time and funds may feel he is only scratching the surface of Polynesia. In a sense, this is true. To get "way out" isn't easy; neither is managing the necessities when you *are* "way out" on a far-flung out-island. For these reasons, the itinerary chosen by our Pacific traveler is quite specific; it will, however, enable the traveler to dig well beneath the surface.

Domestic airlines take you to the outliers: Air Tahiti, Cook Islandair and Air Rarotonga in the Cooks, and Friendly Islands Airways in Tonga. South Pacific Island Airways—SPIA—also links many of the Tongan out-islands, as well as serving the Samoas. Air Nauru, one of the Pacific's several on-again, off-again airlines, may also connect some of the Tongan outliers along one of its international routes.

A variety of interisland ferries and cargo ships also ply these waters, linking the outliers to the gateway, and often traveling between these nations—fine if you have a lot of time. French Polynesia also features decidedly passenger-oriented cruise ships.

Polynesia is closed on Sunday—nowhere more so than in Tonga.

## CHAPTER 6

# FRENCH POLYNESIA

*Name:* Territoire d'Outre-Mer de Polynésie Française
*Political status:* Overseas territory of France
*Island groups:* Society Islands, Marquesas, Australs,
    Gambiers, Tuamotus
*Gateway island:* Tahiti
*Capital:* Papeete
*Population:* ca. 180,000
*Land area:* 3567 square kilometers
*Language:* Polynesian (Tahitian), French
*Currency:* Cour du franc Pacifique franc (CFPF)

French Polynesia assaults the senses, although not, at first, in the way the traveler might have expected. Papeete and the sprawl of its suburbs, fast cars on fast roads, French menus and French fashions, lavish waterfront hotels and hordes of tourists abruptly and effectively give the lie to the myth of South Seas languor. On the most accessible of the out-islands, the decibel level is lower, but the glitz often persists. Hang on; once you're no longer blinded by the dazzle, you can look with more accepting eyes on the extraordinary physical beauty of these islands. When you're back home next winter, it's this that you'll remember.

## GEOGRAPHY, TOPOGRAPHY, CLIMATE

French Polynesia, an overseas territory of France, consists of some 130 islands and islets totalling approximately 3567 square kilometers of land across more than 4 million square kilometers of the south-central Pacific. The whole of Europe could fit easily into this vast area. Europe, however, is 18,000 kilometers away. The west coast of the U.S. and the east coast of Australia are each about 6500 kilometers distant.

The islands lie in a northwest-to-southeast orientation between latitudes 10 and 30 degrees south and longitudes 120 and 160 degrees west. The Cook Islands are to the west. Pitcairn, inhabited by the descendants of the *Bounty* mutineers, is to the southeast. North are the Line Islands, and if you continue south from tiny Rupa, the "bottom" of French Polynesia, your next landfall, a long way away, will be Antarctica.

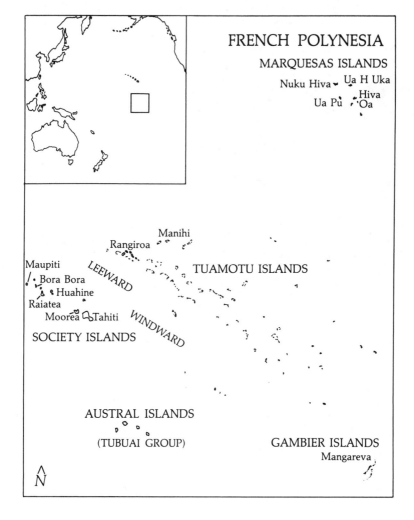

FRENCH POLYNESIA

MARQUESAS ISLANDS

Nuku Hiva ⬢ Ua H Uka
Ua Pu ⬢ Hiva 'Oa

Manihi
Rangiroa

Maupiti     LEEWARD     TUAMOTU ISLANDS
Bora Bora
Huahine
Raiatea
Moorea ⬢Tahiti    WINDWARD
SOCIETY ISLANDS

AUSTRAL ISLANDS

(TUBUAI GROUP)     GAMBIER ISLANDS

Mangareva

N

The islands fall into five distinctive archipelagoes. The most famous, and the center of administration, commerce, and action in the territory, are the Society Islands (Iles de la Société, or Archipel de la Société). The Society Islands are in turn divided into Windward and Leeward groups. The Windwards, Iles du Vent, number five islands, including Tahiti and Moorea. The Leewards, Iles sous le Vent, include Bora Bora, Huahine, Raiatea, and six others. The ten Marquesas Islands in the Archipel des Marquises, some 1500 kilometers northeast of Tahiti, include Nuku Hiva, Hiva Oa, where both Paul Gauguin and Belgian singer Jacques Brel are buried, and Fatu Hiva, where Thor Heyerdahl and his young bride spent the year of 1936 (about which experience Heyerdahl also wrote a book). The five islands of the Austral group, Iles Australes, also called the Tubuai group, are to the south of the Society Islands. The Gambier Islands, or Mangareva group, consist of a small cluster of four principal islands about 1700 kilometers southeast of Tahiti. Finally, there are the Tuamotus, 76 small islands lying between the Societies and the Marquesas.

Some authorities consider the Tuamotus and the Gambiers one group. Indeed, a look at the map confirms the appearance of a single sweep of islands between the Society and Marquesas archipelagoes. But the archipelagoes of French Polynesia are divided by more than just water—water to a depth exceeding 2000 meters in places. They are also divided geologically and topographically into either high islands, volcanic formations, or low islands, mostly coral atolls. The Society Islands, Marquesas, Australs, and Gambiers are high islands, though a few atolls disperse themselves among them. The Tuamotus are a string of low coral islands, all but one of them atolls, and they thus contrast strikingly with the cluster around Mangareva in the Gambiers to the southeast.

The high, volcanic islands are dramatically jagged in outline and present a relief of sharp peaks and deep valleys. Streams, small rivers, and waterfalls tumble or rush down the hillsides, draining out into the lagoon and forcing passes in the coral reefs. These are the travel-poster islands, the earthly paradises of green and blue and gold so alluring to Western imagination. The low islands are barely above sea level—and often go below it during storms. Their limestone soils and inadequate freshwater resources keep vegetation scanty, though many were planted thickly with stands of coconut during the height of the copra era. Their beauty is of a different kind, harsher and less forgiving perhaps, but extraordinary nevertheless.

The territory's climate is basically humid and tropical, but such factors as latitude, elevation, and position relative to prevailing winds cause significant weather variations among the islands. Generally speaking, the period November to April brings the greatest heat and humidity, while the rest of the year tends to be cooler and drier. Hurricane season traditionally begins in January; the yachties settle in at some island or other, planning to be off again around April 15, when the storms *traditionally* end. The other weather rules of thumb also apply here: the closer you are to the equator, the hotter it is (viz., the Marquesas are hotter than Tahiti, which in turn is more tropical than the Australs); the windward side of an island, the southeastward face, will be wetter—and more lush—than the leeward.

# THE NATURAL ENVIRONMENT

Two facts inform the natural history of French Polynesia. First, as the easternmost land in the Pacific, these islands are the least in variety of species, although the flora, to be sure, make up in abundance and health what they lack in variety. Second, many of the species of plants and animals introduced by man—both Polynesian voyager and European—have had and continue to have a destructive or at least altering effect on the natural environment.

## Flora and Fauna

The first European explorers had an impression of a wealth of vegetation in the islands of French Polynesia. Much of it was the fruit of human skill and labor—islanders cultivating the plants that had been carefully transported in their ancestors' canoes. The islanders were evidently quite remarkable horticulturists; living on isolated islands, they took care to select and improve their most useful plants. Among these were breadfruit, taro, yam, coconut, papaya, and the sweet potato.

The early settlers had also brought the pig, dog, and chicken, all of which were bred for food. The horse, cow, rat, goat, and cat came later with the Europeans. Cats killed off several species of birds, and rats attacked the coconuts. Throughout French Polynesia today, the traveler sees metal bands on the trunks of coconut trees; these are antirat devices. The wild descendants of those pigs that escaped domestication or the knife still roam the interior of these islands and are sought eagerly by hunters.

The giant snail, also an introduced species, ravages vegetation and has eliminated local snails; introduced into Tahiti, it has spread to other islands. The sheep brought by Europeans, and allowed to roam freely, destroyed the vegetation on numerous islands—especially the Marquesas. The introduction of destructive species of animal continued into the 20th century; the mynah bird (*Acridotheres tristis*), brought in to ward off flies and other insects, bred rapidly and chased indigenous birds from the coastline into valleys, from which many have now completely disappeared. The bird also makes a terrific racket.

Introduced plants have often proven destructive as well. It is estimated that the Europeans effectively destroyed virtually 80 percent of existing forest cover on a number of islands, planting such new species as the guava, lantana, and various ornamental plants. This severe change affected not only local plant life but also local fauna and especially birds. On the high islands, one can sometimes find upriver a few original trees—candlenut, for example; along the coast, the traveler can find such original survivors as Barringtonia, Calophyllum, casuarina, ficus, hibiscus.

The environmental equilibrium that exists today is as fragile as ever. The lovely croton plant, for example, brought from Asia and used by almost everybody as garden borders, has moved up from the coast into the valleys and onto the slopes of the mountains, where it greedily crowds out other plant species, depriving them of needed sunlight and water.

But the plant and flower life of the islands of French Polynesia is still a joy for the traveler's eye. Along the shore, ironwood trees are interspersed among the coconut groves, while breadfruit, taro, yam, and other domestic plants are cultivated in the coastal plain. On the steep slopes of high mountains, look for the extravagant orange flowers of the tulip tree. The *mape*, chestnut, grows along rivers and streams.

The blossoms of French Polynesia's vegetation are brilliant, extravagant—flame trees and calliandra, poinsettia, bougainvillea, hibiscus, and frangipani. The most famous of all the blossoms, and one native to these islands, is the *tiare apetahi*, emblem of French Polynesia. The tiare is a species of gardenia, and it flowers nearly all year round. Legend has it that its petals represent the fingers of a lovesick Tahitian maiden, whose low birth prevented her from marrying her prince. It is used for garlands and is worn in the evening behind the ear. The tiare is velvet to the touch and is even more fragrant the second day than when freshly picked.

Fruit trees are cultivated on plantations and are abundant at almost every home—an important staple of the diet. Bananas, mangoes, papayas, avocado, custard apples, and pineapples are prevalent.

## Avifauna

The birds of French Polynesia are few in number, but then, if you had to fly all the way from Southeast Asia or New Guinea to get here, you too might drop by the wayside. The paucity of species in fact lends a particular importance to these birds, at least in the eyes of ornithologists—most of them can be found nowhere else. It is estimated that 90 species live in these islands, some 59 of those species in the Society Archipelago. Most show affinities with the birds of Australia, Asia, and, principally, New Guinea. Because they are birds with no particular talent for long flights, it is posited that they were literally blown here by cyclones or other violent atmospheric conditions.

Having arrived, and being scattered among numerous far-flung and isolated islands, the birds of French Polynesia developed in response to the particular milieu of their particular island or island group—often by undergoing fairly spectacular mutations. Able to exploit to the fullest their ecological possibilities without competition from other species, many changed their feeding habits and alimentary systems. Others were able to simplify the structure of certain organs or the pigmentation of their plumage. A number of birds, in the absence of predators, even lost the ability to fly. No wonder the cats and rats later introduced had such a field day of bird destruction.

In gardens and up the valleys, one sees—hears, anyway—the mynah, the little vini (*Peruviana*), and the zebra dove. Seabirds are numerous: white terns lay their eggs on the branches of breadfruit trees; white-tailed tropicbirds nest in the cavities of cliffs on the high islands; brown noddies call at night among the coconut groves of the coast; boobies—gannets—ply the barrier reefs and are eagerly followed by fishermen, whom they lead to shoals of fish. In the lagoons, look for crested terns, often perched on the thorn bushes of the *motus* (coral islets), and reef herons, also to be found on river banks and in swamp areas. Off Tahiti and Moorea—and only there— you may also see the Tahiti petrel, while crimson-backed tanagers can be spotted among the banana trees on the windward side of these islands.

Perhaps the best vantage for viewing a variety of the birds of French Polynesia is Point Venus on Tahiti. Most species pass overhead from season to season. For a species like the New Zealand cuckoo, French Polynesia is the eastern limit of the winter journey; at the right time of year, you may see these birds as they end a flight of several thousand kilometers.

## Underwater

Fringing reefs and barrier reefs coexist in the Society Islands and in the Gambiers; they exist separately in most other islands, except in the Marquesas, where there are no barrier reefs.

The smaller passes in reefs are called *hoa;* larger channels may be as much as 30 meters deep. Around the high islands, the hoa are usually opposite freshwater creeks or streams; on atolls, hoa are typically on the leeward side of the island.

The reef flats, on the seaward side of a motu or coral islet, are like a coral foundation. They are poor in algae but have many mollusks, crustacea, pencil sea urchins, and holothurians. At high tide, the flats are visited by parrotfish, surgeonfish, angelfish, and the small white black-tipped and white-tipped sharks called lagoon sharks.

On the sandy-bottomed lagoon slopes, look for sponges, sand crabs, oysters, cowries, cones, starfish, and ceriths, among other species.

Bivalve mollusks are at home on the corral outcrops and pinnacles, as are surgeonfish, angelfish, butterflyfish, soldierfish, harpfish, trumpetfish, and more. The fish tend to hover over a particular pinnacle—to the delight of the snorkeler.

Lagoon bottoms are almost devoid of living coral and algae and are colonized mostly by mollusks. Razor clams lie here almost buried. Most shells remain hidden during the day; only the traces of their nocturnal wanderings are visible.

In the open lagoons, the roving fishes rove—lagoon sharks and stingrays; some, like jacks and mullets, come and go between lagoon and ocean.

Fringing reefs are rich in numerous species of flora. Trochus are abundant, and you can see moray eels, rock eels, surgeonfish, and angelfish. The fringing reefs are mostly alternate substrates of dead and living coral.

# HISTORY

From the Tonga-Samoa cradle, the ancestors of the people of French Polynesia first settled the Marquesas, probably around 300 A.D., then spread southward to the Society, Tuamotu, Gambier, and Austral groups. Primarily because of their size and resources, the Society Islands—and particularly Tahiti and Raiatea—became the cultural center of the region, while Marquesan culture, developing in some isolation, flourished separately until the early 19th century.

Arii, or ariki, or alii—local chieftains—were in charge in these early societies and ruled major territorial divisions, which often were defined by valleys on the larger volcanic islands. Lesser chiefs were those who, through heredity or great skill, had some measure of mana and held sway over territorial subdivisions. Commoners formed the great majority and were prohibited contact with the upper orders. The child of a union between arii and commoner was killed or left to die.

Territorial wars between arii were not uncommon, but no one chief gained hegemony. Resources were abundant, and the systems for distributing wealth seemed to work, while some craftsmen and specialized workers—canoe builders, fishermen, priests—were given special tasks and often had their own "guild" maraes. You can see remains of these maraes today on Huahine.

Oro, the war diety, had become, by the 18th century, the premier god in the pantheon of mythical gods. His cult was centered on Raiatea, and his priests held special status. The *arioi* were a society of actors and singers dedicated to Oro; they traveled among the islands giving performances in return for tribute from the local populations.

In the rather more isolated Marquesas, there were but two social divisions, arii and commoners. Warfare was frequent and bloody; resources here were scarce, and periodic droughts led to food shortages. Cannibalism was practiced.

Some members of Magellan's expedition were the first Europeans to touch these islands; a few landed on Pukapuka in the Tuamotus (not to be confused with Pukapuka in the northern Cook Islands) in 1521. The Marquesas were next; Mendaña reached here in 1595, spending just enough time to name the islands (for the Spanish viceroy of Peru) and for some of his men to kill a few hundred inhabitants. It was a long while till the next contact: Wallis on the *Dolphin* happened upon Tahiti in 1767. His men traded nails, which the natives bent into fishhooks, for sexual relations with the willing young Tahitian girls and became the first to carry homeward their story of a sailor's dream come true in the earthly paradise of "Otaheite." Bougainville in *La Boudeuse* arrived on the eastern side of Tahiti in 1768, and his men had similar experiences. Bougainville called the island Le Nouveau Cythère, after the Mediterranean island onto which Venus rose from the sea. The French and the English have been accusing each other of introducing venereal disease into French Polynesia ever since.

Science and secret orders to look for the southern continent were the purposes of Cook's three voyages—in 1769, 1773, and 1777. Among other activities, Cook befriended the chieftan Tu, who thereby obtained tools and weapons and was able to gain ascendancy over the other chiefs. Europeans found it convenient to deal with a single "monarch," and Tu, now calling himself Pomare, took advantage of this fact. Missionaries—the first were sent by the London Missionary Society—arrived in 1797 and made little headway at first. But when Pomare II, the aggressive son of Pomare, was unable to conquer all Tahiti, he turned to the Christian god for aid; most of the population of Moorea, where Pomare had fled, converted with him, and in 1815, Pomare did indeed succeed in becoming ruler of Tahiti and several outliers.

While the missionaries brought about a cultural revolution— preaching against "licentiousness" and dressing native women in Mother Hubbards—a lively trade in salt pork, copra, pearls, sandalwood, and arrowroot flour was proceeding apace. Pomare II died in 1821, his infant son died in 1824, and the rule of Tahiti passed to Pomare II's sister, Aimata, Queen Pomare IV.

In 1836, French Catholic missionaries attempted to come to the islands and were rebuffed by British-Protestant interests. The French sent a warship to demand reparations, seized the Marquesas, and, eventually, forced Queen Pomare to sign her nation over to the protection of France. A year later, she renounced the agreement and begged British assistance, but none was forthcoming. The Tahitians themselves kept up resistance until 1846, but Tahiti became a protectorate of France in 1847. When, in 1880, the dead queen's son, Pomare V, abdicated, Tahiti became a French colony. Over the next several years, French power was extended to the other island groups of present-day French Polynesia.

During the American Civil War, Chinese immigrants were brought to the islands to work cotton. At the end of the war, the Chinese stayed, becoming shopkeepers and moneylenders. Today, nearly every island of French Polynesia has its Chinese store.

The latter part of the 19th century was also the era when the fame of French Polynesia was spread through literature—Melville, Robert Louis Stevenson, Pierre Loti (Julien Viaud), and poet Rupert Brooke, who could still write of "the brown lovely people who sing strange slumbrous South Sea songs and bathe in the soft lagoons by moonlight." Gauguin arrived in 1891 and found in Papeete "an absurd, almost caricatural imitation of our customs, fashions, vices and civilized absurdities. . . . To have traveled so far to find this, this which I was running away from!" He pressed on, first to the Maiatea district of Tahiti, then to the Marquesas, putting thousands of miles between himself and "this deceptive and conventional European civilization," and preserving, in the paintings he made, a Polynesian civilization now virtually impossible to find.

Colonial society, though Gauguin might abhor it, was well entrenched. At the top were French officials, military officers, and businessmen. Then came other Europeans, the Chinese, and the demis—those of mixed European and Tahitian parentage. At the bottom were the indigenes, maohi.

In World War I, Polynesian soldiers served in the Pacific Battalion of the French Army in Europe, while German cruisers shelled Papeete briefly. In World War II, the local population supported the Free French, forcing the resignation of a pro-Vichy governor. Another Pacific Battalion was formed, and although the territory happily was not a battleground, Bora Bora was used as a base for U.S military forces and as a staging area for men and equipment fighting further west.

The postwar period saw the rise of a popular nationalist movement under Pouvanaa a Oopa, though the majority of the population elected to remain a French overseas territory in the 1958 referendum. It should be noted that the *métropolitains*—people from France living or working even temporarily in French Polynesia—have the right to vote in territorial elections. In 1977, under threat of another independence campaign, the French granted partial internal self-government: a 30-member territorial Assembly elects six of the seven members of a Government Council. The high commissioner, appointed by Paris, presides over the council and controls defense, foreign affairs, immigration, internal security, the civil service, foreign trade, TV and radio, and secondary education. Forty-eight *communes* elect municipal councils and mayors, but administration is effectively in the hands of appointed French civil servants who run five administrative subdivisions, one for each archipelago.

Though French Polynesia has not reached the political boiling point that New Caledonia has, the French policy seems to be to make some concessions to popular rule while digging in to protect France's interests—particularly the Pacific Test Center, which, until 1974, carried on atmospheric nuclear testing on the islands of Mururoa and Fangataufa in the Tuamotus. (Underground testing has continued since 1974.) Despite growing protests around the Pacific and around the world, no French government, whatever its political stripe, has shown evidence of any willingness to close the test center, and a great number of people, both local and expatriate, find employment there.

Tourism provides another boost to the economy, as does the bureaucracy itself. Exports include copra, oysters, and vanilla. A great deal is imported. There is no taxation in the territory.

Though the population of French Polynesia continues to grow, the proportions of each group and their roles in the structure are typical of colonial society. Europeans make up about 15 percent of the population and are at the top of the social structure. Asians represent some 5 percent of the population. Though the categories are not clear-cut, the split between demis and maohi is about 18 percent and 62 percent, and, in fact, the indigene population is becoming increasingly westernized. The highest concentration of population is of course in and around Papeete, a magnet for many young people from the outliers, and few traces remain of traditional Polynesian social organization.

# FRENCH POLYNESIA TODAY

In appearance at any rate, French Polynesia today is perhaps the extreme example of what's been termed the rape of Oceania. A colonial government is in charge; large-scale tourism has pretty much

run amuck; there is video in every village; and young people, having seen or heard about Papeete's Paree, are unwilling to be kept
down on the farms of their native outliers. They even have a word
for it—*fiu*—expressing the frustration, if not despair, of living on
a small island in the middle of a great sea, and of living lives of little
stimulation despite the sunshine and tradewinds Westerners find so
delightful.

The traveler cannot—at least, he should not—avoid exploring
this, for it is at the heart of what must be, for those living it, a certainly confusing and possibly terrifying moment in their history. Exploring it, however, isn't easy. Contradictions and anomalies abound,
throwing perplexing shadows across the traveler's field of vision.

In the main, this is a tolerant society. If ever another argument
against racial purity were needed, it is in the faces of the people here.
Mixtures of Polynesian, European, and Oriental going back hundreds
of years have produced people of great beauty. Yet despite this mixing, the social pecking order keeps the *kaina*, those with mostly
Polynesian ancestry, at the bottom.

Then there is the phenomenon of the *mahu*, the male trans-
vestites first described for Westerners by Captain Bligh. By choice
and/or at parental urging, a young boy assumes a female role from
an early age, performing the traditionally female household tasks,
taking women's parts in dancing—or performing male striptease acts
in the nightclubs of Papeete, and working at jobs that are traditionally women's. There is no stigma attached to this, and Polynesians
show no homophobia; that is, the mahu's sexual orientation is seen
as valid, and the mahu is a fully accepted member of society, if frequently a figure of fun. Today, however, more and more Papeete-
based mahus are turning to homosexual prostitution, and this is seen
as a corruption of the original thrust of this long-held tradition, a
culturally undesirable development in the light of both traditional
and contemporary mores.

Sexual mores have been a confusing issue in these islands since
the first sailors brought back tales of orgies and the first missionaries
thundered against nudity. A recent American visitor to Huahine was
warned off a secluded beach where a young European woman had,
one week earlier, been raped. The young woman had been sunbathing
topless on what undoubtedly looked to her the quintessential South
Seas strand when she was attacked by three men. No police action
had been taken because of the intricate political and family connections on the island, and because, in the words of one islander, the
*young woman's behavior* was considered "absolutely unacceptable."

Returning to Tahiti, the American visitor decided to spend an
afternoon relaxing on the black sand of Mahina Beach. It was a week-

day, and the beach was crowded with members of the French community—energetic children and their mothers. Almost without exception, the mothers were topless. The juxtaposition with Huahine struck the American visitor as bizarre in the extreme. Here were Europeans who had "advanced" to the very state of sophistication they had once found objectionable in Polynesians. Here were Polynesians, receiving horribly mixed signals, whose distaste for a European custom had led to the most brutal results.

Aggressiveness is never too far beneath the surface here. The statistics on wife beating and child battering are frightening. Stripped of their traditional dominant role, often finding that their wives—working in service positions—are the breadwinners of the family, some men seem to need to demonstrate their machismo in violence.

In the past, warfare provided a release for these tensions. So did traditional dancing, which evidence shows to have been very aggressive in nature. Today, almost every native of these islands still learns the *tamure,* the forceful and often erotic hip-shaking movement that is at the heart of the dance of French Polynesia. Traditionally, such dances enacted legends of events—battles, acts of heroism, fishing and sailing. The musical accompaniment was heavily percussive, relying mostly on the *toere,* the long, hollowed-out wooden drum played with sticks. Yet it's almost impossible for the traveler today to see such dancing in French Polynesia; hotel "shows" are slick, looking more like popularized Hawaiian hula dances than traditional Polynesian, accompanied by strings as well as the toere.

It is heartening to know that, in the face of this gloss of blandness, a back-to-the-roots movement is taking hold. Local politicians espouse traditional values; the Polynesian language is now taught at school; ancient crafts are being revived in workshops; a group known as Pupu Arioi specializes in educating children in the traditions that once were the heart of their culture.

It remains to be seen whether this reinfusion of values will succeed against the glitz of Western society and the often terrible identity crisis it has caused. The question may be less what French Polynesia was than what it is going to be. The question is also whether what exists today—a rootless culture for the natives, an economy that seems to be pretty much dependent on a self-perpetuating French bureaucracy—is worth preserving.

On the verandah of a home near Papeete one May night, a group of people was gathered—three Tahitian couples and one French couple, all professional colleagues employed by the government, and an American visitor. Fine French brandy and liqueurs had been served. Frangipani and tiare sweetened the air, and a cool breeze blew.

It was the end of a long, pleasant, enlightening evening. Dinner at one of Papeete's fine Chinese restaurants, Le Dragon d'Or, had proceeded through numerous courses and several bottles of wine. The conversation had been lively and amusing, although the French couple had taken some heat, at first good natured, then less so, as representatives of the clearly resented colonial regime. One man had told how he and his wife, French citizens by dint of their Polynesian birth, had gone to France some years before, arriving late at night after their long journey to find that, despite the French passports, no hotel would accept them because of the color of their skin. Finally, in desperation, the man had pocketed his passport and told a hotelier that he and his wife were Brazilians. They got a room.

On the verandah, the friendly humor was less in evidence. When the young Frenchman asked why he could not find in the newspapers here, as he could at home in Toulouse, discussion of political issues, he was answered almost coldly. "You think we read newspapers?" one man replied. "We do not. We keep current in the old way, by oral tradition. Every district has its center. People wait there, at the store or beneath the tree, for the person who would know about an event. He tells us."

He went on more angrily. "You whites think you know us. You *don't* know us, even the ones who have lived here a long time. You can never know us. Our life is with our people, not where you see us, and you can't go where we are."

The outburst threw a monkey wrench into the evening's pleasantness, though this was quickly recovered. Indeed, the eventual farewells were warm and gracious all around. But as the French couple and their American guest were leaving, the angry Tahitian man took the American by the arm and said, plaintively, *"Vous voyez,* we are the victims of a myth conceived in the imagination of foreigners." He shrugged.

# THE TRAVELER IN FRENCH POLYNESIA

For a number of reasons, French Polynesia can seem unmanageable to the traveler. Start with size. If you're going to explore even a few of these archipelagoes, you are going to be taking several airplane rides, and you are going to be logging a lot of kilometers. Nor will the traveler be the only one logging these kilometers. The territory's highly developed tourism often seems to be a matter of propelling waves of tourists, luggage, and transfer vans into an insufficient number of channels. The independent traveler may occasionally feel caught up in this tidal flow; in French Polynesia, he is in the minority, and little is geared to his particular needs.

Moreover, for the hypothetical Pacific traveler of this book, French Polynesia is the gateway to Oceania—the first stop in the journey. The beginnings of any journey to a strange land can be overwhelming, until you find your feet.

Even with your feet found, there are certain facts of travel life in French Polynesia that the traveler should be prepared for in advance.

## The Price of Fame

The one overriding caveat to keep in mind is cost. Virtually anything you want to do here costs money, and virtually everything that costs money costs a lot.

One explanation, the favorite of tourists, is that since French Polynesians pay no taxes, it is the tourists who are helping to subsidize the economy through the high prices charged for everything they want to do.

The expense may also be due in part to the singular reputation of Tahiti, which surely surpasses that of any other island in the Pacific, if not the world. (Even the French Polynesians, whatever their native island, routinely refer to themselves as "Tahitians," and the term is used universally to mean all the natives of these islands.) For this fame we have to thank the accounts of early explorers, the paintings of Gauguin, and the works of such great writers as Melville, Rupert Brooke, Jack London, and Somerset Maugham. Perhaps above all, we must give credit for this fame to two not overly great writers, the Americans Charles Nordhoff and James Norman Hall, authors of the *Bounty* trilogy (see Chapter 5, The Literary Pacific).

*Mutiny on the Bounty* became the most famous seagoing novel of the 20th century. The longevity of its appeal is reflected in the fact that three generations of movie producers have seen fit to create *Bounty* movies. It is impossible to estimate the numbers of people worldwide who have watched Charles Laughton and Clark Gable, then Trevor Howard and Marlon Brando, then Anthony Hopkins and Mel Gibson fight it out in an exquisite Tahitian setting—real or contrived. Brando, of course, succumbed to the spell of the islands, married a Tahitian woman, and took possession of Tetioara, now a nature preserve which the traveler can visit on a package tour. (Alternatively, the traveler might consider buying the island, which, at the time of this writing, was for sale.)

Tahiti has thus long been a popular tourist destination; indeed, local airlines have flown routes to and from destinations in the western Pacific since 1947. The upgrading of facilities at Faaa Airport in the 1960s, however, at last made possible regular, direct flights between Tahiti and North America, thus sparking a new burst of

American tourism; today, travelers from North America represent some 70 percent of Tahiti's visitors.

Because it was looking primarily to the U.S., Canada, and, to some extent, Australia and Europe for tourism growth, the thrust of tourism in French Polynesia was toward meeting the recreational needs of relatively affluent travelers from the world's richest countries. These people, it was assumed, were looking for a tropical island holiday, and tourism in Tahiti was going to give it to them. The big tourist hotel and the package tour became the beaten track of tourism in French Polynesia; it is not easy to get off the beaten track.

## Accommodations

On almost all the outlying islands served by the domestic airline, Air Tahiti, there are resortlike tourist hotels. Indeed, that is why Air Tahiti flies there. Such hotels are also of course the rule on Tahiti itself. There is nothing intrinsically wrong with these hotels: they are undoubtedly comfortable, occasionally pretty, and equipped with all sorts of facilities. Club Med is in the islands in force, and the Bali Ha'i Boys, three good-old-boy Americans, have built a chain of luxury hotels—and a fortune—in French Polynesia. But for the traveler seeking the adventure of getting off the beaten track in these islands there are at least two things wrong with these large westernized hotels.

First, they tend to be overpriced. Since even the cheapest accommodation in French Polynesia is not cheap, it is worthwhile examining whether the stiff tariffs of the big hotels are worth it. The short answer is: in the big hotels, you're probably paying for more, or other, than you need or want.

Second, they do not encourage or easily enable the traveler to touch or be touched by the life of the island—nor are they intended to. They are intended to be vacation centers; as such, they are pretty much all the same, whether on Tahiti or Bora Bora or Huahine or, for that matter, Oahu or Jamaica or Miami Beach. You will have a spacious room with ceiling fans—no air conditioning, except on Tahiti itself; a private bathroom where the hot water will likely be iffy; a mosquito coil that is supposedly changed each day, or maybe a mosquito net; a restaurant where you can get hamburgers at lunch, steak at dinner, and, on occasion, as a special treat, a "Tahitian meal." The hotel will run tours—an Around the Island Tour, a Glass-Bottom Boat Tour of the Lagoon, and so on—during which the tour leader's well-worn spiel will cater to the lowest common denominator and will tend to include a lot of sexual innuendo about Polynesian women. There will be a swimming pool and a beach or access to a beach. (Beware here: some of these hotels really have just a smidgin of waterfront sand.) There will be a bar, and once a week there will

be a staged "Polynesian show" of music and dancing du
a number of spectators will be hauled onstage to bump anu g-
with the pros. In the hotel shop, you will be able to buy pareus,
T-shirts, black pearls, and souvenirs. You will receive a flower
garland and free drink on arrival and a shell necklace on departure.
You will be able to make arrangements for almost anything you want
to do, and you will be able to make such arrangements in English.

In other words, you really didn't have to leave home. As one
American visitor put it, "If all I wanted was an island, water sports,
and a bar, I could have gone to Hawaii or the Caribbean with far
less trouble and for far less money."

The middle range of hostelries—and more of these are being
developed—tends to be French owned and French run and caters to
French tourists or expats down for the weekend. The Ibis and Mahana
chains are examples of these.

By far the best bet, both for price and for giving you the feeling
that you're on an island of Polynesia, are the *pensions familles,* listed
in English as "accommodation in private homes." These are the
cheapest accommodations in the islands, save the youth hostel in
Papeete, and they offer the adventure traveler the best value for
money in French Polynesia.

At a pension, you will have your own bungalow or room,
possibly with a private bath, although not always with hot water.
You will likely be on the beach, and very often you will be on the
best stretch of natural beach the island has to offer. You will have
three plentiful, good meals a day, taken *en famille* or with the other
guests at the pension. The people running the pension will be able
to make any arrangements you want made—for a bicycle, a tour,
a hike, diving, and the like. But you will not be able to count on
any English being spoken at all, so, if you are not a French-speaker,
you will have to rely on your high school French and/or a phrase
book. At one-seventh the price of a hotel where English *will* be
spoken, it seems little enough effort—especially given the compensations of getting to know some Polynesian families, living something
close to island life, and achieving the tranquillity you have probably
come here for in the first place.

To find out about pensions, go to OPATTI (Office de promotion et d'animation touristiques de Tahiti et ses iles—i.e., the tourist
bureau) in Papeete and ask for, beg, or demand recommendations
for pensions on the islands you intend to visit. Or, if you have
booked flights to the outliers in advance, write to OPATTI about
pensions in advance as well. In fact, the OPATTI staff, who are
courteous, competent, and English speaking, may be induced to
reserve space for you. Indeed, there is evidence that Polynesians
on the OPATTI staff, including those in high positions, agree with

the American visitor who complained that there ought to be more to tourism in French Polynesia than a westernized resort hotel.

## Where to Go

There are beaches near Papeete on Tahiti where it is not safe to swim because the water has been polluted by industrial and residential wastes and by the detritus from the lively maritime activity of the port. A sadder comment is that there is some polluted water off Bora Bora, an island claimed by some to be the most beautiful in the world. As with Tahiti, the original sin in this pollution is the rapid and thoughtless development of these islands. The more immediate sin is tourism development, which has proved so destructive of environment, culture, and tradition that a nearby island, Maupiti, simply refuses to allow a hotel. (Yes, you *can* get to Maupiti, and you can find "accommodation in private homes.")

Here is the harshest possible example of the typical Pacific island conflict between development to benefit the local economy and preservation of traditional values. Too often, travelers from developed countries, looking for someplace unspoiled on earth, are all too ready to shake their heads in disgust when they discover that their notion of a place bears little relation to the reality. Such travelers probably have little sense of reality to begin with. But in the case of tourism development in French Polynesia, two questions are worth asking: is the development wrecking or transforming the very things that made people want to come here in the first place? and is the local economy indeed being benefited? It is possible to answer yes to the first and no to the second. In the long run, the conventional sort of packaged luxury tourism may not be enough—you can get that sort of thing anywhere. In the long run, the outflow of tourist dollars back to the developers' home countries may only further impoverish these struggling islands.

Given all this, and given the vastness of the territory and the expense of being here, where should the traveler to French Polynesia go to find some of the things that make these islands distinctive? Our Pacific traveler visits Tahiti—to get a glimpse of history, a good look at today, and to make arrangements; Moorea—for its beauty and because it is so close to Tahiti; Huahine—for its archaeological interest; Bora Bora—for its fame; and Rangiroa—to gain an idea of atoll living.

A note about the Marquesas: these alluring islands, a favorite haunt of yachties despite the rough anchorages, are difficult of access for just about everyone else. Air Tahiti runs one roundtrip flight per week, Papeete to Nuku Hiva. The flight is heavily booked and *very* costly, and you must spend at least the seven days between air flights in the Marquesas. Staying there and getting around can also be extremely expensive.

These ten wild and rugged islands—only six are inhabited—lack protective reefs and coastal plains; most of the inhabitants live in the narrow river valleys. As the northernmost islands of the South Pacific, remote from the rest of Polynesia, the Marquesas developed a somewhat separate culture, though clearly Polynesian. The people lived in houses built on platforms, called *paepae,* and each valley was ruled by its own chief. You can still see (if you can find them among the junglelike vegetation) the stone temples *(me'ae),* terraces, and fortifications *(akua)* of this lost civilization. The artistic style developed in these narrow valleys reveals the powerful, warlike (and cannibalistic) nature of the people—particularly the great stone tikis. It is worth remembering that it was from the Marquesas that canoes went forth to settle, eventually, in Hawaii and Easter Island.

Herman Melville sealed the fame of Nuku Hiva with *Typee,* his classic account of Marquesan life. Melville described what most people would consider a paradise, and he described what it was like to be an unwilling prisoner in paradise. Like many Melville fans, Jack London wanted to retrace the author's route to the Typee Valley; what he found was a depopulated, overgrown, insect-infested, rather unpleasant swamp.

Gauguin came to Hiva Oa in his ongoing attempt to remove himself further and further from civilization. He is buried here. So is the great Belgian singer Jacques Brel, who died in 1978.

There are basically two schools of thought about travel to the Marquesas. One school holds that the ruggedness and remoteness of these islands make them something very special indeed. Others contend that a week there is a dreadful way to spend time, that island life is backward, that islanders are grasping and unfriendly, and that unless you've brought plenty of cash you're reduced to eating pork and beans out of the can—purchased, of course, at the local Chinese shop. Both views are true, in their fashion; you *do* have to overcome some obstacles to enjoy life in the Marquesas, but the intrepid adventurer may indeed find this worthwhile. Still, because of the cost and length of time required for a visit here, the Marquesas do not form part of the itinerary for the Pacific traveler of this book.

## Getting Around French Polynesia

Air Tahiti serves all of the archipelagoes of French Polynesia. Obviously, not every island has an airstrip, but if you can get nearby, you can hop an interisland boat to get to your destination. Flights to the islands visited by our Pacific traveler are often heavily booked; if at all possible, make your reservations from home and *reconfirm immediately upon arrival* in Papeete.

Air Tahiti flies the ATR 42, the Fokker F27, the Twin Otter, and the Britten-Norman Islander—going from big to little. Not all flights are direct. The main route is Papeete-Huahine-Raiatea-Bora Bora. But you must come back to Papeete again to catch a flight to Rangiroa.

Prices are high. Air Tahiti offers a few special 21-day fares if you have or want to spend the time. The most expensive, going to the most islands—Moorea, Huahine, Raiatea, Bora Bora, Rangiroa, and Manihi—cost $360 in 1987.

Interisland sea travel varies from snazzy passenger ships—the *Raromotai* and the new *Liberté*, with six- and seven-day cruises to the main tourist islands—to a range of cargo vessels with passenger accommodation to the copra boats that mostly offer deck passage. Trips on the interisland steamers are inexpensive but can take weeks or even months. (Of course, if you jump ship on an island with air service, you can take your chances on booking a flight back to Papeete, thus shortening your sojourn.) To find and book a cargo steamer, which tends to be a relatively comfortable way to travel, check the offices along the waterfront, mostly at Motu Uta or Fare Ute and the streets behind it. To find and book a copra boat, invariably uncomfortable, but fun, go to where they are moored, beyond Fare Ute, and talk to a likely looking skipper.

On-island, as the Pacific term goes, many islands of French Polynesia offer one of the most effective and ingenious modes of transportation in the Pacific—*le truck*.

Le truck is just that. The driver sits in the cab, and passengers are ranged down two long benches that line the sides in back. The sides have windows that can be opened for air or closed against dust or rain. On Tahiti itself, the trucks are typically equipped with radios that blare forth loud rock music. You climb on from the back or from just behind the cab, take your seat, listen to the music, and enjoy the ride. When you want to get off, press the buzzer, hop out, and pay the stated fare through the passenger window of the cab. There are no scheduled stops—hail and farewell the truck from anywhere, although there are usually traditional and obvious stopping points along the busier sections of road. In the rest of French Polynesia, and indeed in many of the Polynesian nations, the truck may be less raucous than on Tahiti, but it is equally useful.

# LANGUAGE

French and Polynesian are the official languages. Polynesian here means Tahitian, for other dialects are spoken elsewhere: Paumotu in the Tuamotus, Mangarevan in the Gambiers, Marquesan in the Marquesas.

The first Europeans in French Polynesia thought the language easy. One of the reasons the London Missionary Society chose Tahiti was because its language seemed simple to learn. They were wrong. For one thing, slight changes in pronunciation, at first not even discerned by the Europeans, altered meaning entirely. The vocabulary, assumed by Bougainville to have been no more than five hundred words, was in fact vast. Although it lacked words for Western ideas, the shades of meaning used in describing the environment were extraordinary. Another problem for Europeans was the custom of *pi'i*, avoidance of certain words considered tabu—a chief's last words, for example, or the name of the illness that felled him.

Finally, Polynesian was not a written language; it relied on an oral tradition that was remarkable. When an American anthropologist from Hawaii's Bishop Museum asked a man aged 40, Paea by name, to recite genealogies of Tuamotu, Paea was able to recite them all, accurately, though he had no memory of having learned them. As a child, he had absorbed them almost unconsciously from his own father, who had learned them from his father, and so on.

Throughout French Polynesia, the traveler can get by with French, but here are a few Tahitian phrases; using them may enrich your trip. "E" is pronounced more or less as *ay*; "i" is spoken more or less as *ee*. Pronounce each syllable, except in Ia ora na, which derives from "Your honor," and sounds like it.

| | |
|---|---|
| Ia ora na (from "your honor") | Good morning |
| Vahine | Woman |
| Tane | Man |
| Maruru | Thank you |
| Marite | American |
| Aita pe'ape'a | No problem—don't worry |
| Maita'i | Good |
| Hehenehe | Pretty |
| Nana | Goodbye |
| Motu | Islet |
| Moana (ere ere) | Sea |
| Roto | Lagoon |
| Tamaui | Shark |

## French Polynesia Addresses

In the U.S.:
Tahiti Tourist Promotion Board
12233 West Olympic Blvd., Ste. 110
Los Angeles, CA 90064
Tel. (213) 207–1919
Telex 4971603

For information on Air Tahiti, apply to the above, or ask your trans-Pacific carrier, through which Air Tahiti tickets are arranged.

In Papeete:

> OPATTI (Office de promotion et d'animation touristiques de Tahiti et ses iles)
> Fare Manihini
> P.O. Box 65
> Papeete, Tahiti
> French Polynesia
> Tel. 2 96 26
> Telex ODDTOUT 254 FP

# TAHITI

Tahiti is two volcanic formations joined by the low isthmus of Taravao. It looks like a gourd oriented northwest to southeast, with Tahiti Iti, the peninsula, as the handle to Tahiti Nui. From the air, the traveler gains a good impression of the ruggedness of the landscape—an interior of precipitous green peaks, limned by rivers and valleys, ringed by a narrow coastal plain. A fringing reef (*récif*, in French) hugs the coastline, with numerous passes where the fresh waters flow down to the sea. The island's highest points are Mount Orohena (2241 meters) and Mount Aorai (2066 meters) on Tahiti Nui; both are almost always shrouded in mist. Mount Rooniu (1332 meters) is Tahiti Iti's highest peak.

A paved highway circles all of Tahiti Nui. Road signs periodically indicate the PK (*point kilométrique*, distance in kilometers) from Papeete. The distance around Tahiti Nui is 117 kilometers. After crossing the isthmus, one road proceeds for 19 kilometers along the north coast of Tahiti Iti as far as Tautira; another edges the south coast to just past Teahupoo, also 19 kilometers, before dead-ending. The rest of Tahiti Iti is rugged, often cliffbound coast.

You will need at least one full day in Papeete (pronounced pah-peh-*eh*-teh), the capital of French Polynesia, to arrange the logistics of your travel around the outliers or to reconfirm arrangements already made. Excursions to other parts of the island—including an essential visit to the Museum of Tahiti and the Islands—can take anywhere from one day to several days, depending on what and how much you want to see. If you plan to do some hiking, you'll need yet more time. There are indeed beaches to flop onto here, but you may want to save that for the more tranquil outliers.

## Arriving in Tahiti

Even arrival in Tahiti may seem a bit overwhelming, what with

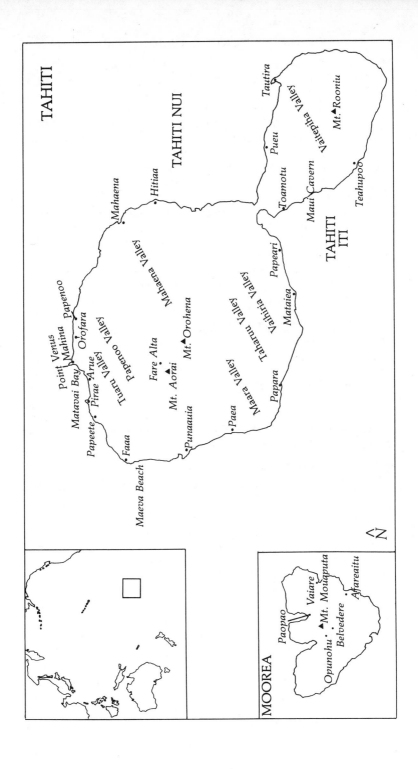

most travelers being met by agents tagged with color-coded badges while activity proceeds apace in this, the gateway to French Polynesia. Faaa Airport is some six kilometers southwest of Papeete.

(Travelers who *embarked* on their flight at Samoa or Fiji may be held up for as much as two hours while their luggage is fumigated. However, since they are free to pass through Immigration and Customs while the fumigating is going on, the best bet for these travelers is to keep enough in their carry-on luggage, which need not be fumigated, for a night's stay. Come back for the big stuff tomorrow. The fumigation is aimed at protecting Tahiti's coconut crop against Fijian and Samoan pests.)

If you have no Pacific francs, which often are obtainable in U.S. west coast money centers, you should change money at the airport. A bank is supposedly open for the arrival and departure of all international flights; so is a welcome booth for tourists run by OPATTI. Don't count on the latter, especially since many flights arrive in the middle of the night, and if the bank is for some reason *not* open— anything is possible in the Pacific—you can usually get by with dollars, especially in a taxi. If OPATTI is open, they can book lodgings for you; be sure to ask how much a taxi to your destination should cost. If OPATTI is not open and it is the middle of the night and you have no idea where you will spend your first night—never a good travel principle—ask somebody; you can always change hotels later. To take le truck to town, head out of the airport, walk up to the road, cross to the other side for trucks heading northeast to Papeete, and hail the first one you see.

## First Things First

Since it is recommended that the traveler use much of his time in Tahiti to arrange travel to the outliers, it is also recommended that he stay in downtown Papeete, the arena of arrangement-making operations and the logical starting point for excursions on Tahiti itself. Downtown offers a variety of lodgings, from businessmen's hotels on the waterfront to family-run pensions. If you haven't been able to book accommodation from the airport, make OPATTI your first stop and do so there. It's right on the waterfront on Boulevard Pomare, just a few blocks from the market where the truck comes to its final stop.

Otherwise, your first stop must be the airline office of Air Tahiti, across Pomare from OPATTI and a few blocks west. Like most business offices throughout French Polynesia, Air Tahiti opens early, at around 7:30 or 7:45, closes at noon for an hour and a half or so, and reopens at 1:30 or 2:00 until 4:00 or 4:30. Here you *must* reconfirm your ongoing flights to the outliers—if you have not already done so at the airport—or try to make reservations. Usually, you can only reconfirm your first flight out, so that at each outlier, you reconfirm the next onward booking. As if that weren't enough aggravation, the Air Tahiti office is monstrously crowded at almost any hour. Get there early and get on line; your turn will come.

You should also reconfirm your international flight onward from Tahiti. As in most cities, airline offices are clustered together—either along Pomare itself or in the Vaima Center, a large urban shopping mall right in the heart of town. You cannot miss Vaima—downtown Papeete is not a big place—and you can enter from Pomare or from the Rue Général de Gaulle, which parallels Pomare inland one block.

Once you are as reliably booked as possible, head back over to OPATTI, tell them the islands you are heading for, and ask them to find you pension accommodations on each or to reconfirm any reservations you may have arranged by mail. Be sure to ask them to arrange also that you be met at the airport on arrival; not only the large hotelkeepers, but also guesthouse proprietors do this routinely throughout the Pacific. While you're at OPATTI, ask any questions you have on your mind—perhaps about activities you particularly want to do; OPATTI is an efficient operation with a lot more resources and savvy than the slick brochures on display would indicate.

With arrangements behind you and a place to lay your head at night, you're free to explore Papeete and the rest of the island.

## Papeete

This is the center of action on Tahiti and for all of French Polynesia, and the traveler perforce will be spending some time here. The name means "water from a basket"; the early Tahitians probably came here for fresh water, though Cook and Wallis found it a marshland. In the 1820s, however, Queen Pomare made it her capital, and sea captains began to frequent its protected harbor in preference to Matavai Bay to the north, where Cook and the missionaries first put in. A variety of waterfront establishments grew up to service the whaling trade and whalers' R&R, and when the French military moved in to protect Tahiti in 1842–43, this is where they moved.

Today, Papeete and its suburbs—Faaa, Pirae, and Arue—are home to over half of Tahiti's population. The construction boom of the 1960s that answered the population boom, with immigrants from both France and the outliers pouring into the big city, sacrificed much of the natural beauty of the site. It is easy to malign Papeete for being modern and busy and not at all what you had in mind, but it is a lively and enjoyable town and the only real city in French Polynesia.

It's a good walking town. Armed with a city map, which is free from OPATTI and most airline offices and hotels, you can quickly orient yourself. The market (*marché* in French) is the liveliest place in town, especially on Sunday mornings when out-of-towners arrive to sell the week's produce or crafts. The rule of thumb about the market is that Polynesians sell Polynesian foods—fish, taro, and yams; the Chinese sell vegetables; and the Europeans and Chinese sell baked goods and meat.

Wander the waterfront. What with yachts, fishing boats, ferries, and freighters, there is usually a lot of activity on and just beside the water. To see the copra boats that may be in—you'll smell them first—go past the naval yard to Fare Ute, where the coconut-oil processing plant is located. The coconuts come off the freighter, and sacks and drums and cartons of store-bought commodities get loaded on.

Sights to see in town include the Territorial Assembly back inland; Bougainville Park next to the post office; and the Catholic Cathedral and the Catholic Archbishop's Palace, not at all near one another. All these preserve the feeling of the old colonial days.

## Food

Food is one of the true advantages of being in Papeete. Not only is there fine French cuisine—not surprising, perhaps, but welcome anyway—there are also good Chinese, Vietnamese, and Tahitian restaurants. Price is, as always, an issue. At the famed Acajou, on the waterfront, a major gathering place during and between all meals of the day, fine French cuisine and great steaks from Down Under do not come cheap. Neither does elegant dining at Le Belvédère, high above the city at the end of the road up the Hamuta Valley, although there you're also paying for the spectacular view and gardenlike atmosphere. Hotel food is also pricey and tends to taste like hotel food. It should be added that the high-priced restaurants of Tahiti are not as costly as the high-priced restaurants of New York or Paris.

Snack bars and cafeterias ranged along Rue Général de Gaulle and tucked back in side streets are typically short on ambience and long on value. But some places calling themselves "snacks" are actually bistrolike restaurants with a counter up front. Sit at a table and you can enjoy a leisurely meal at a reasonable price.

One of the best bets for eating is right on the waterfront quai where the Moorea Ferry departs and arrives. In the evening, and usually whenever a cruise ship is loading up, a string of food trucks pulls up, and the drivers open up the panels of the pickup, and start cooking. The variety is staggering—*steak/frites*, *gaufres* (Belgian waffles), Chinese food, banana splits. This is a great way to beat the high cost of eating in Papeete—in intriguing surroundings, watching the boats and the parade of people.

*The* beer is Hinano, brewed locally by Heineken. Fr
are available at very steep prices.

## Getting Things Done and Shopping

In addition to OPATTI and the airlines offices, downtown
Papeete is richly supplied with resources, and as the outliers are not,
you're well advised to do what needs to be done here.

Banking hours are more or less 8:00 A.M. to 3:30 P.M., although
they vary from bank to bank. A few stay open Saturday mornings.
CFP notes come in denominations of 500, 1000, and 5000; coins are
in denominations of 1, 2, 4, 10, 20, 50, and 100 francs.

A few photo shops offer one-day processing of color film.

The post office on Boulevard Pomare is open from 8:00 to 11:00
A.M. and 2:00 to 5:00 P.M. Mail, telephone, telegram, and telex services are available. The stamps of French Polynesia are beautiful;
even if you're not a collector, these make good souvenirs.

There is a Hachette bookstore in Vaima and another on Avenue
Bruat. These stock an abundance of books and booklets about French
Polynesia as well as maps. They also carry some English-language
books—Michener and a few paperbacks of the best-seller, airplane-
reading variety. Hotel shops also carry English-language books and
newspapers; the latter are more conveniently available at news shops
in Vaima.

Shopping in Tahiti runs the gamut. Clothing, jewelry, and artifacts range from Paris imports to locally made. Black pearls from
the Tuamotus are heavily advertised. Check out the shell and pareu
vendors along the quai. If your Tahiti trip is part of a long Pacific
journey, you probably won't want to load up on souvenirs, but,
as always, a local T-shirt is a recommended purchase, and a pareu
or two will serve you well anywhere in Oceania. Baskets, best at
the market, make good carry-on luggage. For duty-free shopping,
you'll do well to have both passport and onward ticket on hand.
Hold on to the invoice to show to Customs on departure; you may
also need to exhibit the purchases themselves.

### Around Tahiti

Car and motorbike rentals are expensive. Pedal bicycles, in the
thick traffic of Papeete and along the fast, curving coastal highway,
are not a great idea, and rentals are not available. If you have brought
your own bike for riding around the outliers, think hard about using
it to see Tahiti. Cheaper than a car or organized tour, and more
interesting if also more difficult, is travel by le truck, that most
ingenious Pacific institution.

The departure point for les trucks is the market—actually, streets alongside the market. Trucks heading north and east line the east side of the street; their noses face the waterfront. Those heading south and west line the west side of the street and look inland. Destinations are shown on the sides of the trucks.

The trucks are absolutely the best way to get to points not too far out of Papeete. You'll need to inquire in French to make sure your truck is going to or beyond your destination, but driver and fellow passengers are all delightfully courteous—this *is* Polynesia, after all. Truck travel becomes difficult if you want to get way out— to Tahiti Iti, for example. Such long hauls are made infrequently; in fact, they usually bring out-of-town workers into Papeete in the morning and take them back in the afternoon. So if you want to take le truck out to Tautira or Teahupoo, you may have to arrange to spend a night out there. Of course, if you are planning a walk around the coast of the peninsula (see "Hiking," below), that is exactly what you want to do anyway.

If you do the circle-island tour by truck, you must do it in two stages: north coast (Papeete to Taravao to Tautira) and south coast (Papeete to Taravao to Teahupoo). It's time consuming. A good suggestion is to take one of the full-day organized tours of the island (arranged at any hotel travel desk or travel agent) to get a feel for the whole, then return by truck over the next days to places you'd *really* like to see more of.

Renting a car or hiring a car and driver is most convenient and most costly. A suggestion if you do your own driving, or if you *do* want to bike around: start off going northeast—clockwise around the island. This will put you on the inside lane going around some of the more startlingly precipitous hairpin curves.

However you go, you should equip yourself with one of the numerous available guidebooks to island sights; the best of these is Bengt Danielsson's *Tahiti Circle Island Tour Guide.*

Here, going clockwise out of Papeete, are some of the more famous and/or interesting stops to make:

- The Bain Loti, where a bust of Pierre Loti is all that remains of the site where he first saw Rarahu, heroine of *The Marriage of Loti.*
- Tomb of King Pomare V, one of the less noble of Tahiti's rulers.
- Home of James Norman Hall, coauthor of the *Bounty* books; he died here in 1951 and is buried on Herai Hill above.
- Point Venus, where Captain Cook inaccurately measured the transit of Venus on June 3, 1769. It is on Matavai Bay, where Wallis, Cook, and Bligh all put in, and where the first missionaries landed. The lighthouse has stood here since 1868. Here too is the black sand beach of Mahina.

- The Orofara leper colony.
- Papenoo Village, at the mouth of the island's biggest river—a village that still preserves some of the old look.
- The blowhole of Arahoho and the Faarumai waterfalls; of the latter, one is easily accessible, while the others require a hike.
- The battlefield at Mahaena, where, on April 17, 1844, French weapons superiority marked the end of formal armed resistance by the Tahitians. After Mahaena, the Tahitians practiced guerrilla warfare for two more years until the end came in 1846, when the French moved up the valley of Fautaua and—somehow—climbed the stubbly rock cliff to assault the natives' last stronghold.
- Bougainville's anchorage, visible from Hitiaa. Oputotara, the nearer or more southerly of the two islets (the other is Variaruru), was the rather bad anchorage Bougainville chose in April 1768.
- Fa'atautia Waterfall.
- Vaitepiha Bay at Tautira, where Cook's second expedition very nearly came a cropper, and where Robert Louis Stevenson lived briefly and worked on *The Master of Ballantrae*—a bizarre setting for the writing of a gloomy, weather-beaten Scottish horror story.
- Zane Grey's fishing camp at Toahotu, off which the pulp writer, a fishing fanatic, hauled in a gargantuan silver marlin. Grey writes about fishing in Tahiti in *Tales of Tahitian Waters.*
- Maui's footprints, where, according to tradition, the Polynesian hero Maui slowed the sun so Tahitians would have time to cook before dark. He lassoed the sun, using a rope made from the pubic hair of his sister Hina, then tied the earth-end to a beach boulder. The proof is in the footprints, still visible on the reef.
- Debarkation point of the ancient Tahitians at Paperari, where the ancient Polynesians first settled Tahiti over a thousand years ago.
- Gauguin Museum and botanical gardens. The gardens were the work of an American, Harrison Smith, a physics professor at MIT who threw it all over to come to Tahiti in 1919 and devote himself to botany. Some years after Smith's death, philanthropist Cornelius Crane, also American, donated the gardens to the public. The museum is on the grounds; its exhibits chronicle the artist's life. A few of his works are here—something from just about every medium in which he worked, although not necessarily created in Tahiti: painting, drawing, woodcarving, ceramic. A New York–based foundation raises funds to try to bring back to Tahiti some of Gauguin's Tahitian paintings from museums in Europe and the U.S. As curator Gilles Artur told the author, "It would be a completely different experience to view those paintings here in Tahiti."
- Mataiea Village, where Gauguin painted some of his most famous masterpieces, most of them now in U.S. museums. Somerset Maugham came here researching *The Moon and Sixpence*, his novel

about Gauguin, and found three glass doors painted by the artist and forgotten. He bought one for what in today's prices would be a little over a dollar (U.S.), shipped it to England, and later sold it at Sotheby's for £13,000.

Rupert Brooke also came to Mataiea to search for lost Gauguins. Here he fell in love with "Mamua," the Tahitian woman who inspired the poem "Tiare Tahiti."

• Site of the Marae Mahaiatea at Papara. Now in ruins, the dimensions of the site give evidence of the monumentality it once possessed: 90 meters long, 29 meters wide, 15 meters high.

• Irihonu crafts center at Paea, housing workshops of artisans skilled at traditional crafts—woodcarving, mat-weaving, and quilting. The last was introduced by the missionaries. The beach here is a popular surfing spot. It was also the site of a marae where Cook witnessed a human sacrifice in 1777.

## Le Musée de Tahiti et des Iles

The must-see sight for the traveler to French Polynesia is the Museum of Tahiti and the Islands. Make for it as soon as you're settled in Papeete; it will illumine everything else you see in these islands.

The museum is in the high-rent district of Punaauia. Take a truck and watch the PK signs. At PK 14, just about at the bridge over the Punaruu River, get ready. The MUSEE sign is on the right just past the bridge. Ring the buzzer, head down the road, and turn right. The museum is open every day except Monday from 9:00 A.M. to 6:00 P.M. with no lunch break.

Here are superb collections superbly displayed to inform the visitor about the human and natural history of the islands of French Polynesia. The museum also rotates shows of the works of Tahitian artists, or those inspired by Tahiti, and it puts on demonstrations of traditional arts and crafts.

### Beaches

Mahina for black sand and for reliably clean water. At Maeva, in the opposite direction from Papeete, the sand is white, but the pollution is often severe enough to close the beach.

### Hiking

Pierre Florentin, guide par excellence to the interior of Tahiti and to the other islands of French Polynesia, listens politely to the many Europeans and Americans, like the author, who tell him what good, strong hikers they are. He will tell them in turn that the terrain in Tahiti is difficult and that the heat can be severe. Well, they will argue, the mountains here are no higher or steeper than the Alps, the Himalayas, the Rockies—and we can take the heat. He will then tell them that an eight-kilometer uphill walk can take six hours—more, if it has just rained—and he will not be believed.

Believe him. The hiking here is as tough as it gets, and *everyone* has trouble with it.

The trail up Mount Aorai, for example, is perhaps the best mountain trail on the island. At first, as you head up the hill from Le Belvédère restaurant past the place where French Army mountaineering troops train, you think it might be a saunter. The trail, originally a hunting track, is lined by mango trees planted to point the way. A raspberry bush provides a second breakfast. Tulip trees, ixora, and gorgeous wild orchids abound. Spanish moss hangs from branches on which vini perform their nervous little mating dances accompanied by their energetic singing. The views take in the coastal plain and Papeete, the valleys to either side, the sea and Moorea in the distance.

Then you contour a ridge to lose sight of the sea, and the path becomes an obstacle course. That is, if you can find the path. Pierre Florentin can find it even after a rain, but then, he has been hiking these mountains since he was a little boy, and he knows the way. If path this is, it is obscured by thick underbrush, beneath which there may be—and often are—sudden holes. The hillside is eroded; a slide downhill looks like it might be a fast trip and a long one. Slick mud, slippery rocks, and curling roots, also hidden by the brush, catch your feet in any number of unpleasant ways. Insects buzz in the heat, and while they don't bite, the thorns along the way do. Exposed on the slope, in fierce heat, with infernal sun beating relentlessly and only relieved on occasion by a small cluster of green trees that suddenly block the trail, you're on a rigorous hand-over-hand scramble. Six hours of this get you to the refuge Fare Ata; it's another two hours to the summit at 2066 meters. No wonder it's usually a two-day hike.

Hiking the high peaks of Tahiti is not easy, but after a time, even this strenuous walking develops a rhythm of its own. In any event, it offers an unsurpassed chance to see into the heart of this island.

Pierre Florentin (B.P. 5323, Pirae, Tahiti; tel. 43 72 01) offers 18 set excursions. Five are classified as easy, use 4×4 vehicles, and take a day—except for the two-day trek around Te Pari, the cliffs of the peninsula, when a boat is used. On the other 13 guided hikes, Pierre handles all guiding arrangements, and while he can also arrange food and equipment for you, these are not part of the guide's fee. The cost is high, like everything else in Tahiti, and the prices are geared for small groups, so if less than the maximum number of people sign up, you pay more.

Essential equipment includes long trousers, long-sleeved shirt, gloves, lots of water, and food.

Pierre's favorites are the two- to three-day cross-island traverses, both of Tahiti and of the peninsula. These walks tend to be along valleys and are not quite as demanding as the peak-bagging treks, although length alone makes them strenuous. The walk up Mount Orohena, Tahiti's highest peak, is not only difficult but dangerous. The knife-edge summit is extremely narrow, and ropes are required. Another favorite is a trip involving a helicopter lift onto Orohena for a two-day descent. Pierre provides time for artifact hunting; because Orohena is just up-valley from Matavai Bay, where so many early explorers landed, the plateau is thought to be rich in artifacts— sabers, rifles, coins, and the like. Pierre works this trip in coopera- tion with ORSTOM, the Office de Recherches Scientifiques de Ter- ritoire d'Outre-Mer.

There is no mountaineering in Tahiti; the crumbly nature of the basalt rock makes this too perilous.

Hiking on your own in Tahiti is certainly possible, but hiking absolutely solo is not recommended. What was a trail yesterday can disappear under the instant growth produced by an overnight rain. If you lose your way, or fall, or slip, you can be in real trouble.

What is more, many of the valleys that look like great places to wander along are in fact restricted areas; official authorization is required to go there. However, that still leaves a lot of valleys; some of the best for day hikes are: Taharau, Vaihiria, Maara, Ma- haena, Papenoo, Tuauru, and Vaitepiha.

Lots of people try to do the walk around the peninsula, atop the Te Pari cliffs. Be aware that it is a hard two-day walk. You have to walk in the water for a bit of the way, or swim it at high tide— this is where Pierre uses the boat. Despite the presence of good warning signs put up by the government, a number of people have calculated the number of kilometers for this walk, decided there wasn't much to it, and set off unprepared. There used to be an American expatriate with a house along the walk who frequently had to give emergency shelter to exhausted, starved, thirsty hikers. Be warned.

Other than Pierre Florentin, who can also arrange treks on any other islands, including the Marquesas, few outfits are geared specif- ically for hikers. Mafatu Fenua Excursions, B.P. 108, Papeete, tel. 42 06 17 or 42 54 78 or 58 25 69, specializes in 4×4 excursions into the interior and may be able to help. There is a chapter of the Club Alpin Français on the island, and you may be able to hook up with one of their trips. As always, ask at your hotel and press OPATTI for information.

## Underwater

*La plongée libre* (snorkeling) and *la plongée avec équipement* (scuba diving) are widely available, and all sorts of equipment and supervision go along with it. Ask at OPATTI, try any of the major hotels, or get in touch with Tahiti Plongée, B.P. 3506 Papeete, tel. 43 62 51, or the Yacht Club d'Arue, Club de Plongée, B.P. 1456 Papeete, tel. 42 78 03.

# MOOREA

The other major island of the Windward Group is Moorea, a spectacularly beautiful island some 16 miles west of Tahiti. Shuttle flights lasting about 11 minutes leave every 20 minutes from Faaa; ferry boats, including the swift passenger ferries of the Keke Line, depart daily from the quai of Papeete. You can get a morning ferry at a reasonable hour and return late afternoon or evening.

The surviving south rim of an ancient volcano, Moorea is twice as old as Tahiti, and its topography is more weathered. The island is a thick *W,* or a downward-pointing triangle into whose hypotenuse Opunohu Bay and Cook's Bay have carved their jagged cul-de-sacs. From the air, it is a lushly green island surrounded by a luminous lagoon and fringed by an azure sea. A typically high island, it is cut by deep valleys, in which pineapple plantations have pretty much replaced the cultivation of vanilla. The island's dramatic ridges and clefts of valleys are evident from almost anywhere on the ground, and watching the mountaintops enter and leave the clouds that pass over them is quite a spectacle.

Inhabited since about 1600, the island was the scene of ongoing internal warfare by the time Cook arrived in 1774. It wasn't until Pomare I, who had taken refuge here, was able to conquer Tahiti that Moorea knew peace; by then, it was nothing more than a province of the new kingdom. Colonists arrived in the 19th century, planting cotton and coconut. The 20th century saw the arrival of vanilla and coffee cultivation, and of tourism—in a big way.

Luxury-style tourism is well entrenched on Moorea, with more planned. Most facilities for tourists are in fact part of the big hotels, but it is possible to rent cars, bikes, or scooters near the Club Med, where most of the hotels are located, and in Paopao, the main town. An airport bus operates every two hours, stopping at hotels and villages, between 6:00 A.M. and 4:30 P.M., and trucks also operate. Warning: trucks and the very pricey taxis tend to stop operation during the lunch hour.

It requires no more than a day to see Moorea, if seeing it is all you want to do here. Although the circuit—about 61 kilometers—

makes a long bike trip, it is an easy turn by car or scooter. If you're willing to give up the idea of making it all around, Moorea is a good place for walking; indeed, the strong walker can eschew all motorized transportation, or combine walking with wheels, and, in one day, get a good feel for the island and see what are probably its most important sights, the marae of Opunohu Valley, the Belvedere Lookout, and Cook's Bay.

## The Moorea Day Trip:
## On Foot (Partly, Anyway)

Take the earliest Keke III ferry, leaving at around 7:00 A.M., from Papeete to Vaiare. Walk left from the ferry landing, cross the bridge, then turn right almost immediately, heading inland up the dirt road with a stream on your right. At the fork in the road, keep right—you will see here the first of the orange-red disks that mark a fine trail over the shoulder of Mount Mouaputa to Paopao.

At the single remaining post of a gateway, fork right onto a path that is actually a somewhat overgrown jeep route. If you find yourself passing some new, sleek-looking meeting houses, you've gone too far; go back and find the jeep track. Follow this, keeping the stream on your right, till you see the sign marked PAOPAO. Cross the stream now, and continue to follow the markers and arrows, looking for them on tree trunks, often fallen tree trunks, or rocks. The trail contours a hill more or less southwest through thick undergrowth, then suddenly darts uphill due west. It becomes very steep just before achieving the top. A sign welcomes you here: "OAHA—Moi, j'aime la nature." Walk south along the ridge for views into the heart of Moorea and to the peak of Mount Mouaputa (830 meters). A well-marked trail leads downhill and ends by crossing a stream and proceeding along a line of houses. Keep veering more or less right to meet, eventually, the paved road on which the Paopao school and town hall stand.

This lovely hike should take about three hours. Once you've arrived at the road, you can turn right to the coast road and Paopao for some refreshment and, if you so choose, to rent a bike, scooter, or car for heading back uphill.

If you want to continue on foot, eschew the right turn down to the coast, instead continuing west on the dirt road to achieve, in three to four uphill kilometers, the maraes at the top of Opunohu Valley.

The sites of over 500 ancient structures have been identified here, confirming that before the arrival of the Europeans the valley as a whole teemed with people. But early in the 19th century, with traditional religion giving way to Christianity, both the valley's importance and its population declined.

Six maraes, a council platform, and two archery platforms have been reconstructed by the Bishop Museum's Y. H. Sinoto, the great archaeologist of eastern Polynesia. The most elaborate marae is the Ahu-o-Mahine, once the community marae for the valley, featuring a three-stepped *ahu*, or platform. The archery platforms are crescent shaped at one end, enabling archers to perch on one knee as they drew their bows; distance, not accuracy, was prized.

Up the road from the archery platform is the Belvedere Lookout, offering stupendous views of the valley. *The Bounty*, the Anthony Hopkins–Mel Gibson cinematic version of the *Bounty* story, used the Belvedere as a setting.

On foot or on wheels, head down the Opunohu Valley. You might think you're in the countryside of Britain; cows graze in grassy meadows, and agriculture proceeds apace. This is in fact a protected zone—no hunting or fishing allowed. The presence of The Center for the Environment, the Office of Rural Economy, and the agricultural school confirm the point. When the road reaches the coast, turn left to see more of the island, time permitting, or right to return your rental at Paopao before finding a truck back to the ferry. If you're on foot and tired, don't go all the way downhill to the valley floor. Look for a dirt road on your right; it cuts the looping meander the road follows around the point of land formed by the two bays and gets you back to Paopao, right on Cook's Bay.

Indeed, instead of returning from Vaiare to Papeete, take the ferry from Cook's Bay and watch it recede as you head for home; it is one of the loveliest sights in the Pacific.

## Exploring All of Moorea

There are 28 kilometers of good paved road along the north coast of Moorea, and another 33 or so of what is called Moorea *sauvage* in the south. Life is more rural here, among scattered copra plantations and tranquil villages. The best beaches are here, particularly in the southwest. Here also are the majority of deep valleys, many with roads running at least partway up. Afareatiu is the island's administrative center while Haapiti offers a Catholic mission.

Most hotels are ranged along the north of the island, and it's here that you can arrange for the variety of water sports—diving, sailboarding, fishing—that brings visitors here in droves. The town of Papetoai is noted for its octagonal Protestant church.

# BORA BORA

In the beginning was the god Ta'aroa. He created the islands, first among them Bora Bora Fanautahi, an island surrounded by motus (coral islets). He also gave birth to the demigods, among them Maui, whose footprints the traveler may have seen on the reef off Tahiti, and Ru, the navigator. Ru tried to lift up the sky to relieve the darkness. He succeeded only partly, became hunchbacked from the effort, and ruptured himself so badly that his intestines floated away to settle forever as clouds above the mountains of Bora Bora. These are called *rua nu'u a Ru*.

Hiro, the sorcerer, kept a hideout on the southern tip of Toopua, one of the encircling islands of the Bora Bora lagoon. He tried to steal the island one night and was about to hurl a chunk of it away when the cock crowed. Since Hiro's powers worked only between sunset

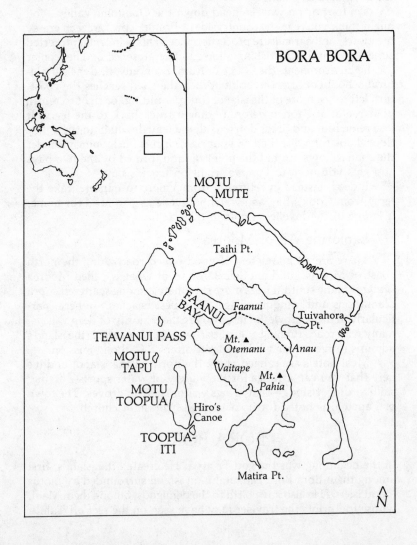

BORA BORA

MOTU MUTE

Taihi Pt.

FAANUI BAY

Faanui

Tuivahora Pt.

TEAVANUI PASS

Mt. ▲ Otemanu

Anau

MOTU TAPU

Vaitape

MOTU TOOPUA

Mt. ▲ Pahia

Hiro's Canoe

TOOPUA-ITI

Matira Pt.

N

and cockcrow, he was thwarted in his purpose; he abandoned his double canoe and fled. Toopua-Iti is the chunk of land Hiro tried to steal, and the parallel rocks between it and Toopua are called Hiro's canoe.

The turtle stone, *ofai honu,* mated with the cliff of Mount Pahia to begin the royal dynasty of the island in the person of Firiamata o Vava'u, a great navigator. The island Vava'u in the Tongan Group may also take its name from Firiamata, and there is other legendary evidence of the Tongan connection.

Bora Bora came to be known as a great warrior state, conquering numerous nearby islands and some not so nearby. Her military strength stemmed in particular from her warriors' ability to achieve surprise; this they did by muffling the paddles of their canoes, staging swift, silent, nocturnal raids. Some say Bora Bora means "fleet of canoes with silent paddles."

When Ru returned from a great journey to New Zealand in the canoe *Te apori,* the voyage was immortalized in this chant:

O Ru, what land is this rising upon the horizon?
It is Porapora, let its watchword be,
Porapora the great, the first born,
Porapora with the fleet that strikes both ways,
Porapora of the silent, muffled paddles,
Porapora of the pink leaf,
Porapora the destroyer of fleets.

Bora Bora, some 260 kilometers and 50 minutes by plane from Tahiti, has been called the most beautiful island in the world, though its beauty has not always been the first priority of its visitors. For early Polynesians, it was a place of exile for outcasts. Cook found it "difficult of access"; he came here to recover Bougainville's anchor and, with the concurrence of the local powers, was able to do so. Darwin in the *Beagle* came to study the local barrier reef structure; his diagram of Bora Bora illustrated his theory of the formation of coral reefs. In 1942, the U.S. Navy chose Bora Bora as its central Pacific fueling and staging base; the island's barrier reef, with only a single pass, formed a deep and secure harbor for a giant fleet. The operation, Bobcat, brought some sixty thousand troops; they left behind ship landing and loading facilities, guns, the airstrip of Motu Mute, and a number of half-American children. The island was again occupied in 1977, this time by the cast and crew of Dino De Laurentiis' *Hurricane.* The movie was not exactly memorable, but the hotel built at the time, the Marara, remains.

The beauty of Bora Bora has not itself been diminished by these arrivals. Born about seven million years ago, part of the chain of extinct volcanoes that compose the Society Archipelago, Bora Bora consists primarily of one large island some 10 kilometers long and only about 4 kilometers wide. A high, craggy spine of mountains rides from north to south along the island; Mount Otemanu is the highest point at 725 meters, and double-peaked Mount Pahia, at 660 meters, is the most distinctive.

Toopua and Toopua-Iti, Hiro's islands, complete the eroded remnant of the volcanic wall. The three islands define the deep harbor that once was the center of the volcano. A barrier reef encircles all the islands at a distance of from one to two miles. It is broken by a single pass, Teavanui, the great channel, in the middle of the western reef to the leeward, allowing passage for most ships. Within the barrier reef are a number of small motus; the most northerly, Motu Mute, accommodates the airstrip where the traveler arrives. Motu Tapu, just south of Teavanui, a sacred site of old, is often seen on posters—the quintessential paradise island of the South Seas.

Only small craft can navigate the lagoon, which is filled with coral and built-up sand banks. Fringing reefs hug the shore of the island almost all the way around; in the south, at Raititi Point and Matira Point, the fringing reef is interrupted long enough for two wide strands of white beach.

There are no rivers on Bora Bora, and there is little soil. Especially on the west, the mixture of volcanic debris and coral sand supports abundant vegetation—coconut, pandanus, lime, hibiscus, tiare—while the lower slopes of the interior grow banana, breadfruit, mango, papaya, grapefruit, ironwood, and rosewood.

The principal village is Vaitape, on the west; Faanui to the north

Bora Bora, French Polynesia. *Photo by Susanna Margolis.*

and Anau to the east are the other main population and commercial centers. The whole island is about 32 kilometers around—a pleasant bike ride, which is how most people make the tour.

For a small island, Bora Bora boasts a lot of luxury hotels. Unhappily, most facilities for the traveler are geared to life in these hotels; the trucks, for example, are run by the hotels as shuttle services. They are buzzerless, meant to accommodate the particular hotel's residents who, it is assumed, just want to be taken back to their room. You can, however, ride one and ask to be dropped at the destination of your choice, if it is en route. Most of the island's activities are also run by the hotels—trips around the lagoon, picnics on a motu, diving, and the like.

Still, if you choose to stay at a pension famille, as is recommended, the proprietor will usually be able to arrange any activity for you—and you can always sign up for something at one of the big hotels, even if you're not staying there.

Yet more tourist development is slated for Bora Bora, so that this once quiet retreat seems well on its way to becoming a major stopover for packaged tourists who come and go in droves. Among other effects, this may increase the already jaded attitude of the natives toward travelers. It may also make Bora Bora increasingly difficult for the independent traveler; getting flight reservations promises to grow even tougher, and it is no picnic now. One thing that might slow development a bit is the fate of the 154-room Hyatt Regency. Due for opening in 1986, and intended to be the largest hotel complex on the island, the project came to a dead halt due to structural problems in construction and the inadequacy of the water supply. At this writing, the Hyatt remained a ghostly shell, just beginning to get ramshackle around the edges, looking like doom. It is, it should be noted, just beside the Bora Bora Bungalows, a set of condos that, it is said, have been purchased by movie stars and rock stars as tax write-offs.

The lagoon of Bora Bora alone is worth a couple of days of exploration. Some of the best snorkeling anywhere is just off Matira Point—that is, if development doesn't pollute the waters. Give the island sights a day, and spend at least one more on the water, and plan your stay accordingly.

The 35-minute launch ride from the airport to Vaitape is part of the price of your airplane ticket. On arrival, the launch will likely be met by a horde of hawkers and hotel shills. Unless you are staying at one of the resort hotels, tell whoever meets you that you want to rent a bicycle *now*, and do so in one of the many places in town— you will not require motorized transportation on Bora Bora.

Vaitape also contains the Air Tahiti office, where you must of course reconfirm your onward flight, and the *mairie*, town hall, where you may be able to arrange for a guide to take you up Mount Pahia, should you decide to do so. There are also numerous grocery stores here, including "the Chinaman's," Chin Lee, biggest market on the island and a gathering place as well as a store. Anau, halfway around the island, also boasts a grocery. Vaitape is home also to the post office (international calls possible), boutiques, and to numerous snack bars and restaurants. Other restaurants are scattered between Vaitape and the big hotels; Bloody Mary's is legendary, although its schedule of opening hours has grown erratic.

## Biking Bora Bora

Head counterclockwise to bike the island, stopping as and when you wish. Just past Chez Lulu, a very good restaurant about a kilometer out of Vaitape, is the mansion built by De Laurentiis as a replica of the governor's residence on American Samoa. A few kilometers further along, you will see the two large hulks of ships on the reef, a collection of anchors, a Mark II gun, and varied military detritus: Tatu's Museum. Tatu lives in the A-frame behind the collection. Bike on past Bloody Mary's and the Moana Arts shop, run by Tahiti's famed photographer, Erwin Christian, and the swank Hotel Bora Bora next door.

In another two kilometers you come to Matira Point, the best beach on the island, and another kilometer brings you to the Marara Hotel. Anau is five kilometers further, the second town of Bora Bora. You reach the summit of the road some three kilometers later; don't race downhill, as the road is often rutted. You are now on that part of the island where habitation is scarce. There is hardly any water here, and little electricity. But the area is rich in maraes, though you may have to descend from your bike and walk a bit to reach them.

Marae Aehua-tai is down a path from the top of the road's summit. Past the Hyatt Hotel site some two kilometers is Marae Fare-Opu, visible from the road: look for the turtle petroglyphs. At Faanui Bay and village, you can see some of the remains of the American presence from War War II. A kilometer out of the town is the path to Marae Marotetini, the most important temple on Bora Bora, with a stone ahu three meters high; the marae was restored in 1968 by Yoshi Sinoto. Nearby are two tombs built for the royal family during the 19th century.

## Hiking Bora Bora

The cross-island hike goes from Faanui to just above Anau. Start at Faanui's garbage dump—ask for the road leading to it, pass some marae ruins, and keep going. Thick as the vegetation can be, you will see your objective—the saddle of the ridge, with a single coconut palm atop it—and the trail is fairly clear.

Pahia can be climbed from a trailhead just north of Vaitape, though there is no marked trail. Best is to find a guide. Ask about one at your pension or at the mairie, especially if there has been a recent rain.

A walk up to the American gun emplacements—the trail is easily found just across from the Club Med entrance—is a quick, easy saunter, rewarding the walker with fine views as well as the eerie look of these rusty guns aimed out at an enemy who, fortunately, never came.

In climbing anywhere, beware of *tupa pau,* the spirits of the mountain that don't want you there. They make this clear, one expat told the author, "by making your hair stand on end when you try to descend." *Tupa* is also the very prevalent sand crab on the island.

## On the Lagoon

Apart from snorkeling off Matira, you may want to join up with a hotel trip to see the lagoon. Most of the hotels run a half-day trip that takes you in a motorized outrigger and offers a series of "events." You'll get a chance to walk on the reef and to hover, holding a line and wearing snorkel and mask, while the crew tosses raw mahi-mahi into the water so that you can watch lagoon sharks scrambling for it. You'll probably be taken to a motu where one of the crew will climb a tree for coconuts. Midlagoon, you'll watch a couple of the crew dive for huge black mussels; you'll be treated to the meat, and you'll be able to fondle the crude black pearls from inside. In this way, you'll travel all around the island.

Dive trips can be arranged through the dive shops at the hotels.

## Hanging Out

The hotels all have bars and shows, and some—the Club Med, for instance—run discos. Locals drink in a nameless bar opposite the Banque de Polynesie in Vaitape. The Oa Oa is one of the nicer gathering places, possibly because the American couple that runs the place has made it a haven for yachties. The scrapbook reads like a travelogue, with autographs from far-flung provenances. The crowds in the bar and dining room confirm the informal, international atmosphere.

# HUAHINE

Huahine where the eye of the North rises
Huahine in the froth of the waves
Moonlight on the broken shells
Obstinacy is their pasttime

The eye of the North refers to one of the best-known maraes on this marae-rich island. Nearby, on the shore, the "sand" is composed of small shells broken and whitened by erosion, a favorite spot for religious ceremonies in moonlight. That obstinacy is a Huahine pastime is attested, not only in this ancient poem, but by no less than Captain James Cook, whose ships were pillaged and attacked here in both 1769 and 1777.

In more recent Polynesian history, Huahine is famed as the birthplace of Pouvanaa a Oopa, the great advocate of the Tahitian Independence Movement. Pouvanaa, the son of a Danish sailor and a Polynesian woman, and a decorated veteran of World War I, became the most powerful politician in the Territorial Assembly. At the height of his power, Metua, as he was known—"beloved father of the Tahitians"—was convicted of conspiracy in a plot to burn down Papeete. He was sent to the Baumette prison in Marseilles and, at age 64, was sentenced to 8 years of solitary confinement. He was also banished from Polynesia for another 15 years. Pardoned after 10 years, Pouvanaa returned to Tahiti and to politics. He died in 1976.

About 170 kilometers and 40 minutes from Tahiti, Huahine is two island formations, Huahine Nui and Huahine Iti (big and little, respectively), linked by a low isthmus. At high tide, the isthmus becomes a narrow channel, so a bridge connects the two parts of the land mass. "Hua" means phallus; the relevant rock formation juts up from Huahine Iti. "Hine," as in "vahine," refers to a woman; a three-peaked hill on Huahine Nui can be seen to be the chin, breasts, and stomach of a woman. This is a lush, mountainous island, with varied scenery, fine beaches—especially inside the barrier reef to the north, the best surfing in French Polynesia, and a colorful main town, Fare. Above all, Huahine is rich in archaeological remains.

There are four villages on Huahine Nui and four more on Huahine Iti. Fare, on Huahine Nui, is the action town, with its quay serving both passenger ships and copra boats, its snack bars and restaurants, pensions and hotels, a supermarket, shops, offices, churches. It is one of those sleepy, dusty "main towns" that become dear to Pacific travelers. Maeva (same name as Tahiti's white-sand beach) also has stores, but, more importantly, it is the center for exploring a number of maraes. From Faie, the third village of Huahine Nui, a steep road leads over the hill to Fitii, the final town.

On Huahine Iti, there are Maroe, Tefarerii, Parea, and Haapu. Resortlike hotels are scattered here as well as on Huahine Nui, and Parea boasts a few pensions. There is little in the way of commerce on Huahine Iti, save a tiny counter-store at Haapu and a Chinese grocery truck that comes through a few times a day. Between Tefarerii and Parea live a number of victims of elephantiasis; they are typically shunned by their village neighbors.

Most eating on the island is in the hotels. Since a number of these are French run, the standard tends to be fairly high. In Fare, there is a beachfront snack bar, Temarara, which caters to both tourists and locals, and Chez Enite, where the food is so good, reservations are necessary.

Huahine is thickly planted with taro, vanilla, banana, and coconut. Some three thousand people inhabit the island; only about half are employed—in tourism, commerce, transportation (trucks), and government.

## Seeing Huahine

If you plan to tour the entire island, you might want to go with a hotel tour or rent a car. Scooters are available, but the only gas stations are in Fare, so if you run out of fuel on the other side of the island, you have also run out of luck. A bicycle circuit of the island is certainly possible, but, although the island is only some 16 kilometers from stem to stern, the hills and jagged coast make this a long and rigorous ride.

One of the best ways to see the island is from the back of a horse. La Petite Ferme runs a variety of rides. In fact, they can arrange just about anything you want, and you will pay accordingly. You can go for as little as a few hours, take a day tour to the maraes, spend three days touring Huahine Nui (and camping out at night), or four days to take in Huahine Iti as well. You don't need to know how to ride, and the proprietors can help you improvise equipment if you have not brought sleeping bag, long pants, etc. Two days on horseback to see the maraes and get a feel for the island, then another two relaxing on a beach or at a quiet pension or hotel would make a very nice stay on Huahine.

## Archaeological Huahine

However you choose to see the island, the must-see sights are the maraes. These are grouped, conveniently, into two areas: those along the coast at Fare Pote'e, and those in Maeva. (There is another at the bottom of Huahine Iti.) At least 16 of these maraes have been restored—by Sinoto—and you can also see fortification walls and the stone fish weir traps of Maeva Lake.

In addition, on the grounds of the Bali Ha'i Hotel near Fare are the remains of a village believed to have been settled between 650 and 850 and thought to be the oldest known settlement in the Society Islands. These finds confirm Huahine's status as the richest archaeological site in French Polynesia; it is an open-air museum for the traveler.

As an important center of ancient Polynesian culture, Huahine was centrally governed and remained free of the internecine warfare that plagued many of the other islands. Each of its eight royal families was given its own coastal area for worship. These are the maraes at Fare Pote'e, northeast of Fare. By bike, car, scooter, or truck, you can't miss them. Across the road from the maraes, look for the remains of fortification walls, just up the slope a little.

The slope is Matairea Hill, on which is located, among other sites, the second most important temple in all of French Polynesia (the first is on Raiatea). Proceed into the town of Maeva, and look for the church named Galilea. Just opposite it is a house, blue at the time of this writing, behind which you may discern a railing lining a trail leading uphill. The trail switchbacks rightward at first, then you walk pleasantly uphill in shade for perhaps 15 minutes to arrive at Matairea-rahi, most significant of the temples in the Society Islands prior to the construction of Taputaputea in Raiatea. The upright stones— one is missing—represent ten districts. Behind these is the ahu, throne for the gods. Below the ahu is the sacrifice platform, where, on occasion, humans were sacrificed. A second structure of the marae is the site of a house, built on posts, in which the images of the gods were kept.

Beyond this marae is Marae Tefano, with another huge ahu standing under an enormous banyan tree. To see more maraes, come back to Matairea-rahi and head south along the path. At a fork, your choice is to go left and straight down the mountain or right to see more maraes on the open slope. Go right, then follow the trail down to the road and head left, back toward Maeva. Along the way, check out the stone fish weir traps in the water.

Cross the bridge, marked by a monument commemorating the islanders' resistance to the French in 1846, and head toward the ocean and left to see Marae Manunu, the two-tiered structure which became the community marae after Matairea-rahi. Next to it is the grave of Taiti, the last high priest of Maeva. At his death, in 1915, a huge slab fell from the marae.

Another marae, Anini, at the tip of Huahine Iti, was a place of worship for Oro and Hiro, and was also a center of human sacrifice.

What makes these finds so important is that they provide a missing link between the cultures of the Leeward and Windward islands. Prior to the discoveries on Huahine, the known maraes of the two groups had been of distinctively different construction, despite the clear political and cultural ties between Windward and Leeward. The finds on Matairea Hill indicate that the maraes of the Windward Group probably originated in Huahine.

Equally enlightening were the finds of Vaito'otia/Fa'ahia at the Bali Ha'i Hotel. Sinoto believes that the village was destroyed around the year 1100 by some natural catastrophe, probably a tidal wave. The villagers evacuated fast, leaving behind their possessions, which were buried and preserved in the mud. Fishermen's tools, canoe parts, coconut graters, pendants, pearl and shell objects manufactured for trade, the detritus of daily living have all been unearthed here, and the Bali Ha'i exhibits some of the finds. Among the most fascinating are two planks of a canoe Sinoto dates to 1100 years ago—the fiber lashings are still visible—and a 4-meter-long steering paddle, dating from about 1300 years ago, that must have propelled a 25-meter-long canoe. That such items were being constructed here that long ago is evidence of an advanced seagoing community. The style of the artifacts is remarkably like the Marquesan style, thus reinforcing Sinoto's theory that the first settlers came from the Marquesas to the Society Archipelago and from there emigrated to New Zealand.

# Rangiroa

The Tuamotu Archipelago, also called Paumoto and, by sailors, the Dangerous Archipelago, comprises 78 islands, 41 of which are inhabited. The islands total 726 square kilometers of land spread across some 720,000 square kilometers of ocean. They include one upthrust coral island, Makatea (the word means "raised reef" or "plateau"), and the largest group of coral atolls in the world, as well as numerous small atolls and reefs. Rangiroa is a prime example of the large atoll island, and it can be a prime setting for the traveler's discovery that there *is* something different about an atoll.

Nearly 360 kilometers from Tahiti, one hour by plane, Rangiroa is 77 kilometers long, 24 kilometers wide, and not 2 meters above sea level. It does have something in common with the high island of Tahiti; the lagoon of Rangiroa has a larger surface than the big island. Indeed, from one side of the lagoon, it is impossible to see the opposite shore. Strong tidal currents sweep through the two passes into the lagoon, generating flows of from three to six knots and providing an exceptional variety and quantity of marine life. Rangiroa is a snorkeling/diving paradise, as well as a beachcomber's dream.

There are three big—and costly—hotels on Rangi, as it is universally called. One of the three, Village San Souci, is on a motu about an hour away from the main island. The Bouteille de la Mer is on a beach facing the lagoon. Kia Ora Village caters mainly to divers; it is very like a Club Med, with which organization it is in fact affiliated. If you're doing a Club Med tour of French Polynesia, you stay at Kia Ora on Rangi.

But Rangi abounds in pensions familles, run by Rangi natives and catering, to a great extent, to French families who have come over for the weekend. Many are right on the beach, so that you can walk out of your private bungalow right into the water. The food is fine—fresh fish every day; beer and wine are plentiful; the atmosphere is delightful; access to facilities is excellent—"everything can be arranged"; and the price is one-tenth what you would pay at a Kia Ora.

There are two towns on the atoll, facing each other across the pass. Avatoru has a single store and a few churches. Titupa, the administrative center, has a mairie, post office, *gendarmerie*, clinic, schools, and more churches. It is a pretty town, with neat houses fronting almost manicured green lawns, whitewashed walls lining the street, lots of flowering trees.

If you have not yet spent a Sunday observing or participating in Polynesian church services, Titupa is a good place to do it. As you walk along the main drag, you will hear some familiar hymns, and some not so familiar, pouring from the open doors and windows and denoting a variety of denominations, though all the singing is typically and harmoniously Polynesian. Stop in at the tall, colorful Catholic church for mass, and you may be lucky enough to hear the rather funereal hymn that is sung in French to the tune of Auld Lang Syne. Perhaps a single female voice will start the song, answered by the men in chorus providing the harmony while the women together take up the melody. *Restons toujours unis, mes frères*, the song says—let us remain united, my brothers. With warm air carrying the scent of frangipani, stillness without, rich music lushly sung within, you might consider how narrow and minute is this speck of coral you are on and how, indeed, an atoll is different.

From the air, Rangiroa is a circlet of desert, with a few green patches, ringing the azure lagoon. It is pretty much that way when you land, too, except that the "desert" sand is pulverized coral—hot looking, harsh, biting. The green patches are coconut palms, and copra, as in most of the Tuamotus, has long been a staple industry of this island, now being complemented by tourism. Around the island, you can still see the copra being harvested. The ripe coconuts are split with a machete and dried in the sun, then the meat is removed and dried again, usually in overhead racks to keep it from the coconut crabs. These crabs, *kaveu*, are large creatures who live in rocks and emerge at night to feed on coconuts. They can break one open with their claws, so if you see kaveu, avoid the claws.

Once harvested, the copra is bagged in burlap and weighed and recorded by the Chinese shopkeepers, who are still the main merchants of Titupa. If the copra boat is in, you can watch, with almost everybody else, as the bags are loaded and the staples and luxuries from the mainland unloaded under the watchful eye of the supervisor.

Another industry of these islands, developed in the last two decades, is the cultured pearl industry. The natives of Rangi are said to be able to dive to 30 meters with just snorkel and mask in search of the tasty fish of the lagoon; this is a feat they had been perfecting for years before the cultured pearl industry. Find one of these divers to help you explore the lagoon of Rangiroa.

Don mask and snorkel and drop over the side of the outrigger or motorboat. You will see a lot of fish—jack, surgeonfish, mullet, pompano, parrotfish, grouper, butterflyfish, trumpetfish, eels. Where the reef drops off, look down at the sharks shuttling anxiously back and forth. Look with impunity; the small lagoon sharks of the Pacific have not proved dangerous to people, as the daring underwater activity of local divers attests.

The diver's spear gun is typically a piece of wood perhaps three-and-a-half-feet long, one end of it carved to form a handle. The lethal metal arrow lies against it, held to the wood, slackly, with twine. Surgical tubing provides the force when the arrow is released. Seeing a fish, the diver heads straight downward, extending his gun. It is one straight vertical line, the readied spear and the man behind it. Straight down and down and down, then plink! The hovering snorkeler hears a slight noise: the fish has been speared. In the author's experience, these divers never miss. Novices, like the author, almost always do.

Even without the hunting, of course, the lagoon is a mecca for snorkelers and divers who enjoy watching underwater life proceed apace—coral, fish, the sunlight creating a pattern like a sparkling net, the perfect clarity of the water, the periodic gentle current, and that absolute and most wondrous silence—except for the occasional plink of death.

Once you have explored the lagoon, try shooting the passes. It is, of course, dangerous to do this on an outgoing tide, but when the tide comes in, and with a boat following for safety, this is one of the great adventures in the Pacific, and a rare opportunity for observing underwater activity.

# CHAPTER 7

# THE COOK ISLANDS

*Name:* Cook Islands
*Political status:* Self-governing, in free association with New
   Zealand
*Island groups:* Northern Cooks, Southern Cooks
*Gateway island:* Rarotonga
*Capital:* Avarua
*Population:* 15,000
*Land area:* 240 square kilometers
*Language:* Polynesian (Maori), English
*Currency:* New Zealand dollar ($NZ), Cook Island coins

The traveler who arrives in Rarotonga from Tahiti—a popular and
heavily booked flight—may have the impression that someone has
just turned off a very loud radio. After the glitz of Papeete, the complexity of tensions in French Polynesian society, the distances and
difficulties involved in travel among those far-flung islands, the
Cooks will seem downright tranquil, easygoing, relaxed. Here is a
self-governing people who routinely—in the Southern Cooks, at
least—speak a rhythmic Kiwi English. Prices in this heavily subsi-
dized economy are reasonable. Tourist facilities are easy to access;
indeed, the Southern Cooks are a major vacation destination for
packaged New Zealanders looking for winter warmth and duty-free
shopping.
   The contrast with eastern Polynesia is indeed vivid, and it is
perhaps profound. Tahiti, despite its luxury-hotel veneer, maintains
a certain seductive sensuousness, a savagery, something elemental
in its very terrain. There, the dark recesses of a moody Polynesian
past combine with the intrigue of Gallic circumlocution to produce
mystery layered over mystery. Rarotonga is more amiable turf, its
central mountains not nearly so high, its lushness not nearly as extravagant or wild. It is more straightforward, less brooding, with
proper little lawns properly cared for—little English-style gardens
tended each weekend. If life seems less dramatic here, it is also, from
the traveler's point of view, somewhat less stimulating.
   Drive, bike, or walk around the 32-kilometer coast road of
Rarotonga and you will see village after pleasant village, markets,
video shops, and motels carefully spaced virtually every inch of the
way. The houses of coral lime and concrete block may not, by law,
exceed the height of a palm tree. Where there are no houses for the
living, there are often cemeteries for the dead, although here, as

throughout Polynesia, family members are also buried in the yards of their homes. Ride a horse up into the interior and you will see hills with savannahlike grass slopes, while under high trees and shrubs there is ground to walk on.

The Cook Islands, in short, are a manageable place, where the traveler's senses, and his mind, are lightly caressed, not assaulted. Those austere, puritanical missionaries did a good job, although in the dancing here—among the very best in the Pacific—and in the Banana Court Bar on a Friday night the traveler can see the energetic, erotic muscularity that underlies the impeccable friendliness of the islanders. Still, the Cooks seem quiet, informal, controlled, and controllable.

# GEOGRAPHY, TOPOGRAPHY, CLIMATE

The 15 Cook Islands are dispersed over some 1.8 million square kilometers of ocean between 8 and 23 degrees south latitude and 156 and 167 degrees west longitude. From Penrhyn in the north to Mangaia in the south, the chain runs a distance of 1400 kilometers. The islands are west southwest of Tahiti by more than 1200 kilometers, and are to the east of Tonga by about the same distance. To the north northeast is Kiribati, while the Samoas lie northwest. Avarua, the capital of the Cook Islands, is approximately 3700 kilometers from Wellington, the capital of New Zealand, which is well to the southwest and across the International Dateline. More Cook Islanders live in New Zealand than in their native islands.

Almost every type of island formation can be found in the two groups of Cook Islands. The six Northern Cooks are mainly coral atolls; most are but a few square kilometers in area. Except for Nassau, all have central lagoons. The largest island of the Northern Group is Rakahanga, at 11 square kilometers, while Penrhyn, the northernmost island, though only six square kilometers in area, encloses a lagoon that is 280 kilometers square.

The nine islands of the Southern Group are volcanic in origin, a continuation of the Austral Islands to the east, formed when volcanic material escaped from a southeast-to-northwest fracture in the earth's crust. Atiu, Mangaia, Mauke, and Mitiaro are uplifted atolls; their high coral rings enclose volcanic soil. Atiu and Mangaia boast rolling hills, however, while Mauke and Mitiaro are flat. Aitutaki, though a volcanic island, is surrounded by an atoll-like barrier reef sheltering a lagoon defined by many small islets. Only Rarotonga, the main island, is a high volcanic island in the true sense; the traveler gets a good impression of this if he makes the cross-island hike.

The low atolls of the Northern Cooks have little variety of

vegetation. Their limestone-based soils are unable to hold much water or to provide needed nutrients. Coconut trees do grow here, however, and copra is exported.

The topography of the high islands of the Southern Cooks is characterized by steep valleys cut by rapid freshwater streams. The rich volcanic soils nourish a wealth of vegetation, giving these islands a lush, verdant look even up the slopes of the hills. There are well-defined peaks and pinnacles here; the highest point on Rarotonga is Te Manga, at 653 meters, and the summit of the cross-island walk is at the formation fittingly known as the Needle.

The islands have a humid, tropical climate—less so in the Southern Group because of its greater distance from the equator. Trade-winds blow from the southeast in the Southern Cooks and from the east in the Northern Cooks. The storm season runs from November to March. The hurricane of December 1986, bringing winds of up to 150 miles per hour and 30-foot waves, left some 1000 islanders homeless and destroyed buildings and crops, setting back the island nation's economy by years. Nearly 80 percent of Avarua was severely damaged. No one was killed.

# THE NATURAL ENVIRONMENT

According to legend, the *au*, a native yellow-flowered hibiscus, is connected with fire. Papa Manu, who was said to have powers that let him see in the darkness, promised his grandson, Tama, that when he died, he would give the gift of fire through his veins. "Bury me next to my favorite breadfruit tree," Papa Manu ordered. "Dry me in the sun so that I might capture its power. Rub me so that I can demonstrate its power. On my skin, you will find another gift; strips of it will enable you to weave whatever you desire."

The au remains an all-purpose plant. Though rubbing two au sticks together is no longer the primary source of heat and light in the Cook Islands, the flower makes medicine, the leaves are used to cover the earth oven (*umu*), the branches wall native cottages, and the fiber is indeed used to weave skirts, sandals, and rope.

The lush vegetation of these islands also includes taro, banana, grapefruit, orange, and so many avocados and papaya that the islanders feed them to their pigs. All were introduced by either early settlers or Europeans, and all are grown in well-tended plantations on those islands where soil and water permit—viz., the high, volcanic islands. Tropical fruit is, in fact, the Cooks' largest export, and a cannery on Rarotonga processes citrus and papaya to produce "Raro juice" under the brand name Sunfresh. It's good.

The Ministry of Agriculture works hard at urging diversification of planting, to beans, peppers, corn, tomatoes, watermelons, and other vegetables and fruits known to produce well in the islands. Informative leaflets tell both commercial planters and home gardeners which varieties of plant are good for export and which for the local market, how to prepare the soil, and what pesticides, fungicides, and fertilizers to use.

The most prevalent bird is the mynah, an introduced species that aggressively feeds and breeds, thus driving out other species. It was brought to the islands to kill insects, and while the traveler may indeed feel less bug-plagued here than in other parts of Oceania, it is also true that, on Rarotonga, at least, a pest control company does a lively business.

The traveler will note that there are few, if any, dogs on the Cook Islands. Considered a culinary delicacy, they have mostly disappeared down the gullets of the islanders.

For the traveler to the Cooks, perhaps the most interesting aspect of the environment is underwater. Reef walks off Rarotonga, and even more spectacularly off the west coast of Aitutaki, provide an extraordinary look at living reefs. Brilliant blue starfish, angelfish, butterflyfish, cod, parrotfish, black sea slugs *(bêches de mer)*, trochus, and the routinely eaten clams abound in these waters, but it is the living coral itself that is most striking. Latitude, water temperature, the high salinity of the water, and its clarity, calm, and oxygen richness have combined here to produce varied and colorful miniature forests the traveler can observe up close.

# THE ENVIRONMENTAL DILEMMA

Yet even in the Cook Islands, billed by the tourist promotion slogan as "the last heaven on earth," environmental problems are not absent. On Rarotonga, the worst problem is coastline erosion. It is caused mostly by sand mining, the sand being used in concrete mix for construction. A small Conservation Service, a fairly recent creation of the Internal Affairs Ministry, despairs of being able to do much about the problem. The sand is seen as private property; Conservation's argument that it originally comes from below the mean high water mark and is therefore Crown land has thus far carried little weight.

Inland, the biggest issue is the protection of water catchment areas, which are increasingly coming under cultivation as people look for more room for agriculture. Bad enough on Rarotonga, the problem is particularly acute on Atiu, an island where, unlike most of Oceania, the people live in the center, not on the coast. Cultivation here, completely unplanned, has resulted in serious erosion, silting the lagoon and creating swamp areas.

Another problem is overfishing. On a small island, many of whose inhabitants live off fishing, this is difficult to regulate. On the other hand, the future ramifications of overfishing are potentially very serious. In addition, it has long been a tradition in the islands to kill fish by poisoning; the *utu* tree, with its large, green, pear-shaped fruit, is typically used, and it poisons and kills the coral as well as the targeted fish. Poisoning has become a particular problem in the Southern Group, where the more sophisticated fishermen now use chemicals.

Even the Cook Islands are thus discovering, in their turn, the two horns—one marked conservation, the other marked economic development—of a widespread dilemma. The creation of the Conservation Service is a welcome forward step. Its primary effort for the time being is to promote public awareness, particularly in the schools. In the words of Conservation Officer Teariki Rongo, "We hope the next generation will be able to deal better with the problems; at least we can point them out."

# HISTORY

Today's Cook Islanders are Polynesian Maoris, British subjects, citizens of New Zealand, and self-governing. A lot of history is bound up in these facts.

The ancient legend tells of the meeting at sea of Karika, offspring of a chiefly Samoan family, and Tangiia, from Tahiti. Both were heading toward the Cook Islands and decided to join forces. With the Rarotongan resistance overcome, the two chiefs contested in a canoe race to determine the division of power. Karikia headed south, and Tangiia headed north, both attempting to circle the island beyond the outer fringe of reef. The territory each chief traced in his canoe would be his to rule. The outcome gave an equal share to each, and the two chiefs lived in harmony, even joining up again to repel an invasion by the Tongan Tuatapu.

Other legends tell of the arrival of Ru on Aitutaki after a long, arduous journey from eastern Polynesia; of the Cook Islanders' resistance against Marquesan invasions; and of the departure of Avaiki's canoes to New Zealand.

The first settlers probably arrived in these islands around the eighth century, and they did indeed come from the Society Islands, Samoa, and the Marquesas. Archaeology also confirms that islanders left from the Cooks to settle New Zealand. It is perhaps not surprising that these islands at the heart of the Polynesian triangle should see so much to-ing and fro-ing, nor that tribes in the Cooks still refer to themselves as *vaka*—canoes, nor that the Maori-dialect Cook

Islanders and the Tahitian-dialect French Polynesian islanders are able to understand each other's languages, which come from a single Polynesian source.

The first Europeans to make contact were Mendaña in 1595 and Quirós in 1606. Cook discovered five islands of the Southern Group in the 1770s; it was the Russian cartographer Johann von Krusenstern who named the islands for Cook on an 1824 map. Some of the islands, including Rarotonga, which Cook never saw, were visited by the *Bounty* mutineers in 1789. They brought the seeds for the islands' first orange trees.

In 1821, John Williams of the London Missionary Society stopped at Aitutaki and dropped off two Tahitian missionaries. On a return trip in 1823, Williams took one of the missionaries (both had proved successful) to Rarotonga, leaving him there for four years. Again, the missionary, Papeiha, was inordinately successful; his method was to convert the *ariki*, the chiefs, who then ordered their subjects to follow their example. Thus was formed the Cook Islands Christian Church (CICC), to which nearly 70 percent of today's Cook Islanders still belong. Its main building on Rarotonga dates from 1829.

The coming of Christianity profoundly transformed society in the Cook Islands. The early missionaries toppled statues; dissolved all forms of ancestral power and imposed Western dress, housing styles, and legal codes; enacted numerous blue laws against dancing, kava, and the wearing of flowers. These last, happily, do not seem to have had too serious or lasting an effect, but religion in the Cook Islands today is still a formidable force. Not only the CICC, but also Catholic, Mormon, Baha'i, Jehovah's Witness, and Presbyterian churches make the typical Polynesian Sunday closing particularly tight in the Cooks (Saturday for the Seventh-Day Adventists).

The dominance of these Protestant missionaries and the islands' proximity to New Zealand drew them increasingly into Britain's sphere of influence. When, in 1888, it looked as if the French might be preparing to intrude westward from Tahiti, the Southern Group was declared a British protectorate. In 1901, both north and south islands were annexed by New Zealand, with the agreement of the British Crown and the consent of the islands' ariki. (One of the measures promulgated at once by the New Zealand government was a prohibition against Chinese immigration; even today, there are few Chinese evident in the Cooks.)

In World War II, U.S. forces were based on Aitutaki, while numerous islanders enlisted in New Zealand's forces. Demands for self-government grew louder and more articulate after the war, voiced most eloquently by Albert Royle Henry, son of an Aitutaki chief. Self-government was phased in starting in 1946. By an act of the

New Zealand Parliament promulgated in 1965, the islands were declared a self-governing nation in domestic matters, with New Zealand responsible for defense and available for consultation on foreign affairs. Albert Henry became the first prime minister of the new nation.

Henry's story doesn't end there. During the campaign preceding the elections of 1978, he was accused of corruption and abuses of power. The charge was that Henry had used public monies to charter aircraft to bring expatriate islanders home from New Zealand to vote. The opposition had also brought supporters home, but with party funds. Henry was removed from office by the chief justice of the High Court, he was stripped of his knighthood by Queen Elizabeth, and he eventually lost the election—though it took the Privy Council in London to render the final decision on the change in government. This was the first time in Commonwealth history that a court ruling had in fact changed a government. Henry died in 1981, reputedly of a broken heart.

The connection with New Zealand deprives the Cook Islands of a seat in the United Nations, but it brings enormous subsidies from that country, subsidies on which the Cooks' economy is highly dependent. Remittances from expatriates living in New Zealand also prop up the economy, as does tourism. By 1970, there were more Cook Islanders living and working in New Zealand than at home; in 1982, the number of foreign tourists to visit the islands exceeded the total population.

The British monarch is the head of state in the islands, and a six-member cabinet is responsible to a 24-member parliament, elected for four-year terms by universal adult suffrage. One member of Parliament represents the overseas islanders. An upper house, the House of Ariki, comprises 15 ariki who may consult only, particularly on issues of custom or land tenure. Local government is carried out through island councils and village committees, although most administration is in the hands of the chief administrative officer appointed by the government. Government control is strict; indeed, control is a watchword for the Cook Islands in many ways.

## THE TRAVELER IN THE COOK ISLANDS

For one thing, control is the word for travel in these islands. One of the reasons you may have trouble getting a plane reservation is that the government limits the number of flights into the country. It also licenses the hotels, restaurants, and tourist facilities. The laudable objective of all this is to ensure that tourism here will not overwhelm the ability of the infrastructure to deal with it; a side effect is an ability to keep tabs on the *type* of tourists. Customs agents are on the lookout for drugs, and no camping is permitted in these islands. Indeed, a reservation at a licensed hostelry is a requirement of entry to the Cooks.

Fortunately, there is a range of accommodations, from resort style to guesthouse by way of motels. The last are very much like American motels—or at least, as American motels were before the glitzy chains got hold of them. Most units have kitchens, and a few motels have restaurants and bars. You choose your accommodations when you make your flight reservation; the airline or travel agent will have a list, with details and prices, and will make the booking for you.

On the outliers, there are fewer lodging and restaurant facilities; the Cook Islands Tourist Authority, right on the coast road in Avarua, has a complete listing of what's available, and varied travel and tour agencies in Avarua can also make arrangements for you.

On Rarotonga itself, restaurants abound, serving everything from Italian to Chinese to continental cuisine. In addition, most of the bigger hotels offer an "island night." You eat a traditional meal—*umukai*—cooked on the umu, and watch sensational native dancing. Although these are hotel floor shows geared to tourists, the dancing is genuine and quite fantastic, and the evenings provide good-humored fun.

Travel in the Cooks is effectively travel in the Southern Cooks. Between Cook Islandair and Air Rarotonga there are flights to Aitutaki, Atiu, Mitiaro, Mauke, and Mangaia, with some special combination fares offered, and with interisland flights between Atiu, Mauke, and Mitiaro. For the Northern Group, you must rely on interisland steamer travel out of Avatiu, Rarotonga's harbor. Schedules are erratic, the journeys are long, and the comfort level is low.

Rarotonga, the visitor soon discovers, is filled with vacationing New Zealanders, many of them prepackaged into the larger resort hotels. One can hardly blame them, since this is an extremely pleasant place, offering interesting sights and varied activities. But as always in the Pacific the traveler will also want to experience at least one of the outliers.

Aitutaki is an obvious choice. There are frequent flights, there is good accommodation, and its reef is wonderful to explore. It is also the outlier most visited by the prepackaged Kiwis and other tourists, for just these reasons.

Atiu is of interest because its inhabitants prefer the interior to the shore—not surprisingly, since the interior is a high central plateau surrounded by low swamps and ringed by a raised coral reef (*makatea*). Atiu also has exquisite beaches. Mitiaro is a low and quite swampy island, whose inhabitants all live in one village. There are some pleasant walks here and some marae ruins to observe, and the church in the village is worth a look. Mauke, easternmost of the Cooks, is a raised atoll with another interesting church and more superb beaches, particularly on the south end of the island. Mangaia, southernmost Cook, is a geological curiosity: its raised makatea forms a 60-meter ring around the island. On all of these islands, you will live somewhat more primitively than on Rarotonga and Aitutaki. Our Pacific traveler limits his Cook Islands visit to those two.

## LANGUAGE

Cook Islanders are Maori Polynesians and speak a Maori dialect. They can, however, understand Tahitian Polynesian, and Polynesians of Tahitian dialect can understand the Cook Islanders. Here are a few useful terms:

| | |
|---|---|
| Kia orana | Hello |
| Aere ra | Goodbye |
| Kia manuia | Good luck (a toast) |
| Meitaki | Thank you |
| Maori | Polynesian person or language |
| Papa'a | Foreigner, foreign language (the word actually means four layers, derived from the dress of the early Europeans: jacket, vest, shirt, undershirt) |

# RAROTONGA

You will be met at the airport by someone from your chosen hotel—or you should be: be sure to confirm this when the airline or travel agent makes your reservation. As you are driven to your destination, and particularly if you go via Avarua, you will notice numerous car/bike/scooter rental agencies.

This is a reminder that the second thing you should do—after reconfirming your flight—is to arrange wheels for yourself. As almost everywhere in the Pacific, your hotel manager will be able to help with these arrangements. Motor scooter is the most prevalent form of transportation, for both islanders and tourists. If you rent a car, you must have a Cook Islands driver's license. Present yourself and your home driver's license at the police station, and, for a nominal charge, you get the required document. It's an excellent souvenir.

There is also a minibus service that travels counterclockwise around the island regularly, though not to any schedule, from 6:00 A.M. to 4:00 P.M. weekdays, till 11:30 A.M. Saturdays. Never on

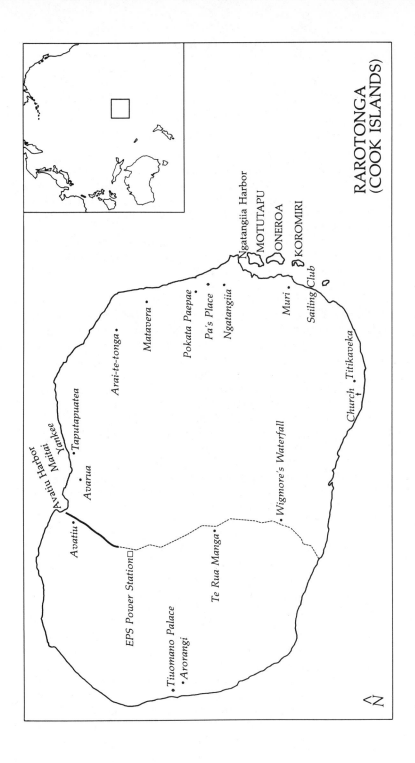

RAROTONGA
(COOK ISLANDS)

Sunday, here in the deeply religious Cooks. It stops when you hail it; the primary starting place is in Avarua, just opposite the police station.

Everyone calls the island Raro.

## Avarua

Avarua, capital of the Cooks and main town of Rarotonga, has all the resources you could need. There are supermarkets, and the local outdoor market is held on Saturdays. Near the harbor at Avatiu there is even a huge liquor supermarket stocking New Zealand beers; wines from Down Under, California, and France; liquor, brandy, rum, the lot.

The Bank of New Zealand in Avarua opens from 9:00 A.M. to 3:00 P.M. weekdays. Be sure to buy some Cook Islands dollar coins with the image of the noticeably virile god Tangaroa—another good souvenir.

Duty-free shops abound and are a mecca for Kiwis eager for appliances cheaper than they can buy at home, though for Americans used to discount stores there are no real bargains. Excellent crafts—baskets, pandanus hats, mother-of-pearl jewelry, wood carvings—are available at the Women's Development Center, an upright organization fostering traditional morals and the domestic arts, anomalously located in the same building as the notorious Banana Court Bar.

There are numerous shops all around the island selling T-shirts, pareus, hand-printed fashions, various knickknacks, books, and magazines. There is as well a variety of snack bars, beach bars, and restaurants—even two movie theaters showing movies of uncertain provenance according to an uncertain schedule.

All international telephone and mail services are available at the post office, as are Cook Islands stamps. A special Philatelic Bureau also caters to philatelists worldwide; stamps are a major source of revenue.

The tourist bureau's visitor center is open weekdays from 8:00 A.M. to 4:00 P.M., 9:00 to noon on Saturdays. A hard-working office, the staff is both competent and courteous and can provide any information you need. For topographic maps, apply at the Survey Office behind the Ministry of Internal Affairs in the government buildings area.

The two wrecks you see in the water are the *Yankee*, a world-famous brig that ran aground on July 24, 1964, while its crew was partying below decks, and, further out, the *Maitai*, a trading vessel wrecked in 1916.

The other sights of Avarua are easily seen in a slow walk. Don't miss the Cook Islands Christian Church with its massive wooden balcony, and check out the churchyard and Albert Henry's memorial.

The museum and library are worth a visit; the artifacts and mementos of the missionaries are interesting, and you can actually arrange to borrow something to read. You can also visit the Takamoa Mission House, at the end of the road, where locals are trained as ministers and from which numerous missions have been sent out to the wider world. Note, not far from the town's movie theaters, the ruins of Taputaputea, once the palace of the one-time Queen Makea; the name is the same as that of the most important temple in French Polynesia, on Raiatea.

## Around the Island

Two roads go around Rarotonga: the new coastal road and the old inland road, the Ara Metua, or Great Road of Toi, said to be the oldest road in Polynesia. Paved in coral blocks nearly a thousand years ago, the Ara Metua was an all-weather thoroughfare through the swamps. Most Rarotongans once lived along its inland side, until the missionaries of the 19th century concentrated the population around the churches near the coast. Where Toi came from, and why he built such a road, is still not known, but his road goes almost all the way around the island and can be followed on foot or in a vehicle (preferably 4×4 if it's rainy season).

Here are some of the sights to look for as you tour the island, going clockwise from Avarua (note that village signs are wooden, reddish, with the town name and either KIA ORANA, "hello," or AERE RA, "good-bye," in stylized letters):

• Araei-Te-Tonga, on the Ara Metua. These stone structures were once chiefly courts where ariki were invested and where offerings to ancient gods were first assembled before being conveyed to the marae. These ruins are considered sacred sites—take that, missionaries!—and should not be walked on.

• In the Takitumu district, look for the Pakata *paepae*, platform or meeting place, and for the palace of Pa, the district's one-time high chief, built with coral and lime. The harbor of Ngatangiia, across the way, was the departure point for the Great Migration of Maori Canoes in 1350. Seven of them reached New Zealand; one was named Takitumu. The CICC building along here (1865) is in a lovely setting, with its solid, earthy look given vigor by the whitewash and colored windows.

• Muri Beach, a great place for beaching and the site of the bareback horse races occasionally run on Rarotonga. The Sailing Club here is a favorite hangout, especially for youthful Kiwis.

• The Titikaveka CICC Church, built in 1841 of coral slabs. The coral was hewn by hand from the Tikioki reef and hauled here by chain. The lagoon at Titikaveka offers the best snorkeling on Rarotonga.

• In Aorangi, look for the departure point of the Great Migration canoes—their first stop after Ngatangiia and before New Zealand; the four-cluster Tinomana Tribe settlement; the Preaching Stone where Papeiha, John Williams' Tahitian missionary, first preached; the Tinomana Palace, built near the church when Christianity was introduced.

• Black Rock. In a coral lagoon off the northwest coast, this is Tuoro, "welcome," the leaping-off point where souls begin their journey back to the fatherland, Avaiki.

## The Cross-Island Hike

This is a delightful jaunt of about four hours. There is considerable steepness at times, and after a rain, as the author can attest, the walk can be muddy, slick, and very slippery. But with good tread soles and clothing that you don't intend to wear out that evening, the hike in or after a rain is still quite splendid.

Take the road behind the main wharf and continue heading up past the power station to a small hut. You can drive this far, then start walking. The path moves along quite easily—very verdant, thick with ferns, pocked with some roots and rocks, but a real trail, open and evident. Then it begins to ascend, increasingly steeply, though there are plenty of roots and young trees for handholds, and numerous footholds, even if the reddish soil has turned to clayey mud. It's about an hour's walk to the Needle, where there is a chimney formation and a track up the rock. Be careful if this is wet; it can be a treacherous climb. Better just to pause to look out on the island, all of which is visible from here, before going on with the walk.

The downhill heading south is a longer walk, taking at least two hours, and the first descent is steep and serious. You cross the stream at least half a dozen times. After a rain, when the stream is fast and full, some of the stepping stones across it are underwater, while those that are visible are mighty slippery. Moreover, the rain tends to erode the banks, so at some crossings you may just be hauling yourself up any which way. Plan on getting wet and muddy.

You can, however, clean yourself and your clothing off entirely by hurling yourself into Wigmore's Waterfall, the island's only cascade and the end point of the cross-island hike. From there, walk another 20 minutes or so to the road, making sure to turn left at the fork. At the road, a right turn gets you to the Rarotongan Hotel in another kilometer and a half—a good place for a cold beer while you wait for a taxi or the bus. Taxis, by the way, will return you to the trailhead, if you have left a car or scooter there.

## Other Activities

Guided reef walks are conducted along various parts of the reef—a good way to learn about marine life here. And, of course, it's easy enough to do on your own. Be sure you have shoes on. There is nothing out there that can cause serious or permanent damage, but the stonefish and crown-of-thorns starfish can cause painful wounds, and some coral seems to bite as well.

Diving and snorkeling—plus gear and supervision—are readily available; ask at your hotel or the tourist bureau. Sailing and fishing outside the sheltering reef are excellent. Bonito, blue marlin, and barracuda have all been caught here.

Horseback riding takes you up the Avana Valley—a good way to see into the heart of this island.

Do not under any circumstances miss seeing the traditional dancing here, and do not miss the Banana Court Bar, in the center of Avarua, open Monday through Saturday from 11:00, with dancing Wednesday through Saturday. Friday night, the joint really jumps; keep low to stay out of the line of fire. With Quinn's of Papeete gone, the Banana Court may be the last of the great watering holes of the Pacific.

# AITUTAKI

The pace is yet slower in the Aitutaki atoll, a fishhook formation whose hook end is a high volcanic island, while the line end comprises 12 small motus. A triangular reef 45 kilometers around surrounds it all, defining a broad lagoon.

Legend has it that Maungapu, the island's highest point at 120 meters, is the top of Raemaru on Rarotonga, from which it was stolen by victorious Aitutaki warriors. In historical times, Aitutaki received its first European contact from the famous Captain Bligh, in 1789. It was here that Papeiha and Vahapata, the Tahitian convert missionaries, were put ashore by John Williams to convert the natives; Aitutaki was thus the first Christian island in the Cooks.

The airstrip on which you land was built, as were so many Pacific airstrips, by U.S. Seabees during World War II. Akaiami, in the lagoon, was used as a refueling base by Tasman Empire Airways (now Air New Zealand, which still carries the two-letter code TE) in the 1950s—the first time that an uninhabited island was visited by an international airline.

There are two resort hotels here (meaning meals, bar, activities arranged), one on Akitua atoll over a causeway, the other near the main town of Arutanga. There are also numerous guesthouses, almost all of them strung along the main drag of Arutanga.

Arutanga also has a few stores, post office, public hall, and churches. Do not forget to reconfirm your onward flight at Cook Islandair or Air Rarotonga; the agent radios back to Raro to ensure your place. This is a delightfully sleepy town; the action, such as it is, is concentrated around the wharf. Because the coral heads and currents make passage through the reef dangerous, interisland vessels put cargo and passengers on lighters—short-haul transport barges—for the trip to shore.

Almost everyone gets around on scooters, which you can easily rent. The road is pretty good almost all the way around the island. Villages on the east side of Aitutaki are noticeably poorer than on the west, though the well-tended gardens and carefully mown lawns persist, and there are lots of banana plantations and coconut groves. Look for seabirds along the lagoon.

If you're on Aitutaki on a Sunday, do go to church. It can be an all-day affair (though you can dash out at any time), with music-filled services punctuated by eating.

*The* thing to do here is to reef walk (and/or snorkel or dive). At low tide you can walk along the sandbar from the Rapae Cottage Motel right onto the reef; at high tide, arrange for an outrigger. Park yourself on a clump of coral or at a tidepool, or walk along, taking care where you set your feet. Here are bushlike acropora, white, red, and violet; flowerlike montipora spreading its "petals" wide; porites in purple, yellow, beige, white; pachyseris like lined shells; cactuslike pavona; all sorts of favia and diploria and platygyra—all living coral, often growing like an outer layer around dead skeleton but a very vital garden nevertheless.

See if you can get your outrigger "driver" to take you over the pass, or at least try to watch somebody do it. It is quite something to see these frail canoes wait for the moment, then shoot the pass and head out to the wide sea. The pass is also a good place for snorkeling when the tide is incoming; hang on to a piece of the wall and watch the world go by.

You might try to help out with the clam gathering. The implement is a T-junction metal spear. The top of the T is the handle, and the spear itself is perhaps two feet in length, a long, thick nail. Dive, and look for the royal blue wavy line that is the mouth of the clam, *pahua*. Aim, then send the point of the spear very fast into the mouth, before it can close up, and continue spearing down through the shell so you can wrest the clam from the coral. The trick is to be fast enough; the wavy mouth closes quickly and irrevocably if you hesitate. Open with a knife, cut off the black connecting membrane, and eat raw—delicious. So too the reef mussels, which you can just pluck from the coral on your walk.

Across from the Rapae Cottage is Big J's, a popular watering hole where you can watch and/or participate in both traditional dance and contemporary disco.

On Aitutaki, as on Raro and Arui, archaeological work—and restoration—are proceeding apace in an attempt to find and preserve evidence of the early settlement of the Cooks.

### Cook Islands Address

Cook Islands Tourist Authority
P.O. Box 14
Rarotonga, Cook Islands
Tel. 29435
Cable "Cooktour"
Telex RG62054

Air New Zealand offices and U.S. travel agents may be able to provide you advance information about lodgings and assistance with making reservations.

CHAPTER 8

# WESTERN SAMOA

*Name:* Independent State of Western Samoa
*Political status:* Independent (1962)
*Island groups:* Nine islands, four of them inhabited
*Gateway island:* Upolu
*Capital:* Apia
*Population:* 162,000
*Land area:* 2849 square kilometers
*Language:* Polynesian (Samoan), English
*Currency:* Western Samoa tala ($WS); 1 tala =100 sene

Western Samoa is one of the great travel destinations of the Pacific. It is a treat for the traveler interested in traditional culture, for the traveler interested in natural history, for the traveler interested in political history, for the traveler interested in shopping, for the traveler interested in finding enchanting locales, and for the traveler who has none of these interests, if such a person exists. You can sightsee, swim, snorkel, hike, boat, fish, wander, and get to know people in lovely surroundings in an easygoing atmosphere. At a level matched by only a few other nations of Oceania, Western Samoa is the Pacific you have come to see.

## GEOGRAPHY, TOPOGRAPHY, CLIMATE

The nine volcanic islands of Western Samoa lie about two-thirds of the way from Honolulu to Auckland, between 171 and 173 degrees west longitude and 13 and 15 degrees south latitude. Savai'i is the largest island, but Upolu is where 75 percent of the population lives, and it is the site of the capital, Apia. Between the two are Manono, within Upolu's reef system, and Apolima, outside the reef in the Apolima Strait. Fanuatapu, Namu'a, Nuutele, Nuulua, and Nuusafee, small islands off the east and south coasts of Upolu, are home only to seabirds. Fringing reefs encircle the two big islands, creating a calm and protected shoreline.

The islands emerged from the ocean about three million years ago as a chain of volcanic cones, the Fagaloa volcanics. (It is not too early to state that the Samoan "g" is pronounced "ng"—a good thing for *palagis*, pronounced "palangis" and meaning foreigners, to know.) Two successive eras of significant volcanic activity followed—the Salani, about a hundred thousand years ago, and the

Ocean beach, Western Samoa. *Photo by Susanna Margolis.*

Pu'apu'a, some three thousand years ago. The lava flows left a rain forest heritage, reduced by centuries of land clearing for croplands and villages.

Savai'i is less lush and more rugged than Opolu. It is higher; Mount Silisili, its highest point, rises to 1858 meters. Silisili is a cinder crater, probably dating to the Pu'apu'a era. Savai'i's most recent volcanic eruption occurred in 1911; vast lava fields can still be seen.

Upolu presents a less aggressive topography. Its highest point, Mount Fito, is 1100 meters, and Upolu also has less *area* of highland than Savai'i. The island boasts streams and cascades, and the wide Vaisigano River empties into the sea to create the major pass in the fringing reef. At the mouth of the Vaisigano are the harbor and capital city of Apia, once a haven for Pacific trading schooners.

The Samoan Chain is outside the normal path of hurricanes, and severe storms strike only infrequently. When they come, it is the eastern ends of the islands that receive the most rainfall; due to the slightly northwest/southeast orientation of the islands, that's where the prevailing tradewinds drop their load of moisture.

Samoa is a fitting place in which to scan the night skies for the Southern Cross, which is featured on the nation's flag—a white constellation on a blue rectangle in a red field. (See Chapter 4, Travel in Oceania.)

# THE NATURAL ENVIRONMENT

Western Samoa has, in greater proportion than almost anywhere else in the Pacific, an impressive system of national parks and preserves. In these are protected virtually all of the species of plants, trees, birds, coral, and fish that the islands nurture. The first and thus far only national park was created in 1978—O Le Pupu-Pu'e. *Pupu* means seacoast, and *pu'e* means mountaintop, and the seven thousand acres of O Le Pupu-Pu'e run from the south coast of Upolu to the top of Mount Fito. As a national territory, the park is deemed to have "special scientific, educational, recreational, and scenic interest," in the words of the Department of Agriculture and Forests, and thus to merit being "properly controlled and protected by the highest competent authority in the country." That authority, created under the 1974 National Parks and Reserves Act, is the National Parks and Reserves section of the Forestry Division, Department of Agriculture and Forests.

In addition to O Le Pupu-Pu'e, there are five reserves. Similarly protected as having national importance, the reserves are usually sites with a particular environmental or historical value. Robert Louis Stevenson's tomb, the Stevenson Memorial Reserve, has obvious

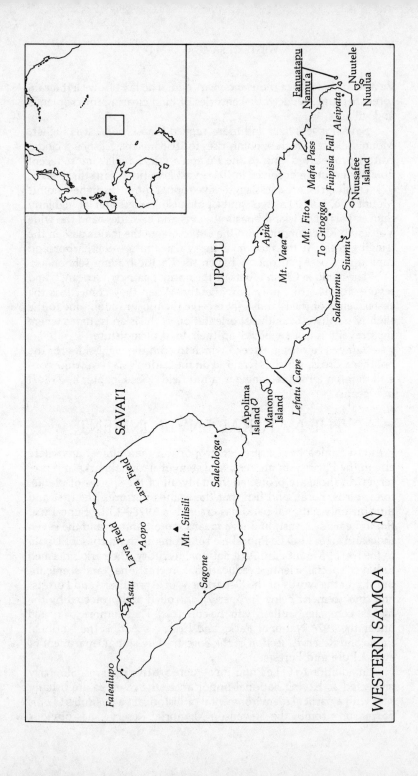

historical importance, and the government has turned the hill on which the writer is buried, Mount Vaea, into a scenic reserve as well. Nearby is the Vailima Botanical Garden, in which the government has planted a variety of species representative of the Pacific. Togitogiga Recreation Reserve, a popular picnic area, preserves a falls and pool. Palolo Deep Marine Reserve, just a mile from the center of Apia, protects a huge hole in the reef where divers and snorkelers can see a superb display of coral and small fish.

*Palolo* is Samoan for the reefworm or coral worm *(Eunice viridis)*, perhaps the most interesting creature of Western Samoa. For two days every year, at the end of October or beginning of November, when the moon and tide are just right, the worms emerge from the reef to propagate the species. This rising of the palolo occurs at night, and Samoans, who consider the reefworm a great delicacy, the so-called "caviar of the Pacific," gather with lanterns, nets, and cheesecloth to claim a portion for feasting. It is only then that the traveler can see the palolo, but if you're there for "the rising," do try to participate; the only other place in the Pacific to observe this rite is Fiji.

Other varieties of marine life are easily seen in Palolo, however—and in other snorkeling and diving spots around Opolu. Look for parrotfish, nibbling at the coral with their strong beaks; long, thin pipefish, which forage down into the coral to feed; clownfish, which seek protection in the poisonous tentacles of the sea anemone, luring other fish that in turn become the anemone's meal.

Vegetation in Western Samoa can be divided into three general categories: littoral, rain forest, and crater. The scrubby plants of the iron-bound littoral, which battle against wind and salinity, are mostly low and herbaceous, burrowed into rock crevices and shallow sand pockets. Look for maritime grass, sedge, coarse ferns, the tiny yellow-flowered succulent known as *tamole (Portulaca australis),* and lavender-flowered beach morning glory. You will also see waxy-leaved shrubs with white fruits and flowers, hibiscus, ficus, and clerodendrum. Littoral forests are of pandanus, Barringtonia, and Calophyllum.

The rain-forest vegetation that *seems,* at any rate, to cover Upolu, presents a varied picture. At higher elevations, the raintree, *tamaligi,* seems to stretch as far as the eye can see. *Tava,* a red wood that is the primary fuel of the islanders, eucalyptus, and teak are evident. *Ifilele* is the wood used for most carvings. To at least one visitor, the prevalent *mamalava (Planchonella torricellensis)* has always looked like a tree that Dr. Seuss might have invented.

Crater vegetation includes such marsh plants as water chestnut, coarse sedge, sunflower, herbaceous species, and a few trees, as well as swamp forest, mostly of pandanus.

Wildlife is particularly abundant in O Le Pupu-Pu'e, where more than 50 species have been identified. Among this wildlife, birds are the most prevalent. The Pacific pigeon, *lupe*, is found here in its highest concentration. Indeed, the lupe has been named the symbol of environmental awareness for Western Samoa; the environmental slogan is *O lo tu le lupe*, which means "Standing and crying, the lupe." The traveler may see signs and posters depicting the lupe "standing and crying" and offering environmental messages. Although a protected species, the lupe is also considered a great delicacy and is still, illegally, shot; White Sunday, the October holiday that is like an additional Christmas for children, is a favorite time for eating this bird.

Also in the park in abundance are the crimson-crowned fruit dove, the wattled honey-eater, white-rumped swiftlet, and Samoan starling.

Numerous seabirds frequent the coast of Western Samoa. Look for tropicbirds, tern, brown noddy, boobies (both red-footed and brown), frigates (both great and lesser). The boobies and frigatebirds nest on the islands at the eastern tip of Upolu.

Thirty-five species of waterfowl, marsh, and land birds include herons, ducks, rails, plovers, sandpipers, pigeons and doves, parrots, cuckoos, barn owls, swifts, kingfishers, cuckoo-shrikes, bulbuls, thrushes, finches, and starlings.

When walking in Western Samoa, and particularly in O Le Pupu-Pu'e, look over your head for flying fox, fruit bat, or sheath-tailed bat, and under your feet for rats. Also under your feet, as well as on tree trunks and branches, look for the skink, called *pili*, very common.

# THE ENVIRONMENTAL DILEMMA

Social realities as much as anything shape the environmental dilemma of Western Samoa. First, subsistence activity is still prevalent in both fishing and agriculture. Second, this is a society where tradition is still of primary importance and is occasionally at odds with the central government's legislation. Sometimes, law and tradition work hand in hand to support subsistence activity, and sometimes that support also reinforces conservation efforts. Sometimes, conservation efforts undermine subsistence activity—sometimes not. Sometimes, law and tradition oppose one another, in which case very little gets done.

For example, teak was once so prevalent here that it was exported. The lands on which the teak grew were controlled by village chiefs, the *matai*, who could not sell but could and did lease the land to outside interests. Teak has now become scarce, and the central government has stopped its export. The matai, however, can and do still order that it be cut. Moreover, a reforestation project has been halted because of a dispute between matai over land ownership.

The problem is particularly acute where fishing is concerned, perhaps because Samoans, it is said, will eat anything from the sea. Indeed, fish are a major source of protein for the islanders, who have long fished both the lagoon and the open ocean. In 1888, a European observer wrote of Samoa that "there are fishes throughout the whole year, for the sea is as inexhaustible as the land." That is no longer the case, but subsistence fishery continues to be crucial to the majority of Samoans living in rural areas. Where marine resources were once under the control of the matai, a village controlling "its" part of the lagoon as far as the reef, the law now states that land below the high-water mark is public. The result, or in any event an uncanny coincidence, has been the uncontrolled cutting of mangrove trees for firewood, dynamiting and chemical poisoning to catch fish, dredging, and direct discharge of pollutants from factories into the sea.

Lui A. J. Bell, a marine biologist with the Fisheries Division, claims that there has been significant overfishing in Samoan waters. There are no statistics on this as yet, but Bell says that anyone who has fished here since boyhood, as he has, can state from experience that there are far fewer mullet, that giant clams are decreasing in number, that the number of rabbitfish is way down. Bell attributes much of the problem to dynamiting and poisoning, especially in the lagoon, but he notes that trawlers with foreign flags have routinely abused the coastal waters off Western Samoa.

Bell took charge of a project initiated in 1981 to culture the Philippine green mussel (Perna viridis), actually imported from Tahiti. The mussels were attached to ropes and suspended from bamboo rafts. Thus far, the results have been good, so the Philippine mussel may prove a cheap supply of protein for fish-loving Samoans whose waters have been depleted—in part by themselves, but in great measure by foreign commercial fishing vessels.

Here as elsewhere in the Pacific, it is a sad commentary that fish must be imported to a place whose fishermen were once so skilled and so daring offshore that one of the first Europeans to these islands dubbed them the Isles of the Navigators.

# HISTORY

There are numerous theories as to the origin of the name Samoa. Perhaps the most common is that it derives from the sacred (sa) hens (moa) of Lu, son of Tagaloa or Tagaloalagi, ruler of all beings in the descending heavens. Having behaved badly, Lu was banished from the tenth heaven and settled at the village of Uafato, on the mountain called Malata, in Atua, at the eastern end of Upolu. One day, Tagaloa, who loved fish, sent down two of his fishermen to try their luck in the lagoon. As the men were returning with their catch, the sa moa of Lu pecked at the fish, and the fishermen seized the hens and brought them to heaven. When Lu discovered the theft, he chased the hens through all the heavens to the tenth, the place of rest. Declaring that there must be no strife in heaven, Tagaloa stopped his son from killing the two fishermen, promising to send him back to earth with the title of King of Heaven, and giving him for his wife Lagituavalu, the eighth heaven. The two indeed returned to earth, where they had a son whom they named Samoa, thus preserving the memory of the sacred hens.

Perhaps more lyrical is the cosmogony myth. First, of course, there was nothing. From it sprang fragrance, then dust, then the perceivable, the obtainable, earth, high rocks, small stones, and mountains. The rocks married the earth, and earth became pregnant. Salevao, god of the rocks, could see motion in the *moa*, or center, of the earth, and the child that was born was called Moa. Salevao then provided water for washing the child and made it sa, sacred, to Moa.

Following creation, legend concentrates on Pili, who lived around 850. Through his marriage to Sinaletavae and as a result of his own prowess, Pili became a powerful and beneficent ruler. But after his death, his four sons, to whom he had bequeathed Samoa, engaged in frequent wars to settle territorial disputes. It is a theme that recurs constantly in Samoan history.

The Tongans came in about 950, and the line of their great chief, the Tuitoga, ruled the Samoans for some three hundred years, until driven out in around 1250. The expulsion also seems to mark the beginning of the extensive oral history of Samoa, much of it repressed and/or lost in the islanders' enthusiastic acceptance of Christianity centuries later. The parting words of the Tuitoga, preserved by this oral tradition, provide the origin of the important Samoan chiefly title, *malietoa:* "Malie toa, malie tau, afai ae toe oo mai Toga, e sau i le aoauli folau ae le o le aoauli tau—"Brave warrior, bravely fought! If the Tongans ever come back again, it will be for a friendly visit, never again to fight you."

Salamasina was the great legendary queen of Samoa. In around 1500, a time of more interdistrict and tribal warfare, she reached the height of power by dint of her descent from all four paramount families. She is one of the few Samoan rulers, and the only woman, to have held all four of the highest chiefly titles.

Archaeology disputes the early legendary history of Samoa only slightly, though science may dispute the cosmogony myths. While legend insists that the Samoans originated in Samoa, in the common homeland of Hawaiki (Savai'i), most historians agree that they, like all Polynesians, are descended from peoples of southeastern Asia. History accepts, however, that these islands were among the first in Polynesia to be settled and that they maintained contact with both Fiji and Tonga; indeed, the Tongan language and the Samoan remain similar today.

The Dutch explorer Jacob Roggeveen was the first European to sight the islands; he charted Manu'a, now part of American Samoa, in 1722. Next came Bougainville in 1768, naming these islands the Navigator Isles, and the Compte de la Pérouse in 1787, the first to land. In 1791, the H.M.S. *Pandora,* skippered by Captain Edwards of the British Admiralty, arrived in Samoa in search of mutineers from the *Bounty.* In the wake of these explorers came sailors, whalers, beachcombers, traders, and, in 1830, missionaries under the ubiquitous John Williams of the London Missionary Society. Arriving on Savai'i just at the end of a violent internal struggle, Williams managed to convert the victorious chief, Malietoa Vai'inupo, who was followed by the matai and the villagers. It may have helped Williams' efforts that a myth had foretold that Samoa should await the kingdom which would come from heaven.

While the rule of God was being established, so was the power of commerce. Whales were scarce in Samoan waters, but coconut was abundant on land. John Williams, Jr., son of the missionary, established a copra exporting trade and became the U.S.'s first commercial agent and consul in Samoa. In 1855, a branch of the German trading firm Godeffroy & Sons was established in Apia and eventually became Godeffroy's Pacific headquarters.

The American Civil War prompted efforts at growing cotton, a successful export until about 1890. The foreign owners of the copra and cotton plantations, finding the native Samoans to be unwilling laborers, recruited workers from Niue, Rarotonga, the Solomon Islands, and Micronesia. Blackbirding became a flourishing business, and Bully Hayes, reputed to have been one of the most nefarious of the blackbirders, came through Apia often on his wild, buccaneering Pacific journeys. It was in Samoa that Hayes met Louis Becke, perhaps the singularly most colorful and most vivid teller of tales about the Pacific in its trading heyday. (See Chapter 5, The Literary Pacific.)

As plantation agriculture and trading grew apace, foreign interests—mostly American, British, and German—were increasingly involved in internal politics. The matai were not averse to selling land to the planters, often without the consent of the rest of the village or kinship group, and just as often in order to buy firearms for use in the intermittent warfare of the time. The outrage over this, the frequent disputes over the rights foreign landholders understood they had obtained and the rights the islanders felt were theirs by custom, and the ongoing internal squabbles among traditional leaders combined to create serious turmoil in the islands.

In 1873, Albert Steinberger, a U.S. Department of State official, entered the picture. Steinberger became a trusted adviser in the islands and arranged an informal agreement, seen by the islanders as a treaty, between the U.S. and Samoa. Germany was not wild about this idea, and in 1874, with Steinberger away, a German warship intervened to support a land claim of Godeffroy. Steinberger was unquestionably an opportunist who involved himself in a number of conflicting business interests, but he may have been something more as well. In any event, on his return to Samoa, in 1875, he managed to get himself named premier of the islands. Neither the U.S. nor the British consul was willing to accept this, and Steinberger was deported on trumped-up charges.

Meanwhile, the three foreign interests and warring local factions continued to jockey for power in a complex web of intrigues. Finally, on March 15, 1889, three German ships, three American, and one British vessel lay at anchor off Apia, each nation thereby asserting its claim and warning the others. What averted war was a hurricane, in which only the British *Calliope*, racing out to sea, escaped destruction. It was time for a conference.

The three-power joint administration established by the Berlin Conference of 1889 lasted just ten years. In 1899, the three agreed on complete partition: Britain withdrew her claims in return for recognition of claims elsewhere in the Pacific, Germany retained control of the western Samoan islands, and the U.S. Navy took Tutuila, the large island in the east with its superb harbor of Pago Pago, and the isolated Manu'a group. On March 1, 1900, the German flag was raised at Apia.

German rule continued until the outbreak of World War I in 1914, when New Zealand forces seized the country. New Zealand had long entertained ambitions toward Western Samoa, but its wartime administration was necessarily limited. It was also tragic. On November 7, 1918, the ship *Talune* arrived from Auckland; on board was an influenza that proceeded to kill one-fifth of Western Samoa's population, mostly the elderly.

Partly as a result, the Mau movement for self-government, first founded in 1908, reemerged with greater strength. The New Zealand government outlawed the movement and exiled its leaders, including

O. F. Nelson, part Samoan, the most successful merchant in the country and holder of a Samoan title. In 1929, shots were fired when New Zealand officials attempted to arrest several Mau members; 11 Samoans, including several title holders, were killed. Relations between the government and the populace declined further.

In 1935, a new Labor government in New Zealand effected several reforms, reinstating the Mau, bringing back Nelson and other leaders, establishing more local autonomy. World War II brought a halt to most of these efforts. It also brought U.S. troops to Upolu, the construction of the airstrip at Faleolo by the Seabees, and one other extremely important result. In 1942, in a weatherboard building near the mouth of the Vaisigano, a part-Samoan woman named Aggie Grey started selling hamburgers and coffee to the Yanks at a quarter a meal. The short-term impact was phenomenal; the long-term impact was overwhelming. Aggie Grey's Hotel—Aggie's, to absolutely everybody—eventually became what has been called "the Raffles of the Pacific," a landmark hostelry and gathering place and one of the most amiable places in the whole wide ocean.

Among the Americans who used to hop over to Aggie's to escape the rigid military style of Pago Pago was James Michener, and the word got around that Aggie Grey was the prototype for the Tonkinese Bloody Mary in *Tales of the South Pacific* and the Rodgers and Hammerstein musical based on it. Aggie Grey and the Grey family were not pleased that Aggie should be thought of as a madam. Michener also more or less denies that that was the case. He told Nelson Eustis, Aggie's biographer (*Aggie Grey of Samoa*, Hobby Investments Pty. Ltd., Adelaide, South Australia, 1979), that the character of Bloody Mary was "on paper long before I met Aggie. But it was Aggie, and she alone, who fortified my writing in the editing stage, who remained as the visualization of the island manipulator when the play was in formation, and who lives, in a curious way, as the real-life Bloody Mary." The kind of manipulation Michener refers to is a way of life in Samoa, so that it is a compliment to be referred to as a manipulator. Michener also told Eustis that Aggie was "ebullient, effervescent, outrageous, illegal, and terribly bright. She and her crew must have bilked the American forces out of a couple of million dollars worth of services, and never was wartime money better spent." In 1971, Western Samoa honored Aggie Grey with a special postage stamp, and, in 1983, she was awarded the Queen's Service Order by Queen Elizabeth II.

At the end of World War II, Western Samoa became a United Nations trust territory under New Zealand administration, and the government in Wellington began to prepare the islands for eventual self-rule. In 1947, the legislative assembly, the Fono, was established, and the New Zealand administrator became the high commissioner. A constitution was completed in 1960, and independence was declared on January 1, 1962. To avoid the holiday rush, Western Samoans sensibly celebrate their national holiday in June.

The system of government is parliamentary, with a prime minister and cabinet chosen from among the members. Forty-five of the 47 members of the Fono are elected by the matai, and only matai may stand as candidates for those seats. The other two members are chosen by non-Samoan residents. A head of state is selected by the Fono from among the four paramount chiefs. Even in a modern parliamentary system, tradition still governs, and custom rules.

## Tusitala

Robert Louis Stevenson—to Samoans, "Tusitala," the teller of tales—is so connected with these islands that no history can fail to mention him. He first came here in 1889, after a year of travel around the Pacific. He began his book, *In the South Seas*, which does *not* touch on Samoa, at sea, and finished it where he found "life most pleasant and man most interesting," in the house called Vailima, a few miles south of Apia.

Here, in what he called "my beautiful shining windy house," Stevenson, his wife, Fanny, and Fanny's mother and son lived a life of some elegance. Their furniture came from Scotland, as did the Royal Stuart tartan cloth made into lavalavas—the elegant saronglike skirts worn by men in Samoa—for the Stevenson servants. Their wines came from France. Their friends came from various levels of colonial and local society.

It is generally accepted that Stevenson left Europe for reasons of health; he as much as says so, and it is a fact that he suffered ill health for many years. Yet there is also evidence that the illness was under control when Stevenson decided to leave Europe and that other forces pulled him from Scotland, then from London, New York, and San Francisco. Art, he had written, catches "the ear, among the far louder voices of experience." Stevenson went listening from one continent to another, from one island to another, restlessly, until he came to Samoa. He worked nearly every day of the five years he spent here, dying on December 3, 1894.

His lovely house, Vailima, is now the official residence of the head of state, as it was when the head of state was a New Zealand resident officer. The daughter of Sir Alfred Turnbull, governor of the islands from the midthirties to midwar in 1943, recalls the cow paddocks on the grounds in those days, and the Chinese who served as grounds-keepers and house servants. The three large wings included, downstairs, a living area in the middle, a dining wing, and a large verandah that was used as a ballroom. Tourists routinely walked around the grounds of the house and signed the visitors' book. Mount Vaea was then, as it is today, a frequent excursion—long before its National Reserve status gave it its well-maintained trail. Turnbull's daughter remembers "running up the hill" with some friends at night, in celebration of her birthday.

"A German millionaire had lived there before us," she recalls, "and he left a lot of nice books"—including, fittingly, a complete edition of Robert Louis Stevenson.

# FA'A SAMOA

Western Samoa is the first independent nation of Polynesia and claims to shelter the largest concentration of full-blooded Polynesians in the world. Some 89 percent of the population is categorized as Samoan, and another 10 percent is part Samoan. For the traveler, these islands constitute a unique look at traditional Polynesian society and culture—*fa'a Samoa*, the Samoan way.

Fa'a Samoa includes a complicated system of genealogies and hierarchical nuances; it rejoices in elaborate ceremony and occasionally arcane customs. Yet it is based in the simple concept of collective life within the village.

The central unit of Samoan life is the *aiga* (pronounced ah-*ing*-a), an extended family of blood relatives, in-laws, and adopted members. Authority is vested in the matai, who is responsible for the aiga's lands, assets, and distribution of same. Aiga welfare comes first, and the matai must see to it that no member of the aiga is in need. He or she—there are numerous female matai—also represents the aiga on the village council, or fono. The matai is chosen by consensus of the aiga, and although heredity counts, it is not a guarantee of election; titles are given on merit.

Titles can also be split, allowed to fade in importance, or newly created. Adding to this social flexibility is the system of adoption, which is common and widespread. An aiga member's ability to move in with another branch of the aiga, in another location and even overseas, tends to temper the authority of the matai.

Several aiga comprise a village, *nu'u*, or subvillage, *pitonu'u*, and each village has its own matai. There are some 362 villages in Western Samoa today, and there are an estimated 12,600 matai. The matai come in two categories: the *ali'i* titular leader and final decision-maker, and the *tulafele*, the talking chief. Talking chiefs preside at ceremonies, wielding their characteristic "fly whisk" scepters of office, and are responsible for keeping track of the complexities of rank and title.

These complexities are significant. Vaasili Tevaga Moelagi Jackson—the first two are titles—a savvy, sophisticated, energetic woman the traveler to Savai'i should try to meet, was asked by a visitor to explain the meaning of the four chiefly titles. "It takes four volumes," Moelagi replied, "one volume per title."

Somewhat easier to understand are the four types of land ownership in Western Samoa. There is a small amount of freehold in and around Apia. There is government-owned land in the national park and reserves, although some of this is disputed. There is Westec land (for Western Samoa Trust Estates Corporation), plantation land originally taken and planted by the Germans and now administered by a quasi-governmental corporation. And there is the bulk of Samoan land, customary land, administered by the matai who may lease the land, but may never sell it, for the benefit of the aiga.

Samoans and Samoa watchers agree that when customary law and tradition meet head-on with the Fono's legislation, the Fono invariably gives way. An example is the Fono's prohibition against the cultivation or cutting of firewood in water catchment areas. The law simply has no force among people who have been planting this land and chopping its trees for centuries and who see officialdom as violating their land rights. As a result, according to one Forestry Division official, "After a big rain, the tap water here runs chocolate brown, it's so full of sediment."

Western Samoans live in traditional *fales*—open-sided houses, set on platforms of coral or concrete, with pillars made from the wood of tree fern or myrtle supporting roofs that often come to a high central peak and are thatched with palm or pandanus or, increasingly, made of corrugated tin. Mats cover the pebble floor of the platform and are the mainstay of furniture, although chairs and tables are increasingly making their way into Samoan life.

Similarly, enclosed fales are more and more to be seen in Western Samoa—less so the further you go from Apia. Often with jalousie windows, these European-style homes resemble the housing that is so prevalent in American Samoa. In other cases, open fales have been rather ingeniously turned into the front porches of European-style houses. Some very snazzy new residences are made of bricks and mortar but follow the fale's architectural shape and style.

Round fales, often set in the center of a village, are the guest fales. Here, in the past, a traveler on foot or by sea would come to rest or find shelter from inclement weather. He could be certain that he would receive every hospitality from the villagers. In return, he was expected to give a gift; if he had nothing to give, he was in debt to the village and owed a favor. It was, says Moelagi Jackson, "a perfect system in a noncash economy. Everything in Samoan life was based on giving and receiving gifts." This has not, of course, entirely died out, nor is it so very different, in many respects, from practices followed in much of the Western world, where it is called politics.

Oblong fales are the talking chiefs' fales. The tulafeles sit on the long sides, while the ali'i take the round ends. Hence, tulafeles can always outnumber ali'i in their own fales.

In Western Samoan villages today, the fono meets in the *fale taimalo*, various other matai have *their* fales, the men's council has *its* fale, the women's council meets in *its* own fale.

It is important to note that economic and political power is shared in Western Samoan life—many matai are women—while labor is divided according to gender or individual talent or desire. The men's councils, for example, have decision-making power over education, training in skills, and the like. The women's councils have powers that carefully do not overlap those of the men—health, for example. Thus, if the women's council decides a new health clinic is needed, that's the end of it, although the men will be asked to contribute labor. Similarly, if the men decide on a new school, the women may be set the task of collecting stones, something at which they excel. There are three orders of membership in the women's council: wives of titled men, wives of untitled men, women born in the village. A woman may be the wife of an untitled man in her husband's village, the village to which she goes upon marriage, but in her home village, she sits in the women's fale as a woman of the village, a higher rank.

The social structure, as noted, can be Byzantine in its complexity.

The traveler will see the men and women of Western Samoa meeting in their respective council fales throughout these islands— the men in their handsome wraparound lavalavas, the women in their tunic and long skirt outfits known as *puletasi.* Everyone will be talking, and the women may be fashioning some handicrafts, weaving pandanus into mats or stringing shells on fishline for *ula sisis*, shell leis. Centers of power and decision-making the council fales may be, but they are also social centers.

Family fales are also symbols of wealth and status. The aiga's guest fale will be front and center, flanked by the living fale, cooking fale, and, in a well-to-do aiga, a European-style house to enclose possessions. Asked about the lack of privacy in the traditional open-sided fale, Moelagi Jackson replies with a smile: "We grow up to be very quiet lovers."

Another extremely powerful and important institution in Western Samoa is religion. About half of the population belongs to the Congregational Church, direct successor to the London Missionary Society. A quarter are Catholic. The Catholic cathedral in Apia has long been a landmark for ships entering the harbor. Methodists and Mormons make up the rest of the population; the erection of a Mormon temple in Apia, with its gold statue of Moroni, established Samoa as the center of Mormonia. (Although not a major religion here, the Baha'is have built an exceptional house of worship, one of six in the world, on the cross-island road south of Apia. A dome of coral limestone sits, falelike, on nine pairs of soft red granite buttresses. The textured interior is of white concrete and ifilele timbers.) Every village has at least one church, and the pastor is a figure of authority, often living in the biggest fale. On Sundays, the nation becomes a sea of white lavalavas and puletasi. The men often complement the lavalava with white jacket over white shirt and white tie; the women wear white wide-brimmed hats. It makes for a very pretty picture, reflective of the fact that the Christian religion has here fused brilliantly with traditional values, reinforcing the notions of collective welfare and of each person's role in the community.

Nevertheless, the belief in *aitu*, a kind of witch, has not been entirely wiped out. Aitu might be the spirits of dead relatives or national identities. Overseas Samoans in California, Hawaii, and New Zealand seem to be particularly bedeviled by aitu. Old atavisms die hard.

Something else that seems endemic to Samoan life is *musu*, a moody state of mind equivalent to Tahiti's *fiu*. Sulky intractability can suddenly erupt in a person who was a moment before gracious to the point of excess. It fades just as rapidly and inexplicably.

Also in common with French Polynesia is the Samoan *fa'afafine*, the transvestite (*mahu* in French Polynesia). Boys reared as girls even from birth by families wishing or needing to balance the distribution of males and females, they dress as girls from an early age and later take up traditionally female roles or jobs. They also, like their Tahitian equivalents, have formed entertainment troupes.

As the traveler explores the fascinating traditional culture of Western Samoa, he should also keep in mind some of the dark side of contemporary life here. Western Samoa is classified by the United Nations as a least developed country; it thus has the dubious distinction of being among the poorest countries on earth. Economic planning by the central government has been ineffective, perhaps because initiatives have yet to develop local industry and products but have rather been based on importing new industries—tobacco and brewing, for example.

Imports of foods are also on the increase, and so are such imported diseases as hypertension, heart disease, diabetes, and ulcers. Perhaps the most alarming health trend in recent times has been the rising suicide rate among young people. Juvenile delinquency has been so serious that many villages have imposed curfews on the young. A number of youths leave each year for American Samoa, the U.S., and New Zealand. The country offers such people few motivations for returning home.

But then there is someone like Moelagi Jackson, committed to both preserving the old and taking from the new whatever can be fitted harmoniously into the traditional cultural pattern. It is a delicate balancing act, but Moelagi, among many others, seems to be succeeding at it despite economic obstacles and incursions from an outside world that, in its desire to package what is central to fa'a Samoa, threatens to destroy it.

# TRAVELER'S CODE OF BEHAVIOR

*Caveat viator!* Samoan tradition and the power of the churches have combined to enforce a code of behavior for travelers to Western Samoa (and to American Samoa). Do not panic if you cannot keep all these caveats straight; no one is going to chop off your head if you violate one—it will likely be obvious that you are not a native of the islands—but your visit will be more enjoyable if you follow the code as much as possible.

For example, travelers are asked by the government not to wear shorts or revealing clothing except on the beach. In fact, disapproval of shorts is waning, and in the streets of Apia, young palagi women wear them almost routinely. But these young women are very probably offending a number of people, and perhaps foreigners, as guests in the country, have a duty to be extra sensitive. When Samoan women start wearing shorts, foreigners can follow their lead.

Other caveats:

- *In a home.* In a Samoan home, don't speak or eat while standing or walking. Sit down cross-legged on a mat first. And don't stretch out your legs while sitting; it's considered rude to point your feet at anyone. If you must stretch your legs, place a mat over them first. Do not walk on mats—go around them.
- *En Route.* Don't eat while walking through a village.

If you pass an open fale where chiefs are meeting, lower any load you may be carrying or an umbrella to hip level (fold the umbrella).

Don't enter a fale when prayers are being offered.

- *Prayers and Sunday.* Evening *sa* time, prayer session, lasts about 10 to 15 minutes. The signal for it is sounded on those oxyacetylene cylinders or conch shells you see hanging from trees. The first gong signals a return to the house, the second is for prayer, the third is the all-clear. When you hear the gong, stop whatever you're doing: driving, swimming, walking, talking. Wait for the all-clear.

Don't wear flowers in church. Don't undertake any manual work on Sundays. Many villages also disapprove of swimming or of anything seen to disturb the peace of the Sabbath.

• *Kava.* The kava ceremony of Western Samoa, unlike that of Fiji or Tonga, is an exceptional ritual rarely witnessed by outsiders. If you are invited to one, you should not sip from the cup until you tip a little onto the ground in front of you while saying *manuia*, "good fortune." Nor should you drain the cup. Leave a bit and empty it onto the ground before handing it back to the server.

• *Hospitality.* If you are invited to stay in a Samoan fale with a family, remember that hospitality requires a gift—a *mea alofa*, thing of love. This might be shirts, belts, fabrics, or money—a certain amount per night; ask at the tourist bureau before you go, but at least US$10 per person per night. Make the giving of the mea alofa a ceremony so that it does not in fact look like payment for accommodations. You might say just that: "Hospitality cannot be paid for, but I would like to leave this mea alofa to show my appreciation." If neighbors of the family you stay with invite you to stay with *them*, do not accept, as this will shame your primary hosts. In Western Samoa, shame is more important than guilt; don't be the cause of any.

# THE TRAVELER IN WESTERN SAMOA

Friendly, comfortable, limited in scope, reasonably priced, and evidently intended to stay that way: that is pretty much the good news for travelers to Western Samoa. There are a few hotels, a few restaurants, a few shops, a few things to do, and an enchanting atmosphere. The traveler will not want to rush his visit here.

Everything essentially happens from Apia, and unless the traveler wants to hide away at Upolu's only beach resort on the south coast of the island, this is the place to stay and the launching pad for activities and excursions to Savai'i and Manono as well as around Upolu. The accommodations, though few in number, are varied enough—from the "big" hotels, which are neither outsized nor overpriced, to guesthouses and rock-bottom budget accommodations. If you haven't arranged a place before arriving, ask at the airport or in town at the visitors bureau next to the market.

Once established in Apia, the traveler can make plans and arrangements for his stay in these islands.

One important warning for the *end* of your stay: do not neglect to change tala to dollars—New Zealand, Australian, or U.S.—or to the currency of your next port of call, if possible. Tala may not be exported from Western Samoa; more to the point, they are useless outside of Western Samoa. Keep enough for your return trip to the airport and for airport tax—WS$20, at this writing—and get rid of the rest.

## LANGUAGE

| | |
|---|---|
| Talofa | Hello, welcome |
| Fa'amolemole | Please |
| Sa | Taboo, sacred |
| Tofa | Goodbye |
| Ioe | Yes |
| Leai | No |

At least learn to say and understand *fa'amolemole*—fah-*moe*-lay-*moe*-lay. It is said that you can buy anything here with a fa'amolemole, a reference to the manipulative nature, at least in Western perceptions, of the culture here. Be careful how you use the word, and be firm when asked fa'amolemole to give up something you own and may need. On the other hand, when seeking assistance, it is always proper to ask "please" in this way.

# APIA

Apia is open more or less from 8:00 A.M. to noon and again from 1:30 to 4:30 P.M., post office 9:00 A.M. to 4:30 P.M. The town itself runs from Mulinu'u Point on the west, site of the Fono, yacht club, and various monuments, eastward beyond Aggie's to the wharf and Vaiala Beach. It is concentrated along the waterfront and a few blocks inland. The traditional center is the Town Clock, a World War I memorial and traffic circle.

It is easy to see Apia quickly, but it deserves more time for a thorough if languid exploration. Armed with a map from the visitors bureau or one of the several bookshops, check out its nooks and crannies and get a feel for its one-time status as a trading center—Burns Philp still dominates the "skyline," though Godeffroy is gone.

All needed resources are here: banks and agencies to cash travelers' checks; post office and telephone bureau; restaurants and bars—Vailima is the excellent local beer. The market offers more in the way of character than consumer goods, but there is fine shopping in Apia for handicrafts. The Western Samoa Handicraft Center offers tapa (called *siapo* here), woodcarvings, kava bowls, baskets, and handbags. A number of commercial shops also offer a range of very good handicrafts. Look for the *tuluma*, a watertight wooden box for carrying valuables on canoe journeys. Clothing is also available—lavalavas, puletasi, T-shirts—both in Apia and at Island Styles, on the cross-island road south of town. You can find English-language books, especially Michener, in a number of places. Look for works by Samoa's leading novelist, Albert Wendt.

Wendt (see Chapter 5, The Literary Pacific) is one of the most interesting, prolific, and best known of contemporary Pacific writers. His work in a sense traces his life: he broke with his aiga, eventually going so far as to spend 13 years in New Zealand, before feeling the pull to return home. His early books reveal numerous aspects of the sense of dislocation. In New Zealand, he experienced "that intellectual solitude so peculiar to the disinherited souls of the west." Back home, he was disturbed by the "erupting materialism" of Samoa. He turns to myth, fable, the riches of fa'a Samoa, triumphantly synthesizing these with contemporary realities in exploring a purpose for the community as a whole, beyond personal salvation. Perhaps his most famous book is the novel *Sons for the Return Home*, availble in Apia's bookstores.

There is swinging disco nightlife at a number of Apia clubs—ask at your hotel, or anywhere else for that matter. Friday night is the *fia fia*—Samoan feast plus Samoan dancing culminating in the graceful, beautiful, sensuous *siva*—at Aggie's and at the Tusitala, the other major hotel of Apia. At the fia fia, be sure to try *palusami*, here consisting of coconut cream, onions, the tinned corned beef called pisupo, and taro leaves, wrapped in breadfruit leaf and baked on hot stones. It is served on slices of baked taro. *Oka* is Samoa's raw fish dish; *taofolo* is kneaded breadfruit and sweet coconut wrapped in taro leaves and baked; *fa'ausi* is grated taro and coconut pudding; and *suafa'i* is uncooked bananas with coconut cream.

Friday night is also the night the evangelists preach down at the market, accompanied by a religious choir and more graceful dancing.

Samoans are mad for cricket, which you can see Saturday afternoons in virtually every village. In Apia, there are often practice matches behind the clock tower. It's called *kirikiti* here.

# AROUND UPOLU

Sightseeing in Western Samoa begins on the ride into Apia from Faleolo Airport. Outside your bus or taxi window, village life proceeds. You look into fales to see people seated on mats, working, talking, cooking, caring for children. Kids play on the village cricket ground. Perhaps the chiefs are meeting in a communal fale, or maybe there is a prayer meeting or choir practice. This is what you have come to see, but there are other sights and activities worth pursuing on Upolu. A note on pursuing them: in many villages, outsiders are required to pay a fee to swim, visit a cave, climb the waterfall, and so on. Signs may state the fee, but you may just be asked to pay.

If you have any doubt about the authenticity of the price—which should be nominal—or the person asking for it, either leave altogether or say courteously that you would like to give the money directly to the village mayor. These are called custom fees, another sign of the remarkable power of traditional rights here.

One recommendation for seeing Upolu is to take a packaged around-the-island tour to get a feel for the place. Then rent a car or take public transportation to head back to key spots. The public bus station is at the market, though long-distance buses leave from the field opposite Burns Philp.

Here are points of major interest.

East from Apia, the traveler proceeds through some of the island's loveliest scenery. After 27 kilometers, you come to Piula College, where for a small admission charge you can swim in the Piula Cave Pool on the college grounds. Two kilometers further on is Falefa Falls, impressive especially after a rain. Continue over Mafa Pass, with its spectacular view of the coast, to Fuipisia Falls. The island ends in the easternmost district of Aleipata, from which you can see the uninhabited offshore islands of Nuulua, Nuutele, Fanuatapu, and Namu'a.

Continue south and then head west on the south coast. In the southwest are the villages of Lefaga and Salamumu. Here is the famous Return to Paradise Beach, where Gary Cooper and Roberta Haynes filmed the movie *Return to Paradise,* based on a Michener story. The two stars stayed in eponymous fales at Aggie's. At the western end of the island is the lovely Lefatu Cape; look for Manono, which some Pacific observers say was Michener's inspiration for Bali Ha'i.

Along the cross-island road, south from Apia to Siumu, the traveler rides the high middle of the island. Here are the Baha'i Temple and Tiavi Falls, both visible from the road. Above all, quite close to Apia, is Mount Vaea, worth a special pilgrimage.

To get there, take a bus from the market for Vailima. Bus fare is a few *sene* (100 sene = 1 tala). Pull the wire when you see the sign; a red button will light up on the driver's dashboard, and a shrieking noise will sound. Head up the Trail of the Loving Hearts, a pretty path well constructed and well maintained, nicely switchbacked and with occasional steps. A bench along a somewhat steep stretch rewards you with a view eastward of valley and hills.

At the summit, the tomb of both Stevenson and his wife, Fanny, sits on a neatly mown clearing, edged by a forest of shade trees to south and west, but clear for magnificent views to north and east. A peaceful place. The well-known requiem reads:

Under the wide and starry sky
Dig the grave and let me die.
Glad did I live and gladly die,
And I laid me down with a will.

This be the verse you grave for me:
Here he lies where he longed to be;
Home is the sailor, home from the sea,
And the hunter home from the hill.

When Fanny died in 1914 in California, her ashes were brought back to Samoa for burial at the foot of Stevenson's grave. His words to her, Aolele, her Samoan name, are on the plaque:

Teacher, tender comrade, wife,
A fellow-farer true through life
Heart-whole and soul-free
The August Father gave to me.

Palolo Deep is another must stop for the traveler. Take the bus or walk one mile from the center of Apia eastward to Pilot Point beyond the wharf. There is a small shop for postcards, beer, and snorkel gear rentals, and there are changing rooms. You can walk (wear shoes) across to the hole; a fale and platform mark the spot. Spend some time hovering in the pale blue coolness of this exceptional spot; the reef wall drops off sharply to a great depth, but along the wall, the snorkeler can explore extravagant coral and other marine life.

## Other Activities

There is very good diving off the south coast, especially at Nuusafee Islet, and off Aleipata to the east, also around the islets. The Hideaway Beach Resort Hotel, half an hour from Apia, on the south coast, is essentially the island's scuba center. There is also an all-day Palolo Deep dive from Apia; Five Mile Reef, however, has been somewhat destroyed by dynamiting to bring up fish.

The best beaches are also on the south and southwest coasts. If you swim off the north coast, be careful of the often strong undertow.

If you want to do some serious hiking or camping in the national park, apply at the Forestry Division, National Parks and Reserves section, near the market. For camping, you will require a permit, and you will also need food, a kerosene stove, and maybe a bush knife. You can purchase everything. You can also arrange for guides up Mount Fito, where it's easy to get lost. For routes of shorter walks, you should also ask at Forestry, or find some staff in or around the visitor's center at the entrance to O Le Pupu-Pu'e. There is an informative display there, by the way. Spending some time in the park is a great way to see a good bit of Upolu and its flora and fauna, cheaply. You can even arrange a ride there if you wait for the pickup truck to leave the Department of Economic Development's parking lot. Planning a visit to O Le Pupu-Pu'e, as with everything in the Pacific, "can be arranged."

# MANONO

There are scheduled packaged tours here, but you can also take the outboard from Manono'uta near Lefatu Cape. You can walk around the island in about an hour, calmly and safely; there are no cars on Manono. The beaches, though few in number, are relatively unspoiled. Check out the grave with 99 stones, one for each of the deceased's wives.

# SAVAI'I

Try to spend at least one night here—the feeling is quite different from Apia. The ferry from Mulifanua on Upolu takes an hour and a half; several flights a day from Fagali'i airstrip, east of Apia, take about half an hour.

This is a big island, and its sights are widely dispersed. There are lava fields to see in the north, and blowholes to see in the south, not to mention Mount Silisili in the center. The unabashed recommendation here is to arrange, from Upolu or from home, to put yourself in the capable hands of Moelagi Jackson, who also happens to own a few hostelries—with open-sided fales—on Savai'i. Moelagi's "tours" of the island are cultural immersion experiences— tapa-making, a night with a family, a dance performance, if available, guides to Mount Silisili, or anything else that's available or that the traveler might wish. In this way, you also get to meet Moelagi, one of Western Samoa's great treasures.

### Western Samoa Addresses

Western Samoa Visitors Bureau
Department of Economic Development
P.O. Box 862
Apia, Western Samoa
Tel. 20 471

Vaasili Tevaga Moelagi Jackson
Box 5002
Salelologa P.O.
Savai'i, Western Samoa
Tel. 0685 24262
Cable "SAFUA"

# CHAPTER 9

# AMERICAN SAMOA

*Name:* Territory of American Samoa
*Political status:* Unorganized, unincorporated territory of
  the U.S.
*Island groups:* Tutuila, Manu'a Group, Swains, Rose
*Gateway island:* Tutuila
*Capital:* Pago Pago
*Population:* 36,500
*Land area:* 201 square kilometers
*Language:* English, Polynesian (Samoan)
*Currency:* U.S. dollar ($US)

American Samoa seems, at first blush, very American. Sloganeers who rail against the various American "isms"—materialism, imperialism, etc.—and the attendant lack of taste are quick to dismiss American Samoa out of hand. It is true enough that the traveler must look harder, and travel off the gateway, to find the "old" Pacific. On the other hand, in entering into the life of American Samoa today, and into the lives of American Samoans, the traveler engages with some of the realities of a small island that is pretty much at the tail end of a huge nation's priorities—except among football recruiters, who put American Samoa pretty high on their list.

This is a congenial place. Tutuila offers the traveler interesting sights, some excellent hiking, and numerous resources for handling any number of chores. The Manu'a Group offers something very different—unspoiled island living in delightful settings. In the end, American Samoa cannot be dismissed; it's here, as real a part of the Pacific, its history and culture, as any other.

## GEOGRAPHY, TOPOGRAPHY, CLIMATE

The seven islands of American Samoa stretch some 300 kilometers from west to east at 13–15 degrees south latitude and 171–173 degrees west longitude. About equidistant from Honolulu and Sydney, American Samoa is the only U.S. soil below the equator. In more ways than one, it finds itself caught or perhaps adrift between the newly emerging island nations of the Pacific—Western Samoa, Kiribati, Vanuatu, Tuvalu, the Cook Islands, the Solomons—and the continental United States, to which it is politically, economically, and socially linked.

The largest of the seven islands is Tutuila, at 137 square kilo-

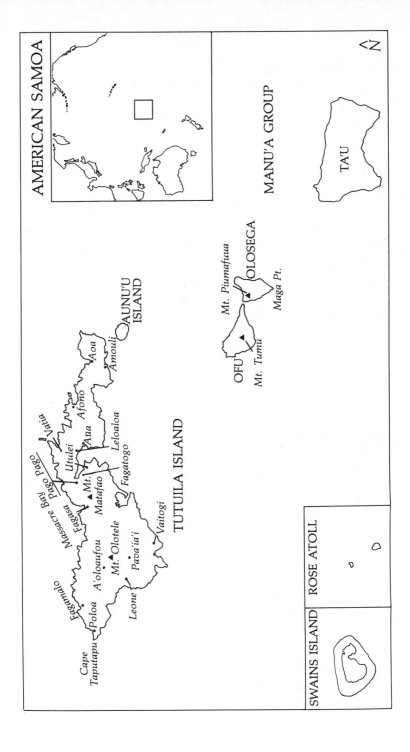

meters. Just off Tutuila's eastern tip is Aunu'u, two kilometers square. To the southeast are the islands of the Manu'a Group: Ofu, Olosega, and Ta'u. Tiny Rose Atoll, uninhabited by humans but a sanctuary for wildlife and marine life, is about 145 kilometers further to the east and south. Over 360 kilometers north of Tutuila is Swains Island, also a coral atoll, and not part of the Samoan Chain.

Except for Rose and Swains, the islands of American Samoa are high volcanic islands, their cone-shaped mountains arising with abrupt steepness. The superb harbor of Pago Pago (the reader already knows that this must be pronounced "Pango Pango"), very nearly bisecting Tutuila, is a submerged crater whose southern wall collapsed millions of years ago. These high islands are stunningly green, the hillsides carpeted thickly with coconut palms, breadfruit, and mango.

The humidity of Tutuila is a major feature of the tropical climate. Somerset Maugham entitled his famous story about Sadie Thompson "Rain" for good reason. As warm easterlies are forced up and over the 491-meter Mount Pioa on the east side of the harbor, clouds drop their moisture over the bay and the interior. Little wonder that Pioa is known as Rainmaker Mountain.

# HISTORY

Archaeologists and Samoan traditionalists still dispute whether Savai'i in Western Samoa or the islands of the Manu'a Group were the first landfall of the ancestors of present-day Samoans and later the jumping-off point for settlement of eastern Polynesia. Another candidate is Tula, on the eastern tip of Tutuila, where, evidence shows, there was an established settlement by at least 600 B.C. What seems clear about the otherwise joint history of the Samoas (see Chapter 8, Western Samoa) is that Tutuila was really a subdivision of a district on Upolu, while Manu'a remained somewhat outside the mainstream of Samoan development. The Tuimanu'a, or ruler of Manu'a, was one of the strongest and most powerful leaders of ancient Samoa; despite a cultural affinity with the rest of Samoa, Manu'a remained apart, at least until recent history.

Otherwise, the history of American Samoa departs from that of Western Samoa on April 17, 1900, when the U.S. flag first flew over Tutuila; the deed of cession, from all the chiefs except the Tuimanu'a, was accepted by the U.S. Navy, which was using Pago Pago Harbor as a coaling station. The Tuimanu'a finally signed over his islands in 1904 so that his people might share in the benefits of American association. Before his death, however, he willed that his title die with him; to this day, it has not been revived.

Swains Island, a coral atoll with a large lagoon in the center and a population that hovers at or around 30, was at one time owned by Tokelau and was incorporated into the British Gilbert and Ellice islands in 1916. When Britain transferred the atoll to New Zealand administration in 1925, the U.S. simply annexed it. In 1980, the Tokelauans officially signed the island over to U.S. sovereignty in return for the withdrawal of U.S. claims to Tokelau and its fishing zone.

In 1940, American Samoa became an advanced training and staging area for the U.S. Marine Corps. Roads, airstrips, docks, and medical facilities were built. The traveler can still see much of this construction, as well as concrete bunkers around the coastline and gun emplacements over Pago Pago Harbor. The military presence also made the local economy boom, and there was little battle action—just a few shells from a Japanese submarine on January 11, 1942; ironically, they hit the store of one of Tutuila's few Japanese residents, Frank Shimasaki. Numerous Samoans enlisted in the Marines; today, military service remains a common form of out-migration for American Samoans, who thereby become U.S. citizens.

The departure of the troops was a blow to the economy but ushered in some political reforms, including the formation of the bicameral legislature, the Fono. A further blow to the economy was the 1951 closing of the naval station, at which time administrative responsibility for the islands was transferred to the U.S. Department of the Interior. By 1956, the islands had their first native-born governor, Peter Tali Coleman, and the Fono had created a constitutional convention. Then in 1961 President John F. Kennedy appointed H. Rex Lee governor of American Samoa, and Lee proceeded to dispense significant federal funds in a massive program of public works, housing, electrification, tourism facilities, and communications, including television. It was the Americanization of American Samoa.

In 1966, a new constitution was ratified. It contained a bill of rights, confirmed the legislative authority of the Fono, and established laws protecting fa'a Samoa and above all prohibiting the alienation of customary land to foreign ownership.

Three times, the people of American Samoa voted down referenda for increased home rule. Finally, in 1976, they voted to elect their own governor; a year later, Coleman became the territory's first popularly elected governor. In 1981, American Samoa's first nonvoting delegate to the U.S. Congress was sworn in in Washington.

American Samoa is defined as an unincorporated and unorganized territory of the United States. It has not been *incorporated* into the 50 states; and since Congress has not enacted organic legislation mandating powers of self-government, it is *unorganized.*

But it is, of course, governed. Today, the territory's executive is vested in a governor and lieutenant governor elected for four-year terms. The bicameral Fono comprises 18 senators, elected by 12 councils of matai to four-year terms, and 20 representatives elected by popular vote to two-year terms.

American Samoans, alone among the peoples of U.S. territories, are U.S. nationals, not U.S. citizens. They may not vote in U.S. national elections. However, they have free entry to the U.S.; indeed, there are more than twice as many American Samoans in the United States as in American Samoa.

This is mostly due to economics. Subsistence agriculture and fishing have all but disappeared here, and the islands of American Samoa are poor in natural resources, far poorer than Upolu and Savai'i. The fish processing and export industry provides a major share of the private-sector payroll, but nearly half of the adult population is employed by the government. Attempts to develop alternate local employment opportunities have been beset by mismanagement and corruption.

# AMERICAN SAMOA TODAY

Culturally and ethnically, the people of the two Samoas are one. The boats and airplanes that ply the route between Apia and Pago Pago are filled with folks visiting relatives and friends; about ten thousand Western Samoans now live and work in American Samoa. The two peoples share a language, traditions, the values of communal living.

But to the traveler, the difference between Apia and Pago Pago, between Upolu and Tutuila, is stark and dramatic. It is not just a political difference. Apia is of course far larger than Pago Pago. It is also at once more vibrant and more dreamy, or at least more evocative of a Pacific past. Pago is spread out, its exquisite harbor is too obviously covered by oil slicks, its main road is clogged with traffic. To Americans at least, who will see much here that is familiar, it seems to lack a hoped-for charm and character associated with the Pacific.

On the other hand, one of the familiar things about Pago Pago is a kind of raw, informal democracy that is less evident in other Pacific nations. Even in the independent nations of Oceania, the traveler senses a barrier of sorts between expatriate or visiting Westerners and native islanders. Friendships and deeper relationships do abound, of course, in those islands, but Tutuila seems, at least, to be much more of a melting pot.

There are more than four thousand cars on the overburdened 80 kilometers of paved road on Tutuila. Much of the route passes through villages of walled houses of plywood and tin, most built with U.S. emergency funds after the 1966 hurricane destroyed great numbers of thatched fales. The houses have neat lawns and shrubs, and the effect is more of a California bungalow suburb than of the exotic islands Maugham and Margaret Mead wrote about. The traditional fales so evident throughout Western Samoa are extremely limited in number on Tutuila, though the visitor can see them aplenty in the Manu'a Group.

American Samoa is also a communications center for the region, site of a COMSAT installation and a center for television broadcasting. National television was established by Governor Lee in 1964, and commercial viewing soon followed. TV is today government run, and the news was, until recently, effectively government controlled. Also until recently, nothing was live. Tapes are flown in from the States twice a week to provide week-old shows from CBS, NBC, ABC, and PBS. You can see favorite sitcoms, soaps, specials, "Masterpiece Theater," etc. Daytime viewing is educational, including two shows a day of *Sesame Street*, and evening is reserved for entertainment and for religious programming. The recent change to all this, effected by a new chief engineer from the States, Bob Blauvelt, was an agreement with CNN allowing the local station to carry *live* news, via a new satellite receiver system on Tutuila. For travelers, in any event, this is a boon, unless you're the type of traveler who spurns news when on the road, in which case you won't care.

There are those who disparage television, along with the cars and walled houses, as evils that threaten to destroy fa'a Samoa. If they are threats, they are not the first threats fa'a Samoa has come up against. Certainly, traditional life has been undermined here, as throughout the Pacific, but it is just as certain that it is simply not possible to roll back a century of reality. The issue for Samoans, and for concerned Americans as well, is not only what from the past should be preserved but how it should be preserved.

Participatory democracy, for example, probably will not go away, even if the Americans do. How can it be made to work with, or alongside, or even in tension against, the traditional systems of aiga and matai? Political development in American Samoa today seems aimed toward the phasing out of U.S. authority without sacrificing the economic benefits and the close social ties with the numerous overseas Samoans living in the U.S. How is that to work?

Reunification with Western Samoa is at present a sentimental wish, and, as more than one Samoan has pointed out, there is a question whether Samoa was ever unified in the first place. The matai of American Samoa (except for those of Manu'a) are of lesser rank than those of Western Samoa and may not be eager to give up their present authority. Meanwhile, Western Samoan leaders, while perhaps desirous of the kind of economic aid American Samoa enjoys, wonder about the Western institutions already entrenched in American Samoa and their potential effects both on the people and the much richer natural resources of the west.

Traditional life has not entirely disappeared from American Samoa, and numerous organizations are at work to rejuvenate it. Among other efforts is a project funded by the American Samoa Arts Council and run by the students of American Samoa Community College. The project is called Faasamoa Pea—Continuation of the Samoan Way—and its purpose is "to collect, record, and preserve Samoan folklore, including legends, proverbs, riddles, place name stories, and the like" in order to display "the variety and richness of the Samoan culture." Twice a year, the group publishes its collected data.

Here, as in Western Samoa, traditional values combine with the prevalent potency of religion to enforce a code of behavior travelers would do well to follow (see Chapter 8, Western Samoa). Traditional dancing and handicrafts are also to be found here.

# MARGARET MEAD, ETC.

It is impossible to talk about tradition in American Samoa without mentioning Margaret Mead, whose classic study, *Coming of Age in Samoa* (1928), was researched in three villages on the coast of Ta'u in the Manu'a Group. And it is now impossible to talk about Mead without talking about Derek Freeman, whose 1983 book, *Margaret Mead and Samoa: The Making and Unmaking of an Anthropological Myth* (Harvard University Press), sought to demolish Mead's methods and findings *and* the whole concept of cultural determinism she espoused. You can get into any number of lively discussions about Mead, Freeman, and sexual mores with Samoans of west and east, finding virtually every shade of opinion—one side, the other, or the well-worn middle.

The questions Mead set herself, as she writes in the introduction to her book, were these: "Are the disturbances which vex our adolescents due to the nature of adolescence itself or to the civilization? Under different conditions does adolescence present a different picture?" Her findings convinced her that yes, it is the conditions of a culture that "vex" adolescents. Comparing the young girls she studied on Ta'u with American girls, Mead found a number of factors that kept Samoan adolescence from being the stressful time it often is among young Americans. The casual attitude toward life ("the lesson of not caring"), the narrowness of choices, the lack of contradiction, the slower pace of education and upbringing, and, above all, the organization of the family and the attitude toward sex seemed to Mead to have equipped the young child in Samoa "particularly well for passing through life without nervous instability." Her portrait of how culture shapes the experience of adolescence made and continues to make an enormous impact on readers of her work.

Freeman claimed that Mead had quite simply been deceived. His detailed work attempted to show the fallacy of Mead's case by undermining the accuracy of the data she reported. In contrast to the portrait she presented, Freeman showed an aggressive, violent, and sexually inhibited Samoa. His larger purpose, however, was to restore what he called balance to the nature-nurture debate. He wanted to unmask the notion of cultural determinism as a fallacy and to reestablish the role of biology in human behavior. The publication of his book was preceded by more media hype than that which followed, although scholarly reviews by anthropologists were, in the main, critical of Freeman.

Yet another book, *Quest for the Real Samoa*, by Lowell D. Holmes (Bergin and Garvey Press, South Hadley, Massachusetts, 1986), treats the Mead/Freeman controversy itself and is also a republication of Holmes' 1954 restudy of Ta'u, where Mead had worked. Holmes' purpose in that study was methodological; he wanted to show how the age, sex, and personal status of a researcher could in fact affect the data. For example, what he learned about matters that were considered the prerogatives of older men differed from what Mead had learned, but Holmes concluded that Mead had an advantage in the areas of adolescence and female sexuality, which were the focus of her work. Holmes also concludes that Mead's research, contrary to Freeman's claim, was of a very high standard of quality and that her depiction of coming of age in Samoa in 1925 was essentially correct. But Holmes also accepts that since every study is indeed shaped by the personal attributes, background, and training of the researcher, juxtaposing accounts enrich our understanding of a culture.

Whatever the picture of Samoan life that emerges from these studies, Margaret Mead's message about cultural differences and the human potential are still valid and always timely. If this is what she learned on Ta'u, the world ought to be grateful to Ta'u.

# THE TRAVELER IN AMERICAN SAMOA

The friendly and effective staff of American Samoa's Office of Tourism have their work cut out for them. Tourism here is not yet a growth industry. Accommodations have long been sparse, and the one big hotel, the Rainmaker, keeps changing hands. Similarly, air service to and from Pago has been spotty, as has passenger ship service.

Most travelers here have typically been business people, for Pago Pago, boasting one of the world's finest natural harbors, is a regional center of business and commerce and perhaps the country's most valuable natural resource. The harbor's well-developed port facilities are a haven from hurricanes and a major port of call for everything from yachts to the huge purse-seiners that now do the bulk of the tuna fishing.

Give Tutuila a reasonable amount of time. Sixty of American Samoa's 76 villages are here—most of its population—and although the island is small, it takes at least a few days to get a feel for it. If you have been traveling for a while, Pago is an excellent place in which to regroup. If you want to mail things off, do so here, at a U.S. post office promising the low prices and good service we take for granted at home.

For something approaching a fabled South Seas holiday, the Manu'a Group is the place. You will need to arrange travel and accommodations with the tourism office, but here are some unspoiled islands for lolling, beachcombing, walking—a nice adventure. NOTE: a new set of television equipment has recently been installed on Ofu, if that sort of thing bothers you. It is aimed at greatly improving reception for the people there.

# TUTUILA

Twenty-nine kilometers long and ten kilometers wide, Tutuila has one of the scraggliest coastlines imaginable. Pago Pago Harbor nearly cuts the island in two, and various other bays thrust in and out of the coastline sharply. Only the southwestern part of the island, where Tafuna Airport is, is flat.

Pago Pago is actually the name of a small village more or less up the hill from the narrow end of the harbor. The *real* capital of American Samoa is Fagotogo, center of commercial life, spread along the southern shore of the harbor. Around the eastern point of this bit of shore—Goat Island Point, where the Rainmaker Hotel is located—is Utulei, a kind of extension of Fagotogo. Together, all are known as Pago Pago, and since the distance from the village at the end of the harbor to Utulei around the point is all of about three kilometers, that makes sense.

You'll arrive at Tafuna International Airport, and if you're a U.S. citizen, you need neither passport nor visa. Tafuna is some 15 kilometers from town; a taxi ride should take about 20 minutes.

In addition to the Rainmaker, the other hotel of Pago is Herb and Sia's Family Motel in Fagotogo—much friendlier than the Rainmaker. Otherwise, you should ask the tourism office to help you find budget accommodations in private homes, or ask around; it isn't hard to find a place. It is also possible to camp in fales established on the sparsely populated northeastern coast at Aoa; check with the tourism office.

Samoan food is available in Pago at the Friday night fia fia at Herb and Sia's, and at some of the snack bars around town. Otherwise, an Americanized menu is the rule. Soli's, officially Soli and Marks, is a yachtie hangout.

Friday night is traditionally letting-loose night, and there are numerous places for that in Pago. Try the Pago Pago Yacht Club, a small bungalow in Utulei, south of the Rainmaker.

Seeing Tutuila consists of exploring Pago Pago, going west along the south coast, going east along the south coast, and heading cross-island to the north coast. The road only goes 80 kilometers along the south shore, and there are few villages on the north. Much of this sightseeing can be accomplished by bus, but that will take a lot of work meshing schedules—such as they are—and routes, and buses tend to stop rolling at about 4:00 in the afternoon (and never run on Sunday). It is much more convenient to rent a car. Or, as always, go first with a scheduled tour group, then come back on your own by whatever method you choose.

The all-important tourism office is in Utulei, along the road *south* of the Rainmaker.

## Pago Pago

The life of the harbor may be Pago's most exciting attraction. Cargo boats from Western Samoa, from which American Samoa imports a great deal of food, go back and forth several times a week. The *Queen Salamasina* ferry makes the trip in eight hours. Tongan ships touch at several Tongan island groups en route from Pago to home, and a monthly Silk & Boyd steamer goes to Rarotonga. The purse-seiners and long-line fishermen lie at anchor; yachts, looking tiny by comparison, pull at their moorings when a motorboat goes by. Naturally, the town of Pago is filled with all the people from all these boats, filled with the activity of loading and unloading, filled with the sounds and smells from the fish processing plants. Station yourself at the wharf and watch the show.

Real sightseeing in Pago begins best with the tramway ride to Mount Alava. Take the road opposite the Rainmaker up Solo Hill to the Kirwan TV Center—you can tour the studios weekday afternoons from 2:00 to 5:00—and continue to the tramway station. A monument here recalls the 1980 U.S. Navy airplane disaster; the pilot hit the cables and crashed into the Rainmaker Hotel, killing the six servicemen aboard and two paying guests of the hotel. The hotel manager at the time refused to allow the memorial to be erected on the hotel grounds.

The tramway was built in 1965 to transport personnel and heavy equipment for the construction of the television transmitting tower on Mount Alava, rising 491 meters across the harbor. Almost 1500 meters of cable stretch across the harbor, one of the longest non-supported cable spans in the world. You'll feel the car shudder off its mooring, then ride out high but level over the harbor. When it starts upward, it seems to move faster, lurching and slowing just before the top, then banging in—bend your knees. At the top of Alava are the wreck of the old transmitter building, the new building, the transmitters, and a lookout. You can also see the dirt track that heads down and curves all along the top of the ridge to meet the Fagasa cross-island road.

But it is the view of the harbor and out to sea that is so stunning here. On a clear day, the Manu'a Group and Western Samoa are visible; they are both about 130 kilometers from Tutuila, in opposite directions. The water of the harbor from here looks clean and smooth; smooth it is, but more often than not, it is covered by shiny blue oil slicks. The big purse-seiners look minute from here, though they get a little bigger as the tramway heads back down. The tramway ride goes regularly every day from 8:00 A.M. to 4:00 P.M.

Just below Solo Hill and the tramway stop is Maugaoalii, the hill of chiefs, where Government House is located. The two-story house, built in 1903 and since enlarged and restored, is surrounded by coconut and mango trees but can be easily seen—a most colonial-looking place—and you may walk the grounds.

Head for Fagotogo. The Jean M. Haydon Museum, named for the wife of former governor John M., contains numerous ancient artifacts. The building was originally the naval base commissary. Opposite the museum are various travelers' resources: bank, post office, airlines offices. The Fono, built in 1973, blends traditional architecture with modern materials. The middle building is designed after the *fale tele*, round house, and the two flanking buildings are built after the *fale afolau*, oval house. The Fono meets in January and July. In front of the Fono is the *malae*, village green, where the chiefs of Tutuila ceded the island to the Americans in 1900. The police station was once the barracks of the Samoan militia, the Fitafita Guard.

Past the malae is the old courthouse, looking like it belongs in a small town in Alabama. On the water side of the road is the market, lively at almost any time. Pass another few stores, still on the water side, and look up. Atop a grocery store that has undergone numerous changes of ownership and name are the boarding house rooms in which the fictitious characters Sadie Thompson and the rigid and tormented missionary Davidson played out their story against the rain that never stopped.

"Desire is sad," Maugham wrote in "Rain." The author was on

his way from Hawaii to Tahiti in 1916 to research Gauguin's life for his novel *The Moon and Sixpence.* It is almost certain that he stayed in the rooms above the grocery, along with his secretary (and lover), the American Gerald Haxton. The two men had traveled on the steamer *Sonoma,* on which there was indeed an American prostitute who had been thrown out of Hawaii, and two missionary couples. One of the missionaries looked to Maugham like "an embalmer of cadavers," and he began to imagine the trollop and the missionary "coming into emotional conflict." Like the characters in the story, Maugham, Haxton, and the other *Sonoma* passengers were held up in Pago because of a measles epidemic and were lodged together in the rooms above the grocery. "Rain," published in Maugham's collection of stories *The Trembling of a Leaf,* was turned into a play and a film and turned its author into a rich man.

On past Sadie Thompson's is the side road leading uphill to the Happy Valley; you can see numerous World War II bunkers up along here, but many are now inhabited. Back down to the water, continue west to Pago Pago Village at the end of the harbor. There are a number of handicraft fales here. The tuna plants are on the north of the harbor, along with the marine railway used for the maintenance and repair of the fishing fleet.

Shopping and office hours are typically 8:00 A.M. to 4:00 P.M. Banks are open from 9:00 to 3:00, as in the U.S. There is not typically a lunch closing, but Sunday sees a total shutdown. The public market is liveliest on Saturday.

If you're going to get sick, Pago Pago is the place to do it; the Lyndon B. Johnson Tropical Medical Center is one of the best hospitals in the Pacific, and doctors see outpatients for a nominal fee. If you are going on to a malaria-infested area anytime soon, this is a good place to load up on malaria prophylaxis, if they have it in stock.

## West

Heading west from Pago, you pass through a highly built-up area, complete with shopping malls, before you get a chance to see the dramatic coast. Leone is the second town of Tutuila and has a monument to missionary John Williams, commemorating his landing on October 18, 1832. Further west to Cape Taputapu, the road is spectacularly scenic; check the black lava cliffs at Vailoatai. You need to leave the main road to reach Vaitogi, site of spectacular blowholes, high waves, and the legend of the turtle and the shark. The legend says that blind Fonuea and her granddaughter, unable to find help in time of famine, leaped off the cliff into the sea. The old lady turned into a turtle, and her granddaughter turned into a shark. When their family couldn't find them, they went up to the cliff and called their names and chanted; the turtle and the shark came up, as they still do, if you have a guide who can find someone to do the right chanting.

Inland in the west, a road leads up from Pava'ia'i to A'oloaufou, where there is a botanical park, and Mount Olotele, where there are radio towers and a view. A track, often muddy, leads north from here to arrive in about an hour at Aasu Village on Massacre Bay. Here, in 1787, 11 members of La Pérouse's crew on the *Astrolabe* and *Boussole* were killed in an encounter with Samoans. So were an estimated 39 Samoans and a Chinese member of the French expedition. A French monument, erected in 1883, commemorates the Frenchmen only. In fact, the Western world was so outraged by word of this disaster that Samoa was avoided for decades.

Or, track west from Olotele to Fagamalo on the west coast, a longer walk, and follow southwestward to reach the road at Poloa.

## East

The eastern ride shows the traveler numerous sleepy coast-side villages, as well as wrecks of war bunkers on the beach. The surf here is fast, often rough, often high, and the undertow can be perilous. There are lovely white beaches at the far eastern end, at Tula, and the road continues over rocky promontory to the northeast of the island. You can get out of your car and walk along here to Aoa, where the camping fales are located—or, reach Aoa via road from the south at Amouli. Even if you have no destination in mind, the walking here is good, as plantation tracks lead through the vegetation or along streams, while a beaten track follows the north coast.

From the southeast of Tutuila, you can see Aunu'u, where there is a single village. Motorboats shuttle there and back if you want a ride, but the seas are often very rough. The island is cliffbound to the south, marshy—with quicksand—elsewhere. If you can manage to get to it, Pofala Hill, only about 70 meters high, has an eel-infested lake, Red Lake, in its central crater.

## Cross-Island

The road from Pago snakes across Fagasa Pass; from the top, you can see both the north and south shores of the island before heading to the north coast at Fagasa Bay.

## Hiking

Mount Matafao, at 653 meters Tutuila's highest peak, is easily climbed, but be careful of slick mud and beware of snarling canines; pack a stick or some pebbles just in case. The usual route is from the pass on the Fagasa Road. You scramble up any which way until you find the trail at the top. Preferable is to come up from Faga'alu.

Take the Dr. John P. Turner Drive inland past the LBJ Hospital, past the houses and dogs, over a stream to the end of the road itself. Find the uphill path along the stream, past some falls, and at the top of the ridge, make a left turn for the summit. A right turn from here takes you back down to Fagotogo. It's a walk of perhaps three hours to the top, about two getting down.

Another hike goes along the ridge from the Fagasa Road, or from Fagale'a on Fagasa Bay, to Mount Alava. Then take the tram down. Or vice versa: tram up and walk down.

A track leads from the road at Leloaloa, on the north of the harbor, to Vatia Village and Bay on the island's north coast. The uphill from Leloaloa to the ridgeline is *extremely* steep. A day's walk; hitch or get a bus back.

Another daylong walk (it is also driven by 4×4s) heads from A'ua, also on the north shore of the harbor, over the ridge of Rainmaker Mountain—not its summit—to Afono Village and Bay on the north coast. Going this way makes for a very steep downhill on the north side of the ridge.

You can make a nice two-day walk out of these two.

Rainmaker's summit can be climbed; in any event, it has been climbed.

### Other Activities

Underwater visibility averages 30 meters in the clear waters off American Samoa, and the tourism office or your hotel can put you on to supervised, equipment-providing dive facilities. The best spots are Taema Banks about 3 kilometers outside Pago Pago Harbor and Nafuna Bank about 2 kilometers off Aunu'u Island.

Snorkeling is typically done off Utulei and Faga'alu beaches. It can be treacherous because of strong undertow through the numerous *avas*, the channels through the reef.

Fishing prospects are excellent—for tuna, obviously, marlin, mahi-mahi, sailfish, and broadbill. Again, check with the tourism office or your hotel.

Windsurfing in Pago Pago Harbor is, in the words of one who has windsurfed there, "primo," but exercise caution in the windy winter months.

# MANU'A GROUP

Ta'u Island has guest fale accommodations. You can also camp. Wander all over on foot. Find tracks if you must, but you don't really need them; the vegetation is less thick than on Tutuila, and the area is small enough that you can cover a lot of it in a couple of days. Hills to walk, lagoons to swim in, beaches to lie on.

Ofu and Olosega are two very high volcanic islands linked by a bridge; there's tourist accommodation at Olosega. The east coast of Olosega is too rugged to walk, but the rest is easy, and there is a trail from the south of the island, Maga Point, to the top of Mount Piumafu'a at 639 meters. Ask a local where to find it. You can also walk up Ofu's Tumu Mountain, at 494 meters.

There are day or overnight package tours to the Manu'a Group, daily flights, and weekly interisland boats.

### American Samoa Addresses

Economic Development & Planning Office
Tourism Division
American Samoa Government
Pago Pago, American Samoa 96799

Department of the Interior
Washington, DC 20402

# CHAPTER 10
# TONGA

*Name:* Kingdom of Tonga
*Political status:* Independent state, constitutional monarchy
*Island groups:* Tongatapu, Ha'apai, Vava'u, the Niuas
*Gateway island:* Tongatapu
*Capital:* Nuku'alofa
*Population:* 95,000
*Land area:* 670 square kilometers
*Language:* Polynesian (Tongan), English
*Currency:* Pa'anga (PT)

Tongans enjoy the world's lowest death rate. Although all Tongans die eventually, they do it in just that way—eventually. The traveler can't blame them. Although life here is not without its difficulties and stresses, it does seem to be inordinately pleasant, producing inordinately pleasant people. Not surprisingly, this makes for inordinately pleasant travel; lovely Tonga, slow paced and sweet natured, is one of the treasures of the Pacific.

## GEOGRAPHY, TOPOGRAPHY, CLIMATE

The borders of the Kingdom of Tonga, as defined by King George Tupou I in 1887, are between 15 and 23.3 degrees south latitude and between 173 and 177 degrees west longitude. Within this long, narrow kingdom are 170 islands, of which 36 are inhabited. The total

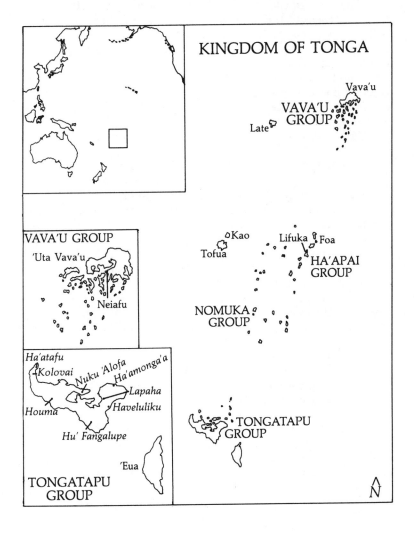

landmass of the islands comes to just under 670 square kilometers sprinkled over an area of ocean estimated at 362,500 square kilometers. The Kingdom of Tonga is the oldest and last surviving kingdom of Polynesia, and it is the only nation in the Pacific that was never colonized by a European power.

There are four groups of islands in Tonga, representing a variety of island types. The southernmost group is Tongatapu—"Sacred Tonga"—including the eponymous gateway island, a flat raised atoll; 'Eua, a high, cliffbound island of streams and forests; and a few coral motus.

One hundred and sixty kilometers to the north is the thin, curving archipelago of the Ha'apai Group. Here are the highest point in Tonga, the 1046-meter extinct volcano on the island of Kao; the flat-topped 500-meter-high Tofua Island; and two stringing clusters of low coral islands.

Another 112 kilometers to the north is the Vava'u Group, 34 elevated limestone islands tilting up to high cliffs in the north, and cut by numerous waterways, including the 11-kilometer channel that leads to the aptly named Port of Refuge (Puerto de Refugio) on Vava'u Island, one of the most famous and picturesque harbors in the Pacific.

You must travel north another 285 kilometers to arrive at the isolated Niuas: Niuatoputapu, a long central ridge surrounded by plain; Niuafo'ou, a collapsed volcanic cone reaching to 210 meters; and surrounding small islands. The Niuas are closer to Samoa and Fiji than to the rest of Tonga. Politically, they form part of the Vava'u District and are administered from Neiafu, Vava'u's main town.

These varied formations of islands constitute an island arc that follows the curve of the Tongan Trench, one of the deepest valleys of the Pacific, in places reaching down ten thousand meters. The trench borders the Pacific Ring of Fire, an area marked by intense volcanic activity. Tonga sits at the point where the Ring, coming north from New Zealand, makes a sharp westward turn toward New Guinea before again heading north, across the Marianas Chain. Although the Ring's primary line of activity is now to the northwest of Tonga, small earthquakes are not uncommon.

Along the Tongan Trench, the Pacific Plate pushes up under the Australian Plate. The melting and rejoining of plate materials and sediments produced the original volcanic explosions here. Then the volcanoes sank, becoming submerged to greater or lesser degree, and coral polyps gradually built up islands. The Ha'apai Group probably subsided first, Lifuka, the main island of the group, remaining less submerged than the others. The action of the subsidence caused Vava'u to the north and Tongatapu to the south to tilt toward the center; hence the cliffs on the outer edges of these groups and the half-submerged islands within.

The word tonga means south, and temperatures here are cooler than in other parts of Polynesia, and cooler in the southern islands than up north. Southeast tradewinds blow from May to November, while summertime sees easterlies with hot weather and numerous squalls—especially when moist warning breezes blow in from the north. A hurricane in 1982 devastated the islands, causing serious damage and setting back numerous development projects.

## THE NATURAL ENVIRONMENT

The traveler can see numerous birds and insects here—watch out for biting centipedes underfoot—and a famous species of flying bat. Pigs and chickens, favorite foods, were brought here before the Europeans; so was the rat. Coconut, banana, vanilla, taro, yams, watermelons, and other crops are all widely cultivated. Most natural vegetation consists of small pines and low-lying plants. In 1986, Tonga opened its first two national forest reserves. One, at Vaomapa on Tongatapu, is believed to be primary rain forest.

A network of marine and beach reserves and island parks covers Tongatapu. (More reserves have been planned for 'Eua and Vava'u.)

On the westernmost tip of Tongatapu Island is Ha'atafu Beach Reserve. Here, at a point where windward and leeward meet, the snorkeler can observe some one hundred species of fish. Stay within the reef unless you're a strong swimmer.

Four reef reserves are short boat rides from Nuku'alofa. At Hakaumama'o, the furthest away, you can see a population of fish exposed to strong wave action. Brilliant parrotfish are numerous. At Malinoa, also a historical site, are blue damselfish, clownfish, groupers, snappers, octopus, giant clams, and other shellfish. Monuafe shows the traveler typical strand plants and animals—hermit crabs, marine snails, and numerous butterflyfish in the lagoon. Pangaimotu, containing an inner shallow reef and an outer reef, supports mangrove, shellfish, and the numerous species that feed on the abundant eelgrass.

Outside the reef, Tongan waters are virtually forested with black coral; divers might join a scuba trip out to the seabed.

## HISTORY

Tongan legend preserves no tale of ancient migrations, claiming instead that the hero Maui yanked the Tongan Islands from the sea with a fishhook acquired from the Samoans. Archaeological evidence suggests that the first settlers here, probably around 1000 B.C., were members of the Lapita pottery culture and originated in Fiji or the Samoan Group, though their pottery skills disappeared over the years.

Legend does have an explanation for the origin of Tongan monarchy, describing how Tagaloa, the creator, descended to earth and married Va'epopua. Their son, Aho'eitu, became the first Tu'i Tonga (sometimes "tuitoga"), or hereditary king, around 950. The Tu'i Tonga's fierce warriors roamed Polynesia in their double-hulled canoes, the *kalia*, capable of transporting two hundred people, and eventually extended Tonga's empire from Rotuma, in the west, through the Lau Islands of Fiji, Wallis and Futuna, Samoa, and Tokelau, to Niue in the east.

But monarchy often proved unhealthy, and numerous Tu'i Tonga were assassinated. The 24th Tu'i Tonga, fearing such a fate, transferred political power to his brother, thus creating a new line, the Tu'i Ha'atakalaua. The seventh king of this line did the same and established the Tu'i Kanokupolu title. Today's Tongan nobility presumably descends from branches of these lines.

In 1616, the Niuas were sighted by the Dutchmen Schouten and Le Maire, after which virtually every name in Pacific exploration passed through here: Tasman, Wallis, Cook (three times), the Spaniard Mourello (who named the Puerto de Refugio in Vava'u), La Pérouse, Bligh, who was mutinied against in Tongan waters, the *Pandora* in search of the mutineers, d'Entrecasteaux, and the missionaries of the *Duff*. In Cook's three visits of 1773, 1774, and 1777, he and his crew were greeted with such hospitality that he dubbed these "The Friendly Islands," although it is said that he only escaped the islanders' original purpose, cannibalism, through the profuseness of his all-unknowing thanks. Cook presented the Tu'i Tonga with a male Galapagos tortoise, which wandered blind in the garden of the royal palace at Nuku'alofa until its death in 1966.

In November 1806, the ship *Port au Prince*, out of Gravesend, England, found a harbor on the island of Lifuka, in the Ha'apai Group, where it was soon set upon by armed natives who took possession and killed most of the crew. One of the survivors was William Mariner, who lived among the natives for the next four years as the adopted son of the warrior king Finau 'Ulukalala II. Mariner's life on Lifuka was filled with adventure, to say the least; he also had a keen eye for detail and, having learned the language, he was able to explore native customs in some depth. An account of his stay on Lifuka was written by John Martin, a physician, and published in England in 1817, causing something of a sensation. It remains today a valuable source of history and a classic adventure tale. Mariner himself, who returned to England and became a stockbroker, drowned in the Surrey Canal—not the Thames, as is popularly supposed—in 1853.

Back in Tonga, European contact had the usual effect of introducing weaponry that spurred rival chiefs to new warfare, and civil war raged from 1799 to 1852. It was during this period that the London Missionary Society first sent missionaries, who, perhaps because of the civil strife, failed miserably. The Wesleyans tried during the 1820s, with somewhat more success. They managed to convert a brilliant soldier named Taufa'ahau, nephew of the holder of the Tu'i Kanokupolu title. In 1831, Taufa'ahau christened himself King George, after the British monarch, and proceeded to establish strategic alliances and to create new converts around Ha'apai and Vava'u. In 1845, King George succeeded his uncle, overwhelmed the opposition to seize Tongatapu, and made himself undisputed Tu'i Tonga with the name King George Tupou I. The new king freed the commoners from enforced labor to the nobility, and in 1875 he promulgated the constitution that still rules Tonga today.

The drafter of the constitution was the Wesleyan missionary Shirley Baker, who in 1880 gave up his religious ministry for more immediate rewards as dictator of Tonga, ruling in the king's name. One of Baker's first acts was to establish the Free Wesleyan Church, the official church of Tonga; in so doing, Baker no longer had to send a proportion of weekly church offerings to the Wesleyan home office in Australia. Baker's high-handedness eventually provoked the British into demanding his deportation; a British administrator was appointed to aid Baker's successor in the premier's slot. King George Tupou I died in 1893 and was succeeded by his grandson.

King George Tupou II was almost universally disliked, so much so that the British declared a protectorate over the kingdom in 1901, extending their powers in 1905 but leaving the king at least nominally autonomous.

## The Twentieth Century

King George's daughter succeeded on his death in 1918. Queen Salote Tupou III was only 18 when she became queen, reigning till her death in 1965. The world knew her as the charmer who rode in an open carriage, in the rain, at the coronation of Queen Elizabeth II of Britain—a sign of respect, she said. But she was, and her memory still is, unabashedly adored by her own people. During her reign, she achieved the reunion of the Free Wesleyan Church and its predecessor. She diversified the economy and expanded public health services. She also extended the educational system, making primary education mandatory, providing scholarships for overseas study, and establishing a teachers college. She ruled through World War II, at which time Tonga established a defense force, some of whom fought in the Solomon Islands.

Having married a direct descendant of one of the competing royal lines, Salote ensured the legitimacy of her heirs; she was succeeded by her son, King Taufa'ahau Tupou IV, the present ruler, who continued his mother's development programs and ended Britain's protectorate in 1970. The king, a man of huge girth, is the first Tongan to have earned a college degree and is something of a scholar of his nation's traditions and archaeology.

He is also considered a fairly canny politician. In 1976, finding he was getting short shrift from the West, he established diplomatic relations with the USSR. At once, the Australians came through with a project; New Zealand development specialists arrived by the planeload; American aid began pouring in. Today, a single roving official serves as the nation's high commissioner to Britain, its representative to the European Economic Community (EEC), and simultaneously as ambassador to both the U.S. and the USSR.

The king's eldest son and heir, the crown prince, is unfortunately held in less than high esteem by the Tongan people. He is said to spend more time abroad than at home, to neglect his governmental duties, to be a playboy. His unforgivable sin was to refuse to marry the hugely popular woman chosen for him. She ended by marrying the king's younger son, and it is said the Tongans would rather see that couple ascend the throne, when the time comes.

The monarch rules; he is the head of government as well as of state. He directly appoints his cabinet, in which much of his family serves and with whom he sits in Privy Council, and he also appoints the speaker of the legislative assembly. Seven members of the legislature are elected by the 33 nobles, and another 7 by the commoners. There are no political parties. The real source of the ruling family's power is its ownership of all land in Tonga, which the nobles allocate to commoners in the system known as *tax'api*, and although the institution of the monarchy seems popular as a symbol of continuity and independence, the nobility is less appreciated. According to the constitution, every male Tongan is entitled to 3.34 hectares of agricultural land and at least .08 hectares of town property at the taxable age of 16. Many commoners feel the nobles withhold land; although older sons inherit their father's portion, younger sons must apply. The population increase—some 3.6 percent a year, more than twice the world average—has aggravated the pressure on land allocation even further, and failure to receive an allotment is seen as a major impetus for out-migration—which isn't easy to accomplish—to the U.S. and New Zealand.

Agriculture—mainly copra—remains a mainstay of the economy, although urban industries have recently been expanded. Almost all households in Tonga meet some subsistence needs through cultivation, using the copra as a cash crop.

Tongans are intensely religious, and Sunday prohibitions are strictly enforced: planes do not land or take off, boats may not offload, there is no driving (except by nobles), and tourism comes to a virtual halt. (Some short tours to islands off Nuku'alofa are permitted.) Most Tongans are Wesleyans, but the so-called "new religions" are gathering strength here. It is said that the royal family opposes the highly successful incursion of the Mormons in Tonga, but as the constitution guarantees religious freedom, there is little the king can do about it. Cynics say many Tongans are only "school Mormons," joining up to take advantage of the good educational opportunities for their children, dropping out again when the kids have graduated from Brigham Young U. in Hawaii. In the mid-1980s, a group of ex-Mormons went on the rampage against their former coreligionists, whom they dubbed "the God-Makers." They made a propaganda film which the king was one of the first to see; he ordered it shown all over. Despite the scorn of some and outright opposition by others, the Mormon presence is pervasive. Their standard-issue cream-colored cinder-block churches, schools, meeting houses, and—always—basketball courts are everywhere. One old Tongan hand says the Mormon strength stems primarily from a willingness to value ancient traditions and a tolerance of local ways that other missionaries neither demonstrated nor possessed.

The Seventh-Day Adventists have made an interesting adjustment to the Tongan loop in the International Dateline. Although Tonga is east of the 180th meridian, it is within a loop that puts it west of the dateline—a day ahead of Samoa, which is due north. The Adventists have determined that the loop is fallacious and that Sunday in Tonga is really Saturday—their Sabbath. The Tongan Sunday thus neatly becomes every Christian's Sabbath.

# THE TRAVELER IN TONGA

Tonga's tourist bureau has taken advantage of the country's position just west of the dateline to coin a slogan describing Tonga as "the place where time begins." The traveler may find instead that, here, time ends. Or stands still. Or doesn't matter. Even on the gateway island of Tongatapu, as well as on the outliers, the traveler can—indeed, *must*—relax into "island time," taking things at an island pace—*fakatonga*, in the Tongan way.

There can be few more affable places on earth. Cook's notion of friendly isles, also now a tourist slogan, finds very real expression in the language, which seems to have an inordinate number of ways of describing a contented life, *mo 'ui fiemalie;* a peaceful life, *m'ui nonga;* living happily, *nofo fiefia;* making others feel at home, *nofo fakalata.* You will routinely be greeted with *malo e lelei* ("hello") and a smile, and you will certainly want to reciprocate. *Malo* also means "thank you," a useful phrase.

The traveler will see many Tongans dressed in the *ta'ovala,* the distinctive traditional skirt made of pandanus mat and worn over the wraparound *vala.* The men secure their short ta'ovalas with a *kafa,* a belt of coconut fiber, and women may wear a *kiekie,* a highly decorative waistband, to hold their long ta'ovalas. They are worn to show respect, on formal occasions, and, with black, are often a sign of mourning. Many are very old, handed down from generation to generation; these are the most prized, the "best" ta'ovalas, worn on the most important occasions. It is said that the custom of the ta'ovala derives from an ancient sea custom. Sailors returning from long voyages cut the mat sails from their canoes to cover their nakedness as a sign of respect before seeing the chief.

Tonga seems particularly clean; on the outlying islands, this is especially the case if a member of the royal family is about to or has just come through—an occasion for a major cleanup. Tonga is also a relatively quiet place. Though old-timers decry the recent sprawl of Nuku'alofa, the first-time visitor will find it a sleepy, dusty, small town. The market can get lively, and the buses and *ve'etolus*—three-wheeled, open-sided taxis—rev their motors from time to time, and the entryways to Burns Philp and Morris Hedstrom may seem positively congested, but basically this is as tranquil a capital as you can find. On a Friday night, however, even the outliers go in for rocking and rolling and a good deal of beer drinking.

The tranquil dead rest in cemeteries vibrantly decorated with recycled beer bottles, seashells, artificial flowers, religious banners.

The traveler should try to see some Tongan dancing, for Tongans are among the most accomplished and devoted dancers in Oceania. In Tongan dance, the story is all—the dance illustrates it. For that reason, the *punake,* or poet-composer-choreographer, reigns supreme. He composes the song and the movements, then trains and supervises the dancers. Punakes are among the most revered members of Tongan society; the beloved Queen Salote was considered a major punake.

In general, the style of dance here is not the hipswinging of Hawaii or the aggressive tamure of French Polynesia and the Cooks; rather, the hands and feet convey the message, and in the case of sitting-down dances, the hands alone tell the story. Women's movements tend to be graceful and soft; they step delicately, pointing their toes, but with elaborate hand and arm gestures. Men's movements are more vigorous, with real stomping and swirling.

There are forms to Tongan dance. The *lakalaka*, perhaps the most famous, is commonly an all-male group dance. It starts off as a slow and majestic movement, building to an intense, ecstatic finish; with perhaps 150 often very large people participating, the lakalaka seems like mesmerizing waves of rhythm. The *ma'ulu'ulu*, typically all female, is a sitting-down dance. The *tau'olunga* is a solo dance by a woman; the knees are held together in a uniquely Tongan posture. The *kailao*, war dance, has no accompanying song, just the shouted instructions of the leader, feet stamping the ground, and the insistent rhythm of pounding on a *pate* or toere, a hollowed-out log, and on a huge, skin-clad drum.

Tongan dance traditionally goes on for hours. The groups in group dancing can range into the hundreds, with subgroups spelling one another from time to time. Adding to the spectacle are the costumes, often made of tapa, or covered in leaves, with feather headdresses and bracelets and anklets of rattling shells that add to the musical "accompaniment." The accompaniment is usually a huge drum—often made of cowhide stretched over barrels. One person holds the drum, while the drummer beats it hard and fast with padded sticks—wide-arcing, powerful arm movements that cause the drummer to sweat more profusely than anyone around.

The traveler will quickly become aware of the custom of *faka-pale*, which means to give a prize to a dancer. If you admire the skill of a dancer or musician, by all means, show it through fakapale. Walk over to the performer, whose body is by now slick with coconut oil and perspiration, and stick paper money to his or her skin. It will be appreciated.

There are dance "shows" at some of the hotels on Tongatapu, but they are shortened versions contrived for the tourists. If you can, try to see the real thing.

If you do, it may be accompanied by a feast. Gargantuan amounts of food will be placed on *polas*, long trays made from plaited coconut fronds. The food is baked in the umu, and coconut cream is the basic lubricant with everything. Tongan feasts also typically feature roast suckling pig, one per person at major events.

Should you chance to be here between June and October, you may be able to watch whale hunting. Tonga is one of the last places on earth where humpbacks are still hunted from gaff-rigged boats and harpooned by hand. The news of a catch is announced by a black flag flying from the boat. The whale, its mouth sewn up, is hauled in offshore, and people wade out to make their purchases as its carcass is cut up. The heart of a large whale is presented to the king; the rest of the *tofua'a* is baked in the umu—a great delicacy. Only three or four may be caught in a year.

Time should be invested in Tonga. A tour of the interesting historical and cultural sights of Tongatapu can be accomplished in a day. Take more than that. Fly to Vava'u for some good walking and wandering. On Ha'apai, there is literally nothing to do, but there are beaches where you can do it in almost perfect isolation. Prices are ridiculously reasonable. If you want luxury, it is entirely affordable here, but as always, the smaller guesthouses possess more local charm.

Tonga is also a premier place in which to shop for handicrafts. Its baskets are world renowned, as are the pandanus-weave mats. Tapa may be purchased in shops; when you see it being made in the villages—you'll hear the pounding of the mallets first—you might ask to buy some directly from the makers. Jewelry of shell, black coral, and scrimshaw is also good value here. The growth of tourism and the arrival of cruise ships have introduced some phony tiki manufacture, but, in general, the Tongans seem to value the worth of their traditional handicrafts as being of particular interest to tourists, and this in turn has inspired a very high quality of creativity and workmanship.

Some caveats. There is a dark underside to what may appear to the traveler the paradise of Tonga. You may indeed hear people complain about the lack of social mobility and about economic scarcity. One of the best of the contemporary Pacific writers, Epeli Hau'ofa, is a Tongan. (No Pacific traveler should miss his *Tales of the Tikongs;* see Chapter 5, The Literary Pacific.) In a heartfelt essay, "Our Crowded Islands," first published in 1977 by the Institute of Pacific Studies in Fiji, Hau'ofa describes what he sees as the adverse impact of overpopulation and "westernization" on Tonga's physical environment, the political milieu, the social life. "The glaring reality is this," Hau'ofa writes: "We are losing the best in us while adopting the cheapest, the most superficial, and often dangerous, aspects of other civilizations. Mutton flaps from New Zealand, second-hand clothes and shoes from America, and karate films from Hong Kong, are minor examples of the kinds of imported rubbish with which we have littered our country. We are polluting, desecrating and destroying what we already have through our misdirected aspirations."

The traveler will draw his own conclusions, but he should keep an eye open for the kind of thing Hau'ofa is talking about.

There is also an underside to travel in Tonga. Tongatapu offers numerous facilities for tourism, even resortlike accommodations and activities. Vava'u has a lively little center in Neiafu, and it too provides a number of activities. Ha'apai is different. Patricia Ledyard Matheson, a native Californian who came to Tonga in 1949 and stayed, writing several books about the place, describes Ha'apai in *Friendly Isles* as, "after Tongatapu . . . figuratively and literally, a breath of fresh air." She also warned an American visitor en route there that "Ha'apai is a good place if you have something inside you to fall back on, but palagis tend to go off their rockers there." Take some stock of yourself before you commit to a long time on these outlier islands.

In Tonga, the Pacific traveler explores Tongatapu and the main islands of the Vava'u and Ha'apai groups.

### Language

| | |
|---|---|
| Malo e lelei | Hello |
| Talitali fiefia | Welcome |
| Fefe hake | How do you do? |
| Malo | Thank you |
| Lelei | Good |
| Io | Yes |
| Ikai | No |
| 'Alu a | Goodbye |
| Nofo a | Goodbye (in reply) |
| Palagi/papalagi | Foreigner |

## TONGATAPU

The traveler arrives in Tonga at Fua'amotu Airport, which lacks both a tourist information desk and a bank, although it does have a duty-free shop. A sign on the wall of the luggage claim room, however, lists the available hostelries, with prices. The van from the International Dateline Hotel serves as a shuttle bus from airport to Nuku'alofa; there are also taxis and private cars, and an occasional airport bus.

The island is shaped like a very pregnant swimmer floating on her back. Fua'amotu is to the southeast, right on the swimmer's rump, some 21 kilometers from the capital in the north, around the curve of the Fanga Uta Lagoon, more or less on the distended belly of the swimmer. The road seems flat, although in fact the island tilts slightly downward from south to north.

In addition to a range of lodgings in Nuku'alofa, there are accommodations on the lagoon, near the jetty for 'Eua, and, for excellent resort-style value, at Kolovai and Ha'atafu beaches. There is also superior-value resort living at Pangaimotu and Fafa, islets off Nuku'alofa. Both provide fale living, and the Fafa resort, German owned and a bit more expensive, offers a full range of water activities, a good restaurant, and an excellent wine cellar. Even if you don't stay, make a day trip to either or both of these islands; launches go on Sunday, if you want to escape the piety of the Tongan Sabbath.

In addition to the above-named beaches, there are excellent swimming, snorkeling, and beachcombing at 'Oholei, Ha'amalo, Monotapu, Laulea, 'Utukehe, Fahefa, and Fua'amotu.

## Nuku'alofa

Nuku'alofa—the name means "abode of love"—looks a neatly laid out town, with its broad avenues and dissecting streets. There are a number of new and rather snazzy buildings—the Tonga Development Bank, for one—but much of the endearingly ramshackle look of the Pacific persists in weathered buildings with hand-painted signs.

A range of lodgings is available. A number of delightful guesthouses are clustered near the International Dateline Hotel, government owned and a major gathering place, on Vuna Road along the water. A good bet is to stay at one of these and pay a nominal fee for the use of the Dateline's pool.

Nuku'alofa offers a surprisingly wide range of cuisines, from continental to Chinese and Japanese. There are disco palaces, dance halls, even movie theaters. Tuesday and Saturday are barbecue and show nights at the Dateline, while Wednesday and Friday are the nights for the *very* stagey Tongan feast at 'Oholei Beach. Book these—as you can book almost anything—at the Dateline, or ask at the tourist office, also on Vuna Road, just a couple of blocks closer to the center of town than the Dateline.

The tourist office is also a good place to find information about trips to Vava'u and Ha'apai, trips that you should try to arrange as soon as possible in Nuku'alofa if you have not already done so. Flights and accommodations are often heavily booked, and communications to these outliers is by radio, so time may be needed to confirm and reconfirm arrangements.

"Town" is not a big place, despite the fact that it continues to spread outward. The activity along Vuna Road stretches from the Royal Palace on the west to the Yacht Club on the east, with the Dateline Hotel in the middle. The center of town moves inland from Vuna Road only a few blocks; Salote, Wellington, and Laifone roads parallel Vuna. The main intersecting road is Taufa'ahau, along which are many shops and offices. Government offices are concentrated near the water. The market is on Salote Road, in the middle of everything. Town opens early—at around 8:30 A.M., takes a lunch break from around 12:30 to 1:30, and closes down for good at 4:30; nightlife takes over a couple of hours later.

The tourist office has an excellent brochure on a walking tour of Nuku'alofa as well as a variety of maps and brochures on Tongan life and sights to see. Perhaps the major urban attraction is the Royal Palace, a pleasant-looking house, all gables and gingerbread, surrounded by a low wall and only partially hidden by ironwood and other trees. A single guardhouse stands at the gate through which cars enter. This is an understated monarch's residence.

For the superior baskets, tapa, mats, and shellwork of Tonga, browse in Langa Fonua, the Tongan Women's Association Handicraft Center on Taufa'ahua Road, near the office of Friendly Islands Airway (with a branch in Neiafu on Vava'u). Commercial shops also sell fine handicrafts, and do not neglect to look in the market. Langa Fonua and the shops will wrap and ship items, but the pile-up of tagged baskets waiting for a ship is not a reassuring sight. Air mail postage of a large Tongan basket can be almost as costly as the basket; it is, however, quite reliable as well as fast—this may be worth the money to you. Artisans set up "shop" along Vuna Road, clustering on the malae, or village green, where they sell black coral, shellwork, and scrimshaw. The work is often exceptional. Scrimshaw in particular, taught to the islanders centuries ago by whalers, here depicts tropical images—hibiscus, coconut palms—and the artisanship is often very fine. Look for the work of Feao Fehoko, a talented young man, whose jewelry has graced the person of the Queen of Tonga, among others.

Philately is a major source of revenue here as on so many Pacific islands; even if you're not a collector, you'll appreciate both the beauty of the average stamp and the ingenious "stickum" technology.

The Friendly Islands bookstore, also on Taufa'ahau Road, has a good collection of English-language books. Look here for the works of Patricia Ledyard Matheson and Epeli Hau'ofa.

## Around the Island

Tongatapu has an area of 275 square kilometers, well crossed by 190 kilometers of road. Buses blaring rock music leave from the market and reach all parts of the island very cheaply—head east from the East Terminal, west from the West Terminal. Be aware that the last bus *leaves* from either end of the island to return to Nuku'alofa at 3:00 P.M. There is no bus service on Sunday. Bicycles may be available, either through a licensed agent—check at the tourism office or at the Dateline—or through a private deal. Scooters are not usually for rent; to rent a car, you need a Tonga license, obtainable at the Police Traffic Office on presentation of your domestic license and a small fee.

Perhaps the best way to see the island is to negotiate a deal with a taxi driver or ve'etolu driver, although the latter conveyance may be somewhat lacking in comfort. If your driver suddenly pulls to the side of the road and lurches to a halt, keep your eyes on the road; a member of the royal family is passing.

Head east in the morning and west in the afternoon, or vice versa, but be sure to see the following:

• Cook's landing place, where a monument commemorates the arrival of the *Endeavor* in 1777 and the banyan tree, *ovava,* under which Cook rested. It was, according to the monument, the time of the gathering of fruits, and Cook came to honor the Tu'i Tonga.

• Lapaha, the ancient capital, one of the richest archaeological sites in western Polynesia. From around 1200 to around 1800, this was the home of Tonga's chiefly rulers and center of Tongan culture. Of the original living and working quarters, only a few scattered foundation mounds remain, but 28 *langi,* burial mounds, can still be seen. While commoners were buried in shallow sand mounds, the langi of the nobility were built to last—stone foundation mounds on which stone-lined burial vaults rested. The stones, cut from coral sandstone common along the reefs, were cut and transported on double canoes (*tongiaki* or *kalia*) and hauled into place using sennit ropes, sledges, roller, levers, and slave labor. Final shaping and cutting were done when the stones were in place.

Langi of the nobility have been found as far north as Vava'u and through Ha'apai, but those on Tongatapu are the most striking. Note particularly the pyramid tombs Paepae-'o-Tele'a and Namoala, and the mound dubbed Hehea. As in all cultural and historical sites on Tongatapu, these are well marked.

• Ha'amonga'a Maui, a trilithon, a huge, three-stone structure consisting of two vertical uprights each five meters high and a lintel nearly six meters long mortised into the top of the uprights. Myth says the trilithon was brought here by the hero Maui, who transported it on a pole across his shoulders from Wallis Island, three or four tons of rock being a mere bagatelle to a hero. Archaeology says it was built by the Tu'i Tonga Tu'itatiu around 1200. The trilithon's uprights are said to represent his sons, with the lintel symbolizing the unity he hoped they would demonstrate. Most likely, it was the gateway to the old royal compound, for this spot was the capital of Tonga before Tu'itatiu's sons moved it to Lapaha, where there was better anchorage for their canoes.

In 1967, at the summer solstice, Tonga's king installed himself atop the lintel to observe the sunrise, which corresponded exactly with a groove drawn in the lintel. This confirmed his theory that the trilithon was an instrument for determining the seasons.

- Haveluliku. Here are the *makatolo,* huge stones which Maui threw across from 'Eua island at an errant chicken, and the stalactite cave of 'Anahulu. There is fine beach here, continuing south to 'Oholei.
- Hufangalupe ("Pigeon's Doorway"), a dramatic cliffbound coast; the doorway is a natural coral bridge with a sandy cove flanked by cliffs.
- The blowholes at Houma. Called Mapu'a a Vaca—the chief's whistle—the blowholes are best seen at high tide, when surf forced through natural air vents can send up shoots as high as 30 meters.
- The memorial to the landing of the first Christian missionaries, at the westernmost tip of the island, and Ha'afatu Beach.
- The flying foxes of Kolovai, actually bats with foxlike heads, hanging upside down from casuarina trees. They are said to be sacred—a love gift from the Samoan maiden Hina to an ancient Tongan chief, according to legend—and may be hunted only by the royal family.

### Other Activities

Scuba diving for exploring the reefs and beyond is superb here, especially off Malinoa and Hakaumama'o reefs. The tourism office will have a list of reliable dive operators. Snorkeling from most beaches and at the marine reserves is excellent. Deep-sea fishing trips can also be arranged through the tourism office or your hotel; catches include barracuda, tuna, marlin, and sailfish.

# VAVA'U

The 34 islands of the Vava'u group cover 117 square kilometers, most of them hilly and verdant like Vava'u itself. Neiafu, the capital, is nestled at the bottom of one of the hills overlooking the Port of Refuge. The fjordlike harbor entrance at the end of an 11-kilometer channel is one of the most beautiful sights in the Pacific.

There are two tourist hotels here, one small and useful, the Stowaway Village, the other huge and more or less fashionable, the Paradise International. In addition, there are numerous delightful guest houses.

To get around, you may rent a scooter or bicycle from the Paradise International or in a private deal, or hire a taxi. Passenger trucks and mini-buses crisscross the island on an unscheduled basis; catch them outgoing at the Neiafu market.

Vava'u is a fine place to explore on foot. To help you out, get hold of *A Walking Tour of Neiafu, Vava'u,* by Pesi and Mary Fonua, available at the hotels, at Robyn's gift shop-cum-coffee shop, in town at Burns Philp and Morris Hedstrom, and at the Friendly Islands bookstore back in Nuku'alofa. The not-to-be-missed walk is the one up the 131-meter Mt. Talau, from which the view over the harbor is sensational. At this writing, Talau had been named a national reserve, and there were plans to improve the eroding trail. Even if you go barefoot, however, the view is worth it.

Vava'u is a yachtie haven and a center for bareboat chartering. The sailors tend to congregate at the Paradise bar or Vava'u Club in the evening, and at Robyn's during the day; the latter serves the best cup of coffee east of Papua New Guinea and west of Hawaii.

For water sports, it's the Paradise International Hotel, which rents out boats and sailboards and organizes scuba and snorkel trips. If you are not staying there, it is still possible to join in, though priority is given to hotel guests. The classic tour on Vava'u, to Swallows Cave and Mariners Cave, is actually *off* Vava'u, and it is a good idea to do this one with a supervised group. Mariners Cave is a drowned grotto on Nuapapu island, southwest of Neiafu. The story is that a young chief hid his beloved here, coming each night with food and water, until he could build a canoe in which to spirit her to safety in Fiji. Because the story was first told to the Western world by Will Mariner, the cave is named after him. It's a lovely, blue-lit cavern, with a hard-to-find entrance. The organized trip fits you with snorkel gear and provides guides to take you in. Swallows Cave on Kapa Island, at the end of the Port of Refuge, is a multi-colored, cathedral-like chamber which is in fact a sanctuary for swallows in the autumn. Sea snakes also live here. You enter by boat and can dive down a steep vertical drop-off. The trip to the caves usually ends with a picnic on Nuku Island, which has a beautiful beach.

Back on Vava'u itself, there are beaches a-plenty. The two most popular and accessible are Keitahi and Ene'io, both well out of Neiafu. The villages of Vava'u are small and quiet, and the island is covered with plantations for copra and vanilla. Feletoa, the ancient capital, was the scene of an 1808 battle between Finau 'Ulukalala II and other chiefs of Vava'u. There are some remains of langi here; that of Finau is behind a house opposite the primary school. It was Finau who imprisoned, then adopted Will Mariner; Finau later conquered Tongatapu.

Near Feletoa is Lake Tu'anuku, a huge freshwater lake down a long, rough plantation road. The villagers here call out to the *lapila*, kingfish, and catch them by hand.

Vava'u's northward road seems to stop past Holonga, though a staunch car can carry on through the brush. When you can really go no farther, get out and walk to 'Utula'aina Point, a very beautiful and imposing height from which you can look out to the island of

Toku and down left and right to two beautiful coves. One, Likuone, has a staggeringly lovely beach. There are routes down to this beach, though you may have to beat a path through thigh-high bush. Ask at the village of Holonga, or check out the planted fields for tracks.

Vava'u is the place where the young Patricia Ledyard came, after reading about Will Mariner's voyages during the gloomy cold of a New Zealand winter. Here she met and married the Scottish doctor, Farquhar Matheson; here they raised their family; here Matheson is buried. Their house, with its verandah overlooking the harbor and its shelves of books, stands at 'Utulei.

# HA'APAI

From the air, as you fly over the long cluster of coral islands that make up Ha'apai, you can see the white sandy beaches that outline just about every one of them. From Lifuka, the main island of the group, the one with the airfield and road, you can make your way by causeway to Foa, then on foot—at low tide—to Nukunamo, owned by the king, or by motorboat to Ha'ano. You can go south by motorboat to 'Uiha, where there is a kind of guesthouse. Most likely, you will stay in or near Pangai, the very sleepy main town of Lifuka, where there is a range of guesthouses—in particular, a couple run by Seletute Falevai, a large, lovely Tongan woman of immense charm. If you have made a reservation before coming here, you have reason to hope that someone from your accommodation will meet your plane.

It doesn't much matter if they don't; someone will be heading down the island and will deposit you at your destination. Nothing in Pangai is very far from anything else, and the island itself is a 15-minute walk from side to side, though a good deal more than that from end to end.

There is no place to eat outside the guesthouses, although there are stores in Pangai—the ubiquitous Burns Philp among others— and a market if you want between-meal snacks or beer. There are also an airline office (reconfirm!), a small bank, electric lighting, and what seems a disproportionate number of churches; these, the traveler quickly learns, are the center of cultural and social life, and Sunday here is truly the peak toward which the week builds. The peak may be said to start, however, on Friday night, when some of the church halls turn into discos, and when beer-drinking, despite numerous restrictions, often gets out of hand.

Just north of Pangai is the grave of Shirley Baker, with a monument commemorating his life as adviser to King George Tupou I and his assistance in framing the constitution. The Methodist church in

Pangai is the site of a 1975 miracle, if Methodists have miracles, when a cross appeared on the grass; the spot is marked in cement. Also in town is the palace where the king stays when he comes to Ha'apai; at the least, he does so every autumn for the Agricultural Show. From the waterfront, you can often see Tofua and Kao, steep volcanic islands in the midst of the low-lying atolls of Ha'apai. It was off Tofua that Fletcher Christian and the Bounty mutineers lowered Bligh and 18 loyalists into a longboat. From here, in one of the longest open-boat voyages in maritime history, Bligh brought his crew safely to Timor, 6500 kilometers away. There was only one casualty: just after the mutiny, the boat put in at Tofua, and the crew clashed with the Tongans there; the quartermaster of the Bounty was killed.

That is all there is to see on Ha'apai, and joining in the Friday night beer brawl and the Sunday church-going, with its magnificent singing, is just about all there is to do. But bring a book, and bring those inner resources Pat Matheson talked about, and you can find here the South Seas solace you have dreamed about. At the very north end of Foa, just beyond the village of Faleloa, is one of the world's loveliest beaches; the present author went through a wrenching moral dilemma about whether or not to mention this. There are other astonishing beaches as well, easily found—just walk to the water and along it.

At this writing, a couple of palagis were trying to make a go of a scuba operation out of Pangai. Business in Tonga moves on island time, and the arrangements were going slowly. Meanwhile, the two palagis looked to be in danger of going off their rockers, even as Pat Matheson predicted.

The pandanus weaving of Ha'apai is said to be the best in Tonga. Ask about it when you arrive, as this too moves on island time.

## Tonga Address

Tonga Visitors Bureau
P.O. Box 37
Nuku'alofa
Kingdom of Tonga

# PART
# III

# ADVENTURING IN MELANESIA

FIJI
VANUATU
NEW CALEDONIA
THE SOLOMON ISLANDS
PAPUA NEW GUINEA

Melanesia is an inclined "L" or perhaps a stairway of large steps striding from southeast to northwest from the Tropic of Capricorn to the equator. It is larger and more diverse than Polynesia, smaller and more diverse than Micronesia. Indeed, it defies generalization of any kind. The ten million or so square kilometers of ocean it covers are busy with islands, climate zones, varied biotic communities, and extremely varied cultural communities.

The traveler has the impression from its gateway islands that Melanesia is all large and lush. Seventeen of the 30 biggest islands in the Pacific, including New Zealand and with Tahiti ranked last, are in fact islands of Melanesia. That they are large by Pacific standards may be one reason why the emerging nations of Melanesia seem to play such an important role in regional and international forums.

But Melanesia also includes small, low islands, and even artificial islets man-made on reefs. Its diversity takes in high peaks where you can feel actual cold, sweltering swamps, mossy forests, almost impenetrable jungles, and grassland that makes you wonder if you aren't perhaps in South Dakota. In Fiji, there is even an area of desert sand dunes, windswept and bleak. Add active volcanoes, earthquakes, and typhoons, mix in malaria, dengue, blackwater fever, and various parasites, and you have a region that has long seemed, to outsiders anyway, as inimical as it is varied. That is why Melanesia has to a great extent remained a refuge for primitive cultures. It is also why many of its islands may well be, for today's traveler, the best-kept secrets of the Pacific.

# THE MELANESIANS

Melanesia means the black islands—so named by early explorers because of the dark-skinned inhabitants. The Melanesians are perhaps the original settlers of Pacific islands. It is postulated that some thirty thousand years ago (some say as much as fifty thousand years ago), during one of earth's great ice ages, Old Stone Age tribes of Australoid peoples took advantage of the exposed land bridges to spread through Indonesia and across some of the steps of Melanesia to Australia. When the glaciers receded and the sea rose, these ancient peoples, probably short-statured and black-skinned, were isolated. Thousands of years later, New Stone Age peoples, now traveling in boats and rafts, picked their way from island to island along a similar route. These people were probably larger in stature than their predecessors, and while they blended their genes, cultures, and languages with the earlier settlers, they also tended to push many of them out of the way, up into the interior of the islands. The difficulties of the terrain, which kept even the coastal peoples isolated from one another, cut off the people in the interior from any outside contact—most dramatically in Papua New Guinea, where a huge population was not "discovered" until the 20th century. Today, on many Melanesian islands, coast-dwellers still call inland bush people the Melanesian equivalent of "yokel."

These coastal peoples eventually began to travel to one another's settlements, both for trade and for war, which was typically accompanied by cannibalism. Violence required a "payback," and one payback deserved another, and these ancient blood rites have proven hard to shake off even in modern democracies.

Despite the contacts, peaceful or violent, the isolation persisted, and "traditional" Melanesia was more an aggregation of micosocieties than a single culture. The geographic and cultural fragmentation that in many ways is still a fact of life here is perhaps best illustrated in the fact that more than one thousand languages are spoken in Melanesia. Many are of the Austronesian family that stretches from Madagascar to Easter Island, but some are Papuan, a catchall phrase that differentiates these languages from Austronesian more than it bespeaks any linguistic affinity.

It is virtually impossible to find any generalizations about primitive or contemporary "Melanesian culture," any more than one can find generalizations about Melanesian topography. Ethnographers and anthropologists and linguists have been trying for years. As soon as one comes along and says that such-and-such an object has major significance in certain communities, another finds communities in which the same object plays an entirely different role—or none whatsoever. No single characterization has universal validity. The traveler will note that pigs play an important role in many parts of Melanesia; chiefs or "big men" achieve authority through force of personality and exercise authority with much fanfare and display; taro, yam, and sago palm are widely used as food sources; and a lot of Melanesians chew betel. Looking for patterns to be drawn across all of Melanesia can be very frustrating indeed.

Today, nearly 80 percent of the people who inhabit the tropical Pacific (excluding Hawaii) live in Melanesia. Among the Melanesians themselves, physical appearance is far from uniform. Skin color ranges from golden brown to blue black; hair may be straight or woolly; some Melanesians are short, some tall. Nor is the population of Melanesia all Melanesian. More than half of New Caledonia's population is European or Polynesian; more than half the people of Fiji are ethnically Indian. Indeed, Fiji, the ethnic and cultural crossroads of Oceania, is very much a hybrid, and there are some observers who think that as such, and as the launching pad for Polynesian settlement, it does not really belong to Melanesia. Besides the Fiji dilemma, there have been innumerable back-migrations of Polynesians and Micronesians to islands all along the border of Melanesia; these islands are called Polynesian outliers or, collectively, the Polynesian fringe.

# EUROPEAN CONTACT

To this native ethnic diversity must be added the ethnic diversity of the Europeans who colonized these islands. The Dutch, the British, the French, and the Australians have all had a piece of Melanesia—in the case of Vanuatu, two of them (Britain and France) at once. The first white men to these islands did not, in general, find them friendly places, and tales of cannibalism and hostility kept many Europeans away for many years. Greed eventually proved stronger than fear, however, and Melanesia offered rich pickings in copra, sandalwood, sugar, and *bêche de mer*, the sea slug that is a prized banquet dish of China. One result of the trade was the development of pidgins, convenient trading languages that bridged the gap not only between traders and natives but between different native language groups. The traveler will be introduced to three pidgins in Melanesia—Bislama in Vanuatu, Pidgin in the Solomons, and Tok Pisin in Papua New

Guinea, where it is today effectively the national language.

Another result of trade, however, was that Melanesia became the center for blackbirding, one of the more repellent practices of human history. An Englishman named Benjamin Boyd holds the dubious distinction of having started the practice; Boyd brought some 65 natives from the New Hebrides and the Loyalty Islands—today, Vanuatu and New Caledonia—to Australia in 1847. The recruiters who followed Boyd often simply shanghaied islanders or made deals with chiefs to buy young men for what amounted to slave labor on distant plantations. Many never returned to their home islands; many others who did return introduced some of the less desirable elements of the white man's civilization—liquor, firearms, disease.

In the wake of blackbirding, missionaries were often received with quite final hostility. Many became martyrs to the cause before Christianity was widely received. Even today, traditional practices and ancestor worship persist in the inland regions of many Melanesian islands.

As colonies, the islands of Melanesia of course became pawns in the power politics of the 19th and 20th centuries. Some of the bloodiest battlefields of World War II are to be found here—most notably perhaps, the Kokoda Trail of Papua New Guinea and Guadacanal in the Solomons. In these and other battles, the island natives who fought alongside the Allies and gave them various forms of assistance were conspicuous for their bravery.

One of the more interesting side effects of the war was the growth of cargo cults, which preached the cessation of work on the grounds that a mystery ship or airplane would soon appear, bringing enough necessities and luxuries to make work a thing of the past. The supply ships and cargo planes brought to Allied staging areas in Melanesia, disgorging huge amounts of hitherto unheard-of goods, provided the visual evidence the messiahs of these cults could point to, but in fact the cargo cult is a recent manifestation of a long-standing nativistic impulse. The root cause of these movements, which go back to the 19th century, is the evangelism that sought to revolutionize native religions, replacing them with Western systems of belief that were probably unsuited to life here.

In the postwar period, the nativistic impulse eventually led to agonizing struggles for independence; many of the new Melanesian nations continue to agonize as they try to find their way to new relationships with their former rulers and with other world powers. What is generally considered the political tinder box of the Pacific, New Caledonia, shows the traveler a rather tragic arena in which are being wrestled the dominant political issues in Melanesia today—ethnicity, colonialism, resistance.

# THE TRAVELER IN MELANESIA

Except in Fiji, you will see fewer tourists here than in Polynesia, and more expats: aid officials, contract workers, consultants to ministries of government. Most of the tourists you do meet will be Australian, for these islands are in Australia's backyard, and for east-coast Australians, holidays in Melanesia are often cheaper than trips to the west of their own country. Besides, as Australians will cheerfully tell you, the scuba diving is better here.

For the traveler who is not simply "having a holiday," there are perhaps three things that characterize the experience of travel in Melanesia. One is its very diversity—the almost mind-boggling variety of scenery, peoples, languages, cultures, food, shopping, political situations, places to go, things to do. Another is that here, perhaps more than in any other place on earth except Africa, the traveler has a chance to explore a living laboratory of primitive culture. Papua New Guinea is the preeminent example of this, but the outliers of Vanuatu and the Solomons should not be overlooked. Third, the out-islands of Melanesia in general offer the traveler rich opportunities to live in fact the unspoiled island life of the imagination. Many of these outliers hardly see tourists at all; some that do, as in the Solomons, boast a style of tourism that might be a model for all of the Pacific.

Melanesia is exceptionally rich in its arts and crafts, still linked to magic and the supernatural, still executed with superb skill and creative vitality. The Solomon Islanders are particularly noted for their crafts, but the art of Oceania reaches what is perhaps its zenith in Papua New Guinea. Among the numerous items particular to Melanesia are masks, rarely found elsewhere in the Pacific. These were often totemic displays or, in their hugest forms, representations of supernatural monsters. They were used in religious ceremonies, and their aim was to provide visual excitement, as they still do.

Our hypothetical Pacific traveler begins his itinerary in Fiji, flying from there to New Caledonia and then to Vanuatu. From Port Vila, capital of Vanuatu, he catches a regularly scheduled but infrequent flight to the Solomon Islands. From the Solomons, he proceeds to Papua New Guinea.

Each of these nations has its domestic airline offering flights to outliers. It's Fiji Air or Sunflower in Fiji; Air Calédonie in New Caledonia; Air Melanesia in Vanuatu; Solair in the Solomons; and Air Niugini, also an international carrier, or Talair in Papua New Guinea. Air Niugini's flights offer an on-board snack that has the only chocolate chip cookies in the South Pacific.

# CHAPTER 11

# FIJI

*Name:* Fiji
*Political status:* Independent state
*Island groups:* Viti Levu, Vanua Levu (Northern Group), Yasawa
   Group, Mamanuca Group, Kadavu Group, Ovalau, Lomaiviti
   Group, Yasayasamoala Group, Somosomo Group, Lau Group,
   Rotuma
*Gateway island:* Viti Levu
*Capital:* Suva
*Population:* 680,000
*Land area:* 18,333 square kilometers
*Language:* English, Fijian dialects, Hindi
*Currency:* Fiji dollar ($F)


Fiji is the crossroads of Oceania. It is the arena of transition from
Polynesia to Melanesia. Though settled early by Melanesian peoples,
it was from Fiji that the seeds of Polynesian culture wafted eastward.
Today, the traveler sees signs of both, though on arrival at the air-
port of either Nadi or Suva he may feel that he is in fact in New
Delhi; Indians are the largest population group of Fiji.

The number of Indians in Fiji, their preeminence in business and
commerce, and native Fijian resentment of Indian presence and
power have long constituted the central fact of political and social
life here. In May 1987, this fact exploded; Fiji became the first and
thus far the only nation in Oceania to suffer a military coup d'etat.
The coup was bloodless, and a caretaker government headed by the
army officer who staged the coup promised elections once a new
constitution could be drafted. That constitution, it was understood,
would ensure that the balance of power in Fiji would rest absolutely
with Fijians.

The coup destroyed Fiji's economy, bringing a halt to the sugar
harvest and putting a nearly fatal drag on tourism. But travel to Fiji
soon began to rebound. Aussies and Kiwis weary of winter began
to make their way back to this favorite holiday destination. The U.S.
government's travel advisory suggesting that Americans defer "non-
essential" visits to Fiji was somewhat half-hearted, noting that most
tourist facilities were not located in "disturbed areas." The disturbances themselves died down fairly quickly; three weeks after the
coup, the author was told from Fiji that "everything is the same;
nothing has really changed."

No fatalities resulted from the coup, though some observers
worried that it spelled the death of democracy in Fiji. Others saw

the coup as a safety valve, a penultimate action against Indian dominance of political life, so long feared by the ethnic Fijian community. Had it not been for the bloodless coup, these observers said, more drastic, possibly even final anti-Indian actions would eventually have taken place. In any event, the coup was a swift, clear response to the many complexities of Fijian society.

Those complexities are instantly evident; simplifying patterns are harder to come by. For the traveler, this can make for a confusing experience, but it can also provide a rich one. Fiji is multievery

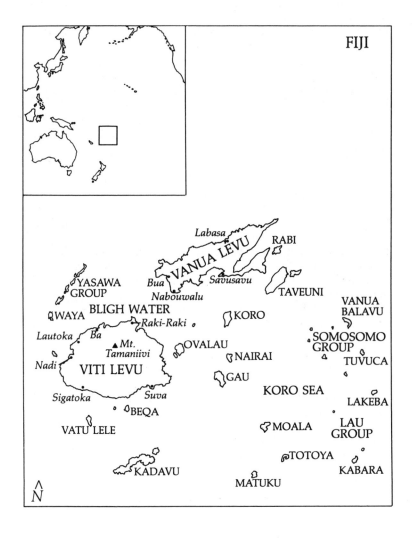

thing: multiethnic, multilingual, multicultural, multifaceted. Even its terrain seems to have everything.

# GEOGRAPHY, TOPOGRAPHY, CLIMATE

Between latitudes 15 degrees south and 21 degrees south, and straddling the 180th meridian from longitudes 177 degrees west to 175 degrees west, lie the 322 islands, about one-third of them inhabited, that make up Fiji. In fact, if you add islets and clods of earth, the number of pieces of land comes to 844, for a total landmass of more than 18,000 square kilometers spread over 1.3 million square kilometers of the South Pacific. The distance from top to bottom of this nation of islands is around 1200 kilometers; from side to side, it measures about 650 kilometers. Fiji's gateway island, Viti Levu, is the seventh biggest island of the Pacific; Vanua Levu, to the north, is the tenth biggest Pacific island. If you remove New Zealand's North and South islands from the rankings, Fiji's two big islands move up in the standings.

The islands of Fiji seem to sweep eastward and downward; en route, they straddle different geologic phenomena. It is as if, after the explosions that created the high volcanic islands of Viti Levu and Vanua Levu, there was only enough energy to scatter small islands around the Koro Sea as far eastward as the Lau Group. In fact, the Laus were formed in the same uplift that created the Ha'apai Group of Tonga, with which, both topographically and ethnically, the Laus have much in common. The volcanic islands to the north and east, by contrast, are vestiges of that sunken continent that today still protrudes as Australia, New Caledonia, Vanuatu, the Solomon Islands, and New Guinea.

The high volcanic islands of the westernmost Yasawa Chain lie in the lee of Viti Levu, itself massive, mountainous, and rugged. Fiji's highest peak is here, Mount Tamaniivi, also called Mount Victoria, and from this and other peaks of the two mountain ranges rush numerous meandering rivers—including the Rewa, the Sigatoka, and the Ba. Key satellites of Viti Levu are Beqa and Yanuca to the south, volcanic islands with reef-rich waters, and the low, limestone island of Vatulele, with a few small outliers.

The northern group that includes Vanua Levu also tends to be rugged; Vanua Levu itself, with several jutting peninsulas, presents a wildly zigzagging coastline, while its elongated neighbor, Taveuni, is almost as high and extremely lush. To the north of Vanua Levu is the Great Sea Reef, one of the largest in the world, while the Rainbow Reef is just off the island's southern coast.

Well to the south of Viti Levu is the Kadavu Group with rich native forest. To the north of the island, in the Kadavu Passage, is the extraordinary Astrolabe Reef; within the Astrolabe Lagoon are the barren island of Ono and numerous islets.

Just east of Viti Levu are the volcanic, forested islands of Ovalau and the Lomaiviti Group, where Koro and Gau islands rise to considerable heights.

East of Kadavu, at the bottom of the Koro Sea, are the three isolated Yasayasamoalas: Moala, Toyota, and Matuku.

The eastern border of Fiji consists of a long, fragmented chain of islands and coral cays. The islands themselves are mostly upthrust coral, with some volcanic formations and a number that are geologically composite. All these islands are routinely referred to as the Lau Group, but in fact they are properly broken into at least two, and sometimes three, distinct chains. To the north, more or less from Nunuku Passage to Lakeba Passage, lies the Somosomo Group or Exploring Islands, dominated by Vanua Balavu with its great system of lagoons, and by the up-flung coral mass of Vatuvara. The Lau Group itself extends from Nayau south across the Lakeba Passage to Onoilau and the Tuvana islets. But these last, and indeed all the islands south of the Bounty Boat Passage, are often referred to as the Southern Laus, distinct from the islands north of the passage.

Finally, some 500 kilometers north of Vanua Levu is Rotuma, geographically isolated and primarily Polynesian in heritage, but politically part of Fiji, though frequently expressing resistance to that fact.

The climate of Fiji is controlled by southeast tradewinds, active from February to November. December through April are the hottest months, and hurricane season, though officially December and January, can run right through these hot, humid months. The 1986 hurricane started battering the islands around April 1, and the system took a few weeks to pass through, causing serious damage.

The most distinctive climatic feature of Fiji is the striking contrast between windward and leeward. The eastern and southeastern windward sides of the large islands get as much as 3500 millimeters of rainfall per year, almost twice as much as that expected on the drier, leeward sides.

# PRONOUNCING FIJI

If you look on a map for the names of Fiji's islands and waters as written above, you conceivably might not find a single one. Travelers who have been told they will arrive at Nandi Airport at such-and-such a time are often surprised when they deplane at Nadi; heading for the island of Beqa to see the famous firewalkers, the traveler may be confused to hear it called something that sounds like—and is often spelled—Mbengga. It all has to do with pronunciation, and with the alphabet constructed by the missionaries, who found sounds in Fijian for which they had no equivalent letters.

The man primarily responsible for the economical Fijian spelling system employed today was David Cargill, a Wesleyan missionary originally stationed on Tonga. Cargill was not actually present at the 1834 meeting at which volunteers were sought for a mission to Fiji; this made him the obvious choice, and he was overwhelmingly elected. With university training in languages and with a fluency in Tongan, the first language of communication between the missionary and the natives, Cargill experimented with a number of systems to find one that was simple, regular, and an aid to the Fijians who were learning to read for the first time. Consonant letters were, for the English-speaker, the main difficulty. Hearing the islanders pronounce the name of an island in the Lau Group "la-kem-ba," Cargill at first wrote it that way. But to the Fijians, each sound is a single consonant, and each consonant is separated by vowels; seeing Lakemba, they pronounced it "la-ke-ma-mba." As Cargill wrote, he then "substituted one consonant for the two, and the natives were quite delighted with the improvement, and joyfully exclaimed, 'You have just now known the nature of our language; we are just now able to read the books which you have written'" (quoted in *Say It in Fijian*, by A. J. Schütz, Pacific Publications, Sydney, 1972).

Here are the consonant letters Cargill came up with, still in use today:

*b*, pronounced *mb*, as in member
*d*, pronounced *nd*, as in Monday
*g*, pronounced *ng*, as in singer
*c*, pronounced *th*, as in father
*q*, pronounced *ng+g*, as in finger.

Thus, Cakobau, a major figure in Fijian history, is "tha-komb-au." *Yaqona*, the national drink known as kava in Polynesia, is "yang-gona." Even the common greeting, *bula*, is rather more "mbula." To get by in Fiji, then, the traveler must remember his Bs and Qs. Here are some other key words:

| | |
|---|---|
| Vinaka | Thank you, good |
| Turaga | Sir |
| Marama | Madam |
| Sa moce | Goodbye |
| Sa bula | Hello |

The corollary to all this pronunciation knowledge, however,

is that contemporary Fiji often adapts its spelling to the needs of outsiders. Thus, you will see Nadi written as both Nadi and Nandi; Sigatoka may also be Singatoka; the Kadavu Passage may appear as Kandavu; Buca may be Mbutha; the Mamanuca Group may appear as Mamanutha. It's another of those moments when Fiji embraces more than one world—confusing, but enjoyable.

Moreover, the traveler may hear Namaste and Achha, Hindi words, as frequently as he hears Bula and Vinaka—a good reason to stick to the official lingua franca of Fiji, English.

One further note on language. The spelling of the name Fiji actually contains two consonants not found in the language. The official name is Viti; the Tongan pronunciation of this at the time of the first Western explorers was something like "Feejee," as some early spellings have it, although Tongans today call the island "Fisi."

# THE NATURAL ENVIRONMENT

In this potpourri of islands, island types, and island topographies is found a corresponding variety of flora and fauna. Of the approximately three thousand species of plants, about a third are indigenous. Most vegetation is similar to that found elsewhere in Melanesia, the seeds of the nonindigenous plants having been blown or

Pandanus-weave house with corrugated tin roof, Fiji.
*Photo by Susanna Margolis.*

transported to the Fiji Islands across the Melanesian Chain. Along the coastlines are the herbaceous plants, shrubs, grasses, and mangrove swamps. Trees, shrubs, and agricultural crops grow further inland. On the high islands, the windward sides tend to be dense with rain forest—an array of trees, bushes, ferns, and vines. The leeward slopes of these islands once sported monsoon forest or bush cover, but centuries-old clearing, often by burning, has mostly destroyed this; the leeward sides of Fiji's islands today are barren grasslands with some growth of pandanus, cycads, and casuarina. The border areas between windward and leeward are typically thick with reed or bamboo and low bush. On the limestone islands, tropical palms predominate.

The extravagant blooms of Fiji are poinciana, bougainvillea, hibiscus, frangipani, and orchids, while breadfruit, mango, and banana grow widely and are an important part of the local diet.

Winged animals dominate among the fauna. Most bird species originated in the islands of Southeast Asia and encountered first the high volcanic islands of the Yasawas, Vanua Levu, and Viti Levu. Ornithologists believe the first avian settlers landed in Fiji during the ice ages, when the sea level had dropped and the ocean was less of a barrier. Some species—the blue-crowned lory, the crimson-crowned fruit-dove, and the Pacific pigeon—probably overflew Fiji to land in western Polynesia, from which they worked their way backward only relatively recently.

Of the 60 species of native land birds—those that arrived without human help—a full 40 percent are endemic, as are four genera. Among these are the three species of a distinctly Fijian fruit-dove (golden, orange, and whistling dove), an endemic genus of musk-parrot (red breasted, sulphur breasted), a rare genus of long-legged warbler, the barking pigeon, collared lory, broadbills, flycatchers, silktail, honeyeaters, and parrot-finches. This high degree of endemism demonstrates that, although avian pioneers may have crossed the ocean at a time when it was relatively low, it nevertheless was a daunting obstacle; having beaten their way across it, against prevailing winds, the birds arriving in Fiji established themselves locally, adapted, and bred in new and unique ways.

No single island or island group boasts the full range of native land bird species. Variety is greatest in the large, forested islands of the west, with variety being markedly reduced even in the Lomaiviti Group and dramatically so by the time you reach the Laus. The bird life of Fiji thus belongs primarily to Fiji's forests, with which avian evolution was closely linked.

Terns are the dominant seabird here, and the traveler will also see petrel, including the rare MacGillivray's Fiji petrel, tropicbird, booby, and the occasional frigate bird.

Perhaps the most evident bird is the mynah, imported as an insect catcher from India. Its noisy, rapid-sequenced call, sounding like nothing so much as a high-pitched sneeze, is an almost constant accompaniment to life in Fiji.

From India also comes the mongoose, imported to control the rat population but responsible for the destruction of several native ground-nesting bird species. Indeed, almost all animal life comes from somewhere else. Goats, cattle, and horses have all established feral populations; goats, in particular, are numerous and constitute a threat to the environment. Rats, mice, and cats are proving almost as disastrous as the mongoose.

The flying fox, a bat, is Fiji's only native land mammal; two insectivorous and four fruit-bat species have been identified. Reptiles are more varied. Two endemic species of frogs live mostly in the rain forest and feed at night; they are rarely seen but are noteworthy for the suction disks on fingers and toes. Fiji's snakes include the venomous elapid, *bolo loa*, and the Pacific boa. There is a range of skinks and geckos, but one of the most interesting lizards is the banded iguana—normally emerald green, the male with blue cross stripes—which grows darker in color in the direct rays of the sun. The iguana is mostly tail, which propels it up the trunks of the trees in which it lives. What makes the banded iguana interesting, apart from its response to light, is that it is related to species found in South America and Madagascar—a Pacific conundrum in the heart of Oceania.

There are seven species of sea turtles in the world; four of them nest in Fiji's waters: the green, the hawksbill, the loggerhead, and the leatherback. From November to February, when the moon is full and the tide high, the female turtle moves laboriously up the beach to dig a hole and lay as many as a hundred eggs. She then proceeds to nest over the hole, protecting the eggs with her hind flippers. It is a serious violation of law to take or injure turtles or their eggs during this nesting period.

Fiji's waters are also outstanding for the many barrier reefs here. The Great Sea Reef, Astrolabe Reef, Rainbow Reef, and the Argo Reef in the Laus are among the most famous, but there are beautiful reefs off the so-called Coral Coast of southern Vanua Levu, all around nearby Beqa Island, and among the Mamanuca and Yasawa chains. The coral cracks and crevices around Fiji's islands are filled with a variety of marine life and with a variety of snorkelers and divers as well, there to explore the silence and beauty of the undersea world; outside the rainy season, when discharge from rivers may muddy the waters slightly, the visibility can be extraordinary.

As do the Samoans, Fijians celebrate the rising of the *balolo*, *Eunice viridis*, the sea worm considered a culinary delicacy. The balolo (*palolo* in Western Samoa) lives in the fissures of coral reefs but rises to the surface of the ocean twice a year to lay its eggs and die. Its fixed appearances take place in the third lunar quarter of October and November, when waiting Fijians scoop up the balolo by the millions. An hour after emerging, the sacs burst, the eggs spurt forth, and the propagating generation comes to an end.

# HISTORY

Some 3500 years ago, sea voyagers first congregated in the Fiji Islands. Archaeologists are agreed that these voyagers had earlier occupied the chain of islands westward as far as Southeast Asia. A site in what is today Papua New Guinea's New Britain yields obsidian, the volcanic glass with which the voyagers probably fashioned tools for making pottery, and pottery shards dating to 1290 B.C. have been found in the sand dunes near Sigatoka on Viti Levu. The style of the pottery and some linguistic features show a link with finds from the Lapita site of New Caledonia. The sand dunes of Sigatoka, meanwhile, are thought to have resulted from deforestation and erosion caused by slash-and-burn cultivation that may date from 2000 B.C. A pattern of linkages may thus be drawn that seems to indicate a stepping-stone process of island discovery and connections among early settlements around Melanesia.

Yet many of the early voyagers either moved on from Fiji or bypassed it entirely to head further east, specifically to Tonga and Samoa in approximately 1300 and 1000 B.C., respectively. There they developed the ethnic group and culture that we today call Polynesian. In Samoa, which is at most a four-day sail from Fiji, the star-track route between the islands is remembered to this day. The double-hulled canoes of the Fijians made extensive interisland contact possible; they were highly prized by the Tongans in particular. From Fiji, Samoans and Tongans imported high-status males as consorts for women of high birth; this consciousness of status is particularly Polynesian.

The first confusion of Fijian history is thus this: it was discovered and first settled by Melanesian peoples who were in fact the forebears of today's Polynesians. The successor migrations—Lapita-ware potters and later peoples from Island Melanesia—gave the islands their Melanesian character. Migrations from Island Melanesia continued at least until the 12th century A.D. Evidence of hill forts, bolstered by the oral tradition, confirms that the interaction among communities was routinely hostile.

By the time the Europeans arrived, the peoples living in these islands had become distinctly Fijian. "The natives of Feejee," wrote Captain Cook in 1774, "are of a color that was a full shade darker than that of the Friendly Islands (Tonga) in general." Cook also saw "clubs and spears . . . carved in a very masterly manner; cloth beautifully checkered; variegated mats, earthen pots, and some other articles all of which had a cast of superiority in the execution." Clearly, the Fijians were materially richer than their one-time relatives and neighbors to the east.

In their political style, however, they closely resembled the Polynesians. Fijians defined status and authority by descent. Power was concentrated in the hands of a chief, *turaga*, living embodiment of the ancestor god, the *vu*, and therefore possessor of great soul. In assuming the chieftainship of his group, *vanua*, the turaga drained the yaqona cup and put on his armband of bark cloth, *masi*, eschewing that ranking by conspicuous display that is found in other Melanesian societies. The turaga ran a society in which functions were ascribed—craftsmen, fishermen, warriors, priests—and at the bottom of which were the *kaisi*, slaves, who, unlike the turaga, had no soul.

This was a male-dominated society, cannibalistic and given to practices that would strike the Europeans as hideously barbaric. When house posts had to be renewed, men were sacrificed so that their bodies might rest beneath the new posts. The *drua*, the 30-meter-long, double-hulled canoes, were launched over the living bodies of young girls. The chiefs held the power of life and death over all, and cannibalism was a major part of ceremonial occasions; the proper ritual greeting of a commoner to a chief was "Eat me!" The turaga offered corpses from outside the vanua to his people in exchange for the first fruits of the season and for wives. Those conquered in battle accepted vassalship by offering women of high rank and baskets of earth. Enemies were routinely cannibalized. A particularly hated enemy might be forced to watch his hand or nose eaten raw or cooked in front of him; sometimes, he was forced to taste a piece of his own flesh. Widows of chiefs were strangled so that they might accompany their husbands to the spirit world; the women's farewells are remembered today in *meke*, action songs (also: an evening of song and dance).

The turaga could lose his office if his vanua did not prosper. Moreover, the competition for leadership was constant, providing a chance to display *kaukauwa*, inner strength. The structure of chiefdoms was so complex that a state economy developed: each household's surplus above subsistence went to support it.

# EUROPEAN CONTACT

Dutch explorer Abel Tasman was the first European to sight Fiji, spotting islands near Taveuni in 1643. Cook was next; he sighted Vatoa in the Southern Laus, but could find no one with whom he could communicate. In 1789, following the mutiny on the *Bounty*, William Bligh sailed through the Fiji Islands from the southeast; in what is today Bligh Water, near the Yasawas, his open boat just managed to outrun a pair of drua. In 1791, the *Pandora*, looking for the *Bounty* mutineers, lay offshore the Southern Laus for some weeks and was hospitably received. For the most part, however, European ships, including the mission vessel *Duff*, showed little inclination to land in Fiji; the perils of its reefs and its reputation as the "cannibal isles" constituted what would today be called a major disincentive.

In 1804, one Oliver Slater, a survivor from the shipwrecked American schooner *Argo*, told a passing ship that sandalwood grew thickly in western Vanua Levu. A lively sandalwood trade lasted till 1814; the Fijians cut the wood for trade goods or European help in warfare, and the traders bartered it in China in return for tea to sell in Europe. After the sandalwood forests had been stripped, traders harvested *bêches de mer* in a trade that commenced in 1822. Firearms had come ashore with about 20 British and American beachcombers by 1810; these beachcombers were admired for their marksmanship, settled down for lives of adventure (sometimes short lives), married native women, and served as go-betweens for the traders. Their headquarters was Levuka, on the island of Ovalau; it would become Fiji's first capital.

The first missionaries arrived from Tonga in 1830—Tahitian converts sent by the London Missionary Society. The Methodists arrived in 1835; it was Methodist missionary David Cargill who developed the writing system. As elsewhere in the Pacific, the conversion of chieftains led to wholesale conversion by the mass of the populace.

Also as elsewhere in the Pacific, a preeminent chieftain used his conversion to Christianity to good effect in consolidating his power. Cakobau, of the island of Bau, the center of power for western Fiji, emerged as a major figure in the 1840s. By 1851, however, a revolt against his authority was having some success; Cakobau converted to Christianity and promptly secured the support of an American vessel and a Christian chief from Tonga. By 1855, he had solidified his control over western Fiji. In the Laus, however, another Christian from Tonga, Ma'afu, continued to wield influence. The Laus had seen significant back-migration of Tongans from the similar islands to the east and were by this time under Tongan political control.

British consul William T. Pritchard, fearing that the French and the Americans might take advantage of the unstable situation, convinced Cakobau to offer the islands to Britain in exchange for protection. Whitehall refused the offer, but the timing of the discussions, which began in 1858, lured to Fiji numerous Australian and New Zealand settlers eager to farm cotton for export to the Civil War–torn United States.

In 1871, Ma'afu swore allegiance to Cakobau, but fiscal crises and assorted other problems worked against stability, and more violence ensued. The British agreed to reexamine the situation, and, in 1874, they voted to annex the country. On October 10, 1874, Cakobau, Ma'afu, and eleven other chiefs signed a deed of cession, and Fiji became a British colony. Early in 1875, a measles epidemic wiped out one-fifth of the Fijian population.

Despite this bad start, the first governor of Fiji, Sir Arthur Gordon, sought to restore native confidence by transforming traditional structures to suit colonial rule. Fijian tradition, as it turned out, was uniquely well suited to adaptation. In the conversion to Christianity, not only had rituals of the old faith adapted to the new, but even the old Fijian gods were presumed to have become Christians. In a later era, colonial Fiji would manage to migrate into the modern world—and a multiethnic modern world at that—without losing tradition or control over tradition, relying instead on the adaptive capacity of traditional values and modes of behavior. Gordon confirmed the principle of native ownership of land. The chiefs remained in charge of the land and of traditional structures. They became, under British colonial rule, the representatives of the colonial government, collectors of government revenue instead of wielders of the life and death prerogative.

What would turn out to be Gordon's most striking move was originally an economic expedient. Fiji would build an economy based on sugarcane, Gordon decided, but blackbirding would not be tolerated. Moreover, native Fijians could not be required to work on European plantations. To provide labor, Gordon sanctioned the indenture of laborers from India; they began arriving in 1879, working as coolies in the fields owned and run as a near monopoly by Australia's Colonial Sugar Refining Company. Fijian history, and certainly Fijian political life, has since been dominated by the fact of the Indian presence; indeed, Fijian democracy may be said to be in large part a balancing act between native Fijians and Fijian Indians—an equilibrium maintained by ensuring that tensions are just taut enough and not one whit tauter. Indians now outnumber native

Fijians, and while other Pacific islanders, Europeans, Chinese, and people of mixed descent, also have sizeable populations here, it is the interaction between the two majority peoples that sweeps all before it.

# THE TWENTIETH CENTURY

In 1904, the first Fijian chiefs, along with the first resident Europeans, were admitted into the Legislative Council, an advisory body to the governor. In 1926, an Indian was appointed to the council, and in 1928, three elective council seats were allotted to the Indian community. Still, power lay with the colonial regime.

Gordon's decree that native land could never be sold did not prohibit its being leased. After 1920, when indenture ceased, many Indians became tenant farmers on land owned by Fijians. Despite a complicated system of ownership and tenure, a pattern was set: the Indians worked the lands, the Fijians received rents, and the Europeans ran the processing plants and controlled trade.

During World War II, many Fijians distinguished themselves, particularly in the Solomon Islands campaign. So adept were they at jungle warfare that it was said a Fijian was not listed as "missing in action" but as "not yet arrived." The postwar climate of anticolonialism did not bypass Fiji, but here the issue was complicated by ethnic divisions. The nation's major political parties were born in this period: the Alliance Party, multiracial but predominantly Fijian, headed by Ratu Sir Kamisese Mara, and the National Federation Party, also multiracial but dominated by Indians. In 1970, Fiji gained her independence from Britain with the Alliance Party and Mara in power; the first Fijian governor general was Ratu Sir George Cakobau, great-grandson of the chief who had ceded the nation to Queen Victoria.

In 1973, the new government bought out the shares of the Colonial Sugar Refining Company and formed the Fiji Sugar Corporation, which holds a monopoly over all sugar milling; a separate government marketing organization sells the milled product overseas. A quarter of Fiji's population is directly employed in the sugarcane industry, and many more depend indirectly on it. Fiji has also been a world leader in research on sugarcane.

Before the 1987 coup and the redrafting of a constitution, Fiji's two major political parties, divided along ethnic lines, were nevertheless agreed on a democratic and free-market approach. The Federation Party, however, held that the constitution impeded the full representation of Indian interests; despite a parliamentary system, certain privileges were reserved to the Fijian community. Land tenure and local government were two such areas protected by the constitution, while legislation ensuring a preference system for Fijians at the university level was an arena of major controversy. Moreover, parliamentary seats were apportioned according to ethnic quotas that did not necessarily reflect the population. The House of Representatives contained 22 Fijians, 22 Indians, and 8 other General Electors. Voters registered on two lists, the Communal Roll and the National Roll. On the Communal Roll, the voter selected one candidate from his ethnic group to fill 12 Fijian, 12 Indian, and three General Elector seats. On the National Roll, the voter chose one candidate in each of the three categories to fill the remaining seats. The Senate, largely advisory, consisted of 8 members nominated by the Fijian Great Council of Chiefs, 7 by the prime minister, 6 by the leader of the opposition, and one by the Council of Rotuma. (Rotuma, mostly Polynesian, was considered a separate community with special constitutional protection. Similar protection was afforded to immigrants from Banaba, in Kiribati, who live on Rabi Island.)

Despite these complexities, or perhaps because of them, Fiji had thus far avoided ethnic violence, and while there had yet to be a coalition of interests between the two major parties, the political life of this democracy seemed lively, if highly charged. In recent years, the issue was complicated by the emergence of the Fijian Nationalist Party, whose slogan is "Fiji for the Fijians." Despite condemnation from the Alliance Party, the FNP managed to garner sizeable support. Third- and fourth-generation Indians on Fiji, who have never been to India and consider themselves Pacific people, sometimes voiced fears of "another Uganda."

## The 1987 Coup d'Etat

This was the situation in 1987 when elections for the first time produced a government dominated by the Indian community. Ratu Sir Kamisese Mara and his Alliance Party, *the* government of Fiji since independence, were defeated by a coalition of the Federation and Labor parties. Timoci Bavadra, a Fijian, became Prime Minister of the new government, but 19 of the 28 members of the government were Indians, well positioned now to effect some of the changes long sought by the Indian community.

On May 14, 1987, Lieutenant Colonel Sitiveni Rabuka, third ranking officer in the Fijian Army, and some 10 soldiers wearing gas masks and brandishing pistols walked into the House of Representatives. Moving quickly to the government side of the chamber, Rabuka asked Bavadra, his cabinet, and other coalition members to follow one of the soldiers outside, where the officials were loaded into army trucks and taken to an unknown destination—effectively under arrest. Later that day, Rabuka named a 15-member council of ministers, including Mara as Foreign Minister, and announced that a new constitution would be drafted.

In the days that followed, strikes by the Indian community and ethnic confrontations in major cities and towns on Viti Levu frequently resulted in violence, while several world powers—Australia, New Zealand, and Great Britain—cautiously denounced the coup. Fiji's Governor General, Ratu Sir Penaia Ganilau, as the representative of Queen Elizabeth II, formally Fiji's head of state, announced that he had assumed power, while Rabuka, quickly promoted to brigadier, claimed he was in charge and promised elections within six months.

The press, after several days of constraint immediately following the takeover, reported that wealthy Indians were lining up at the passport office, presumably planning to emigrate. Qantas, Air New Zealand, and Continental suspended flights to Fiji, although tourists still managed to trickle in via Air Pacific—and found plenty of room in Fiji's hotels when they arrived. Australian longshoremen refused to load goods onto Fiji-bound vessels, and the nation's essential sugar crop remained unharvested in the wake of a strike by Indian cane-cutters.

Yet the flurry of panic and defiance faded in time. A month after the coup, the people of Fiji and the governments of neighboring countries seemed to have accommodated to the fact of the coup; the British queen's refusal to meet with Bavadra, who had gone to London for just that purpose, was widely seen as Commonwealth acceptance of Rabuka and the caretaker government. From the Coral Coast, a Fijian told the author that it was "hard to tell who was running things" but that life was back to normal. At the luxury Fijian Hotel, delegates from all over the South Pacific gathered for the annual Pacific Tourism Conference.

As this book goes to press, it is not clear what kind of government will emerge from the 1987 coup. Of Rabuka himself, only a few facts are known. A graduate of Sandhurst, Britain's premier military academy, and a decorated veteran of Middle East peacekeeping activities, Rabuka is seen as a quintessential military man. He is also a lay preacher and is said to be quiet, contemplative, and extremely courteous in his dealings with people. What does seem clear is that the governance of Fiji, whatever form it takes, faces two overwhelming facts. One is political: the profound resistance of the Fijian community to even the thought of Indian political power. There is nothing new in this. As far back as 1933, the Council of Chiefs articulated an uneasiness that was already mature when it resolved that "the immigrant Indian population should neither directly nor indirectly have any part in the control or direction of matters affecting the control of the Fijian race." The second fact is economic. With 70 percent of the economy in the hands of the Indian community, it is simply not realistic to consider the expulsion of Indians or to make life so difficult for the Indian community that Indians will either emigrate en masse or be stymied in their economic activities. A Fijian traveling in the U.S. at the time of the coup put it this way: "We, Fijians and Indians, have developed this country hand in hand. It is impossible to think of Fiji without Indians."

The coup d'etat in Fiji besmirched the Pacific's clean record on military takeovers and certainly struck a blow against democracy in this, the crossroads of Oceania. It remains to be seen whether the coup was democracy's death knell or just a hitch in the process of figuring out how this multiethnic nation can be made to work.

# THE PEOPLES OF FIJI TODAY

Fiji is less a melting pot than a patchwork of distinct ethnic groups, a collective of cultures, each of which plays out its life in organizations and associations that tend to be ethnically defined. It is a matter of great interest to the traveler to see this disparate society in action.

The term Fijian properly refers only to a member of the Fijian ethnic community. Today just slightly less than 50 percent of the population, indigenous Fijians are basically Melanesian with an admixture of Polynesian physical and cultural characteristics. Among many local variants of the Fijian dialect—Yasawan islanders and Lau islanders are mutually unintelligible—the eastern dialect of Bau, the language into which the Bible was translated, is the official language. The people, like the languages, fall into eastern and western groupings, with easterners particularly involved in government.

The Fijians still consider themselves as belonging to a *yasuva*, a descent group from a common ancestor, further divided into clans called *matagali*. These latter became the basic landowning units during colonial times and remain so today, holding more than 80 percent of unalienated land. Particularly on the outliers, Fijians live in villages along the coast or rivers; they work the communal land, but an individual is assigned his own plot. Many still live in the thatched *bures* that are fast being replaced, hurricane after hurricane, by homes of corrugated tin paneling. In the economy, Fijians make up the great majority of service workers and agricultural workers; they are about a third of industrial workers and clerical staff, while nearly 40 percent of the technical, professional, and managerial work force is Fijian.

Fijian life continues to be rich in ceremony, preserving many ancient customs. One of the most important is yaqona drinking. The ritual ceremony is performed with the utmost gravity and according to elaborate strictures. But social kava drinking is a way of life, and the traveler who visits a Fijian village or home will undoubtedly be invited to participate. If you do, it is customary to present some yaqona root—the act of giving it is called *sevusevu*—usually to the chief or, by placing it on a mat, to the group as a whole. When it's your turn to drink the yaqona, you must *cobo*, clap once with cupped hands, take the cup (*bilo*) in both hands, and drain it in one chug. When you have done so, return the bilo to the person who gave it to you, and cobo three more times. It's a good idea to stock up on yaqona root on Viti Levu; it may be difficult to find elsewhere, and as the Fijians are outstandingly hospitable, you may spend a lot of time drinking yaqona and offering sevusevu.

Indeed, the exchange of gifts, *solevu*, is an important feature of Fijian tradition, and the traveler hoping to experience village life is advised to stock up on useful items. Some travelers have become embroiled in "solevu wars" of a most rewarding kind: villagers have loaded them down with tapa—here called *masi*—carvings, fans, shell necklaces, and the like, and the travelers have been hard pressed to come up with reciprocal treasures. One mechanically adept traveler went around fixing things for several days; another presented instant Polaroid pictures of everyone in the village. But you may want to be well supplied with such standbys as combs, knickknacks, T-shirts, and cloth for *sulus*, the Fijian wrap skirt.

One of the most important traditional items for solevu was the *tambua*, the tooth of the sperm whale, originally exchanged at war or peace conferences and at alliance meetings. Today, tambua still features as a symbolic welcome during chiefly yaqona ceremonies, or as a prelude to contemporary business meetings or official functions. The tambua is also given when marriages are arranged, as a way of requesting a favor, in settling disputes. This is a prized cultural item; it may not be exported without the Prime Minister's permission, while the Endangered Species Act prohibits its import into many countries, including the U.S.

Dance also remains an important ceremony. Wesleyan missionary Thomas Williams, who left an account of Fiji first published in 1858, wrote that "the dance is undoubtedly the most popular pastime of Fiji." Williams added that "the song by which it is regulated is often very dull, and the movements slow and heavy. . . . The dancers are gaily dressed; and as all bear clubs or spears, and perform a series of marchings, steppings, halts, and varied evolutions, a stranger would rather suppose them to be engaged in a military review than a dance. As the performance approaches the close, the speed quickens, and the actions steadily increase in violence, accompanied by a heavy tramping on the ground . . . " (Thomas Williams, *Fiji and the Fijians: The Islands and Their Inhabitants*, 1858; reprinted 1985 by Fiji Museum, Suva, Fiji). Not all Fijian dance is "military," though the war dance, in which the frightening Fijian club is brandished, can be very aggressive indeed. Men and women together perform the *vakamalolo*, Fiji's version of the sitting dance. The *seasea* is danced by women flourishing fans. The *taralala*, in which the traveler may be asked to join, is a gentle, side-to-side shuffle. If you attend an evening of Fijian music and dance, a *meke*, often part of a feast or *magiti*, be aware that the *isa lea* song is the "Good Night, Ladies" of Fiji and generally signals the end of the festivities.

Another ancient custom the traveler may have a chance to see is the fish drive. A whole village may participate in this, the people grouping themselves in a wide circle defined by a ring of connected liana vines. They shout, sing, and beat the water with poles, slowly contracting the ring as the tide comes in until the fish are directed landward into a net or stone weir.

Spearing stingrays is another time-honored tradition—extremely exciting to watch, if you get the chance. Canoes line up along the reef, and if a stingray is spotted, the chase is on, the canoes paddling forward at ferocious speed until close enough for the spearman to shoot. The lethal-looking stingray is a favorite food.

Finally, there is the Fijian custom of firewalking. Legend has it that Tui-na-iviga-lita, a warrior of the Sawau tribe on Beqa Island, promised a famous storyteller that he would give him whatever he caught while fishing. What he caught was an eel that transformed itself into a spirit god and begged for freedom, offering in exchange the gift of immunity to fire. Tui's descendants are the *bete*, the priests of this rite, called *vilavilairevo*—jumping into the oven. Only the Sawau may perform the rite, today mostly at hotels along Viti Levu's Coral Coast. Firewalkers theoretically have no contact with either women or coconuts for two weeks before a performance. An enormous log fire heats the stones in a pit; the wood is removed, and the firewalkers, chanting ritual formulas, walk barefoot over the stones.

In an extraordinary coincidence, the majority people of Fiji, the Indians, also practice a firewalking ritual, though Indian firewalking is the culmination of a ten-day Hindu religious festival—an act of purification. The practice comes from the south of India, origin of many of Fiji's Indians; most others are northerners, Punjabis, and Gujuratis, although these distinctions and many others that remain important in India have dimmed in Fiji. Indeed, the Indians of Fiji may be said to be more homogeneous and unified than the Indians of India. Caste distinctions have lost importance; religious hostilities are virtually nonexistent; even language differences have been subsumed in the general acceptance of Hindi.

The Indian community dominates the sugarcane industry and makes up the great majority of industrial and transportation workers, most managers and administrators, almost half of all professional and technical workers, over two-thirds of sales personnel, and more than one-half of high-level civil servants in the Fiji Public Service, the police force, and the Ministries of Health and Education. More than two-thirds of students who qualify for university studies in Fiji are Indian, and the quota restrictions on Indian admissions are a source of serious resentment by the Indian community.

The Europeans and part Europeans of Fiji are primarily descendants of Australian and New Zealand settlers. Though once plantation owners, they are today active in commerce, industry, and government; the European presence is overrepresented in the professions and management. The part European community is on the increase; many now refer to themselves formally as Part Fijians.

Rotumans are a small, protected Polynesian minority. The people of Banaba in Kiribati and some Tuvaluans purchased islands of Fiji to replace their home islands after Britain compelled sale of the land for phosphate exploitation; these people remain in Fiji under special autonomy. Solomon islanders, Tongans, Samoans, and other Pacific islanders further confirm the crossroads aspect of Fiji. The Chinese, who first arrived in Fiji in the 1870s, were once numerous and economically powerful; many emigrated to Canada in the 1960s.

With this range of nationalities comes a range of religious affiliations. Most Fijians are Methodist, while Roman Catholicism claims not quite 20 percent of the total Christian population. Eighty percent of the Indians are Hindu, and most Muslim Indians are Sunni Muslims.

## THE TRAVELER IN FIJI

Fiji is the most populous of the Pacific nations. It is, after phosphate-rich Nauru, the most economically advanced. It seeks to be a player on the world stage, participating enthusiastically in such international organizations as the British Commonwealth, the South Pacific Forum (whose secretariat is located in Fiji), the South Pacific Conference, the European Economic Community via the Lome Convention, and the United Nations, particularly its peace-keeping force, in which the Royal Fiji Military Forces have played a major role. The main campus of the University of the South Pacific is here, and Fiji is the most important communications center—and arguably the key intellectual center—of Oceania, vying with Papua New Guinea for leadership of the Pacific's island nations.

It is also, after Guam, the most frequented island group in the Pacific. As is the case with Guam, much of this traffic, by business people and recreational travelers, is due to Fiji's role as a gateway and transfer point to other parts of the Pacific. As it was once a stop-off and refueling station along the route of Polynesian migration, it is today a stop-off and refueling station along the main route between Australia and North America. If not exactly the geographical center of the Pacific, it is the region's *logical* center and its most vitally cosmopolitan hub.

One effect of this is a highly developed tourist infrastructure. Fiji gets visitors from all over the world, but it is in Australia's backyard, and for vacationers from Australia's populous east coast, at least, it serves as a frequent playground. Accommodations in the most frequented tourist areas range from citylike international resorts to bathroom-down-the-hall hotels and serve a range of purses. Foster's Lager is as prevalent as Fiji Bitter, the excellent local beer. Well-staffed tourist offices well-stocked with brochures and the hotels themselves offer an array of tour packages, from one-day jaunts upward. There are cruise ships and tourist launches, air-conditioned buses and glass-bottomed boats, staged magitis and visits to native villages, even a "leisure-oriented satellite village" at Pacific Harbor on the Coral Coast.

Recreational activities abound. Fiji is a diving/snorkeling paradise. Fishing goes on year-round. Cricket and rugby are passions here; lawn bowling is also a major sport. Shopping—everything is duty-free—is a favorite pastime. Discos, bars, and nightclubs, both in the hotels and in the major towns, make for a lively night life in those areas frequented by tourists.

At most hotels, the traveler can find undistinguished continental cuisine. Island fare includes the ubiquitous raw fish marinated in coconut milk, here called *kokoda;* the very common *dalo,* a taro root concoction; and a variety of fish, pork, and sweet potatoes baked in the *lovo,* earth oven. If you've been traveling for a while, you can satisfy a possible yearning for spicy taste by eating Indian food—curries, dal, and the like. The *roti* is the prevalent Indian fast food.

Because tourism is so advanced in Fiji, the best way to approach travel here is, first, to know what the main tourist areas are, how to get there, and what they're like, whether you choose to visit or avoid them; and, second, to have some idea also of the less traveled reaches of these islands. Not surprisingly, the main tourist destinations are easily accessible and well supplied with tourist facilities of every kind; the less traveled areas will require more work.

# FIJI MOST FREQUENTED

The Nadi-to-Suva route along the southern coast of Viti Levu, the waters and islands off this coast, the offshore resort islands and the Yasawas to the west of Viti Levu, and two high-priced resort islands to the east of Viti Levu constitute the basic "tourist's Fiji."

## Nadi to Suva

Fiji's international airport is seven kilometers from the town of Nadi, which is little more than a tourist arrival/departure point and duty-free shopping mall. In serving these arrivals and departures, Nadi is also the embarkation point for numerous cruises, and it is a major bus depot. Buses go everywhere on Viti Levu—high up valleys, deep into the interior, and all around the coast—and they are the best way to travel the island. The traveler has his choice among a competitive range of buses, from air-conditioned vehicles that stop at hotels to expresses that bypass small villages and towns to the local public buses that stop almost everywhere and that afford, through their open windows, an excellent experience of the sights, sounds, and smells of Viti Levu.

The fast, well-paved Queens Road between Nadi and Suva is the busiest tourist area of Viti Levu. It rides the Coral Coast, the 50-kilometer, hotel-lined stretch more or less from Sigatoka to Suva. The express bus from the station near Nadi's market to Suva takes five hours, the local bus takes eight. Arm yourself with a good road map of the island, available in Nadi, Suva, or most other good-sized towns. (The *recommended* ride, if time is an issue and you can only choose one, is the longer but more interesting north coast ride along the Kings Road between Nadi and Suva; see below.)

From Nadi, you can hop off at Momi to see the concrete bunkers and huge naval guns that guarded the bay from a World War II invasion force that never came, or, alternatively, take the route that eschews the coast and rides the Nausori Highlands, a verdant plateau broken by outcrops of black lava. Another possible stop, some 35 kilometers south of Nadi, is Natadola Beach. Unless you're a very strong swimmer, however, stick to lying or walking on it; its strong undertow has claimed several lives.

Sigatoka, the first stop of consequence, is a small, riverside community to which hotel guests are routinely bused for duty-free shopping and for trips up the Sigatoka River in launches. The river trips stop at villages where you can buy the Fijian pottery for which Sigatoka is famous but which is not available in Sigatoka itself. The trips also provide a look at life along the river and *on* it; locals travel it in *bilibilis*—bamboo river rafts. Just west of Sigatoka, at Kulukulu, a major surfing area, are the extraordinary, Saharalike sand dunes that extend for several kilometers between highway and sea. Climb to the top—it can be windy up there—and if you find any pottery shards in the sand, remember that they are protected by law and should be left where they are.

The Coral Coast begins in earnest at Korotogo. Villages of corrugated tin houses, often with small shops or roadside stands selling fresh fruit, hug the highway, while seaward are the hotels that lord it over the coral beaches—not as fine here as on the offshore islands. At Korolevu, guests from nearby hotels often set off inland on horseback, bound for hot springs and the beautiful Savu-na-matelaya Waterfalls. (You can also walk in from Biausevu Village—about a kilometer.) Pacific Harbor, a major landmark along the coast, is a combination resort, villa-on-the-golf-green community, visitor attraction, and cultural center and marketplace. It is a world unto itself. Some eight kilometers to the east is Navua, a sugarcane town from which numerous river trips take travelers to native villages for Fijian lunch, kava ceremony, and shopping. The remainder of the ride to Suva may be broken by a stop at Orchid Island, where a garden and recreated village constitute another—and very good—cultural center of traditional Fijian life.

## Suva

Strangely enough, Suva, the intriguing capital city of Fiji, is typically seen but briefly by most tourists. This is a shame, for Suva is something else again—not quite the overgrown village that many Pacific capitals still feel like, not quite India, though the prevalence of Indian merchants urging you to buy is extremely reminiscent, not quite like a European town that happens to be located on an island of sunshine and palms. It is not quite any of these; it is rather more than all of them.

Sitting on a point that juts into Laucala Bay, Suva is a busy port town, and Kings Wharf is routinely jammed with ships, goods, and passengers coming and going—many of them justifiably shopping like mad at the Curio and Handicraft Center along the water. The market and bus station nearby are lively with commuters and shoppers. Downtown Suva is inland from the wharf and along Victoria Parade around Sakuna Park and the triangle formed by Cumming, Thomsen, and Renwick streets. To the north are Burns Philp and Morris Hedstrom and, further east, a great clutch of Indian shops and eateries. To the south are the government buildings, and across from them is the Grand Pacific Hotel, in whose elegant public rooms you can easily imagine finding either Somerset Maugham or Sydney Greenstreet—or both. The government buildings stand on the edge of Albert Park, where aviator Kingsford Smith landed on his epic trans-Pacific flight in 1928; to the south are the Thurston Botanical Gardens, themselves worth a look, and the Fiji Museum.

The museum is a must-see stop for the traveler. Small but extremely well conceived, it takes you from prehistory, with stunning pottery shards, through the coming of the islanders, early culture, European contact, warfare and consolidation and the arrival of the Indians to independence. The centerpiece of exhibits, in the main hall, is one of the last double-hulled canoes ever constructed.

Suva is an excellent place for serious students of the Pacific to stock up on literature not readily available at home. The museum has a good, if small, collection of books, but try also Desai Bookstore—where you can find good airplane reading as well—and the bookstore of the University of the South Pacific, a major center for Pacific scholarship.

The other "must" stop for the traveler in Suva is the Fiji visitors bureau, right in the heart of downtown, at the triangle. Here (or at your hotel), you can arrange a variety of package tours: trips up the Rewa River by launch, visits to native villages, cruises of any duration, round-the-island tours, stays on the offshore islands. One worthwhile excursion from Suva is to Colo-i-Suva, a forest park where the traveler can see much of Fiji's tropical flora. Take the Sawani bus from the station; in only 11 kilometers, you're out of town in more ways than one—the place is breathtaking.

Suva is a major center for dive trips: right out along the Coral Coast; to Beqa Island, whose 80-mile-long barrier reef has been called one of the top five dive spots in the world; to the Astrolabe Reef of Kadavu, with its exceptional visibility; and to Suva's own outer reef, with its coral plateau on which foundered the three-masted barque *Woodburn.*

## Offshore

East and west of Viti Levu are offshore resort islands that make no claims to being anything but that: resorts. Here are, for real, the soft-sand beaches, swaying palm trees, gentle tradewinds, clear, warm, azure waters, and powerful tropical sunshine of every Pacific fantasy. Each resort island has its own style and loyal clientele, and a range of budgets is catered to.

East of Viti Levu is the four-acre speck known as Toberua, a luxury resort that has been rated one of the twelve best in the world by an organization that searches the globe for "intimate hostelries in a uniquely secluded environment, in private settings of extraordinary natural beauty." It is all definitely world class—fresh fruit juice here means the juice has literally just been squeezed from a freshly picked fruit; it is definitely tranquil—there is neither tennis court nor golf course. Water sports are available, however, and the cuisine and service are excellent. But you pay dearly for the Toberua experience.

Also to the east is Naigani, a lush island with lovely beaches and a single Fijian village. The resort here, Islanders Village, can also be pricey, but it offers budget accommodations as well.

West of Viti Levu, the Mamanuca Group offers a variety of resort islands. Castaway is known for its good food and the counteracting "fitness" facilities. Beachcomber is famous for having a young crowd, dormitory-style living, and cheap prices. Turtle Island is for the carriage crowd—couples without children only. Mana Island is another luxury spot. On Malolo Lailai Island are Plantation Island, offering miles of golden sand, Dick's Place, offering simplicity and excellent prices, the moderate Musket Cove, and the luxury Club Naitasi. In fact, all these resorts work hard to keep up with one another, so that virtually all offer water sports, fishing trips, good restaurants and bars.

Most of the resorts maintain their own passenger launches; these may collect guests from Lautoka's Queen's Wharf or from one or another of the hotels near Nadi. There are also regularly scheduled brief flights on Sunflower Airlines. Day-trippers are most welcome, and many of the Coral Coast hotels and Viti Levu travel agents run package tours on passenger cruise ships. Your hotel or the Fiji visitors bureau can make any arrangements, but keep in mind that, especially during Australia's winter—the Northern Hemisphere's summer—both hostelries and transportation can be heavily booked.

Blue Lagoon and Seafarer are the major cruise lines for tours among the Yasawas and Mamanucas, but it is also possible to take village boats from Lautoka's Queen's Wharf and settle in here, if you have the time. The passenger cruises, lasting from three days to a week, are reasonably priced; to the author's knowledge, no one who has ever taken one has regretted it. One of the more interesting is the three-day cruise on the *Tui Tai*, a 140-foot, three-masted steel schooner out of Lautoka.

To stay on an island in the Yasawa Group—Waya and Tavewa have guesthouse-type accommodations—you will need to take most of your own food and plenty of yaqona root for gifts. For Waya (and the other Yasawas), you theoretically need a permit from the district officer of the Department of Agriculture in Lautoka, and to obtain such a permit, you need a letter of invitation from the village. One way to do this is to write ahead to: Turaga-ni-koro (village chief), Village Name (pick one off the map), Yasawa Group, Fiji Islands—and wait for a reply. Another possibility is to wander the Lautoka market, particularly on Friday, in search of a boat captain heading that way or an out-islander willing to invite you. Possibly the best way is to check with the Fiji visitors bureau—they may be able to "arrange" an invitation—well worth it. For Tavewa, in any event, no invitation is necessary: it is freehold land and not subject to the same bureaucracy.

# THE OTHER FIJI

Viti Levu, in many respects unexplored by the tourist, offers some wonderful opportunities for the adventure traveler. The best way to begin exploration of Viti Levu is by the Suva-Nadi bus along the often dusty Kings Road. Local buses take nine hours from Suva to Lautoka alone; the Sunbeam express runs six times a day from Suva to Lautoka and takes six hours. Do it in two days if you have time, stopping for the night at Rakiraki on the north coast. The Kings Road trip is far more interesting and impressive than the rather busy jaunt along Queens Road; if you only have time for one *or* the other, this is definitely the one.

## Suva to Nadi

Viti Levu has four basic kinds of terrain—plateau, mountain, upland, and coastal—and the trip around Kings Road shows the traveler all of them. Out of Suva, the ride winds north on unpaved road heading inland and upward around some serious hairpin curves through undulating coastal hills and upland heavily dissected by waterways. Looking toward the center of the island, the traveler can see the Nadrau Plateau, rising some 900 to 1000 meters above sea level and covering about 130 square kilometers of dense and marshy forest. Along the route, the traveler passes through lovely villages, where woven thatch and bamboo houses have been constructed with great skill, often alternating dark and light thatch in a checkered pattern. Most roofs are pitched and of corrugated tin; many are woven and flat; some are spectacularly thatched and sharply pitched. The landscape is unbelievably green—well, not so unbelievably given the amount of rainfall here to windward. The traveler will see bamboo, chestnut, banana, coconut, lush shrub vegetation, and, for color, bright pink water lilies on rivers and ponds, wild orchids along the roadside, and the omnipresent hibiscus and frangipani.

In the distance loom the two long mountain ranges that run north and south of the plateau, showing peaks that will look mighty high to the traveler who has had a steady diet of flat atolls. Indeed, Mount Tomaniivi (Victoria), at 1424 meters the highest point in Fiji, will be clearly evident—on a clear day.

The northeastern corner of Viti Levu, where rice is grown, shows off the drama of rugged cliff faces, volcanic pinnacles, exciting lava outcrops. The sites of numerous fortified villages are to be found atop these heights, to which Fijian tradition quite naturally ascribes spiritual importance.

Achieving the north coast and turning westward, the road abruptly departs the rain forests of windward and suddenly plants the traveler in what might be the foothills of the Rockies or northern California. It looks like ranch land—low hills yellow with dried grass that waves in the breeze like wheat, a flat, sere plain where cattle ought to be grazing. Cattle *are* grazing here, in the cattle lands of a major ranch, the Yaqara Pastoral Company. But also, everywhere you look, is sugarcane—and the narrow-gauge railway used to cart if off. Passengers can ride the train—free, and just for the asking.

At towns along the north coast, the bus pulls into the market-place area. Strikingly handsome Fijians are selling produce in the market, while Indians man the shops that line the square. Rakiraki is one such town, and though its real name is Vaileka, everyone calls it Rakiraki. It was the haunt of Degei, the spirit leader who first populated the country. Not far from the town center is the tomb of Udre Udre, a chieftain reputed to have eaten a thousand of his people.

The Nakauvadra mountain range towers over the highway here, but the sea is never out of sight, and the villages filled with *bures* (thatched houses) are picturesque. At Tavua, a market town with a delightful colonial-style pub, is the turnoff for Monasavu and the interior. Here also is the road to Vatukoula and the Emperor Gold Mine, the last of three major strikes discovered in 1934. Back along the coast, the road continues through sugarcane and more sugar-cane—the town of Ba, sitting right in the middle, is a delightful community that exists to serve farming and farmers.

Lautoka is Fiji's second city, home of the country's biggest sugar refining mill and of a modern wharf that services the industry and transports tourists to offshore islands. Heading down to Nadi—a drive of less than an hour—you pass through the Sambeto mountain range, among whose crags the traveler may catch a glimpse of feral goats. On the sea side of the road is a huge pine forest, part of the national trust administered by the Fiji Pine Commission in an attempt to create a timber industry. Inland, in the fertile Sambeto River Valley, tobacco is grown. The country surrounding Nadi itself is all fertile delta and, along numerous back roads, small subsistence villages whose populations have evidently learned to live with the roar of 747s overhead.

## Some Wilderness Adventures

"Wilderness" in Viti Levu primarily translates as inland. While trekking here is mostly along a track that 4×4s can negotiate, the numerous stream crossings can make walking across Viti Levu or along the Sigatoka Valley extremely difficult, if not downright impossible after a heavy rain. Viti Levu also has gorges and caves to explore, and waterways that provide brown-water canoeing and whitewater rafting possibilities.

There are two adventure travel outfitters serving Fiji: Wilderness Adventures (P.O. Box 1389, Suva, tel. 313–616) and Fiji Outback Adventure Tours (c/o Sun Tours Limited, P.O. Box 9403, Nadi Airport, tel. 71266, 72723, 72268; in Suva, tel. 312–300). Both run expeditions on Viti Levu and some outliers.

In addition, the Rucksack Club (P.O. Box 2394, Government Buildings, Suva) meets on the second Wednesday of each month in Veiuto Primary School, Suva, where the next jaunt is planned. One of the club's favorite excursions is to Waiqa Gorge, near Naitauvoli Village on the Monasavu Road. Another, usually an overnight trip, goes to Sovi Gorge near Nabukaluka Village.

In the often thick bush of Viti Levu, passing through villages where tradition is still strong, the traveler may indeed feel more comfortable going with outfitters or with a group of people who know the ropes. But you can, of course, strike out on your own. For two of the finest adventure experiences here—the climb up Mount Tomaniivi and the Sigatoka River trek—your first stop should be the Forestry Department at Suva or Lautoka, where you can arrange to stay at the Nadarivatu forestry station on the cross-island road from Tavua. Nadarivatu is the starting point for the climb up Fiji's highest peak— from the forestry station, hitch a ride to Navai, where you can hire a guide, if you like, for the five-hour round trip. The hike from Nadarivatu to Korolevu on the Sigatoka River takes about three days, with nights spent in villages—bring yaqona root and gifts.

You can also explore upward from Sigatoka to Ba or Nadi in this way, following the river—not always easy—or road, until you connect with the tracks east or north to the coast. The valley boasts numerous villages, truly unspoiled; caves that the locals will happily guide you to; ancient temple mounds; and much lush cultivated land.

A wonderful one-day excursion out of Suva takes the traveler to Namosi. Take the Tebara Transport bus in the morning for an afternoon return, or plan to stay overnight as a villager's guest. Or hitch—and be prepared to pay your driver something—along the Waindina River route. Namosi offers spectacularly beautiful scenery—in particular, views of the Korobasabasaga Mountains, called by Rupert Brooke the "Gateway to Hell" and often referred to as "the dragon's teeth."

Inland Viti Levu, whether you go with a group, hire a guide, or just head for a dirt track and start walking, is well worth some exploration.

## Ovalau

Levuka, once the capital of Fiji, looks like a movie-set rendering of a colonial Pacific town. Once so rip-roaring that the *Fiji Times* editorialized about the need to "go about with revolvers" and warned against the "drink-maddened ruffians" who prowled the beaches, Levuka is today a rather sleepy, decidedly *former* capital; hemmed in between sea and hills, it simply couldn't grow, so the action moved to Suva, turning Levuka into a madly picturesque, history-filled traveler's destination.

North and south of the town, the island of Ovalau is easy to explore; happily, it offers little in the way of activity.

Reach Ovalau from Suva's Nausori Airport on Fiji Air or by ferry. Patterson Brothers, which has been plying these waters for years, runs a daily ferry from Natovi Wharf—67 kilometers north of Suva—with connecting bus service from Lautoka or Suva. The *Princess Ashika* leaves regularly from Suva.

From Ovalau, sporadic village boats leave for other Lomaiviti Islands. There are also flights and ships to Koro and Ngau from Viti Levu, though on an irregular basis. Koro is a lush, mountainous island, full of villages where the traveler may ask to stay. Turtle calling is practiced here, often for the cruise ships, and Koro claims to have the best yaqona in Fiji. Ngau is Fiji's fifth largest island and boasts a barrier reef on the west coast that has created a spacious lagoon.

## Vanua Levu

Less regularly shaped than Viti Levu, with lower mountains, lower plains, and smaller rivers, Vanua Levu—"Great Land"—is only half the size of its neighbor to the south. Few tourists come here, and it remains relatively unspoiled, with villages all around the coast that preserve traditional Fijian life, one lively and one sleepy town, and lots of sugarcane and coconut. It cries out for exploration.

Labasa is the lively town, a sugarcane milling center set among the sugarcane fields of the north. Just southeast in the town of Wasavula, accessible on the Nakoroutari bus, are parallel stone platforms bearing large monoliths—an archaeological site of some interest to the traveler, though most locals can tell you little about it, and the site itself is not easy to find.

Labasa is effectively an Indian town, and it is a market town, so it offers an adequate number of reasonably priced hostelries. So does Savusavu, the sleepy but scenic small town in the south. If you plan to spend a few days, do so at the Namale Plantation—book in advance!—a working coconut plantation–cum–beach resort that is a real Pacific find.

Between north and south is the mountain tableland and, in the lower areas, the plantations and tropical vegetation. East from Savusavu, the so-called Hibiscus Highway travels to Karoko via Buca Bay, where there is excellent swimming and snorkeling. Along the highway, just offshore, is the tiny limestone island of Naweni, where large red prawns inhabit a saltwater crescent and are called up by the villagers, who chant to the spirit Urumbuta. At low tide, you can walk to Naweni, but bring a present for the chief. Ask to see the weather stone on the beach. Further east along the Hibiscus Highway, near the village of Ndakunimba, ask to see the petroglyphs that look like an ancient script, as yet undeciphered.

## Taveuni

Fiji's third largest island, Taveuni is called the "garden island." Look here for the tagimaucia flower, found only on the shores of a small crater lake on the mountain behind Waiyevo. Something like a fuchsia, the tagimaucia has red flowers with a white center and is a climbing plant (*Medinilla waterousei*). Taveuni's 1000-meter-high volcanic spine, running 16 kilometers through the island, virtually inhales water from the prevailing tradewinds, causing heavy rain both to the southeast and the northwest—one reason for the abundance of the flora.

Flights from both Suva and Nadi land at Matei airstrip, on the northern tip of the island. There's also ferry service between Taveuni and Vanua Levu. Most tourists are probably heading for the Castaway at Waiyevo, a luxury resort, but there is additional accommodation at Somosomo, the island's chiefly village. Buses run almost all around the island, save for a portion of the rugged east coast.

Taveuni is a diver's paradise, and the major dive operation, Dive Taveuni, near the airstrip, arranges trips to the fabulous Rainbow Reef off the south coast of Vanua Levu. In no more than 30 feet of water, divers can explore, along with the fish and turtles, the crevices, overhangs, and shelves of this astonishing reef.

To see the tagimaucia, hire a guide to help you find and negotiate the right choice out of a number of possible trails. The legend about the flower tells of a young woman who fled home when her father tried to force her to marry an old man she did not love. She ran uphill to the crater lake in the mountain and knelt beside the water to weep. Her tears, of course, turned into the red and white tagimaucia flowers, and her grief so melted her father's heart that he allowed her to marry her young lover.

If you're not staying at the Castaway, you may still be able to hook up with the variety of activities offered there. You may want to do nothing at all on this beautiful, friendly island.

## Eastern Islands

Four remote islands are now accessible by air from Suva-Nausori—Vanua Balavu, Cicia, Lakeba, and Moala. Though all are generally referred to as belonging to the Lau Group, Vanua Balavu and Cicia are part of the Somosomo Chain, while Moala, far away in the south Koro Sea, properly belongs to the Yasayasamoala Group. A lot of water and a lot of air miles separate these islands—government and private ships circulate here, stopping at perhaps half a dozen islands per very long trip—and the air traveler's best bet may limit him to a flight to Vanua Balavu with a connection to Lakeba only. Except for Moala, these islands are more akin in many ways to Tonga than to the Fijian islands to the east. The traveler will notice that even the appearance of the people seems Polynesian, and their skin tends to be lighter in color.

Vanua Balavu, the "long land," alternates a volcanic structure in the south with a northern end of uplifted coral. Where the limestone cliffs give way, there are long stretches of beaches fringed by palms and backed by lush hillsides. A barrier reef to the east encloses a large lagoon; on the other side of the island is the Bay of Islands, long known as a hurricane shelter.

Lomaloma, on the island's southeast, is the major town and was once an important Pacific port. The Tongan chief Ma'afu made his bid against Cakobau from here, as a small monument on the waterfront recalls. Lomaloma was to have been the site of Fiji's first public garden, laid out a century ago, but someone back in Suva probably forgot about Vanua Balavu. There is guesthouse accommodation in Lomaloma, and a small coconut oil factory.

Isolated tropical beaches to the west, and burial caves down south—get a guide—and boats to rent for the short ride to Susui Island: these will occupy your time on Vanua Balavu.

Lakeba is a volcanic, rounded island; the coastal road runs 29 kilometers all around it, and the around-the-island bus runs four times a day. The main town is Tumbou, where there is guesthouse accommodation. The island's interior is primarily pine plantation today, although, in former times, most of the island's population lived on an interior hilltop here. The coast is thick with coconut, and a number of limestone caves have been found, and can be visited, in the coastal cliffs.

East of the island, a barrier reef encloses a wide lagoon, and there is a fine beach at Nukuselal near Tumbou. Forestry roads enable exploration of Lakeba's interior, and there is history to be explored here as well: Ma'afu is buried in Tumbou, as is Ratu Sir Lala Sakuna, an important figure during the colonial era. The Nayau clan of Tonga conquered the island in ancient times, and the Tui Nayau became ruler of all of Lau; more recently, the Tui Nayau, Ratu Sir Kamisese Mara, was the great leader of Fijian independence and its first prime minister.

On Cicia and Moala, the traveler must very much fend for himself where accommodations and activities are concerned; if you plan to go, ask the airline to assist with arrangements.

## Fiji Addresses

NOTE: In writing to Fiji, be sure to write Fiji *Islands* in the address; otherwise, mail tends to be routed to "Fuji," Japan!

Fiji Visitors Bureau
6151 West Century Blvd., Ste. 524
Los Angeles, CA 90045
Tel. (toll-free nationwide) (800) 621-9604
Tel. (toll-free California) (800) 338-5686

Fiji Visitors Bureau
Thomson St.
GPO Box 92
Suva
Fiji Islands
Tel. Suva 22867
 Nadi Airport 72433

Wilderness Adventures
P.O. Box 1389
Suva
Fiji Islands
Tel. Suva 313-616/313-500
 Nadi 72188/72731

Fiji Outback Adventure Tours
c/o Sun Tours Limited
P.O. Box 9403
Nadi Airport
Fiji Islands
Tel. Nadi Airport 72723/72268
 Nadi 71266/71468
 Suva 312-300
 Korolevu 50143

Fiji Rucksack Club
P.O. Box 2394
Government Buildings
Suva
Fiji Islands

# CHAPTER 12

# NEW CALEDONIA

*Name:* Territoire de la Nouvelle-Calédonie et Dépendances
*Political status:* Overseas territory of France
*Island groups:* New Caledonia (Grande Terre), Isle of Pines,
   Loyalty Islands, Belep Islands, Chesterfield Islands
*Gateway island:* New Caledonia
*Capital:* Nouméa
*Population:* 145,000
*Land area:* 19,103 square kilometers
*Language:* French, Kanak
*Currency:* Cours du franc Pacifique franc (CFPF)

Since "les événements de 1984"—violent political upheaval that confirmed New Caledonia as the tinderbox of the Pacific—travel here has been difficult, to say the least. White-skinned visitors are warned not to travel very far from Nouméa. Group package tours barely exist. Scores of hotels have simply shut down; apart from businesslike hotels in downtown Nouméa, those that are left are mostly activity resorts or do-nothing bungalows catering to weekending French and a few Japanese, for whom New Caledonia has traditionally been a favored honeymoon destination.

These obstacles to travel—or at least to carefree travel—are indeed a shame, for New Caledonia offers the traveler one of the most beautiful and intriguing experiences in Oceania. Even the noncautious, however, may feel that the experience is, or ought to be, limited.

## GEOGRAPHY, TOPOGRAPHY, CLIMATE

New Caledonia, in the southwest Pacific, lies between 20 degrees latitude south and the Tropic of Capricorn, and between 160 and 170 degrees west longitude. It is some 1500 kilometers from the east coast of Australia and about 400 kilometers from Vanuatu to the northeast. It is 20,000 kilometers from France, which has ruled it since 1853, first as a colony, then, in 1856, as an overseas territory.

The main island, the Grande Terre, is the fifth largest island in the Pacific (including the North and South islands of New Zealand) and comprises almost 88 percent of the territory's total land area. It was formed as a result of the same great fold in the earth's surface that produced Papua New Guinea's Highlands and New Zealand's northern peninsula. Now 400 kilometers long and 50 kilometers wide, Grande Terre was once much bigger; the barrier reef that sits some

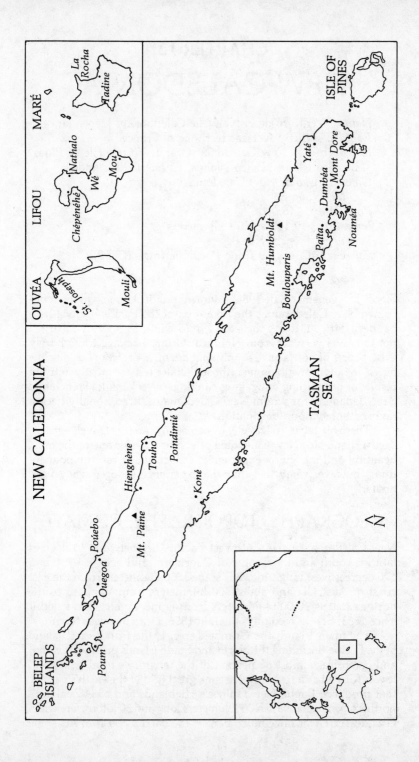

10 kilometers off both east and west coasts, the second longest barrier reef in the world, outlines its original size. The Chaîne Centrale mountain range—scarred by nickel mining—runs the length of the island, creating two distinct climatic and geographic regions. The east coast is wet and lush; rivers plunge down mountainsides to the sea, where they create openings in the reef. The west is savannah, ideal for cattle ranching, and alluvial marshes. Mount Panié in the north at 1628 meters and Mount Humboldt in the south at 1618 meters are the island's highest peaks.

About 100 kilometers east of Grande Terre, and paralleling it in a chain running northwest to southeast, are the drier, uplifted atolls of the Loyalty Islands. The Loyalties include three principal islands— Ouvéa, Lifou, and Maré—and such smaller islands as Tiga, the Astrolabe Reef, Beautemps-Beaupré Atoll, and Walpole Island. Southeast of Grande Terre is Ile des Pins—the Isle of Pines—which makes most lists of the world's most beautiful islands. The Belep Islands are to the northwest of Grande Terre, and the Chesterfields are some 400 kilometers west in the Coral Sea. Both the Isle of Pines and the Beleps are continuations of Grande Terre; the reefs of Grande Terre travel upward through the Beleps to join the d'Entrecasteaux Reefs, two separate lagoons centered on tiny Huon and Surprise islands.

The geology of Grande Terre, based in neither coral deposits nor volcanic activity, is often described as continental because of its similarity to larger landmasses. Locals refer to the island as le Caillou, the Rock, not only for its mountains but for the rock formations, including metamorphic and sedimentary strata. The geological character of Grande Terre accounts for its mineral riches; an estimated quarter to a half of the world's deposits of nickel are here, as well as traces of tungsten, cobalt, copper, manganese, iron, and chromium.

Grande Terre's coastline is 800 kilometers long and often crazily indented, a result of the island's ongoing submergence as the Australian Plate pushes under the Pacific Plate. Along the eastern and southeastern coasts, steep cliffs rise dramatically from the sea. There are several good harbors in the north of the island. In a complex network of waterways, the longest is the Diahot River, navigable for only 32 kilometers.

New Caledonia is one of the southernmost island groups visited in this book. The sunny, moderate climate produced by its distance from the equator is reminiscent, ironically enough, of the south of France. Southeast tradewinds help keep the islands cool. December to March brings the greatest heat, but they also bring cyclones, often serious ones, especially in the northeast of Grande Terre, where the rugged landscape catches the prevailing winds. The seas off this coast are also heavy, with strong currents and rough waves.

# THE NATURAL ENVIRONMENT

The vegetation of New Caledonia is richly diverse, having more in common with Australia than with the rest of Oceania. Because of the island's geographical isolation, more than 80 percent of its 2500 botanic species are endemic. Forests may once have covered almost all of Grande Terre, but overcutting and burning have changed that, although the rain forests to the north remain thick—and still relatively inaccessible. Sandalwood, which once grew plentifully, was almost completely depleted during the 19th-century sandalwood trade. Along the swampy part of the west coast, thick mangrove grows.

The most common tree is the *niaouli*, a low, eucalyptuslike tree, the gum tree of Australia. Its wood is fire resistant—a possible reason for its prevalence in a land of numerous brushfires. *Maquis*, stunted scrub containing numerous species capable of surviving in the red laterite soil, grows in the south of Grande Terre, below 500 meters. But the signature tree of New Caledonia is the indigenous evergreen known as the column pine, *Araucaria cookii*, found in both coastal and upland areas, growing to heights of about 50 meters, with short—two-meter—bristling branches. *Araucaria cookii* strides the shores of the Isle of Pines, which takes its name from Cook's sighting of the tree, as the tree takes its name from the captain himself.

The other outlying islands of New Caledonia boast less diversity of vegetation than Grande Terre, but there are patches of forest, savannah, and scrub as well as coconuts throughout.

Seven native species of mammal, all bats or flying foxes, are found in New Caledonia. Dogs, sheep, cattle, horses, rats, pigs, and deer all came after contact with the Europeans. The deer have become nuisance predators but are routinely hunted.

Of 88 species of birds, 18 are endemic. The Ouvéa parakeet is one, but only a few hundred still exist. The national bird is the *cagou*, a flightless runner that sounds like a barking puppy. Ironically, it faces extinction because grown dogs can often outrun it. As it hatches only one egg a year, New Caledonia may soon lose this traditional symbol.

Another of the most common members of New Caledonia's animal kingdom is the mosquito—bring plenty of repellent.

Sixty kilometers south of Nouméa is the 9045-hectare Parc Territorial de la Rivière Bleue, created by the Territorial Assembly in 1980. The park offers walking trails, picnic areas, camping, and swimming and serves also as a center for research on the natural history of Grande Terre. Such birds as the cagou, flowers including the wild orchid and an indigenous gardenia, the giant tree known as *kaori*, and the stream itself are protected here. Two refuges offer accommodations; reserve in advance by applying to the District Forestry Office in Nouméa, la Flotille, rue Galliéni (B.P. 285, Nouméa, tel. 27 26 74).

The long, riven reefs of New Caledonia, washed by a strong tidal flow, are home to a wide variety of marine life, corals, and sponges. Experienced divers will want particularly to explore Gadji Pass of the Isle of Pines, especially the Gie Island Drop-Off and the Oupère Grotto, a cavern sunk deep in limestone. Ile des Pins also offers the diver freshwater diving among the stalactites and stalagmites of Paradise Cave.

# HISTORY

It is speculated that the islands of New Caledonia were inhabited as long as thirty thousand years ago by Papuans who made their way from the Asian mainland via New Guinea, the Solomons, and Vanuatu. On the Isle of Pines, archaeologists have discovered a cluster of some three hundred earth mounds that may date to 6000 B.C. A wave of Austronesians followed these first settlers in the third millennium B.C.; a thousand years later, another set of migrations began. At the ancient site of Lapita, on the northwest coast of Grande Terre near what is today Koné, pottery carbon-dated to the first millennium B.C. has been found. This Lapita pottery, a key clue in the prehistory of Oceania, is a low-fired ceramic, often intricately decorated. Its trail leads from New Guinea to Samoa, but in Polynesia, the skill of creating it was evidently lost. In New Caledonia, too, a different material culture, a distinctly Melanesian culture, displaced the culture of these earlier peoples during the first ten centuries after Christ.

In this culture, separate clans lived in small villages and farmed their own land, using terracing and irrigation, the vestiges of which may still be seen. The chief dwelled in a large conical house that was also the center for ceremonies and official functions. Religion was animistic. A variety of benevolent and malevolent spirits were believed to inhabit the world. The most powerful of these were the clan's ancestors, who held a key social role, while totemic animals possessed procreative powers. Communities were self-sufficient and isolated from one another. Warfare and cannibalism were common. The dialects of neighboring groups were often mutually unintelligible. Even today, although New Caledonia's 28 indigenous languages are all offshoots of a common Austronesian mother tongue, inhabitants of one island cannot understand the people of another island (except by speaking French, the lingua franca).

Contacts between the Loyalty Islands and Polynesia were frequent in the era before European contact. In back-migrations, Wallisians, Samoans, and Tongans reached the Loyalties and continued west to establish communities on Grande Terre. Wallisians settled Ouvéa in the 18th century. The chiefs of a powerful community on Ile des Pins, however, claimed descent from Melanesian rulers on Vanuatu.

Cook stepped ashore onto Grande Terre's east coast in 1774; the steep cliffs and the pine trees reminded him of the Scottish coast, and he named the island New Caledonia. French interest here began when Louis XVI ordered the Comte de la Pérouse to assess the island's economic potential in 1785. La Pérouse disappeared in 1788, and the French sent d'Entrecasteaux—and, later, others—to find out what had happened. (No one ever did.)

Traders arrived next, and trade got a big boost with the discovery of sandalwood in 1841—by this time, the supplies on other islands of Oceania had been depleted. London Missionary Society efforts in the 1840s succeeded mostly on the Loyalty outliers, where Polynesian peoples proved receptive. French Catholic missionaries arrived on Grande Terre in 1843 but suffered numerous reversals.

French involvement quickened in response to requests to protect the Catholic community and out of fear of British ships in nearby waters. In 1853, the newly enthroned Emperor Napoleon III ordered New Caledonia's annexation; 11 years later, the island became a penal colony. In addition to "hardened criminals" set to work on construction projects and public works, some 3900 political prisoners from the Paris Commune were held here from 1872 to 1879. Among them was the extraordinary Louise Michel, whose memoirs reveal her great interest in and understanding of local Melanesian culture, the culture of the Kanaks.

From the beginning of French rule, the Kanaks were hostile, and from the beginning, the story of French rule is an unpleasant history of plunder and oppression. In 1876, the natives were forced onto native reserves, leaving the best land for French settlers—mostly nickel miners and cattle ranchers. In 1878, the Kanaks revolted, unsuccessfully, and the French instituted the *indigénat*, an administrative system that deprived the Kanaks of the protection of law. The reservation system became yet more oppressive, with many clans forced onto the land of other clans—thus encouraging interclan rivalry. The French government took title to two-thirds of Grande Terre; another quarter went to white *colons,* settlers, and 11 percent of the island, in a grid easily reached by the gendarmes, was left for the natives. Title to these native lands was held by a "Great Chief" appointed by the indigénat. The system of reservations continued until well into the 20th century.

In 1940, after the fall of France, New Caledonia, like French Polynesia, expelled the pro-Vichy governor and declared its support for the Free French. Nouméa became a center for Allied naval operations; the fleet that fought the Battle of the Coral Sea in 1942 was based here. In 1946, Kanaks were granted French citizenship and allowed to live off the reserves, but the French military presence remained strong. Since the events of 1984, it has grown stronger still; young French soldiers man frequent roadblocks on the main highway and otherwise remain highly visible.

Kanak political consciousness rose dramatically in the 1960s— ironically, because of the return of Paris-educated Kanaks wise in the dialectics of American and African black power movements. Demands for independence were expressed through numerous groups, eventually united in the Front de Libération National Kanaké Socialiste (FLNKS). By 1982, the independence forces had gained a majority in the Territorial Assembly. Resistance to independence includes, at its extreme right wing, a rather ugly reactionary element consisting in no small measure of former *pieds-noirs* still angry that they "lost" Algeria, and similar-minded former colonists of Vanuatu, who fled here after those islands were "lost" to independence. Between 1982 and 1984, there were scattered incidents, a few of them violent, and in 1984 the independence forces boycotted the local elections, while FLNKS established what it called a provisional government housed in a storefront bearing the title Government of Kanaky. Serious violence followed, and positions hardened.

The French government has declared its intention to provide eventual self-government while retaining control of defense, the police, and foreign policy; it has also instituted some programs for economic reform. But the issue drags on—it is at the heart of life in New Caledonia. The traveler can hear all shades of opinion from the French expats here—from fourth-generation descendants of colonists or prisoners who say they have no place in France, to entrepreneurs who came here to escape socialism and say they don't care who's in charge so long as they can run their businesses, to right-wingers who say the Kanaks must be taught a lesson. It is harder to find out what the Kanaks say, mostly because it is harder to find them. The Melanesians of New Caledonia are now less than half of the population, and to the majority, they are in many ways invisible. There is virtually no "creole" culture here, and there is minimal interaction between the races. Political and economic power is in the hands of the French; the contrast between their lot and that of the Kanaks—the Ti-va-Ouere, Brothers of the Earth—is obvious and unsettling.

## THE TRAVELER IN NEW CALEDONIA

Tontouta Aiport is 53 kilometers northwest of Nouméa. Special airport buses or the less expensive interurban service takes you into the capital in about an hour. The ride winds past lush, awesome mountains that rise dramatically from a fertile plain. But the traveler will also see the faded, dilapidated signs for now-defunct seaside hotels—victims of the événements and the consequent destruction of New Caledonia's tourist industry.

It is an instant reminder that the traveler out to explore both the physical and social terrain of New Caledonia will find, at best, that his options are somewhat limited—a direct result of the political reality. Nouméa, the capital, which is quite simply a French city with little sense of the Pacific about it, certainly provides a welcome; for the rest of Grande Terre and for the outliers, the traveler is well advised to arrange accommodations beforehand. To do so, apply to the Maison de Tourisme in downtown Nouméa or at the ghostlike offices of travel agents nearby; they have little else to do.

Another limiting aspect to travel here is money. If you have been in French Polynesia, the high cost of living will be familiar, although the variety of possibilities seems greater in New Caledonia. In the French style, the hotels are categorized and priced accordingly; resorts are self-contained communities offering water sports, barbecue night, dining and dancing; camping is prevalent and easy to do; gîtes, consisting of cottages along a beach and often run by Melanesians, provide good accommodations along the coast of Grande Terre and on the outliers; the youth hostel in Nouméa really serves mostly youths—the party atmosphere, sometimes complete with food fights, often continues on the flight from Nouméa to Auckland.

Eating is a pleasure here, especially for the Pacific traveler who may be weary of raw fish and tubers. French cuisine predominates, and supermarkets offer imports, via the European Economic Community, that combine wonderfully for picnics—baguettes, paté, cheese, and French wine. A large Vietnamese community lives here—post–World War II migrants—and they have added their cuisine to the other Oriental fare, mostly Chinese, to be found. The native feast is the *bougna,* a pudding made from sliced root vegetable soaked in the ever-present coconut milk, then wrapped in the equally ubiquitous banana leaves along with pork, chicken, or seafood. It is covered with sand and cooked on white-hot stones.

But the fact is that the traveler will be hard pressed to find a bougna or to experience much of traditional life, which a century of European rule has challenged and in many ways destroyed. Though the current movement for independence is political, it has also become the flashpoint for a resurgence of traditional culture. This culture is best seen outside Nouméa and on the outliers.

If your skin is white, you may be warned not to travel on your own in rented cars around Grande Terre—white drivers, you will be told, are often stoned. You may even hear such warnings if you plan to travel around the island by bus. Yet people do, of course, without mishap or unpleasantness.

If you're worried, book yourself into a gîte on Ile des Pins, which shouldn't be missed in any case, or Ouvéa or Lifou, and fly there. In the current political climate, the outliers are as good a way to experience New Caledonia as any.

In the past, three outfitters offered adventure-style excursions on Grande Terre. Alize-Raid Excursions, located at Anse Vata, offered overland camping trips, while Koné Rodeo and Randonnée Equestre offered horseback expeditions from Koné to Hienghène or into the Pamale Valley. The action fell off after the événements, but if you are interested and have the time, you should certainly try to get in touch. See "New Caledonia Addresses," at chapter end.

# NOUMÉA

On a warm, sunny day, with sports cars racing one another around the curves of the bays, with the billowing sails of windsurfing boards adding their bright colors to the turquoise water off the beach, with a soccer game from Marseilles or the Tour de France on the TV sets of the Café de Paris terrace, you can easily imagine that you are in a town on the French Riviera. Hardly a Melanesian is in sight—except for laughing women in Mother Hubbards in the market, and a few elegantly fashionable youths joining French friends in the cafes of Anse Vata. Yet half of New Caledonia's population lives in Nouméa, a busy port city with a lively downtown surrounded by comfortable suburbs.

The French established Nouméa as the capital of New Caledonia in 1860, moving their administrative facilities from Balade. In 1864, the first convicts arrived on Ile Nou, which was later connected to the city by a land reclamation project. In 1942, the American admiral Halsey established the headquarters of the Allied South Pacific command here; the building today houses the South Pacific Commission.

The city sits on a jut of land that is scalloped all around by pretty bays. The center of the city is concentrated around the Place des Cocotiers and in the so-called Latin Quarter just to the south. You must follow the coast down three bays—Baie de la Moselle, Baie de l'Orphélinat, Baie des Citrons, this last with a beach—to arrive at Anse Vata, *the* beach, where are found most of the luxury hotels, a number of cafes and snack bars, and in the suburban streets inland, a number of superb restaurants. Looking south across the water, you can see the Amédée Lighthouse; on Ouen Toro hill above you, the Australians in 1940 established two six-inch cannons to guard the reef passage near the lighthouse. Continuing east around the "bottom" of Nouméa, the energetic traveler can test his mettle on the fitness track that follows the long, curving promenade Pierre Vernier. The course is well marked (in French) and well used by the locals.

Nouméa's downtown makes for excellent wandering. Start at the Place des Cocotiers, where you can pick up a map at the Maison de Tourisme. The market, being lively and the city's only real pocket of Melanesians, is a must-see visit. Much of the rest of downtown is given over to duty-free shops, offering Paris imports to Japanese tourists, but there are fine bookstores (Maison de la Presse carries the *International Herald Tribune*), a few shops along Rue Anatole France selling locally made crafts, and Prisunic, where you can buy anything. Nouméa is *the* resource center for New Caledonia; if you need anything, get it here.

The streets that cut in from the Old Wharf, east of Place des Cocotiers, are certainly worth a wander. Many of the buildings retain a ramshackle, waterfront appearance—a few have been turned into bars and shops that carefully retain the look—with an architecture reminiscent of New Orleans' French Quarter. Here also are a few buildings in Quonset-hut architecture, leftovers of the war.

The New Caledonia Museum, just off Moselle Bay near the post office, has an outstanding collection of Kanak artifacts and Lapita pottery. The courtyard has been turned into a botanical exhibit, and behind the museum is a traditional *grande case*, big house. You can also visit the former prison on Ile Nou, from whose Fort Tereka there is a splendid view of the interior of Grande Terre, while some five kilometers out of town is the Parc Forestier, where you can see the disappearing cagou, Ouvéa parakeet, local mammals, and more botany. You'll see signs everywhere advertising the Aquarium; it does not live up to its billing, but its collection of reef fish, sponges, cuttlefish, nautilus, *bêches de mer*, sea snakes, and florescent corals is interesting.

Downtown hotels tend to be businesslike; those along Anse Vata are luxurious and extravagantly priced. A number of moderate motels are located inland in Anse Vata, set among the bungalow-style homes of the middle class. The problem here is distance from the center of town, although Nouméa has a very good bus system; you can easily ply the coast between downtown and Anse Vata.

Remember that New Caledonia is effectively France: *everything* closes for the sacred lunch break, which here lasts from about 11:00 A.M. to 2:00 P.M. Everything except the museum and restaurants, of course, which are numerous, offer a range of cuisines, and cater to a range of budgets. Nightlife in Nouméa tends to concentrate in private clubs behind closed doors since the événements—although the Café de Paris, a mecca for young people on loud motorbikes, stays open, as do a few other nearby bars, including the famed Le Hubert. The French of Nouméa say they fear indigene youths prowling around after dark. The motorbikes seem a more obvious menace.

# AROUND NOUMÉA

A few travel and tour agencies still offer tours of Nouméa and environs, geared mostly to cruise ship passengers whose time is perforce limited. The advantage of such a tour is that, since most cruise ships are Australian, the tours are conducted in English. You can see the same sights on your own, of course, either by hiring a driver or renting wheels.

On the eastern outskirts of Nouméa is the high-rise village "reserve," which is a hotbed of Kanaky independence activities—as evidenced in the graffiti sprayed everywhere.

Head north and east through reclaimed mangrove to Conception, where you can see the first church built by the French in New Caledonia. The story is that the bishop originally wanted to build up north. The big chief gave him permission to do so on condition that he feed six hundred villagers for six months. At the end of the six months, however, the big chief demanded three more months, and when the bishop refused, the natives sent him packing. The bishop dreamed of a high mountain; returning south, he saw this mountain and approached the chief of the nearby village. This chief, as it turned out, had also had a dream—this one about a white man in a long tunic—so he willingly ceded the top of his mountain, and the church was built. Although the bishop was eventually shipwrecked while returning to France, the church today is filled with plaques thanking the Blessed Virgin for healing miracles.

Heading inland and uphill, you'll pass through a village of Wallisians, here to work the nickel mines, before arriving at the Saint Louis mission, home to seven monks of a contemplative order. From the grounds of the Melanesian-style chapel is a splendid view of Nouméa. The village of Saint Louis is a native village. Most homes are of mud brick, rich with nickel, and some outbuildings are of thatch. Houses of tin are a sign of wealth. At the entrance to the village—as with most villages on Grande Terre—is the house of the French gendarme, stationed here to "help and protect" the villagers.

The road winds around Mont Dore, so called because gold was found there and because sunset falling on the red-nickel earth makes it appear golden indeed. The hill is hideously scarred by open-cut mining. In some places, the nickel establishment has tried to replant trees to hold the mountain, but the effort looks too little too late. Returning toward Nouméa, you suddenly pass a cluster of new, handsome bungalows, on the hillside just below a mine. These house out-islanders who have been vocal in their opposition to independence. This stand made life at home uncomfortable, since most out-islanders are pro-Kanaky, so the government, as a reward for their loyalty, brought the people here to Grande Terre, gave them the modern houses, and put them to work in the nickel mine. A highly visible object lesson.

## GRANDE TERRE

For travelers game to travel further around New Caledonia, the best way is by bus, from the triangular depot at the market. Schedules tend to be erratic or not clearly posted or both, so be sure to ask in advance. West coast buses to Koumac leave daily, though at different times, and buses all the way to Poum leave three times a week. East coast buses as far as both Poindimié and Hienghène leave daily. Shorter-run services, to Thio on the east, La Foa on the west, and Yaté southward, are frequent. There is also frequent plane service to the further ends of the island.

Indeed, Grande Terre is big enough that a bus trip to its remoter points can take at least a few days. If you must choose one destination, Poindimié is recommended. The administrative center for the northeast coast, Poindimié is 308 kilometers from Nouméa. Its many quonset huts are vestiges of its founding during the war. There is good lodging at Poindimié, and it is a good center for further exploration of the dramatic northeast coast.

## ILE DES PINS

The natives call it Kounié, and it is one of the most beautiful islands in the Pacific, if not the world. From Magenta Airport, the domestic airport five kilometers out of Nouméa, Air Calédonie flies twice daily to Ile des Pins. The 30-minute flight is often heavily booked, and the ten-kilos-per-passenger rule is strictly enforced—well, pretty strictly. If you have booked lodging, as you should have, you will be met at the airfield by someone from your gîte.

The center of the island is a high plateau carpeted with ferns green on top and silver on the underside when the breeze tilts them up. Only a few pines and niaouli punctuate the wide expanse of this plateau, so the vistas are very grand. You can look down to a coastal plain of rain forest, niaouli, and the requisite pines along the shore. The shoreline is an irregular ring of unbelievably bright white sand. The bays are numerous; village life—and tourism—hugs the west and south coasts. The island is not large: the circular road is 42 kilometers long, though on the east it runs inland, while the cross-island road is 24 kilometers long.

The two jewels of Kounié's crown are Kuto and Kanumera, two small adjacent bays with turquoise water and snow-white sand backed by pines, niaouli, casuarinas, coconut palms, and orchids. Kuto, the larger bay, separated from Kanumera by the Kuto Peninsula, offers a hint of surf, while Kanumera is virtually dead calm.

The Ile des Pins also boasts three important caves. Ouatchia is the most difficult, Paradise is often flooded, and Oumagne is the easiest. Guides are a good idea for all of them—ask at your hotel.

Ask also if someone can guide you to Baie de la Courbeille, one of the loveliest spots imaginable.

Other sights of Kounié are the Deportees' Cemetery, with the graves of many Communards imprisoned here for political reasons, and a few remains of the prison itself, behind the bakery at Ouro.

Kuto is a tiny village; the main "town" is Vao, where you can examine some of the extraordinary thatched houses of the natives, remarkable for their architecture and for the skill with which they have been constructed. The dive center is also in Vao; ask at the gendarmerie. The diving off Ile des Pins is exceptional.

# THE LOYALTY ISLANDS

Air Calédonie flies to Ouvéa, Lifou, and Maré, where the traveler can find accommodations, and to Tiga, where, as of this writing, he cannot. Ouvéa is a long, narrow island whose west coast offers some 20 kilometers of gorgeous white sand bordering the lagoon. The ocean side also has some lovely beaches; they interrupt an otherwise rocky, cliffbound coast beaten by heavy surf. Here is a chance to see a good deal of Melanesian village life, after which strenuous activity you can again relax at your beachfront bungalow at one of Fayahoue's gîtes.

Lifou, most important of the Loyalties, is also the chain's administrative center. The "capital" is the town of Wé. A number of villages here merit the traveler's attention: Chépénéhé, with its grottoes, Dueulu, Doking, Mou, for its exquisite beaches, and Nathalo. Here you can see the largest grande case in New Caledonia, and Nathalo Church, with the original and quite lovely decoration.

Maré is the least visited of the Loyalties. Its main town is Tadine, the port, on the west side of the island, opposite where the plane lands. Make your way to Tawainedre, Penaloimedu, and Netche to discover the lovely countryside and some sumptuous beaches.

## New Caledonia Addresses

The first is for the refuges of the Parc Territorial de la Rivière Bleue.

District Forestier de Nouméa
Cider Sud
La Flotille, rue Galliéni
B.P. 285
Nouméa
Tel. 27 26 74 (Thursdays only)

Alize-Raid Excursions
13 rue Tabou
Anse Vata
Tel. 26 26 41

Koné Rodeo
Koné
Tel. 35 51 51

Randonnée Equestre
Koné
Tel. 36 52 55

# CHAPTER 13

# VANUATU

*Name:* Republic blong Vanuatu
*Political status:* Independent
*Island groups:* Northern Group (Torres and Banks, Espiritu
    Santo, Aoba, Maewo), Central Group (Pentecost,
    Ambrym, Malakula, Paama, Epi, Tongoa and Shepherds,
    Efate), Southern Group or Tafea Islands (Tanna, Aniwa,
    Futuna, Erromango, Anatom)
*Gateway island:* Efate
*Capital:* Port-Vila
*Population:* 132,000
*Land area:* 12,000 square kilometers
*Language:* Bislama
*Currency:* Vanuatu vatu (VT)
NOTE: Area is malarial.

Vanuatu is politically, linguistically, and culturally one of the most
interesting places in Oceania. Custom—*kastom* in Bislama—still runs
deep, while the independent government plays the very modern game
of aid and pursues a vocal foreign policy role. During World War
II, the Americans turned much of Vanuatu into a staging area for
some of the war's bloodiest battles; the Americans brought—and
left behind—a wealth of supplies and materials that gave shape to
an emerging cargo cult, still more or less active. One of the Americans
who came here was James Michener, and he celebrated these islands
in that fine book *Tales of the South Pacific,* later turned into a musical and movie seen (and sung) by millions around the world. It is
said that Aoba, visible from Espiritu Santo till it disappears in the
afternoon mists, is Michener's Bali Ha'i, but Michener will neither
confirm nor deny this.

## GEOGRAPHY, TOPOGRAPHY, CLIMATE

The 82 islands and islets of Vanuatu are links in the chain of volcanic
activity—the Pacific Ring of Fire—that stretches up from New Zealand through the Solomons to Papua New Guinea. The two largest
islands, Espiritu Santo (called Santo) and Malakula, which account
for nearly half the total land area of Vanuatu, are ruggedly volcanic,
with sharp peaks and high plateaus. The other large-ish islands are
also volcanic, overlaid with limestone formations. The small islands
are coral and limestone. The five still-active volcanoes are on Lopevi,

Ambrym, Aoba, Santa Maria, and Tanna islands; the one on Tanna, the Yasur Volcano, is, justifiably, a major tourist attraction. There is also a submarine volcano near Tongoa; this the traveler can fly over.

These islands, young in geologic terms, jut up from the western edge of the New Hebrides Trench, 8000 meters deep. Here the Australian Plate is subducting beneath the Pacific Plate—the reverse of what is happening along the Tonga Trench some 1200 kilometers

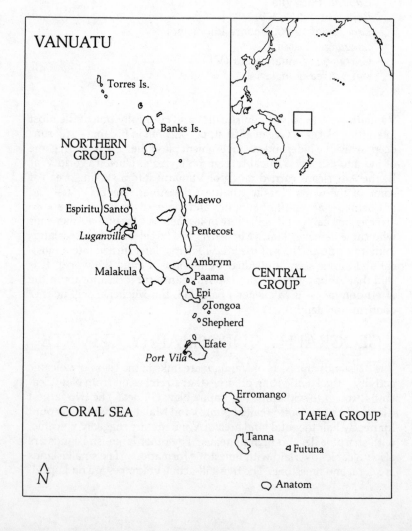

to the east. The subduction process pushes the islands upward an estimated 10 centimeters a year, while sufficient overflow of new lava prevents the development of large-scale reefs along the shores of many islands. The reefs of Efate, however, just offshore from the capital of Port-Vila, constitute one of the world's great dive locations, said to rival Australia's Great Barrier Reef for interest and excitement, and to surpass it in accessibility and in the calmness of the surf.

The climate is hot and humid, less so in the south, where the June-to-September winter can be almost cool. Southeast tradewinds prevail, with periods of calm from November to April when the moist northerlies or easterlies blow. That is also the period for hurricanes, which primarily affect the southern islands. The devastating hurricane of February 1987 left 49 dead and 10,000 homeless and destroyed the copra harvest, the nation's main cash crop. The storm lasted eight hours, had winds of 160 kilometers an hour, and badly damaged the capital and the southern islands.

# THE NATURAL ENVIRONMENT

Vanuatu's vegetation splits into windward and leeward—rain forest to the windward east, tropical woodland and even savannah on the leeward west. *Nabangas* are the giant banyan trees, which often mark the central meeting places—*nakamals*—of country villages. The banyan starts as an epiphyte and eventually strangles its host in a twisting labyrinth of branches and vines. Banyans can be colossal; indeed, they are among earth's largest living organisms.

Indigenous fauna include flying foxes, lizards, and mosquitoes—including the malarial mosquito. Fifty-four species of native bird include pigeons, parrots, warblers, fantails, robins, peregrine falcons, goshawks, island thrushes, and trillers. Most bird life and the best bird watching are concentrated on Efate, the gateway island, and Espiritu Santo. Marine life in Vanuatu's waters is particularly rich—an opportunity not only for the diver but also for the economic future of the islands.

Domesticated pigs, as elsewhere in Melanesia, play an important role in traditional life. Certain male pigs are chosen and first castrated. Their lower incisors are then extracted so that the upper incisors will grow abnormally long, curling back in a circle. A virtually complete circle of pig tusk, often worn as a bracelet, is a sign of wealth, still used in marriage payments and in pig-killing ceremonies, where they are given away as a means to advance in rank.

# HISTORY

Early prehistory in these islands remains vague. Lapita pottery dating from as far back as 1300 B.C. to as recently as 350 B.C. has been found in both northern and southern islands, while the central islands yield a wholly different style of pottery—incised, with applied relief designs; this dates from at least 700 B.C. and is believed to have a Solomon Islands provenance.

Around 1200, the existing culture, whatever it was, was abruptly replaced, at least in the central islands, by immigrants led by a chief known as Roymata. Burials from the period have been found; the ritual seems to have involved the voluntary sacrifice of people close to the dead person. Clan groups of this period inhabited small villages, each of which was an autonomous universe. These early peoples thus developed a remarkable variety of languages and customs. Clans dealt with one another through gift-giving ceremonies or hostility; cannibalism was practiced—some say, up until 1977. The role of the pig was developed during this Roymata period. To become a Big Man or chief, a man had to supply pigs for slaughter at festivals; a complex system of pig-borrowing developed, creating bonds that strengthened the clan. Women were property, exchanged between clans during peaceful intervals. Everyone drank kava.

The first European contact came in 1606 when Portuguese captain Pedro Fernandez de Quirós, on assignment from the king of Spain to find the great southern continent, knelt to kiss the ground he believed was the goal of his trip, naming it La Terra Australia del Espiritu Santo. The members of the expedition spent a month on the island, suffering illness, dissension among themselves, and trouble with the natives; they never discovered that they were on an island, not a continent. Nobody back in Spain seemed terribly interested in the place anyway.

Bougainville in 1768 sailed between Santo and Malakula, thus discovering Quirós' mistake, and in 1774, Cook, on his second voyage, charted the island group, naming it, after Scotland, the New Hebrides.

In 1825, English trader Peter Dillon discovered sandalwood on Erromango, and the rush was on, soon spreading to the other islands and bringing its usual accompaniments of firearms, alcohol, and depopulating European diseases. Along with sandalwood, the traders began to deal in the sea slug or *trepang*—in Portuguese, *bicho de mar*. But in order to trade with the natives, the traders had to be able to talk to them. In the New Hebrides, this was no easy task. In a social system characterized by isolated villages, the islanders had developed what was—and still is—the world's most complex linguistic jumble;

today's Vanuatu boasts the highest ratio of languages to speakers of any nation in the world. To facilitate commerce, a pidgin English was developed as a lingua franca. Some called it sandalwood English, but most called it after the sea slug—beach la mar or bichelamar or bishlamar. The natives called it *Bislama*—today the national language of Vanuatu.

The first missionaries landed on Erromango in 1839 and were promptly killed and eaten; the London Missionary Society continued to lose both European and Polynesian missionaries for several years. The Presbyterians made more headway, assisted by bombardments of resistant villages. But antipathy to Christianity—or loyalty to tradition—still persists today in Vanuatu, where conflicts between "white" religion and *kastom* are not infrequent.

Blackbirding, which began in the 1860s, did not help missionary efforts, especially since many recruiters disguised themselves in clerical garb to demonstrate false good intentions. At the height of the labor trade, more than half of the adult male population of several islands was abroad, mostly in Australia's Queensland, Fiji, and New Caledonia. The reverse process—planters settling in Vanuatu—began tentatively in the 1870s. When the price of cotton collapsed, the planters switched to coffee, cacao, bananas, and copra. Most planters were British, but in 1882, French *colons* from New Caledonia formed the Compagnie Calédonienne des Nouvelles Hebrides and began buying up land; many British nationals went to work for the French company, while Australia's Burns Philp got into the land-grabbing act in 1895. Officially, the land was not sold; rather, its use was temporarily assigned, but the islanders had little understanding of what was going on. The French and British did nothing to enlighten the Melanesians; indeed, the Melanesians were hardly an issue. The issue was the rivalry between the two powers and the wariness each felt of the other. When the natives began to recognize and resist the alienation of their land, however, both British and French warships showed up to bombard coastal villages.

Both European governments were petitioned by their nationals to annex the islands, and, in 1878, both agreed *not* to annex without consulting each nother. Nine years later, the two established a Joint Naval Commission to police the area. By 1906, further discussions seemed in order, especially since the Germans had begun to show an interest in the islands, prompting the dispatch of both British and French resident commissioners. The result of the discussions was the Anglo-French Condominium of the New Hebrides, a unique form of government, colonial or otherwise. Called by one historian an "elaborate joke," the condominium was popularly referred to as the Anglo-French Pandemonium.

## Condominium and Independence

Formalized in the Protocol of 1911 and proclaimed in 1923, the condominium's first 50 years were primarily a matter of each resident commissioner looking out for the interests of "his" nationals—and of the British Protestants and French Roman Catholics respectively. Each power created its own administrative structure; the insane result was two education systems, two health services, two militias, two legal systems. The French were judged by French law, the British by British law, and the Melanesians by whatever law they might run afoul of. There *was* a superior Joint Court to resolve disputes; its first president was an appointee of the king of Spain. One historian observed that this court president was truly neutral, having understood little French, less English, and no Melanesian. Fortunately, the historian went on, this was no particular handicap, as he was also deaf.

Economics and language were two major spheres of rivalry between the European powers. The French, who were allowed to import indentured laborers from French Indochina, took the lead in entrepreneurship. The British, with their policy of localization, had the upper hand in training responsible English-speaking Melanesian leaders.

Except for a minor bombardment of Santo, the islands of the New Hebrides did not suffer during the war; its impact was nonetheless enormous. The traveler to Santo today can see the remnants of the Allied presence—the roads, bridges, platforms, ammo dumps, and airstrips built by the Seabees to support the enormous U.S. staging area that the Americans simply left behind after the war. Much of what they left rests underwater; after giving away as many bulldozers and trucks as the islanders could drive, the Americans dumped the rest into the sea, driving them off what is now called Million Dollar Point.

The seemingly endless supply of military cargo that poured forth from landing craft and airplanes left another legacy—the cargo cult of John Frum. During the war, rumors spread on Tanna that a white man "with bleached hair" had appeared to a number of islanders, promising to reappear with boatloads of the kinds of goods the American troops were bringing in great quantity. Some Tanna islanders built jetties to receive the goods and strung up a "telephone" network of tin cans to speak to Frum, who was possibly the military recruiter on the island. Though the cargo cult is today officially discouraged, and many of its leaders have been jailed, anthropologists believe it bespeaks a deep disillusionment with the breakdown of kastom and with Europeans in general.

That disillusionment began to turn into action in the 1960s with the emergence of the NaGriamel movement on Espiritu Santo under the leadership of Jimmy Stevens (also written Stephens), who urged full political control for Melanesians and repossession of all land held by Europeans. In the 1970s, the National Party, founded as the New Hebrides Cultural Association but with strong ties to the Presbyterian church, emerged as the real local power. The condominium powers, meanwhile, agreed that independence must come but couldn't agree on how. The British wanted out; the French, clinging to DeGaulle's policy of a French presence in the Pacific "forever," wanted to retain some ties of authority. Documents recovered from the French residency after independence confirm that the French policy was to stall the issue. They thus agreed to a British proposal for local elections and a timetable for independence in 1980—while they built a Francophone majority. But French-supported candidates kept losing to the National Party, the Vanuaaku Pati, which was mostly Anglophone, and the French tactic became one of giving covert support to Stevens' NaGriamel, now urging the secession of Santo from the soon-to-be-independent Vanuatu.

Stevens' role is particularly intriguing. Starting out as a opponent of foreign influence, even petitioning the United Nations in 1971 to halt land sales to American tourism developers, Stevens by 1980 had come under the influence of the Phoenix Foundation, an American lunatic-fringe organization that wanted to turn Santo into a tax-free, independent nation that would be run by and for unfettered free enterprise. The French seem to have decided that *they* could run a seceded Espiritu Santo—hence, their covert aid to Stevens.

In May 1980, Stevens' men attacked the British compound in Luganville, seized the airfield, and declared the independence of Espiritu Santo as the Republic of Vemarana. Father Walter Lini, the Vanuaaku Pati leader who would be the new nation's first prime minister, had as yet no troops to put down the rebellion—independence was scheduled for July 30—and though the British sent 200 Royal Marines to Santo, the French, who also brought troops there, would not agree to the use of force. Meanwhile, the leader of a simultaneous secessionist uprising on Tanna was suddenly and mysteriously killed. There was talk of delaying independence, but Lini went ahead with it; a week later, he requested troops from Papua New Guinea who promptly put down the rebellion and threw Stevens into jail in Port-Vila. A number of French planters were invited to leave the country; Lini was firmly in charge. The new nation was named Vanuatu; its people called themselves ni-Vanuatu.

An intriguing novel by the Australian author Thea Astley, *Beach Masters*, tells of a secessionist revolt on a Melanesian island called Kristi. The ni-Kristi, who speak a pidgin called Seaspeak, declare their independence from Trinitas—capital: Port Lena—but are put down by foreign troops. Astley's fictional account is peopled with a good sampling of Pacific characters—French and English district agents and resident commissioners, remittance men and expats who've gone "tropo," priests and demagogues, as well as an array of island-ers. All are dispossessed by the events of the novel, which Astley admits has "historical parallels."

## Vanuatu Today

The new government's tasks have been formidable: integrating three separate governments—English, French, and republican; imple-menting economic and educational reform to link Anglophone and Francophone, rural and urban, Christian and kastom; land reform. Serious progress on all these fronts has yet to be felt.

In the meantime, Lini, who is both a Big Man in his native Pentecost and an Anglican priest, has staked out a role as a Pacific spokesman on the world stage. He has made Vanautu a nuclear-free zone and has been an important voice against French policy in New Caledonia. He has played at keeping the U.S. guessing by negotiating with the USSR over fishing rights in Vanuatu's waters. In 1986, his government signed an accord with Libya's Colonel Qaddafi. Oppo-sition to government policies is low volume, especially since Lini closed down Vanuatu's only opposition paper and sent its editor packing because of criticism of the government.

The economy still rests on copra, and the 1987 hurricane, which destroyed the year's crop, prompted a rash of new aid requests around the world. Exports of fish from the Japanese plant on Santo are another economic mainstay, and the government plans further exploitation of Vanuatu's waters and the development of forestry as future economic opportunities. Tourism is also important, although a variety of factors have combined to keep the number of tourists low. Most tourist facilities are on Efate and Tanna—the latter is also a popular day-trip destination—with Santo a distant third. Many of the tourist hotels and restaurants are often empty shells, waiting for customers. The bulk of the tourists are Australian, and Australian cruise ships stop at Port-Vila and Luganville on Santo.

But the major spur to the economy is Vanuatu's status as a tax haven and offshore banking center. For some 75 banks—only five of which trade locally—about a thousand corporations, and a number of foreign shipping companies, Vanuatu is an on-paper-only home without taxes, auditing, or control.

These businesses are concentrated in filing cabinets on Port-Vila, to which great numbers of ni-Vanuatu have long migrated from the outliers. Following the depopulation of Melanesians under early col-onial rule, the population began to expand by more than 3 percent a year in the 1960s, the time of the greatest urban migration. Today, population growth has stabilized, and some 85 percent of the people live in rural areas. In addition to Melanesians, who make up 93 percent of the population, there are Europeans, Chinese, and Vietnamese. The back-migration of Polynesians a thousand years ago resulted in several Polynesian languages entering the Vanuatu linguistic pool; they are still spoken on Futuna, Aniwa, and Emae islands, and in some villages on Efate. Among the Melanesians, the diversity of cultures is remarkable.

## BISLAMA

The traveler finds himself moving his lips as he reads signs: *Edukaesen Senta, Namba wan aeskrim blong Vanuatu,* and so on (Education Center, Number One Ice Cream of Vanuatu). But Bislama is well beyond quaint; it is indeed a language, with its own grammatical rules and a store of words. It evolved over a period of some fifty years, using a base of mostly English vocabulary and a Melanesian grammar that reflected the structure of the many languages of Vanuatu. Its sister dialects are Papua New Guinea's Tok Pisin and Solomons Pidgin. Note that most ni-Vanuatu do not distinguish between p/b, t/d, and k/g in pronunciation. If you want to hear Bislama spoken at length, attend a session of parliament (if it's sitting).

Here are some useful words and phrases:

| | |
|---|---|
| Tangkyu tumas | Thank you very much |
| Olsem wanen? I gud? | How are things? OK? |
| I gud nomo | Just fine |
| Plis | Please |
| Nem blong mi . . . | My name is . . . |
| You save? | Do you know? |
| Mi glad tumas | I am very pleased/happy |
| Mi wantem sam . . . | I would like some . . . |
| Lukim yu | See you later |
| Gudmoning | Good morning |
| Gudnaet | Good night |
| Tata | Goodbye |

## THE TRAVELER IN VANUATU

Vanuatu offers the traveler an airline—Air Mélanésie—and passenger-carrying interisland freighters that make it possible to get to almost any island in the group. Tourism facilities, however, are concentrated on the gateway island of Efate, on Tanna, some 75 minutes by plane from Port-Vila, and on Espiritu Santo, home of Vanuatu's "second city," Luganville. Malakula, Erromango, Ambrym, and Pentecost also offer hotels or guesthouse accommodation; on the other islands, varied forms of "private" accommodation are possible—check at the visitors bureau in Vila.

On all three of the major islands, it is easy enough to get off the beaten track and in amongst villages where kastom—traditional life—reigns. On all three of them, it's possible to find secluded beaches. Efate offers resorts, superb diving, beaches, and excursions into the interior as well as the resources of Port-Vila. On Tanna, the traveler can hike or drive up to Yasur Volcano, an awesome sight, see the wild horses of White Grass, and visit kastom villages. Santo offers beaches, wild jungle, villages, and the remnants of World War II as well as Luganville. Two other islands offer unique experiences: on Malakula, the traveler may still see the Big Nambas, the last tribesmen of Vanuatu to come into contact with Westerners; on Pentecost during April and May, the traveler can watch land diving, one of the most extraordinary customs—and one of the most phenomenal feats—on earth. Air Mélanésie flies to Santo via Malakula and to Pentecost via Santo. It is possible to connect to Honiara in the Solomons from Santo—at least, it was as of this writing.

An important note about currency: Vanuatu *vatu* are useless anywhere else, except as souvenirs. Be aware that Australian dollars may be used almost universally on the islands that particularly cater to tourists. However, your departure tax *must* be paid in vatu, so be sure to stash 1000 VT per person for departure, and be sure to change all other vatu before leaving.

# EFATE

You arrive at Bauerfield Airport, some six kilometers north of Port-Vila. A tourist desk at the airport can help you with hotel reservations and transportation to town; the hotel bus and taxis are both reasonable. When you enter your hotel, you will probably be entering a world of Aussies—cheerful, informal, friendly—although a Japanese-owned resort caters to Japanese.

A number of these Australians have come to Vila to dive, eschewing their own Great Barrier Reef because, as one put it, "things are just much easier here." Vila is indeed an excellent base for divers, and snorkelers may of course go along for the ride. A number of responsible dive operations are in business here; all are well run and give excellent value. Most offer introductory "resort" courses as well as full certification—on the day a cruise ship is in port, the dive boat may be filled to bursting with first-time divers "having a try." Visibility is excellent, and there is a lot to see just offshore. In addition to such places as Mele Reef, Cathedral Cavern, and Outboard Reef, you can dive the *Star of Russia,* a clipper ship that burned and sank near the main wharf in 1874.

Downtown Port-Vila is concentrated along the main road beside the bay and a few streets running inland, especially those opposite the Cultural Center. The market is here, open Wednesday, Friday, and Saturday mornings—and whenever a passenger ship calls. The town is very busy and quite delightful when a cruise ship is in port, much sleepier but still delightful when the crowds have departed. Businesses and government offices open early and close for a long lunch from about 11:30 A.M. to 2:00 P.M. The visitors bureau is right beside the market; across from it are the government office building with the Department of Tourism and Frank King's Visitors Club. Any or all of these should be able to help with questions and arrangements.

The ni-Vanuatu have a keen interest in the arts, and the level of artistic achievement, as well as taste, is quite high. You can see it in some of the modern architecture, and in the handicrafts and clothing available for purchase. There are also numerous galleries in and around Vila. The capital's Cultural Center, with reading room, handicraft center, natural history museum, and native artifacts collection, shows much of the origins of this vital creative strain.

Food—*kai kai*—is plentiful along Vila's main drag, where there are numerous fast-food places—*kai kai quik taem*—and in the hotels. Several large department stores, including Burns Philp of course, are well stocked with various items. A number of shops sell handicrafts; perhaps the best is the Handikraf Blong Vanuatu next to the Cultural Center. Out-islanders create the lovely bowls, war clubs, carvings, slit gongs, and tapestries here, and the shop will pack them up for you. Packages can be mailed at the post office, where you can also make international phone calls.

Public buses on Efate are short-service; none goes completely around the island. Cars and mopeds may be rented, but be aware that the far side of the island is much less developed, while the road, built by the Americans in World War II and running 132 kilometers around the island, is often steep and frequently rough. Numerous organized tours run numerous excursions, however, and these are a good bet; you may be astonished to see Charolais cattle grazing in the coastal plain—one reason you can get an excellent steak in Vanuatu.

The beauty spot of Efate, apart from the almost inaccessible rain forest of the interior, is Erakor Lagoon, just to the south of Vila. Catch the Le Lagon Hotel bus across from the post office and cross from the hotel to Erakor Island by ferry. Another small island with good beaching is Hideaway—reached from the village of Mele by free launch. North of Mele is Mele Maat, where residents from Ambrym were resettled after a 1951 volcanic eruption.

# TANNA

Tanna is Vanuatu's second most visited island, and your flight there may well be filled with prepackaged day trippers. It will also probably be met on arrival, near Lenakel Village on the west coast, by waiting jeeps, there to transport visitors the 29 kilometers to Yasur. Yasur, and almost everything else you want to see or do, is on the east side of the island, and traffic between Lenakel and White Sands, the east coast's center, is frequent. Accommodations are available on both west and east coasts.

The sights of Tanna may all be toured by prearrangement, but seeing them on your own is easy to do. Yasur may be the world's most accessible volcano. A road goes up the mountain's south side, and a path leads up the north slopes. From the lip of the volcano, the traveler can see and hear boiling geysers and explosive fireworks. The volcano mountain is surrounded by a plain of volcanic dust in the midst of which sits Lake Isiwi, with its black sand beaches darkened by volcanic ash.

There are John Frum churches in Sulphur Bay, just north of Yasur, and at Yaneumakel. Red crosses dotting the countryside are the cult's symbol, being derived from the uniform of a U.S. Medical Corps officer whose arrival on Tanna the believers connected with the coming of Frum.

A trail leads from Sulphur Bay to Port Resolution, landing place of Captain Cook in 1774. The coast along here boasts splendid white beaches.

A network of local trails crisscrosses the interior of Tanna and offers the traveler both good walking and a good chance to see some of the 92 villages where kastom still reigns. The cross-island walk from west to east—Lenakel to White Sands—treks uphill through villages and jungle, then down across the ash plain; it is about a six-hour walk. The plateau in the northern section of the island, at White Grass, is home to a large herd of wild horses, the descendants of stock introduced by missionaries. A road leads here, or you can trek on foot. The horses are magnificent.

The kastom village that is the usual package tour stop is Yaohnanen, where the men still wear *nambas*, penis sheaths, and the women grass skirts. The traveler can pay to see kastom dancing and a kava ceremony. Kava is also drunk routinely, by men only, at the nakamal, the village clearing, most evenings. The kava of Vanuatu is notorious for its potency. In very short order its novocainelike effects take hold, making it virtually impossible to move any part of the body in any direction. After drinking the kava, it is rude to speak in anything above a whisper, but after finishing a cup of Tanna kava, you're lucky to be able to manage even that.

## ESPIRITU SANTO

From the time Quirós first sighted this beautiful island in 1606 to the onset of World War II, little changed here. The work of the Seabees—clearing jungles, building hospitals, barracks, roads, and airfields, bulldozing land to plant gardens—must have seemed like a whirlwind storm to these islanders. Traffic and activity built up until, at one time, there were nearly two hundred thousand American and New Zealand troops stationed here. At war's end, they left as abruptly as they had come, and time and the jungle have reclaimed or damaged or obscured much of the evidence of their sojourn here.

Santo remained a prosperous island, however, at least until the 1980 rebellion by Jimmy Stevens. Since independence, it has tried to bounce back, and a number of hotels, including some offshore island resorts, are evidence of optimism about Santo's potential.

The traveler arrives at Pekoa Airport, five kilometers east of Luganville, the center for exploration of Santo. Luganville sits on Segond Channel, a 13-kilometer waterway that curves around behind Aore Island, thus providing ships a haven from hurricanes. For this reason, you will hear Luganville called Canal by locals. Today, it is the second city of Vanuatu, the main copra port, and site of a meat cannery and fish processing plant—with much of this activity directed from the Quonset huts left by the Allies.

Santo can be explored by truck, although there isn't much road here. A string of islets lines the east coast, and many of these are accessible by motor launch or dugout canoe. Market days in Luganville—Tuesdays for the south Santo people, Thursdays for east Santo goods, Saturdays for everybody—are the best times to look for rides back and forth.

The well-equipped hiker can strike out around the coast for trips of varying length; check with your hotel, the police, or the Local Government Council about a guide—and about the advisability of the trip.

Tanafo, 22 kilometers north of Luganville, was the site of the headquarters of NaGriamel and Jimmy Stevens' ill-fated 1980 rebellion. Package tours are today bused in to see the spot, under a banyan tree, where Stevens was arrested. Some Stevens family members still reside here; a few of them have told visitors that they await Jimmy's return.

Package tours do ply the island and are a fine way to see the sights, but the major attractions here are really underwater—Santo is another scuba paradise. The reefs off Aore and Tutuba are fine, but the real lures are off Million Dollar Point at the wreck of the USAT *Calvin Coolidge*, sunk in a mine explosion in 1942 with four thousand aboard, all but two of whom made it the few feet to the shore and safety. Three hundred yards long, with its stern resting at 70 meters below the surface and its bow up at 20 meters, the *Coolidge* is the largest accessible shipwreck in the world.

For less active types, Palikulo and Champagne beaches are quintessential South Seas sweeps of white sand fringed by swaying palms and kissed by turquoise water.

# MALAKULA

This big, rugged island can be a stopover on the Vila-to-Luganville route. Tourist facilities are neither numerous nor luxurious, and while the beaches are lovely, their waters tend to be shark infested. The real attraction of this island is that it is home to the Big Nambas, resident in the north, and the Small Nambas in the south of the island.

The large red penis sheath gives the tribesmen of the Big Nambas their name. They are the last ni-Vanuatu to be touched by contemporary Western civilization. Those who remain continue to practice the barter of yams and pigs for women and a ritual in which a particularly valued woman is honored by having her two front teeth knocked out. The women wear large headdresses of red fibers, and the men wear, in addition to the namba, bark belts.

Tribal fighting—and cannibalism—characterized Big Namba life until the 1930s and was responsible for many tribespeople leaving the territory, in the northwest of the island, for safer lives around the coast. A road now leads through Big Namba territory, running 20 kilometers from Norsup to Amokh, where you can pay the chief for permission to take photos of the village and the villagers.

The Small Nambas are far less accommodating. No roads penetrate here, and tourists may *not* visit the Small Nambas except for purposes of scholarly research, for which it is necessary to apply well in advance to the government and pay a hefty fee. The men of this tribe wear a small, banana-leaf namba; during funeral rites, they affect gaudy face masks and body paint.

# PENTECOST

The extraordinary land diving of Pentecost has now become a tourism package, with one all-inclusive price for a day trip from Port-Vila. Even if you are not on the tour, you must pay to watch the divers. Flights to Pentecost are via Espiritu Santo; the traveler should check with the visitors bureau in Vila for the dates on which the dives will be held that year.

Though done to ensure a successful yam harvest, the land dive has its origin in legend. A woman kept trying to run away from her husband's mistreatment, only to be brought back each time. Finally, she took refuge in a tree. Her husband, Tamalie, climbed up after her. Just as he reached her, she dared him to follow her and jumped off the tree, landing unhurt. Tamalie followed and was of course killed; he had not known that his wife had tied liana vines to her ankles to break her fall. Today, the Pentecost land dive is exclusively a male prerogative.

A diver constructs his own diving tower, on a hillside around a tree, to a height of about 20 to 25 meters. He builds it by taping the trunks of saplings, bracing the tower horizontally with branches, and lashing it all together and to the core tree with lianas. Each part of the tower is named after a part of the human anatomy, from feet to crown. At the base of the tower, the land must be flat and softened to break the fall. The diver also constructs the platform he will jump from (to be lashed to the tower), and he selects his own vines, calculating the length so that his head will just brush the ground at the end of the jump. Thus, no other person can be held responsible for mishaps. In lashing the platform to the tower, the diver supports it with a branch designed to collapse when the vines are fully extended to help break the diver's fall.

For weeks before the dive, the diver has followed strict taboos; he has maintained a particular diet, refrained from entering his gardens, kept away from kava and sex. On the day of the dive, the men chant and dance while the women, who must remain a certain distance from the tower, whistle to inspire the divers. They take their places one by one. Each diver climbs to his tower, binds the lianas around his ankles, calls for silence and delivers a speech which may be his last. Then he sends a leaf or feather down from the tower's height, claps his hands over his head several times and shouts. Below, the singing and whistling are again taken up. The diver's body begins to fall forward as he crosses his arms over his chest. He arches his body back and plummets earthward.

The idea is of course that the fully extended vines will "stop" the diver just inches from the ground. The length of the vines is crucial; fully stretched, they should enable the diver's head to just graze the softened earth. Too long, and the diver will crash; too short, and he will recoil back into the tower. The action of the dive itself is also critical. Since the platform is on the upper, narrower part of the tower, the diver must push outward as his feet leave the edge of the platform. Too far, and the vines will stretch outward, shooting the diver back against the tower. Too gently, and the diver might collide with the tower as he hurtles downward.

In a day of perhaps 20 dives, there are occasional mishaps—and deaths. One of the most interesting aspects of this ritual is that no shame attaches to a diver who gets cold feet at the last moment, nor is he in any way ridiculed; he simply walks away, and the next diver climbs up to take his place.

### Vanuatu Address

Vanuatu Visitors Bureau
P.O. Box 209
Port-Vila
Vanuatu

# CHAPTER 14

# THE SOLOMON ISLANDS

*Name:* Solomon Islands
*Political status:* Independent state
*Island groups:* Shortland Islands, Treasury Islands, Choiseul, New Georgia Islands, Santa Isabel, Florida Islands, Russell Islands, Malaita, Guadalcanal, Makira, Rennell, Bellona, Santa Cruz Islands, Ontong Java
*Gateway island:* Guadalcanal
*Capital:* Honiara
*Population:* 251,000
*Land area:* 28,530 square kilometers
*Language:* English, Pidgin
*Currency:* Solomon Islands dollar ($SI)
NOTE: Area is malarial.

The story is told of the Australian who, in the 1930s, sensing that the great powers would soon engulf the world in war, looked for a remote place on earth where he and his family might be safe. He chose an obscure Pacific island of rugged mountains and thick

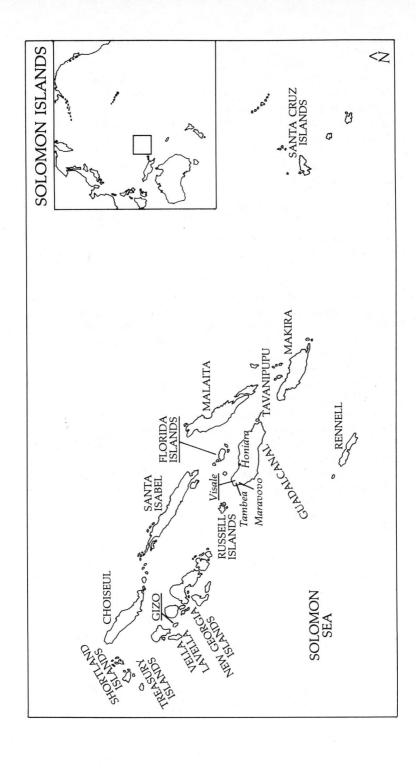

jungle, a place of no interest to anyone, a place called Guadalcanal. It would, of course, become better known, so much better known that the name that once sent puzzled Americans scurrying to their atlases has become irrevocably a grim symbol of bloody fighting. Yet to those who live here, Guadalcanal and the other Solomon Islands are the "Happy Isles," and the few people who visit them may just be right in thinking they have stumbled upon the real secret paradise of the Pacific.

# GEOGRAPHY, TOPOGRAPHY, CLIMATE

The Solomons are a double chain of islands that march, roughly side by side, along a 1400-kilometer northwest-to-southeast chain between 6.5 and 13 degrees south latitude and 155 to 170 degrees east longitude. The six large islands of the double chain—Choiseul, New Georgia, Santa Isabel, Malaita, Guadalcanal, and Makira—comprise some 80 percent of the total landmass. There are about 20 medium-sized islands, nearly 900 other islets and reefs worthy of the name, and numberless tiny clods of earth. Bougainville and Buka islands are geographically part of the Solomons, but politically they belong to Papua New Guinea.

The Solomons constitute a classic island arc, sitting on a curved ridge between the Australian and Pacific plates, fertile ground for volcanic activity. The Santa Cruz Chain is on the Pacific side of the ridge; it has two volcanoes, Vanikolo and Tinakula, as well as numerous fringing and barrier reefs produced by the subsidence activity of other islands. The volcanoes are part of the Ring of Fire that continues through Savo, just north of Guadalcanal, through two submarine volcanoes—Kavachi and Cook—off the east of New Georgia, and through Simbo and Vella Lavella islands in the New Georgia Group. Savo last erupted in 1840, and Tinakula erupted briefly in 1971. Fumaroles and hot springs are scattered throughout these islands. The waters here, the various channels and sounds and straits, are filled with shoals, banks, pinnacles, reefs, and atolls. Particularly around the fringes—Ontong Java and Rennell Island—raised limestone atolls are the rule.

The mountains of the main islands are rugged, in the 1000 to 1500 meter range, and there is little flat land. The exception is Guadalcanal; although its high point, Mount Popomanaseu, reaches to 2330 meters, there is extensive coastal plain along the north. The river systems of the islands tend to run straight and fast downhill, flooding the coasts during heavy rains.

Such rains occur usually between December and March, with the climate hot and humid year-round. The *aras*, southeast trades, predominate during the "dry" season from April to November—they blow hard and long. The rest of the year brings *komburu*, northwesterly monsoonal winds. Up until 1986, it could be said of the Solomons that cyclone buildups normally moved south, causing little damage. In that year, however, Cyclone Manu caused considerable death and destruction; when all those straight, swift rivers swelled and began hurtling their way down the mountainside, they cut a wide path of devastation, bearing before them crops, homes, bridges, lives.

# THE NATURAL ENVIRONMENT

Dense tropical rain forests cover most of the large islands, filled with lianas, ferns, mosses, orchids, various epiphytes, and such flowering shrubs as hibiscus. Sago palms grow in freshwater swamp areas, and many river deltas have formed mangrove swamps. Crocodiles lurk in the latter, and the islands boast numerous lizards, snakes—two are venomous—turtles, skinks, frogs, and toads. Land mammals, mostly nocturnal, include bats, rats, mice, and the cuscus, a monkeylike marsupial.

Unhappily, one of the more prevalent creatures in the Solomon Islands is the female anopheles mosquito, carrier of malaria; Guadalcanal itself is the most malaria-infested island in the world. In addition to taking *some* sort of prophylaxis—which sort is best is a constant topic of discussion among visitors here—be aware that the mosquitoes bite mainly from dusk to dawn, so keep yourself covered, use repellent, and make use of mosquito netting when you go to bed.

Sharks are another potentially unpleasant fact of life in the Solomons. Some people will tell you that white sand beaches are better than black, though there is no real scientific evidence for this. Ask a *responsible* authority before you venture out for a swim. On Malaita, shark worship has long been a part of local culture; many islanders still believe that the souls of their ancestors live on in sharks. There are those who argue that this is why the sharks in Malaita's waters rarely attack. Perhaps. What is certain is that there *are* sharks in these waters and that they are living creatures and therefore unpredictable—even if they *are* somebody's ancestors.

Bird life in the Solomon Islands is rich and varied—at least 148 species and subspecies of land and freshwater birds occur here, as well as the usual seabirds and shorebirds of the Pacific. If you add in all the geographically representative species, the total number of avian fauna comes to some 300, of which about 240 can be identified in the field. Interestingly, there is less literature on the habitats, habits, and voices of Solomon Island birds than on birds of any other region of the Pacific. The bird-watcher should take note, however, that most species are endemic either to a single island or to a few similar islands.

Guadalcanal itself has a range of bird life, including a number of species restricted to the mountains. Cormorants, bitterns, king and pygmy parrots, hawks, ospreys, rails, pigeons, doves, kingfishers, sunbirds, cockatoos—the long list goes on and on. Perhaps the most interesting bird of the Solomons, found particularly on Savo, is the megapode known as the incubator bird (*Megapodius freycinet eremita* Hartlaub). Most common along the seashore, and rarely found above 200 meters, this megapode is small and dark, with a red forehead, a short crest, and olive-green legs and feet. It is called the incubator because it does *not* incubate its eggs; rather, the female deposits the egg—twice the size of a chicken egg—in the soil or sand near a thermal hot spot, in warm volcanic ash, or in heaps of decaying forest litter for an incubation period of 40 days. At the end of that time, the newly hatched young dig themselves out and fly as soon as their feathers are dry; they are completely independent of their parents from the moment of birth.

Rennell Island has a number of species not found elsewhere in the Solomons. The islands of the Santa Cruz Group have fewer indigenous species of all fauna.

Look also for sensational butterflies and moths in these islands.

# HISTORY

Papuan peoples—hunters and food gatherers—may first have come to these islands some ten millennia ago. Probably around 2000 B.C., groups of neolithic Austronesian-speakers arrived and mingled with or displaced the early settlers. Remains found in Fotoruma Cave near the Poha River on Guadalcanal have been carbon-dated to about 1300 B.C. The finds, which contain no pottery, give evidence of an agricultural people who planted taro on shifting plots and raised chickens, dogs, and pigs. There is also evidence that they built outriggers sturdy enough to cross from Makira to the Santa Cruz Group, where Lapita pottery has been found.

How and when those Lapita potters got to the Santa Cruz Group is unknown, but the obsidian trail indicates a migration route from New Britain through the Solomons to Santa Cruz and New Caledonia, probably around 1000 B.C. and probably by the ancestors of today's Polynesians. The so-called Polynesian fringe of the Solomons—ethnic Polynesians resident today in the outlying Santa Cruz Islands, Rennell and Bellona, Sikaiana, and Ontong Java—is not a result of this eastward migration; rather, the forebears of these

Polynesians back-migrated, over the past 1500 years or so, from Wallis and Futuna and from Tuvalu to settle these outposts of the Solomons.

The overwhelming fact of this early period of Solomon Islands history is the isolation of the settlements, reflected in a linguistic diversity still prevalent today. Despite the cultural differences, certain traits were, and are, characteristically Melanesian. The extended family—in today's Pidgin, the *wantok*, as in "one-talk," viz., people who speak your language—was the basis of social life, although descent lines might be patrilineal, matrilineal, or a combination of the two. The possession of land and material wealth was the major indicator of status, gained through ostentatious display in ritual giving. Big Man rank was achieved on merit rather than heredity: success in accumulating wealth and generosity in dispensing it, as well as warrior skills and organizational ability. Another Melanesian characteristic was the delineation of taboos and roles for each sex.

The first Europeans here explored little of this society; indeed, European contact was sparse and not very successful for centuries. The Spaniard Alvaro de Mendaña de Neira put in at Estrella Bay, Santa Isabel, on February 7, 1568, lured from Peru by Incan legends of an Eldorado some 600 leagues westward. Mendaña built a five-ton brigantine to explore nearby islands, giving them the Spanish names they bear today; Guadalcanal he named for his birthplace in Spain. It was on Guadalcanal that some islanders massacred a party of Mendaña's men. Mendaña headed back to Peru, claiming that he had discovered the islands of King Solomon, reeking with wealth.

He returned in 1595, stopping along the way to name the Marquesas, and this time landed in the Santa Cruz Group. Mendaña's plan was to start a colony; for this purpose, a number of unmarried Peruvian women had been brought along, as well as Doña Isabel Barreto, Mendaña's wife—an ambitious, arrogant woman whose aim seems to have been to become queen of the Solomon Islands and all their treasures. The expedition, the colony, and the gold mining were doomed, as was Mendaña himself; he died in Santa Cruz, and the expedition moved on to the Philippines. Another settlement effort failed in 1606. Despite the presence in Mendaña's crew of the fine pilot Pedro Fernandez de Quirós, early charts of the Solomons placed them well to the east of their actual location; even though Carteret passed through in 1767 and Bougainville in 1768, it wasn't until 1838 that they were identified as the islands first explored by Mendaña.

By that time, the whalers and traders had begun to frequent the area, and in 1845, the first missionaries, a group of Marist

Catholic priests, arrived on Makira. After several priests were killed, the Anglicans decided it would be safer and smarter to train some Solomon Islanders for missionary work; despite the murder of the first Anglican bishop, the Anglicans eventually succeeded sufficiently that today's Church of Melanesia, the main church of the Solomons, is Anglican.

Blackbirding was particularly vicious in the Solomons. Recruiters often disguised themselves as missionaries—one reason for the murderous attitude toward priests. They also kidnapped islanders at random and treated their recruits atrociously en route to the canefields of Queensland and Fiji. Between 1870 and 1910, some thirty thousand islanders were blackbirded; ten thousand of them never returned. The practice only really died out in Australia when blacks were expelled in 1904; it ended in Fiji in 1910.

Blackbirding—and the violence and anti-European feelings it engendered—was one of the reasons the British declared a protectorate over New Georgia, Guadalcanal, Makira, and Malaita in 1893. The major reason, however, was to limit German advances in this part of the Pacific; the Germans held New Guinea and had "interests" in the Northern Solomons. The British resident commissioner, Charles Woodford, set up headquarters at Tulagi in the Florida Group, then the capital of the Solomons, and in 1898 and 1899 Britain added Santa Cruz, Rennell, and Bellona to its protectorate. In 1900, in exchange for giving up claims to Western Samoa, Britain received the remaining islands from Germany. Receiving them, it turned out, was not the same as holding them: head-hunting and blood feuds remained frequent, and Choiseul did not come under full administrative control until 1941. It then became part of what was a relatively sleepy group of islands given over to copra plantations owned by Lever Brothers, Burns Philp, and Fairymead—a place where nothing much happened.

## World War II

Following Pearl Harbor, the Japanese had taken Guam, the Philippines, Hong Kong, and Singapore and had advanced through Indonesia. In March 1942, they took Rabaul on New Britain Island (present-day Papua New Guinea), which would become their prime supply depot and staging area, and Bougainville Island. In April, they stepped across from Bougainville to the Shortland Islands in the western Solomons and bombed Gavutu and Tulagi, where there were small detachments of Allied troops. The troops withdrew, and, on May 2, the Japanese took over both islands. On July 1, they landed in strength on Guadalcanal and began to build an airbase. A number of planters, traders, and government officials, with the help of numerous Solomon Islanders, "went bush" and became coast-watchers, radioing out information on Japanese movements in the islands. Their aim was to aid Operation Watchtower, the Allied plan to drive forward into the Solomons and onto Rabaul.

What could the Americans possibly want, a Japanese general staff officer wondered aloud, with an insignificant island inhabited only by natives? What they wanted with Guadalcanal was the air-base. From it, the Japanese could take dead aim at Australia, the last Allied power in the Pacific. Australia was saved, it would later be said, in the jungles of Papua New Guinea and Guadalcanal. On Guadalcanal, the victory would be a long time coming.

American forces landed on August 7, 1942, and seized the air-base, renaming it Henderson Field after a U.S. Marine killed in the battle of Midway. At Red Beach, where the ten thousand Marines landed, the traveler today sees a peaceful prospect, marred only by the rusting debris of landing craft. Indeed, there was little resistance to the Red Beach landing; the real fighting that day was on Blue Beach on Tulagi. While the landings were proceeding, however, a Japanese naval force was en route from Rabaul. The convoy moved down New Georgia Sound, called The Slot, the channel dividing the two main chains of the Solomons, and on August 9 sailed undetected around Savo Island, achieving complete surprise and a resounding victory. The Battle of Savo Island was one of the worst naval defeats ever suffered by the U.S. Four cruisers and two destroyers were sunk, the first of so many ships, planes, and men to be lost here that the waters were later called Ironbottom Sound.

Worst of all, at least to the disbelieving Marines on "The Canal," the battle caused the withdrawal of Allied naval support. The Marines were on their own. Forty-three years after the event, a veteran called it: "Only our deep inexperience of war kept us from realizing our predicament. There were ten thousand troops on the island with no ships to supply them; we were alone and abandoned on a hostile shore" (Nikolai Stevenson, "Four Months on the Front Line," *American Heritage*, vol. 36, no. 6, Oct.-Nov., 1985).

"Bastogne," William Manchester has written (*Goodbye, Darkness: A Memoir of the Pacific*, Little, Brown & Co., Boston, 1979), "was considered an epic. . . . The 101st Airborne was surrounded there for eight days. But the Marines on Guadacanal were to be isolated for over four months. There have been few such stands in history." Japanese supplies and troops kept coming down The Slot in what the Marines dubbed The Tokyo Express. Rations for the Marines were short. They suffered malaria, jungle rot, and dysentery, as well as the tension of what one veteran called "the endless vigil."

The island was bombed constantly. During the day, there were aerial dogfights with Marine aces like Pappy Boyington and Joe Foss fighting off Zeroes, Bettys, and Zekes. At night, there were Louie the Louse, a float plane that dropped pale green flares over the beach, and Washing Machine Charlie, which drove the troops crazy with its whining noise. Pistol Pete was what they called the 155-millimeter Japanese howitzers; Dugout Sunday was the day six-inch guns tried to pin down Allied pilots long enough for bombers from Rabaul to arrive. It didn't work, writes Manchester, "thanks to information brought through the lines by natives, striking men who wore only the lavalava. . . . The battle couldn't have been won without these islanders."

The battle was many battles. In September, the Japanese landed more troops east of the Americans and began to move west toward Henderson. The Marines known as Edson's Raiders were brought over from Tulagi and took up a position on a north-to-south-running ridge south of the airfield. The grass-covered hogback, where today the traveler can see both American and Japanese memorials, was renamed Bloody Ridge or Edson's Ridge after the Marines managed to halt the Japanese advance. There were six major naval engagements during the battle, the most decisive being the Battle of Guadalcanal in November, which prevented the Japanese from landing troops. Still, the Marine war against the enemy in the jungle, malaria, and exhaustion continued until February 1943, when reinforcements were finally brought in and the Japanese withdrew to New Georgia— to be defeated there in July.

Afterward, Guadalcanal would be called a turning point in the war. Along with the fighting in Papua New Guinea, it broke the back of the Japanese advance and enabled the Allies to go on the offensive. Guadalcanal itself became a staging area for those forward actions.

## The Postwar Period to Independence

If Guadalcanal had changed the war, the war had also changed Guadalcanal and all the Solomon Islands. The capital at Tulagi (from which John F. Kennedy's PT-109 had set out) had been destroyed; the administrative center was moved to Guadalcanal, where the Americans had left roads, Quonset huts, wharves and platforms. The place was called Honiara from the native *naho ni ara*, "facing the east and south-east wind."

The immediate postwar period also saw the rise of Maasina Ruru, which is usually translated as "Marching Rule" but which islanders say means "Brotherhood Rule." Sir Frederick Osifelo, MBE, who would chair the Solomon Islands' constitutional convention and would serve as speaker for the constitutional delegation to London, argues that Maasina Ruru was not primarily a cargo cult, as most expats and foreigners would have it. Rather, says Osifelo, "The main aim of the Maasina Ruru movement was self-government," and while it is true that "some of the leaders injected a 'cargo cult' idea into the Movement, this was only a sidetrack" (*Kanaka Boy,* Institute of Pacific Studies, Solomon Islands, 1985). The movement's original objective was to demand a pay raise for Malaitan copra workers; as the movement spread, actions became more radical, with some leaders encouraging people not to pay taxes, to withhold their names from the census, and otherwise to confound and confront the colonial administration. In 1948, the British used force to crush Maasina Ruru, but the movement resurfaced in strength, until finally Britain began to give in to the inevitable, forming local government councils as a first step to the independence finally granted on July 7, 1978. "I am convinced," Osifelo has written in his autobiography, *Kanaka Boy,* "that the war brought about the formation of Maasina Ruru and that the Movement influenced the Colonial Administration to establish Local Government throughout the Solomons. . . ." Today, the Solomons are governed by a National Assembly, seven provincial assemblies, and numerous area councils.

# THE SOLOMON ISLANDS TODAY

The fragmented nature of Solomon Islands society occasionally turns into fractiousness. The road to independence was not entirely smooth; the western islands, with more resources and more wealth, were concerned about losing control, and the constitution arrived at in London had to grant them considerable autonomy. This followed a few threats of secession, and the menace of that possibility still hovers over a political life that is characterized by a good deal of personal infighting.

Customary land accounts for nearly 90 percent of the Solomons, but the *particular* custom affecting ownership differs from place to place, and disputes are frequent. Nine out of ten Solomon Islanders live in villages and practice subsistence agriculture; they work collectively on community projects, and they share within and between wantoks (the extended family groups). An individual's achievements are valued by how much he contributes to the community as a whole; an individual who shows what might be considered too much initiative may come to be resented, while too much ability might be envied.

About 93 percent of the population is Melanesian, but within this ethnic definition is a variety of complexions and appearances. Generally, the people of the west and north are darker skinned, while to the southeast, the color is lighter. Ginger-colored hair is not uncommon, especially on Malaita. Polynesians make up 4 percent of the population and live primarily in the fringe islands where a Polynesian society—patrilineal, hierarchical, and hereditary—prevails. Numerous Micronesians, mostly Gilbertese, settled around Honiara and Gizo in New Georgia in the late 1950s. At the mouth of the Mataniko River in Honiara is a real Chinatown, and a number of Europeans or part Europeans also live in Honiara and in some central province locations. Small minorities of indigenous Papuan-speaking people also remain in the Russell, Santa Cruz, and New Georgia groups. Around the country, there are at least thirty mutually unintelligible languages in use, and the total number of spoken dialects approaches ninety.

What unifies this potpourri of people are regional identities, religion, education, and the growing presence of the central government. Despite rivalries among denominations—including the so-called new religions like Seventh-Day Adventist and Jehovah's Witnesses—Christianity claims most of the population, with only a very few tribal religionists or cargo cultists left. The churches have been primarily responsible for education as well, and they, along with the central government, have fostered the development of modern health and social services. The endemic diseases include malaria, tuberculosis, and leprosy; malaria had been virtually wiped out by DDT, but in 1975, the spray was discontinued, and the number of cases is again of epidemic proportions. Alcoholism and violent crime have also been on the upswing, especially in and around Honiara, where urban migration has threatened to overwhelm the capital.

The economy is based in copra, palm oil, cacao, timber, and fish exports. Lever Brothers still controls much of Guadalcanal's coastal plain where copra and cacao are produced, and the multinational also runs the busy palm oil mill. Forestry, however, is the nation's leading industry, with forests owned by the government but worked by mostly foreign-owned companies.

The country probably has significant mineral resources, and it certainly has excellent potential for geothermal energy— Medaña may have been right after all. But development of these resources would be prohibitively expensive and is probably light-years away.

# THE TRAVELER
# IN THE SOLOMON ISLANDS

The Solomons offer the traveler a menu of two different but easily combined tastes. One is an array of accommodations that might be a model for the kind of holiday resort the Pacific does best. These are often small-island resorts or "resthouses," typically offering self-contained bungalows with few amenities but with central dining facilities and bar, and affording the possibility of arranging a variety of water sports, hikes, sightseeing, or other activities. The atmosphere is laid back and informal. The settings are invariably lovely and very much off the beaten track.

The other dish, equally delectable, is the possibility of striking out, completely on your own, to explore the farther reaches of islands where life is, by any definition, at least thus far unspoiled.

In either case, you will meet few other travelers. They will mostly be Australians or New Zealanders, although you may also run into American Peace Corps volunteers or a variety of aid workers and missionaries. On Guadalcanal itself, you may meet returning American or Japanese veterans, Japanese "bone-hunters" praying for the souls of relatives who died here, aid officials from Down Under or Britain, and, ironically, clutches of young Japanese businessmen on economic missions. There is fine Japanese cuisine in Honiara, and menus in many of the capital's restaurants are in Japanese as well as English.

Indeed, before heading for the outliers, the traveler should explore Guadalcanal. Honiara is the key resource center, the place where you can make most arrangements for the outliers. Change travelers' checks here as well, as it is often difficult to do so in the out-islands. And of course, reconfirm all flights.

### Solomon Islands Pidgin

| | |
|---|---|
| Yumi | We |
| Mifala | Us |
| Gudfala | Nice |
| Save | To know |
| Longwe | Far |
| Hem i stap wea | Where is? |
| Bia blong Solomon | Betel nut |
| Nambawan | The best |
| Nambaten | The worst |
| Wantok | Kinsmen, clan |

NOTE: If you're an American who has been traveling for a while, has met only Aussies and Kiwis, and comes upon a volleyball game played by U.S. Peace Corps volunteers, you've found your wantok.

# GUADALCANAL

Guadalcanal is a flattened S lying on its side. Paved road extends from Lambi on the west to Aola on the east—except where the paving has been washed or rutted away. Motorable tracks head upland and around the southeast, and good trails track all around the island and across its interior. There are villages all around the coastline and following the courses of inland rivers. The southern half of the flattened S is higher and more rugged than the north, dropping sharply to a minute strip of coastal plain.

Henderson Airport is in the north. You step out of it into a small patch of memorials—to the Seabees; the Fiji guerrillas and the South Pacific scouts; the Marine Raiders; the 1st Marine Division; the Solomon Islander coast watchers, scouts, guides, and stretcher bearers. It's a fitting opening to a visit to Guadalcanal.

Henderson is 13 kilometers east of Honiara, and the route is served by airport-hotel bus, taxis, public bus, and passenger truck.

## Honiara

The capital is strung along a narrow strip of coast. The outskirts contain the Pacific equivalent of slums—more-makeshift-than-usual housing for hurricane or volcano refugees or migrants lured by the "bright lights" of the capital. Kukum is the suburb just to the east of Honiara. You pass the very good seaside hospital, still called Number 9 from the days when it was the U.S. Army aid station, then on your left the row of buildings that constitutes Chinatown and runs inland along the Mataniko River, then the waterfront and Point Cruz. Houses climb the hillside, and the main drag, Mendaña Avenue, running east-west, is lined with shops, restaurants, airline offices, government buildings.

There are a number of hotels in Honiara, meeting varied budget needs, but the bar of the Mendana Hotel is a gathering place for resident expatriates, visiting businessmen, and tourists as well. Just next to the Mendana is SITA, the Solomon Islands Tourist Authority. Across from the Mendana are the post office, bank, and courthouse, and behind the courthouse is the office of the Department of Lands and Surveys, where you can find excellent topographic maps to help in planning your travels here. The center of action in town is an almost mall-like minishopping center; across from it is Solair, Solomon Islands Airways Limited, which is the center for all travel arrangements—domestic and international—and your essential stop for booking flights to the outliers and reconfirming your international flight.

Almost all needed items are available in Honiara, which is richly supplied with supermarkets. In among them is an excellent bookstore, the Aruligo Book Center—a delightful find for those travelers hunting down literature on the Pacific, or if you're starved for something really good to read.

The Solomons have been called a museum without walls because of the variety and exceptional skill of the handicrafts produced throughout these islands. Honiara's craft shops offer items from many of the outliers and are excellent places in which to buy. The most sought-after item, now made in miniature for the tourist trade, is the *nguzunguzu*, a carved figurehead, characteristically with mother-of-pearl shell inlay, that was once attached to the prow of war canoes to guide the party to success in headhunting. These and many other fine woodcarvings come particularly from the western Solomons. Look for the "fish-bobs," buoylike carvings usually representing fish or birds, with string and fishhook attached—when a fish is hooked, the carving's head bobs up in the water to indicate to the fisherman where his catch is.

From Malaita come shell money and useful shell items—combs, rattles, flutes, jewelry, fishhooks. From the Polynesian fringe come carved miniature canoes. Makira Province is known particularly for ceremonial bowls, also inlaid with shell. Guadalcanal itself produces the *asa* vine baskets, bags, and trays known collectively as *buka* ware.

## Around the Island

There are three things to see on Guadalcanal. The sites of war are probably best seen on an organized tour by car or van. The interior terrain is probably best seen on foot. The underwater world—reefs, fish, and war wrecks—is best seen by scuba diving, but snorkelers may almost always go along for the ride. When you're tired of looking, Guadalcanal offers two of the loveliest holiday resorts in the Pacific.

A battlefield tour begins with Red Beach, where the Marines landed, and takes in Bloody Ridge, site of the battle that turned the tide. There are now both American and Japanese memorials atop the ridge. On Mount Austen, there is an impressive Japanese gift to the peoples of the Solomon Islands—a statue of a fisherman, the work of Eikichi Takahasi, given in homage by his native city, Ishinomaki. Takahasi was killed in the battle on Guadalcanal. A four-sided plinth, in Japanese and English, has been placed here by the South Pacific Memorial Association and the Solomon Islands Wartime Comrade Association, a plea for peace. The next ridge over, Gifu Ridge, one of the front lines of battle here, takes its name from the city of Gifu, hometown of most of the Japanese soldiers who fought there.

Betikama, where any organized tour will surely take you, was once the U.S. military headquarters on Guadalcanal. Today, it is a Seventh-Day Adventist school and site of an excellent carvings shop. World War II relics, however, are evident on the grounds, and there is also a small war museum. You will also want to see the underground field hospital near the Lungga River, the Japanese command post at Kakambona Village, and Kamimbo Bay, where the Japanese made their escape from Guadalcanal in February 1943.

Many other vestiges of the war are visible all around the island. Marsden matting, used by the Seabees as a bed for airstrips, in bridge building, and in road construction, today forms part of fencing or buildings. Foxholes, airplane wrecks, and the like dot the island; many such remnants are in the flat coastal plain owned by Lever Brothers and are not accessible to the public, although a local war heritage association keeps agitating to build a memorial there.

Walking is an excellent way to see both the major battlefields and some of the scattered wreckage of the war, as well as being a great way to get into the interior and to visit custom villages, centers of traditional Melanesian life. An excellent guide to walking here, *Walks on Guadalcanal*, by J. L. O. Tedder, maps by A. Clayton, has been published by the Solomon Islands Tourist Authority and can be purchased at the SITA office. It's an essential vade mecum for the walker, as is a topographic map available at the Lands and Surveys Office. Both can point the walker to trips of a few hours or a day from easily reached trailheads. For walks of more than a day, the walker will do best to hire a guide. (*Walks on Guadalcanal* has tips on where to find guides for different walks, including Mount Popomanaseu, as well as other good advice.) Whatever the length of your walk, if you pass through a village or even meet an islander along the trail, the etiquette is to ask if it is all right that you proceed.

One of the "sights" of Guadalcanal that combines both war memorabilia and a model custom village is Fred Kona's War Museum at Vilu Village, some 25 kilometers west of Honiara.

Diving off Guadalcanal includes the wrecks of Ironbottom Sound—Japanese transports, a U.S B-17 "Flying Fortress" bomber, a submarine, and more. A few of these wrecks are accessible via walk-in from the beaches. The waters here also offer coral walls, giant clams, and drift dives with school fish. Between Island Dive Services, with sites at both the Mendana Hotel and Tambea Village Resort, and DonTas, the dive sites of Guadalcanal's waters are well and reliably covered—or check with SITA.

Tambea Village Resort, 45 kilometers west of Honiara, is one of the model Pacific resorts in which the Solomons abound. On a curve of beach off which there is fine snorkeling and scuba diving, the Tambea consists of bungalows with plumbing, kerosene lamps for light, a dining room, and bar. You can dive, canoe, ride horseback, bush walk, take a tour, or do absolutely nothing at all in an idyllic setting. The resort was started by a Swedish gymnast who was a medalist in the 1936 Olympics. Asked if he had ever seen Jesse Owens, Tambea's owner told a visitor: "I saw him briefly; I never could catch him." Yet in 1985, at the age of 69, Ole, as he is called, walked into Honiara after a big storm—cars couldn't get through— swimming the swollen rivers along the route. He then sent word back to Tambea that no one should try to come into town—it was too rough. Tambea Village Resort is partly owned by the villagers of nearby Tambea. If you want to relax and get away from it all for a few days, this is the place. Book your stay in Honiara, and someone will come get you.

To get even further away, try another model hostelry, the Tavanipupu Island Resort, on a 40-acre island in Marau Sound, off the southeastern tip of Guadalcanal. You will need food basics and condiments, although you can buy fresh fruit and vegetables from nearby villagers and visiting canoes. All water sports are available.

# THE OUTLIERS

As of this writing, there were eight tourist-oriented hostelries in the Solomons outside of Guadalcanal—on Malaita, Anuha (in the Florida Group), at Munda and Gizo in the New Georgia Group, in the beautiful Marovo Lagoon, and on Pigeon Island in the Reef Islands of the Santa Cruz Group. The traveler can make any or all of these a starting point for further exploration of those islands. In addition, there are numerous other guesthouses and other forms of accommodations on these and various other islands. Check with SITA. The least-frequented islands are three of the big ones—Choiseul, Isabel, and Makira. Guesthouse accommodation is possible here, often run by the Mothers Union. The difficulties of getting to and around these islands is to many their greatest appeal. Though Peace Corps workers are justifiably weary of being regarded as hostels of the Third World for visiting Americans, you might just stop in at PC headquarters in Honiara and see if there's anybody in the outliers who is dying for a visit.

## Central Province

Savo Island is a day trip from Honiara, usually on an organized tour to look for the megapode. It is possible to climb to the crater of the volcano. Find a guide and be prepared for a strenuous and steamy hike.

Malaita is the second largest Solomon island and the most populous. Auki Lodge in Auki, the main town, and Malu'u Rest House, some 80 kilometers north of Auki, are the two fine holiday hostelries. The people of Langa Langa Lagoon still use shell money, with which they trade as far away as Bougainville—at least ceremonially. Shells are broken into small pieces through which holes are then drilled so that the shells can be strung together. The shells are then rubbed into circular shapes. Thousands are strung together to make *tafuliae*, about two to three meters long. Color also determines value: from the most expensive, red, through orange, white, and black. The Malaitans also use dolphin teeth as custom money, diving for dolphins with the help of a sorcerer's magic; the dolphin meat is a delicacy to the islanders.

The major site here is the Langa Langa Lagoon with its man-made islands, most easily visited by organized tour—usually to Laulasi and Alite. Men may enter only the men's custom houses; women may enter only the women's custom houses. These islands are also home to Shark Callers; the calling is done by gongs beaten underwater, and the sharks are fed when they have answered the call. Lau Lagoon also has man-made islands.

Malaita also has an excellent system of roads; exploration with wheels or on foot is possible throughout.

On Anuha Island north of Tulagi, just a 15-minute flight from Honiara, is a small island that an Australian concern has turned into a luxury resort. Diving and all other water sports off the white beaches, comfortable villalike accommodations, and all meals are offered here. Although Anuha Island is world class, its prices are more reasonable than those of most top-of-the-line resorts.

## Western Province

If the Solomons are perhaps the best kept secret of the Pacific, the New Georgia Group is a cryptologist's dream. Solair flies to Munda on New Georgia and to Gizo regularly. Travelers planning to go on to Papua New Guinea may be able to book the flight from Honiara to Kieta via Gizo and thus see the western province en route out of the Solomons.

The main centers of these islands are Munda, Noro, Gizo, and Ringgi Cove, each of which sends a network of roads out into its respective interior. Walking or hitching, you can see a lot. Travel between islands is mostly by boat, but small-plane Solair connections are also possible.

In Munda—the name often refers to all of New Georgia Island—the place to stay is the Munda Rest House, right across from the airport and facing the sea. Noro is about 20 kilometers northeast of Munda and has no official accommodations.

Gizo is the second city of the Solomons, a lively waterfront community with a large number of resettled Gilbertese. The Gizo Hotel is the place to stay in town, and the hotel also operates the Saeraghi

Rest House, to which you transfer via canoe through numerous waterways. The favorite tourist excursion here is to Plum Pudding Island, also called Kennedy Island. It was here that Lieutenant John F. Kennedy found shelter after his PT-109 was cut in half and he was rescued by a Solomon Islander. (Asked by a young boy how he had become a war hero, the campaigning JFK replied: "It was easy. They sank my boat.") Gizo is also one of the major dive centers of the Solomons.

Another great dive center is Uepi Island, in the sparkling Marovo Lagoon, separated from the sea by a huge and varied coral reef and a series of fringing islands. "Once seen," James Michener wrote of Marovo, "it can never be forgotten." It is hard to decide which is more beautiful—the water of the lagoon, the islands that fringe it, the trees that surround it, the birds that rest in the trees, or the underwater world to be explored here. Uepi Island Resort is the place to stay.

Kolombangara Island is a cone-shaped volcanic island; the volcano rises to 1770 meters and can be climbed from Iriri Village. Solair flies to Ringgi Cove, but there is no official hostelry here.

You can reach Vella Lavella by air or outboard canoe from Gizo or by copra boat from Noro. Simbo is also reachable from Gizo by canoe. The attraction of both these islands is their thermal areas—hot springs, bubbling mud, and smoking fumaroles. You can also catch a glimpse of megapodes here. You'll have to make your own way once you've landed, but the islanders will be happy to help with arrangements.

## The Santa Cruz Islands

This is very remote Solomon Islands, quite different in feeling. The outer, low-lying islands are part of the Polynesian fringe, while the larger islands, like Nendo, are primarily Melanesian. On Pigeon Island, one of the Reef Islands, is Ngarando Resort, a real retreat for getting away from it all; Ngarando is served by twice-weekly air service from Honiara.

Nendo, served by Solair, is a hilly and densely wooded island. It was here that Mendaña was killed; his crew found the island "a corner of hell in the claws of the devil."

### Solomon Islands Address

Solomon Islands Tourist Authority
Honiara, Solomon Islands

# CHAPTER 15

# PAPUA NEW GUINEA

*Name:* Papua New Guinea
*Political status:* Independent state
*Island groups:* Eastern half of New Guinea, Bismarck
    Archipelago, North Solomons, D'Entrecasteaux Islands,
    Louisiade Archipelago
*Gateway island:* Papua New Guinea
*Capital:* Port Moresby
*Population:* 3.4 million
*Land area:* 461,690 square kilometers
*Language:* English, Tok Pisin, Hiri Motu, others
*Currency:* Kina (K)
NOTE: Area is malarial.

Every island nation, every island group, even every island in the Pacific is different from every other. But no place is as different as Papua New Guinea. It is not "like" the rest of Oceania, although it is certainly part—a vocal part—of the insular Pacific. It is not like Asia, although the first settlers here probably came from Southeast Asia 40 millennia ago. The Spanish explorer Ynigo Ortis de Retez, who sailed along part of the north coast in 1545, supposed a resemblance between the people he saw and the inhabitants of Africa's Guinea Coast and called the land Nueve Guinea, but despite the resemblance, Papua New Guinea is not really like Africa. It isn't like anyplace you've ever been.

PNG—as it is routinely called—is for the traveler an astonishingly rich destination, a world of diversities. Its terrain offers high peaks, swamps, jungles, and some coastal areas and outlier islands that answer everyone's desire for unspoiled isles. Its vegetation captures species from both continents that flank the country—Asia and Australia—and from other islands in the Pacific. Its animal life is abundant and thrilling, capped by the magnificent bird of paradise, the national symbol. PNG's people provide an extraordinary array of primitive and exotic cultures. For diversity, consider that the population of fewer than four million speaks more than 760 languages. For primitive and exotic, keep in mind that it wasn't until the 1930s that the outside world "discovered" and was discovered by the bulk of the population, while the Sepik River area has long been hailed as a preeminent workshop of primitive art.

It is also a world of color—the brilliant plumage of birds and birdlike headdresses, the striking green of the countryside and its

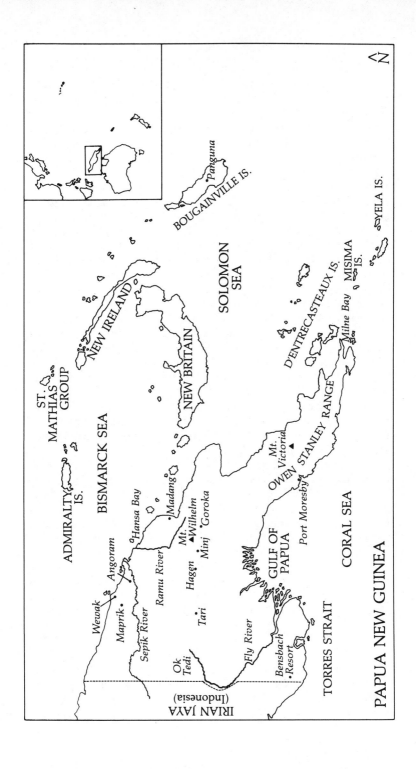

flowering plants, the colors of the *bilums*—the all-purpose woven bags carried by the women. There seems no moderation here; to the Western eye, everything is extreme.

Make no mistake: the traveler here steps into another world. The fascinating people of this country—called nationals, not natives— are a diverse group, but most still live much as they have for thousands of years, although such practices as cannibalism and head-shrinking are said to have been wiped out. The traveler will see women in *asgras*, bunches of leaves tied over their backsides, using digging sticks in their gardens. In traditional tribal cultures, women remain beasts of burden, without status, bought for a bride price in arranged marriages. A few still go off into the bush to bear their babies alone. Their husbands, often shared polygamously, are hunters and virtual lords; they too dress in asgras or *lap-laps*, cloth or fiber aprons hung over the belt. In many villages, men still sleep apart in the men's house. In other villages, nuclear families have their own thatch-roofed huts of woven pandanus leaves, and the main entertainment, apart from church going, is watching videos on the village's one VCR. The traveler will also see young people carrying radios and sporting T-shirts with legends in Tok Pisin—"Mi Laikim Jisas" for born-again Christians, "Nambawan Haus Moni Bilong Papua Niugini" for customers of the PNG Banking Corporation. He will experience the wild terrain that has so affected the development of these people, and he will see some of the extraordinary plant and wildlife with which they have long lived in harmony, and from which they derive their spiritual strengths.

Travel here is neither easy nor cheap. It wants a lot of time. No single chapter in a single book can even begin to do justice to the richness of PNG. Indeed, the body of literature on Papua New Guinea—by historians, art scholars, anthropologists, sociologists, archaeologists, ornithologists, entomologists, zoologists, botanists, ichthyologists, herpetologists, and every other kind of -ist, not to mention explorers, adventurers, and fiction writers—is vast and varied. The present discussion on PNG will try only to introduce the country to the traveler, and vice versa, suggesting how, with limited time at your disposal, you might at least taste some of the richness of this endlessly fascinating place.

## GEOGRAPHY, TOPOGRAPHY, CLIMATE

Papua New Guinea's territory runs from just south of the equator to approximately 12 degrees south latitude, and from 141 to 160 degrees east longitude. The border-to-border distance from east to west is some 2100 kilometers; from north to south, the distance is about 1300 kilometers. The country consists of a large, mountainous island (half-island, actually), much longer than it is wide, with a long, protruding peninsula to the southeast, together with a series of off-shore islands. The whole nation, mainland and island PNG, is administratively divided into 20 provinces that also constitute geographic distinctions.

Nearly 80 percent of the total land area of PNG is accounted for on the main island, where the country occupies the eastern half of New Guinea, second largest noncontinental island on earth (after Greenland). On New Guinea, PNG shares a 730-kilometer land border with Irian Jaya, governed by Indonesia, a matter of no small political concern.

Island PNG rides down the northeast coast of the main island and along its long southeastern peninsula. The Bismarck Archipelago forms a kind of fallen-over J to the north and east of the main island in the Solomon Sea. Here are the Admiralty Islands, including Manus, where Margaret Mead continued her study of adolescence and sex in primitive societies; the Saint Mathias Group; New Ireland, the long, skinny shank of the J; and New Britain, the long, overweight hook of the J. Buka and Bougainville, which nearly abut the J right where it curves, are the North Solomon Islands, while scattered in lines in Milne Bay, like afterthoughts of the main island's peninsula, are the D'Entrecasteaux Islands (including the Trobriands) and the Louisiade Archipelago.

The main island is dominated by a broad central cordillera that is really a complex of mountain ranges interspersed with high, broad valleys. The cordillera starts out narrow in the west, near the border, widens to greatest size in the Western Highlands, then narrows again as it heads down the peninsula toward Milne Bay. Mount Wilhelm (4509 meters) and Mount Giluwe (4368 meters), the two highest points in PNG, lie along the broadest range of the cordillera, the Bismarck Range, but the next highest peak, Mount Victoria, stands in the Owen Stanley Range, the line of mountains that runs down the southeastern peninsula, the line of mountains that became famous—or infamous—to the outside world during the dreadful battles of 1942.

The mountains form a drainage divide between rivers that flow south to the Gulf of Papua or north and east to the Bismarck and Solomon seas. North of the central cordillera is a structural depression that separates the central mountain ranges from the northern coastal ranges. In the west, this depression is occupied primarily by the Sepik River; in the east, by the Ramu and Madang rivers successively. The mouths of the Sepik and Ramu, which both empty into the Bismarck Sea near the border between East Sepik and Madang provinces, constitute the main gap in the rather discontinuous north coastal ranges. South of the main cordillera, a broad, low plain is drained by the Fly River, the nation's largest, flowing almost 1100 kilometers and navigable for nearly 800 kilometers. This low plain joins coastal swamps in the Gulf Province but is wedged out of existence by the mountains of the peninsula, where foothills reach right down to the sea.

The islands of PNG are mostly mountainous; Goodenough Island in the D'Entrecasteaux Group is one of the most mountainous in the world.

From the southernmost point of Gulf Province to Australian territory across the Torres Strait is a distance of little more than a hundred kilometers. The Great Barrier Reef runs into PNG waters where it comes between the Coral Sea and the strait, although the common Australia-PNG boundary in the strait is still disputed.

The climate is tropical, and humidity is a fact of life—even the dry months get a minimum of 50 millimeters of rain—and it takes six separate categories to describe the variations in the rainfall here. The wet season typically runs from December through March, fueled by the intertropical convergence zone, a junction between air streams originating in the northern and southern hemispheres. The ITCZ passes over PNG twice, seeming to lag behind the sun's movement; as it passes southward, the country is hit by northwesterly monsoonal winds. Southeast tradewinds influence the May-to-October dry season. Port Moresby, the capital, lies in a rain shadow of the Owen Stanley Range and remains drier than the rest of the country. Temperatures are not extreme, but evenings in the Highlands can be quite cool.

# THE NATURAL ENVIRONMENT

PNG's incredibly rich vegetation constitutes a paradigm of the Pacific Basin. Indeed, one reason for the richness is that PNG lies in the path of both past and present plant migrations between Asia, Australia, and the islands of the southwest Pacific. In the dense jungles of the country's tropical rain forests grows vegetation that resembles the plant life of Malaysia and Indonesia. In the drier river basins grows a mixed cover of savannah and monsoonal forests that would be familiar to anyone who knows the northern coast of Australia. The central cordillera sports vegetation similar to that of New Zealand and Tasmania.

Nearly 85 percent of the main island is forest. Lowland forest predominates, with a canopy that can reach as high as 40 meters, often matted by strangling figs with huge crowns and thick merging aerial roots. Sheltered under this canopy are palms, woody vines, climbers, masses of ferns, orchids, creepers, and a profusion of other plants. Along the coast are mangrove swamps and coastal forests. Inland in the lowland plains of the rivers are broad freshwater swamps overgrown with cane and swamp grass, herbs, sedge, ferns, paperbark, and the ubiquitous sago palm, whose pith is a staple of the PNG diet. Grasslands of kangaroo grass, *kunai,* and speargrass stride along the Ramu River Valley and across the Markham Plain; the traveler will see wide fields of crops here and cattle grazing on pastureland. Go uphill a thousand meters and you find laurel, red cedar, oak, beech, nutmeg, and mahogany. Continue to three thousand meters and you enter alpine forests of conifers and heath; keep climbing and you'll find equatorial alpine grasslands.

In those typically Malaysian jungles are typically Australian animals, including a number of marsupial species now extinct Down Under. The largest of the more than a hundred marsupial species here is the tree kangaroo, but there are also opossums, wallabies, and bandicoots. Crocodiles can be found here—ask any veteran of the fighting in World War II. The variety of lizards includes the distinctive anglehead, which is hard to find, and PNG also boasts the largest tree frog in the world, the white-lipped tree frog, easily found—look for the white lips. There are more than seventy species of snakes here. Seven land snakes and all the sea snakes are venomous. The traveler should exercise caution when walking through the bush, at least below about 2500 meters, although the most common lowland snake, the carpet python, is *not* dangerous. Still, this snake is habitually killed by PNG nationals, who tend to have a morbid fear of snakes; they will run like mad when one scurries across a road.

The insect to be terrified of is the malarial mosquito. Otherwise, insect life here, which is abundant, is extremely interesting. Look for beetles, jumping and huntsmen spiders (neither of which species builds a web), earwigs, and a variety of spectacular butterflies—the owl butterfly, the jewel butterfly, and the dazzling birdwing.

Most famous of PNG's fauna is the avian sort. Compare the more than 730 species of birds here to a similar number in the whole of Australia and about 800 for the entire North American landmass. The variety of landforms and altitudes, coupled with the abundance of moisture, have created a wide diversity of habitats for a wide diversity of birds. The isolation the terrain often enforces has resulted in evolutionary variants among closely related species, and a number of species are unique to PNG—above all, the bird of paradise.

Among water birds, look for grebes, the black-tailed godwit, lesser egret, gull-billed tern. Birds of prey include the gray or variable goshawk, whistling kite, and New Guinea eagle. In the forests are a variety of fruit pigeons and ground pigeons; such parrots as the black-capped, rainbow, and yellow-streaked; dwarf and hook-billed kingfishers. The blue scrub thrush, the shy hooded pitta, and the not-shy blue-breasted pitta are among the colorful ground birds here. Look also for a variety of flycatchers, gleaners, snatchers, and starlings. In grassland and thicket are found the comic pheasant coucal, wrens, and swallows. Striking bee-eaters, honeyeaters, and the purring peaceful dove are found in suburban gardens and open country.

There are more than thirty species of bird of paradise here; the two most famous are the Raggiana, depicted on the country's national crest, and the emperor. All birds of paradise have been officially protected since 1968, although the nationals may still hunt them with bow and arrow for use in headdresses. The Raggiana, also called the red kumul, is found mostly in lowland and hill forest of the southern two-thirds of the main island. The emperor frequents the mountains of the Huon Peninsula north of Lae, the unique home of three bird of paradise species. A third bird of paradise, the Lawes' six-wired, resides in the lower mountain forests of the central ranges, from the Owen Stanleys west to Tari. Bowerbirds are closely allied to birds of paradise, but instead of evolving plumage to win mates, the males of this species build bowers. They are found in mossy forests above 1150 meters.

Several areas are particularly good for bird watching. The Port Moresby area has a variety of habitats: lowland rain forest near Brown River, hill forest in the Sogeri area (including Varirata National Park and the trailhead of the Kokoda Trail), Moitaka and Waigani Swamp, the surrounding savannah, grasslands, seashore, and mangrove.

Mount Hagen is the primary center for searching out mountain birds. Near here is the Baiyer River Wildlife Sanctuary with a unique collection of PNG wildlife—not to be missed by the bird fancier. Also nearby are the midmountain forest of the Sepik-Wahgi divide, moss forest near Tomba, and midmountain grasslands and gardens of the Wahgi Valley. Wau is another good area for mountain birds, especially on nearby Mount Kaindi.

Bensbach, far to the west near the Irian Jaya border, is another prime wildlife area, and especially good for water birds—a number of species here are unique to this region of the Fly River.

In island PNG, West New Britain is particularly rich in bird life, as a visit to the Pokilli Wildlife Management Area can attest.

Papua New Guinea has long been a mecca for prospectors searching for mineral wealth. The cost of extracting such wealth, however, has usually proved prohibitive, an obstacle to development. On the island of Bougainville, however, the massive open-cut copper mine at Panguna is a mainstay of the PNG economy. Threatening to surpass it is Ok Tedi, the incredibly rich mountain of copper crowned by gold in the remote Star Mountains, near the Irian Jaya border. To develop the project, a road was carved from the mine down to the Fly River. The Fly then serves as a highway, bringing the gold, which is being mined first, downriver by barge to a processing plant at Moresby. Once the gold crown has been completely extracted, the miners will start on the copper. Production at Ok Tedi began in 1985. Before its discovery, the people nearby knew virtually nothing of modern civilization—and vice versa. It is likely that yet more mineral riches lie beneath the jungle-thick, rugged topography of PNG.

# HISTORY

The difficulty of PNG's terrain has limited archaeological efforts on the main island, but the consensus is that man first arrived here some forty thousand years ago in waves of immigration from Southeast Asia via Indonesia. Radiocarbon testing has confirmed human hunting and gathering activity in the peninsula twenty-six thousand years ago; earlier dates are posited for the Highlands. Early agricultural systems in the Wahgi Valley appear to have been in use for the last nine thousand years. Coastal and island sites show human occupation back to at least 4000 B.C. Lapita pottery has been found on Mussau Island in the Saint Mathias Group and on Lou Island in the Admiralties. Lou also forms part of the obsidian trail, which moves on to Fergusson Island in the D'Entrecasteaux Group. This evidence, plus suggestions of pottery exchange among communities of the south coast, may confirm a very ancient antecedent for a major fact of early history here—trade.

The elaborate trade networks and production systems that developed out of economic necessity evolved into religious and political systems as well. The commodities produced and traded included pottery, shell products and currencies, stone axe and adze blades, salt, sago, and probably other food staples. Wars were halted for these exchanges, which assumed major ceremonial significance and spiritual overtones. The networks had names, as follows:

The *hiri* linked the southern coast of the peninsula, moving pots, sago, logs, shells, and axes from site to site. The *kula* route linked the Trobriand Islands and Louisiade Archipelago with one another and with the main island hiri, adding wooden dishes and obsidian to the trade. The Vitiaz Strait network touched at points around the Huon Peninsula, crossing to Umboi Island and West New Britain; shells, dogs teeth, canoes, pots, and carved bowls were among the commodities of this network. In the Western Highlands, the *tee* and *moka* exchanges joined interior areas, later one another, and eventually the coast, moving shells, pigs, salt, and other items. It is likely that the kina shell was introduced into the Highlands along these routes; the kina was highly prized, especially upland, where it was so rare. It has given its name to the currency of contemporary, independent Papua New Guinea.

Of the transactions between trading partners, little is known. What is clear is that the systems that were developed—to move goods great distances through diverse communities and often through difficult terrain—must have been of a very high order.

Portuguese navigators trading in Southeast Asia first sighted the main island of PNG in 1511. In 1526, Jorge de Meneses named the land Ilhos dos Papua, *papua* being a Malayan derivative alluding to the frizzy hair of the inhabitants. It was Retez in 1545 who used the name Nueve Guinea; it appeared on Mercator's world map of 1569. Torres in 1606 coasted the southeast and the Gulf of Papua before passing between Australia and New Guinea via the strait that bears his name, and that ended the period of Portuguese and Spanish navigation.

Discoveries by the Dutch in the 17th century, and by the French and English in the 18th and 19th centuries, added substance to the navigational charts. With D'Entrecasteaux's voyage of 1793, the broad outline of New Guinea was set, and, in the 19th century, detailed mapping of the land was undertaken by men like Owen Stanley and Captain John Moresby. With his work of 1873 and 1874, Moresby considered that he had filled "the last great blank" in the work of the early navigators, but the interior was still unknown to outsiders, and it would be another seventy years before it was fully penetrated. Even the first inland adventurers, the prospectors and explorers who mostly followed the rivers, assumed that toward the center of New Guinea the mountains grew more precipitous and the population more sparse.

In the meantime, the mid-1800s had seen the arrival of European traders, missionaries, scientists, gold miners, and blackbirders. Most stuck to the coastal regions. The missionaries dug in here, bringing European clothing and styles of living; their designated village deacons often became the foremost secular as well as religious leaders of their villages.

Britain resisted several attempts—Moresby's, for one—to stake a claim here, but Australian demands to do something about increasing German commercial activity were eventually persuasive. In a British-German agreement implemented in 1884, the northeastern quadrant of the island became a German protectorate, the southeastern quadrant a British protectorate. The British annexed the territory as a crown colony four years later. Sir William MacGregor's administration, although highly paternalistic, was nevertheless free of many of the abusive practices in German New Guinea, and MacGregor managed to extend British control, often by force, around the coast and somewhat into the interior. In 1906, Britain turned over control of the colony to Australia. Hubert Murray was appointed lieutenant governor in 1908, a post he held until 1940. Murray's administration was for the most part benevolent; while he is faulted for not developing the economic infrastructure, his defense of the rights of the nationals was significant.

German New Guinea consisted of the northeastern main island, called Kaiser-Wilhelmsland, and Buka and Bougainville in the northern Solomons. A private business firm, the New Guinea Company, was chartered to develop a German colony, obtaining land from the villagers for a pittance and selling it to German settlers. Laborers were recruited from Sumatra and Singapore to work plantations around Madang, but they were decimated—as were the colonists— by blackwater fever; the traveler to Madang can see the German cemetery there, the gravestones providing mordant evidence of the power of the disease.

On New Britain, German colonization was more successful, although here the center of the expat community was a Samoan-American woman, Emma Coe Forsayth Kolbe. Queen Emma, as she was known, was one of the many colorful and unconventional characters who have peopled the panorama of Pacific history. She was certainly the mistress of Colonel Albert Steinberger, the American who nearly made himself ruler of Samoa, and she was probably the mistress of a number of other men as well as wife to a few. Her methods were routinely selfish and mostly successful, and she did found a commercial empire that she ruled from a palace, attended by servants and surrounded by family.

German New Guinea became an imperial colony in 1899 and was ruled as a colony for whites, with little attention, if any, given to the welfare of the nationals. German rule ended in September 1914, when Australian troops seized Rabaul. In 1920, the British government, on Australia's behalf, assumed a League of Nations mandate to govern the former German colony. Australia decided to maintain an administrative division between northern New Guinea and southern Papua, and to make the north pay for its own administration through private enterprise development. Australian planters headed north in search of riches, but the worldwide depression felled the price of copra, and most of the copra economy was taken over by Burns Philp or W. R. Carpenter. A gold rush near

Lae in 1926 brought prospectors, a demand for village labor, and some government funds to the north, where the money was spent opening up more areas for mining.

Some of the prospectors pushed inland, and among these were Michael and Dan Leahy. Financed by the New Guinea Goldfields Company, they built an airstrip at Benabena, near Goroka, and in 1933, flew over the Chimbu and Wahgi valleys. Michael Leahy later wrote of the flight that it "laid to rest for all time the theory that the center of New Guinea is a mass of uninhabitable mountains" (quoted in *Papua New Guinea Atlas*, edited by David King and Stephen Rauck, Robert Brown & Associates [Aust] Pty. Ltd., 1982). The Leahys' flight and subsequent expedition with James Taylor were the first discovery by the outside world of the huge Highland population of a million and a half people still living in a Stone Age culture, and it was the first discovery of another world by the Stone Age people of the Highlands.

The Leahys brought a movie camera, recording the expressions and behavior of these peoples as they saw, for the first time, white men, airplanes, radios, and the various other appurtenances of the 20th century. The film is extraordinary, and it is the basis of a dazzling Australian documentary, *First Contact*, which every traveler to PNG should see (most hotels run it frequently). The filmmakers have returned to the point of first contact to interview the old men and women featured in the 1933 film. They tell of their terror and curiosity at seeing these white-skinned people—gods? the ghosts of their ancestors?—and the great bird coming down from the sky. As one old woman puts it, to the laughter-filled agreement of several other women, "We thought these creatures must be gods; then we had sex with them and found they were just men." It must say something about the adaptability and mental keenness of these people, and of their children and grandchildren, that they have gone, in such a short span of time, from the Stone Age to the 20th century. The sons and daughters of a completely primitive people are today auto mechanics, shopkeepers, police constables, government officials; many speak three languages—their own dialect, Tok Pisin, and English; they watch videos and drive buses. In short, they have taken less than half a century to "progress" more than ten millennia. A fascinating story, unique to Papua New Guinea. See the film.

But even with this penetration into the Highlands, Australian control of Papua New Guinea was a hit-and-miss proposition. It still worked by patrol, requiring in many instances epic treks by police, government officials, and missionaries. Many villages might see a patrol once a year, or once in five years. There was no single pattern in the contact between nationals and foreigners; it depended on the community's need, the beliefs held, the foreigners' attitude, past experiences, present realities, and chance. Effective control of communities in the interior of PNG remains a very real issue today.

## World War II

The Japanese bombed Rabaul on January 4, 1942; a small Australian garrison there was overrun within three weeks. Port Moresby was bombed the following month. Japan then quickly occupied New Britain, New Ireland, Manus, and Bougainville, and landed forces at Lae on the main island. Australia established a single military administration at Moresby for the duration.

With most Australian and New Zealand troops fighting in the Middle East, Australia's generals in Melbourne decided on what they called the Brisbane Line theory as a defense against the expected Japanese invasion. They would effectively cede everything north and west of the Tropic of Capricorn to Japan, leaving only scorched earth, and would hold the settled southern and eastern coasts. General Douglas MacArthur, in Melbourne, resisted this decision and eventually won the point. MacArthur believed, correctly as it turned out, that it was precisely in the *southeast* of Australia that the Japanese intended to come ashore. The airfield the Japanese were building on Guadalcanal would be their base for severing Australia's supply lines; the staging area for their invasion would be Port Moresby. In May 1942, the Japanese had set out from Rabaul to seize Moresby by sea; they had been turned back in the Battle of the Coral Sea. But they had landed forces at Milne Bay and at the villages of Buna and Gona on the northeastern coast of the main island's peninsula. Intelligence reports assured MacArthur that no army could be sent south from Buna and Gona through thick, dangerous jungle over the Owen Stanley Range. What the aerial photographs and intelligence patrols had missed was the track that crosses from very near Port Moresby to Kokoda on the edge of the northeastern peninsula's coastal plain. The Japanese *did* come down the Kokoda Trail, and Australian and American troops went up to meet them, stopping the Japanese within sight of Moresby, while other Allied trops were forcing the evacuation of Japanese troops from Milne Bay.

In all, between 1941 and 1945, some 170,000 Japanese troops died in PNG—many from disease. Australian battle casualties were 14,500. Among PNG nationals, 166 soldiers and police were killed, 201 wounded; of the 55,000 nationals conscripted by the Japanese as carriers, of those who voluntarily aided the Allied forces, and among civilians, the number of dead is not known. The Australians had once derisively referred to the native islanders as "fuzzy wuzzies." In the agony along the Kokoda Trail, when native bearers carried innumerable sick and wounded Aussies to safety through nearly impassable bush, they were renamed "fuzzy-wuzzy angels." An Australian film of that name bears homage to the extraordinary bravery of the PNG nationals who aided the Allied war effort.

## The Postwar Period

In 1945, the new Labor government of Australia declared it owed a "debt of gratitude" to the two territories of Papua and New Guinea. Massive new subsidies aided the formidable task of reconstruction—most of the north coast, as well as the islands of Bougainville, New Ireland, and New Britain had been badly bombed—and independence was pronounced a long-term goal. Progress on reconstruction moved forward, not without difficulties, but progress toward independence was slow during the 1950s and 1960s. When Australia's opposition leader, Gough Whitlam, visited Moresby in 1969 and suggested dates for independence, indigenous activism increased dramatically. Self-government was a fact by 1972, in a coalition national government under Michael Somare, and a delayed independence was declared in September 1975.

The course of political life since independence has hardly been smooth. The government's success in preventing the secession of Bougainville was an early triumph, but keeping the coalition government together proved persistently difficult, although it was small potatoes compared to the task of governing a nation with half a dozen roads, limited telephone communications, remote and isolated villages, far-flung outliers, and all those languages. One of the most ingenious methods for dealing with the communication problem took advantage of the widespread passion for *The Phantom* comic book character. With balloons from the Phantom's mouth delivering such messages as "Brada na sussa I laikim go long na kisim sut bilong cholera," thousands were moved to get cholera shots.

The Byzantine politics of PNG often take their cue from personalities. Michael Somare himself, on and off the scene since independence, was an ongoing and important issue. Charges of corruption and incompetence are frequent. Many quasi-government officials or managers of major institutions—banks, hospitals, and the like—are today still expats; the supply of trained nationals has yet to match the demand for administrative and management skills. Tribal warfare remains a major issue, especially in Enga, Western Highlands, and West New Britain provinces. Here, a single dispute—over land or women, for example—may escalate rapidly: an attack requires a payback, and that requires another payback, and so on. On occasion, such disputes have been settled by government intervention that combines traditional concepts of a payout with contemporary negotiating techniques. But in the environment of violence, PNG's "rascals," now most evident in towns and cities, terrorize nationals, expats, and occasionally tourists indiscriminately. Curfews imposed in the early 1980s curbed the general mayhem somewhat, but in PNG, the evening stroll is a remote dream.

Another ongoing issue is the fact of Irian Jaya, where a resistance movement against Indonesian rule has flared repeatedly since 1978. For its part, overpopulated Indonesia may be looking with hungry eyes at the wide open spaces of PNG—and at the kind of potential Ok Tedi represents. The PNG government, while wary of this, would like to maintain good relations with Indonesia, but it must also satisfy the popular sympathy with the rebels, who are racially and ethnically related. There is border tension, and there are occasional clashes— just one more headache in a nation where the simple act of trying to govern a large number of mutually incomprehensible peoples divided by unrelenting terrain is not simple at all.

# THE TRAVELER TO PAPUA NEW GUINEA

NOTE: Visas are required for entry into Papua New Guinea. It is usually possible to obtain the visa on arrival, but the rules do change from time to time. Check before you come. Obtaining a visa from a PNG consulate abroad may also save you time at the airport on arrival.

A word first about safety. The traveler will receive numerous warnings, both around the Pacific and in PNG itself, about the potential danger from rascals. The danger is there. Violent crime—particularly rape, murder, and armed robbery—is prevalent, and it is blind to race, color, creed, or national origin. This is one of the reasons that most travelers to PNG travel on package tours or custom-tailored trips prearranged through reliable tour operators. These forms of "private" travel assure the visitor of guides who know what they're doing, a protective environment, and a range of travel destinations and experiences.

The safety issue is particularly acute for women traveling alone. That being said, it should be noted that the present writer, a woman, has traveled solo throughout PNG—by plane, taxi, riverboat, dugout canoe, and PMV (the blue-licensed Public Motor Vehicles), converted trucks, buses, or vans that ply the separate road networks of Papua New Guinea—and never once sensed the slightest menace from any of the nationals. But the menace, according to a friend who is a PNG national, exists.

Riding the Highland Highway by PMV, quite obviously the only foreigner on the crowded van, I was treated with disproportionate courtesy and kindness, as well as with great friendliness. Yet I was to learn later that, an hour after my PMV had left the town of Kainantu, another PMV had been stopped and its passengers chased and threatened. On another occasion, I went for an afternoon walk in Goroka. It was a lovely, sunny day, market day, and the streets and the market area were lively with people. I had not proceeded far from my hotel when a young man, a teacher, interrupted his walk homeward to his village five kilometers away and attached himself to me—as he said, "for protection." He stayed with me through the afternoon, helping me shop at the market, showing me the sights, helping me deal with chores, and he made sure I was back at my hotel before dusk. I never felt in any peril the entire afternoon; whether it was due to his presence, I cannot say.

The scariest warning—repeated by officials, expats, and nationals alike—is that if you are driving, you must never stop. If you hit something or if you get a flat tire, keep going. Go to the police station or to a gas station or go home, but never stop. If you do, it is said, and the moment you do, people suddenly rise up out of nowhere and set upon both car and you.

In Moresby, the traveler gets the impression that if he wants to become rich, he should move here and go into the home security business. In the wealthier expat areas, barbed wire, electrified fencing, and fortresslike barred gates are the rule. After dark, even taxis may not be safe—especially for a woman alone.

These safety warnings are not intended to frighten. The traveler will make up his own mind about how to deal with the safety issue, but he should be aware that it *is* an issue. If you have made arrangements for organized travel, be guided by what your tour operator tells you. If you are traveling independently, exercise caution and good sense. The cautions may make you feel restricted in your movements, and that may be annoying, but it is a small price to pay, especially given the compensations of the travel experience here.

Think of that experience in four basic categories: bush, Highlands, Sepik, and coastal or out-island PNG. Add Port Moresby for a fifth category. Unless you come by the difficult back route through Kieta—difficult because, when open, the flights are heavily booked—or the illegal route from Irian Jaya, you must come through Moresby, and there is much of interest to see there.

Which of these experiences you "do" will be determined by how much time and money you have to spend. If you must choose among them, the recommendation here is the Sepik and the Highlands; the latter is easily combinable with a bush experience anyway. All of these ways of seeing PNG can be arranged ahead of time through travel agents or airlines; you *must* fly from one part of PNG to another, and internal flights tend to fill quickly, especially during May,

August, and December—Australian school holidays, when the children of expats fly home to PNG from boarding schools Down Under. Even the traveler who wants to stay loose about the exact nature of travel here is well advised to estimate the number of days per category of experience and book flights accordingly ahead of time.

## The Bush

By bush experience is meant a stay in a lodge off the beaten track where you have a chance to explore the interior—terrain, wildlife, villages—in some depth. There are many lodges throughout the country. The four best known and best equipped for travelers very definitely try to provide a "learning experience" of this fascinating country. One traveler likened stays at two different bush lodges to a *National Geographic* expedition, except that the lodges, all of which are expensive, provide every comfort.

Karawari Lodge is on the Karawari River, a Sepik tributary. In a stupendous setting, it features river excursions, *sing sings*—traditional music and dance performances—the chance to see wildlife and explore the region's village life.

Tribal Tops Inn in Minj, in the Wahgi Valley, is somewhat more resort oriented but provides opportunities to visit the Baiyer River Wildlife Sanctuary, to explore Wahgi Valley villages, and to see a performance by the Mudmen, trooped out at night to enact their ghostly war dances.

Ambua Lodge at Tari shows the traveler the Southern Highlands and offers a look at a most unusual tribe, the Huli people, who believe they are descended from birds. They don plumage even if there is no ceremony going on. Here, just 150 kilometers from Mount Hagen, and reachable by road and track (as well as, more conveniently, by plane), only a few people are dressed in Western-style blue jeans and T-shirts. Rather, they wear asgras, a cluster of cordyline leaves covering the posterior and held by a string around the waist.

Bensbach Wildlife Lodge is far to the west, some 25 kilometers from the Irian Jaya border. It serves as a hunting and fishing lodge for those who go in for such sports and provides a unique experience of one of the remotest areas of PNG.

## The Highlands

A look at a map of PNG shows a stunning sparseness of roads. There are some around Moresby, a smidgin near Wewak, another smidgin around Madang on the north coast, and the ambitious Highlands Highway running from Lae on the coast to Mount Hagen, the administrative center of the Western Highlands. Travel the highway by PMV or by organized tour—it is a spectacular ride.

From Lae, at the mouth of the Markham River, you travel north-west across the Markham Plain, big, wide, flat, lush with greenery and thick with villages. The further the distance from Lae, the more prevalent is the bush-material construction of the village houses, often combined with tin. Some houses may be on stilts, and some may be round. They are often elegantly built, the fronds woven together to alternate dark and light or to create a design. The land-scape becomes savannah and pastureland; ahead, the traveler sees foothills folding up from the plain like creased green velvet.

After skirting the hills, the highway climbs abruptly. Finally achieving a summit marked CREST, the terrain opens out into a vast, rolling glen, across which the traveler can see villages and more hills. You have crossed from Morobe Province into the Eastern Highlands Province. There are pine trees here, and a minty edge to the air, but be aware that the sun, if shining, is still fiercely tropical. The highway continues to rise through Kainantu to Goroka. Many of the people you see in villages and along the roadside of the high-way—almost all will wave—wear some variation of Western-style clothing. But many others, especially on market day (usually Satur-day), do not. The women carry bilums, the extraordinary string bags woven, in a most time-consuming manner, from natural fibers—and more recently, from plastic or nylon cord. The women don't actually carry them; rather, the bilum is worn around the forehead. It is an amazingly strong bag, almost infinitely expansible, and can carry everything—including babies. (More than one foreign visitor has described the bilum as the ultimate shoulder bag for busy women who favor such—just keep tossing things in.)

The traveler typically spends the night in Goroka, where he should explore the market, the lovely Raun Raun Theater (see a per-formance if the troupe is not traveling), the J. K. McCarthy Museum (McCarthy was one of the legendary patrol officers), and the coffee mill—Goroka coffee is superb! There are numerous side trips from here; the traveler on a package tour will see many of these sights on the next day's stage from Goroka to Mount Hagen.

The way continues west, always climbing, through fields of cof-fee, *pitpit* grass—wild sugarcane, the kunai grass used to roof houses, the *yarr* tree (casuarina), and the lovely, downcast trumpet flower—so poisonous the nationals say you must wash your hands after touching it. The mountains grow higher, and the highway tops the pass, then heads down to the stream that marks the border between Eastern Highlands and Chimbu (or Simbu) provinces. The stream is called Watabung, "waters meeting." There are views now of the Chimbu Gorge, the notch through which Mount Wilhelm can be reached, cut by the Chimbu River. Beyond Kundiawa is the village where the Chimbu Mudmen and Chimbu Players often perform for

visitors. (Mudmen "performances" may be seen at numerous locations.) The highway continues across high, rolling plateau ringed
by mountains that seem to turn from green to blue as the sun lowers.
There is a high-prairie feeling to this terrain, even a sense of alpine
meadow—rendered disconcerting by all those banana trees, poinsettia, and trumpet flowers.

Mount Hagen has what is reputedly the best market in PNG.
Its slightly Wild West feeling is cut by the businesslike air of new
government buildings and the heavy presence of the constabulary,
reassuring given the area's frequent lawlessness and acts of violence.
Hagen, as it is called, is also a good place to see a sing sing, if you
can find one, and it is the staging area for trips to the 120-hectare
Baiyer River Wildlife Sanctuary, 55 kilometers north. Much of the
wildlife is in enclosures, but birds of paradise and noisy parrots fly
free, and the collection, even if caged, is stunning.

## The Sepik

The Sepik River starts in the mountains along the Irian Jaya
border and runs 1126 kilometers to empty into the Bismarck Sea
at Cape Girgir. With a catchment of 78,000 square kilometers, it
is the largest river system in PNG, although second to the Fly in
length. It is navigable for 500 kilometers by larger vessels, for nearly twice that by small boats. It is the country's main avenue of communications, the center of its flourishing cultural and artistic life.

The Sepik starts off by heading north, then meandering back
and forth across the border before continuing its long, coiling way
to the sea—a huge, slow, brown snake of a river. For most of its
course, it is bordered by wide expanses of lowland through which
the river curves back on itself to create oxbows, lagoons, dead ends,
and lakes that dry into grassland when the river is low.

Starting in 1972, the Sepik was almost choked to death by the
rapid spread of the green water fern salvinia (*Salvinia molesta*), which
can double its mass within a few days. In the lower Sepik region, the
salvinia had so clogged the river that villagers were unable to navigate
essential water routes to markets, schools, and hospitals, while the weed
made fishing difficult and blocked access to swamp lands used for sago
palm production. Many villages were abandoned, and the weed's infestation had reached 250 square kilometers and was still growing.

The search for an effective combatant, one that would not damage other aspects of the river, ended in 1982, when *Cyrtobagous
salviniae*, a rare Brazilian weevil, was introduced. At first, the weevils
did not succeed in damaging the weed mat. Further testing showed
that a nitrogen deficiency in the Sepik water was the problem, so
boosts of nitrogen were given to the weevils, who then began to
multiply sufficiently to kill the weed mat. In a self-perpetuating pro-

cess, the damage the weevils cause encourages the salvinia to relocate its nitrogen reserves to newly developing buds. The buds in turn become weevil food. While it is unlikely that either the salvinia or the weevil will ever completely disappear from the Sepik, the river has been saved from destruction. How the salvinia got there in the first place is unknown, although rumor has it that an expat emptied a fishbowl into the river, and the weed that was decoration for an aquarium began its deadly infestation.

The Sepik is in a sense the soul of PNG, the past and present core of a thriving artistic tradition inextricably linked to a sense of the supernatural. You can travel the river for a day or two weeks, on an elegant passenger cruiser with twin-bedded cabins or in a Spartan river boat (even dugout canoe) staying at lodges or riverside camps. A river trip on the Sepik is a languid procession through the most exotic of civilizations, a living lesson in anthropology and primitive art. Square-backed, narrow, deeply hacked dugout canoes ride back and forth, the pointed bows of even the simplest carved into crocodile heads. The canoes are propelled by equally splendid paddles, carved in a heart shape, lilylike, to a fine thinness and acute point. In addition to the artifacts sold to tourists, the traveler will see small local markets featuring the ever-present betel, its major accompaniment—lime, and potatoes, coconuts, and other edibles. The traveler will wave to the people living on the bank and to the children playing in the water; some of those children may have dis-

Along the Sepik River, Papua New Guinea. *Photo by Susanna Margolis.*

tended bellies, ringworm, and other ailments. He will watch the life of the villages, for which the river is the vital lifeline. In some villages along the river, corpses are burned, not buried—the ground here, such as it is, is far too wet for graves. In the evening along the Sepik, after a day of gardening, sago preparation, or hunting, villagers wash off in the river, then apply gray clay as a kind of perfumed coolant and, in designs along the face and arms, a decoration.

The Lower Sepik runs from the coast to Angoram, an area of small, rather poor villages. From Angoram to just between Pagwi and Ambunti is the Middle Sepik, the cultural treasure house of PNG. Here the traveler finds a great concentration of *haus tamburans*, spirit houses; the most famous of these, those with thrusting-forward facades, are in the Marprik region around Pagwi. Every village along the Middle Sepik route has its own artistic style, but Tambanum is generally considered the river's "artifacts factory." Above Ambunti, the traveler is much more on an expedition than on a river trip. Life here is more primitive as the river climbs, and the villages are fewer and farther apart.

The traveler will do best to arrange his Sepik River experience before he arrives at the river—and according to his resources in time and money. It is possible, however, to make arrangements right at the river—you can even buy a canoe and paddle yourself. Many Sepik trips start at Madang, a pleasant resort town, especially for divers. Many start from Wewak, best known for numerous war relics. Other starting points are Sepik river stations—Angoram and Ambunti can be reached by air.

## Out-Island PNG

Coastal and out-island PNG offer the traveler laid-back holiday time. The outliers are infrequently visited and relatively unspoiled, except perhaps for New Britain, with the spectacularly sited and completely rebuilt city of Rabaul. The scenery on these islands can be breathtaking, and there is little to do—far less than on the sights-abundant main island.

But Rabaul, Stettin Bay on West New Britain, and the main island centers of Madang, Hansa Bay, and Milne Bay offer spectacular water sports, none more spectacular than diving. Even from Port Moresby, the diver can explore the outer barrier reef and inner islands of Bootless Bay as well as an aircraft wreck only discovered in 1980. Madang offers dives within the reef, just a few minutes offshore (check out Magic Passage), and north coast shore dives. Hansa Bay holds some 34 Japanese wrecks, lying mostly upright at a maximum of 25 meters. At Rabaul, the volcanoes have left rock formations to dive, while the war has left 104 wrecks. Milne Bay has so many small islands and reefs that diving is on a safari basis using a fully equipped dive boat. Stettin Bay offers more than 90 reefs, packed with life.

Thus far, PNG remains a relatively uncrowded dive destination. Wrecks and reefs have not yet been picked clean of the intriguing artifacts and coral forms divers love to observe, and the fish life is extraordinarily abundant and varied. Hurry.

## Port Moresby

The must-see sights of the capital are the National Museum and Art Gallery, the architecturally brilliant National Parliament building right next door, and the War Museum. Opening hours for these vary, so check on arrival. The National Museum in particular is an essential introduction to this country. Small and resolute, at least half of it is given over to natural history—exhibits on geology, flora and fauna, ecology, shelter, food. (An excellent exhibit shows how sago is treated, something you'll see a lot of on the Sepik.) The artifacts are exceptional—headdresses, *kundu* (hourglass drums), *garamut* (slit drums), bilums, canoes, canoe models. The room of wood carvings is a spectacular forest of haus tamburans posts, canoe splashboards and paddles, story boards, masks, shields, bowls—a breathtaking display of intricate, elaborate, skillful art.

Moresby also offers the opportunity to stock up on resources, cash travelers' checks, and handle any chores, but do all this in broad daylight. The University of Papua New Guinea is worth a visit, especially its bookstore, which stocks an extensive collection of books of all sorts, and has exceptional resources for those interested in further reading on PNG and the Pacific.

Not far from town is Varirata National Park, with a variety of walking trails and excellent lookouts down and out to Moresby and the coast. If you drive out here, you can easily continue on to the trailhead for Kokoda, although the last stretch of road is a very rutted track. (You can also travel by PMV to the Goldie River to reach the Kokoda.) To say you've been on the trail, walk down to the Goldie River. For a real taste of the trail, try climbing the so-called Golden Stairs. Now imagine doing it with a full pack and people shooting at you. Little wonder the soldiers called Kokoda the Bloody Track and Samuel Eliot Morison described what went on here as the nastiest fighting in the world.

## Wilderness Adventures

Numerous outfitters in the U.S., Australia, and PNG itself run serious adventure expeditions—from bushwalking to whitewater rafting to canoe sailing among the outliers to climbs of Mount Wilhelm. One of the best is Pacific Expeditions, headquartered in Port

Moresby but affiliated with the U.S.-based Sobek Expeditions. In addition to organized tours, Pacific Expeditions will arrange a variety of private expeditions. One of their most interesting and ambitious initiatives is the exploratory expedition; each year, they choose an area little penetrated, if at all, by the outside world. These are usually rugged trips, which is why the area has been so little explored in the past. One of the guides for Pacific Expeditions is Osborne Boga-jiwai, who at this writing held the record for the Kokoda Trail. The trail *can* be done in five days, "if you just look at your feet," as one trail veteran has put it; it is more normally completed in 11 days or two weeks. Bogajiwai, originally from a coastal area, was clock-ed at 28 hours, 14 minutes, 30 seconds.

## Food

The staple food of most villagers is sago, a starchy extract from the pith of the sago palm. The palm is first dried, then softened with water. From the gelatinous paste thus produced, a sort of bread is made, gray and—to the Western eye—unpleasant looking. *Kau kau,* the sweet potato, is another major food; it was introduced into the Highlands some 350 years ago and is said to have been responsible for a population increase there.

In the open-air markets, the traveler will see yams, taro, cassavas, bananas, the sago, and the kau kau. Stores sell canned fish and sacks of rice. Sugarcane, corn, and green vegetables are also grown for food.

At a sing sing or staged feast, the visitor may get to taste local foods prepared in the *mumu,* earth oven. For the most part, the traveler eats the usual undistinguished "continental" cuisine of hotels, although in some of the expensive lodges the food is definitely a cut above the norm.

The local beer is South Pacific. "Be specific," the ad declares, "ask for South Pacific." San Miguel, from the Philippines, is also available, as is Fosters, found, it would seem, wherever more than two Australians congregate.

## Shopping

Arts and artifacts are mostly available along the Sepik and in specialty shops in the main towns, which also stock crafts from the Trobriands, the North Solomons, and other inland areas of PNG. Crafts are also often sold along the street and in local open-air markets—a good place to find bilums. The variety is astonishing— weapons, pottery, spirit boards, story boards, cult hooks, bowls, masks, musical instruments, shell jewelry, and numerous odds and ends. The prices can be high, but if you like the piece and the workmanship seems good, buy it.

## LANGUAGE: TOK PISIN

Papua New Guinea is an exotic land of extraordinary color and extraordinary people—handsome people, with a bearing so dignified it occasionally seems haughty or even fierce, at least until broken by a smile. These people speak in all more than 700 languages. In addition to their native tongue, many nationals also speak Tok Pisin or Hiri Motu and English. Tok Pisin and Hiri Motu are the two main linguae francae of the country, and English is the official language of the government and of education.

Hiri Motu, once called Police Motu, developed out of the contact between policemen and the Motu people around Port Moresby in the late 19th century. Most of its vocabulary derives from village Motu, but it is a real pidgin, spread by the police and others on patrol throughout the southern portion of the country. It is today the unofficial language of administration and the principal lingua franca in this region.

Tok Pisin, which derives from the trading pidgin used throughout Melanesia, is used for broadcasting, playwriting, and song writing and thus threatens to overrun Hiri Motu. Here are some key phrases:

| | |
|---|---|
| Gud dei | Good morning/Good day |
| Apinun | Good afternoon |
| Gud nait | Good night |
| Plis | Please |
| Tenkyu | Thank you |
| Ies | Yes |
| Nogat | No |
| Yu stap gut? | How are you? |
| You save? | Do you understand? |
| Mi no klia | I don't understand |
| Hamas long em? | How much does it cost? |
| Mi laik baim | I want to buy it |
| Taem blong masta | The colonial period |
| Liklik | A little |
| Bikpela | Big |
| Kaikai | Food |
| Mi/yu | I/you |
| Yumi | We (including the person spoken to) |
| Mipela | We (excluding the person spoken to) |
| Yupela | You (plural) |
| Olgeta | Everybody |

*Tru* is officially an adverbial particle giving superlative status, as *moa* contributes comparative status, but you will hear *tru* almost constantly, as in "apinun tru," "tenkyu tru," and the like.

## PNG Addresses

In the U.S.:

PNG Mission to the United States
100 East 42nd St.
New York, NY 10017
(212) 682–6447

Although not a tourist bureau, the mission staff very courteously provide tourist information and answer travel questions.

Air Niugini
5000 Birch St.
Ste. 3000 West Tower
Newport Beach, CA 92660
(714) 752–5440

Sobek Expeditions, Inc.
P.O. Box 761
Angels Camp, CA 95222
(209) 736–4524

In PNG:

Pacific Expeditions
P.O. Box 132
Port Moresby
Papua New Guinea
Tel. 25–7803/25–9796

# PART
# IV

# ADVENTURING IN MICRONESIA

GUAM
THE NORTHERN MARIANAS
PALAU
THE FEDERATED STATES
OF MICRONESIA: YAP, TRUK, PONAPE
THE MARSHALL ISLANDS

To the Pacific traveler who has "done" Polynesia and Melanesia, the experience of Micronesia presents a very different feeling. For one thing, the traveler may no longer properly speak of being in the South Seas. Almost all of the islands of Micronesia are north of the equator; all of the islands visited in this book certainly are. The word summer here refers to the same time of year as in the U.S., and the summer sunsets are splendid.

Since the end of World War II, Micronesia has been called the American lake. It's a convenient label, one that may be becoming less true, but the Americanization of these islands—at least, of the gateway islands—is immediately obvious to the traveler. The automobile is the traveler's most frequent means of transportation. Tipping is back, although not everywhere. You will see more baseball than cricket or soccer. And the almost universal response to "thank you" is "no problem."

In the case of Micronesia, it might be said that location, more than anything else, has been destiny. An islander's location on a tiny speck of atoll in the midst of a vast sea forced him to become an expert mariner and to establish links with other, distant islands—

and to develop items worthy of trade. The location of the string of Micronesian islands, stepping stones between Asia and North America, made them a route of trade and conquest and turned them into some of the worst battlefields and most important staging areas of World War II.

# LAND AND SEA

There are more than two thousand islands in Micronesia, 125 of which are inhabited. These numbers change with time and tide—quite literally, as people move on or the ocean cuts a new channel or rises over a slowly sinking islet. The islands are scattered over 11,649,000 square kilometers of ocean—an area larger than the U.S. Yet the total landmass of just over 3000 square kilometers is about the size of Rhode Island. From Palau in the west to Majuro in the east is a distance of about 2100 kilometers. From the top of the Marianas to the equator, which the Gilbert Archipelago crosses, the distance is about 1300 kilometers.

The stretch of Micronesia moves from the Philippine Sea across the Marianas Trench and the deepest point of the Pacific—11,033 meters—over various ocean ridges and basins just beneath the Mid-Pacific Mountains. From west to east there are four great archipelagoes: the Marianas, the Carolines, the Gilberts (not covered in this itinerary), and the Marshalls. The Marianas form a crescent that is concave on its western side and runs on through Yap and Palau. The Marshalls and the Gilberts follow the southeast-northwest orientation of Pacific Plate movement. The Carolines are more scattered but run generally northwest-southeast over the Eauripik Ridge to the Kapingamarangi Rise, itself following the same sinuous curve as the Marshalls and Gilberts.

Island types vary. The high volcanic islands of the west seem to peter out to a universe of low-lying atolls in the east. The westernmost volcanic islands of Palau, Yap, and the Marianas sit on the western edge of the Marianas Trench—the Palau-Yap Trench is an extension of this—along the Pacific Ring of Fire. These islands erupted along the arc of the trench in this arena of strong volcanic activity. The central and eastern Carolines were formed in what may be a pocket between the Pacific Plate, which moves from southeast to northwest, and the Eurasian Plate. A hot-spot trend line seems to run from Kosrae through Ponape to Truk. From these hot spots, fractures in the earth's crust through which lava escaped, volcanic islands burst forth, then began to sink, while reefs grew upward around them. Kosrae, to the southeast, is the youngest, perhaps a million years old, while Truk, to the northwest, has subsided so much that it is now, at roughly 12 million years of age, an almost-atoll. Furthest east are the classic atolls of the Marshall Islands, most with central lagoons. The islets of these atolls rise to a height of only a few meters, and some may be only a few meters across. The outer slopes of the barrier reefs are the remnants of fringing reefs of the original volcanic islands, now subsided into lagoons. It was Darwin, in his classic work *Coral Reefs*, who first put forward this theory of atoll formation; the realities are well illustrated in Micronesia.

## MICRONESIAN CULTURES AND THE ART OF NAVIGATION

Among these varied islands, historians have distinguished eight different cultural areas: the Chamorro culture of the Marianas (the Chamorros being possibly the first wave of Proto-Malay settlement from New Guinea and Southeast Asia); the Gilbertese; the Marshallese; the east Carolinian; central Carolinian; Yapese; Palauan; and southwest islands—Tobi, Sonsorol, Pul, and Meri, southwest of Palau. Isolation existed even within these culture groups, although there is evidence that the major island in each group exercised some suzerainty by dint of its size and richness.

There has never been a united Micronesia or a uniform Micronesian civilization. The U.S., holding the islands as a United Nations Trust Territory after the war, tried to create a political region of Micronesia, but the islanders resisted. Nevertheless, some similarities can be cited within traditional Micronesian cultures.

Scattered hamlets rather than concentrated villages prevailed, focused around the extended family or clan. Clan lineage was through the mother, and the chief's wife typically exercised strong authority in family matters. Almost all Micronesian cultures had, and retain, a caste organization, and clan and caste met on the issue of land tenure, all important in Micronesia. All lands were clan-owned—indeed, clan and lineage identification was tied to a tract of land. The higher the caste, the larger or better the tract of land; along with this came special prerogatives.

In these small clan residences, subsistence was based on gardening and fishing. But there is also evidence of large-scale organization, highly disciplined—most particularly in the massive stone fortifications of Ponape's Nan Madol, one of the most intriguing archaeological sites of Oceania, if not the world. Similarly, the quarrying and transport of the *latte* stones of the Marianas, though they may only have served as pillars for chiefly houses, indicate both engineering skills and a high level of organized work.

While the high islands offered and still offer lush vegetation and rich volcanic soil for growing breadfruit, taro, yams, coconut, and pandanus, the atolls were—and are—quite limited in resources. To atoll dwellers, the sea was everything, and how to exploit it, how to recover from its force, and how to cross it to find additional resources became the driving force of these cultures. As a result, they developed extraordinary navigational and canoe-building skills, two arts that have almost entirely disappeared but which 11th-hour efforts are attempting to revive.

One such effort is the "voyage of rediscovery" of the *Hokule'a*, a 20-meter, "performance-equivalent" replica of the traditional Polynesian double canoe. Sponsored by the Polynesian Voyaging Society of Hawaii, the *Hokule'a* voyage boasts scientific, cultural, and educational goals—to retrieve and reconstruct knowledge of navigation and canoe performance, to prove that the ancestors of today's Polynesians *did* sail from west to east into the wind and to awaken pride in that, to extend what is learned to islanders throughout Oceania. The *Hokule'a*'s first voyage—there have been several—was in 1976, from Hawaii to Tahiti and back again. To reproduce the exact navigational methods presumably used by the ancient Polynesians (no instruments), the *Hokule'a*'s sponsors chose a Micronesian, Mau Piailug, of Satawal in the Carolines, one of the islands of the state of Yap in the Federated States of Micronesia.

On this coral atoll less than half a kilometer square and only about two meters high, Mau preserves and, as best he can, passes on the ancient art of navigation he labored a dozen years to learn and many more years to master. He can read the shapes and colors of the sky and has memorized more than 150 star routes from Satawal to other islands in Micronesia. The night sky is his compass, on which he finds the rising and setting points of 32 stars known to him in their position around the horizon. Of course, star positions change with the hours—the Southern Cross marks five different steering directions as it tracks the sky. When clouds obscure the stars, the Micronesian navigator turns to the swells of the sea. He knows eight different kinds of swells and identifies each by what the canoe does when the swell hits it, or by the kind of peak formed when swells meet. He also notes wind direction, the patterns on the surface of the sea, the flights of birds. For the most part, such navigation uses dead reckoning, relying on a reference island, called an *etak*, and mentally dividing the voyage into segments marked by the change in bearing of the etak. When Mau agreed to the 1976 *Hokule'a* voyage, he of course was not familiar with the star route, winds, or currents along the course from Hawaii to Tahiti. He had never sailed in latitudes as far north as Hawaii nor as far south as Tahiti. Yet, before landfall in the Tuamotus, Mau accurately reckoned the canoe's position and the time it would take to reach those islands.

For the second and third voyages of *Hokule'a* in 1980 and 1986, Mau trained a young Hawaiian, Nainoa Thompson. Combining what he learned from Mau with his own methods, but still using neither instruments nor modern navigational techniques, Nainoa guided the *Hokule'a* again from Hawaii to Tahiti, and in 1986, from Hawaii to Tahiti, the Cook Islands, New Zealand, Tonga, Samoa, and back to Hawaii—dead-on for every landfall.

The importance of navigational skills to the ancient Micronesian culture imbued it with ritual significance. Indeed, two types of navigators were and still are distinguished: the *falu* who knows only how to sail, and the *po,* who knows both sailing and magic. The navigator was responsible for all the lives on the canoe he directed; if the canoe was sailing to another island or reef for food, the number of lives in his hands was even greater. Where Polynesian society revered ancestors and Melanesian society looked to Big Men whose authority came from their personalities, Micronesians emphasized the skill of the mariner. "Men who can't navigate aren't looked up to," Mau Piaulig has said. "They don't have a name. . . . The ancients had faith in the words of their fathers. This is what we call courage. With this courage, you can sail all over the world."

## HISTORY

Archaeological evidence indicates settlement in the Marianas dating back to 1500 B.C. These Chamorro people, described by the first Europeans to see them as looking very much like Polynesians, may have come from the Bismarck Archipelago off New Guinea or even directly from the Philippines. Little is thus far known of their origins, and over the centuries they absorbed so much interbreeding with other peoples that their origins are even more obscured.

The rape of Oceania began in Micronesia, when Magellan stopped off in Guam and the Southern Marianas. A long succession of discoveries, conquests, and occupations followed, in which four main waves can be distinguished, each leaving its calling card of good and evil—the Spanish wave, the German, the Japanese, and the American.

The first wave was the Spanish, starting really with the establishment of a mission on Guam in 1668. Guam had long been a major port of call on the hemp route between the Philippines and Mexico, but Spanish influence eventually extended to the Marshall Islands. Spain never really ruled here—indeed, Micronesia was an arena for disputes between the Crown and the Jesuits—but she left a legacy of Roman Catholicism, some linguistic influence, and a few pieces of architecture.

Spain sold her Micronesian interests to Germany in 1899, a year after her defeat in the Spanish-American War. Germany was looking for copra and colonies, but her rule also was mostly indirect—a policy that wavered between keeping distant from the natives and oppressing them with force. World War I put a stop to this, and 1914 saw the beginning of the long period of Japanese control.

The League of Nations officially entrusted Micronesia to Japan in a 1922 mandate, but in the years that followed, Japan virtually annexed the islands outright. The islands became Japanese colonies—many of them had more Japanese than native islanders—and enjoyed a level of economic development they had not seen before and have not seen since. The Japanese also militarized the islands in preparation for war.

When it came, it brought to these islands some very fierce and brutal fighting. In addition to land battles, many islands were bombarded before being bypassed and blockaded—islanders as well as Japanese soldiers and civilians died from the bombs and starvation. Economic life, education, health services were all in a state of ruined chaos when the United Nations mandated the islands—except Guam—as a "strategic trust" of the United States in 1947.

The Trust Territory of the Pacific Islands (TTPI) was administered first by the U.S. Navy, then, in 1951, by the Department of the Interior reporting to the U.N. Security Council. Because of the territory's designation as a strategic area, the U.S. was authorized to establish military bases, erect fortifications, and employ troops. It was also obligated to foster the development of political institutions toward the goal of self-government, to promote economic, social, and educational advancement, and to guarantee fundamental freedoms for all inhabitants.

The U.S. trusteeship has received its share of criticism. It is certainly accurate to say that the American policy was virtually no policy at all through the 1950s. Starting in 1962, the policy became one of massive subsidies; the aid both answered very real needs and created a welfare dependency, while little real progress was made in promoting home-grown economic development.

The early 1960s also saw the first steps toward self-government. The Interior Department drafted a charter for a Congress of Micronesia, a TTPI legislature to administer the six district components of the Marianas, the Marshalls, Ponape, Palau, Truk, and Yap. (Guam remained an unincorporated U.S. territory.) In 1965, the Congress established the Future Political Status Commission; five years later, the commission (under another name) recommended the option of self-government in "free association" with the United States.

Free association is something entirely new in U.S. history,

although in the Pacific it may be most closely represented by the link between the Cook Islands and New Zealand. Effectively, it gives the U.S. responsibility for defense of the islands and allows the Americans "strategic denial"—the right to deny access to any other power. In return, the islands receive financial aid and other forms of assistance. It is, in the words of one long-time observer, "strategic colonialism."

The negotiations over the proposed Compact of Free Association proceeded through round after round of talks from 1969 to 1985, punctuated by impasses, changing policies, changing government leaders in both the TTPI and the U.S., changing negotiators, and general weariness. In the early rounds, the people of the Northern Marianas demanded separate negotiations; in 1975, they chose commonwealth status, seeking continued close ties with the U.S. In 1979, the districts of Yap, Truk, Ponape, and Kosrae formed themselves into the Federated States of Micronesia. Meanwhile, the Marshall Islands had decided in 1978 to be constituted as a republic, and Palau followed suit in 1979. Self-determination was now a reality, with each of the four districts having their own governments, but the compact talks dragged on. How long would U.S. aid continue to each separate government? How much aid would there be? What services would the U.S. continue to provide? Such things as airline and airport safety, commercial services, weather prediction, and international postal service were under consideration here. How long would the defense authority last? What about settlement of nuclear claims? All of these subsidiary agreements were laboriously worked out.

Finally, in July 1985, the compact, already approved by the new Micronesian nations, came up for a vote in the U.S. House of Representatives. It was the year of tax reform in the United States, and, suddenly, the House Ways and Means Committee decided to make a point by revising the special trade and tax provisions of the compact to make them less favorable to the Micronesians. The administration, eager to get a tax bill passed, chose not to alienate the committee and its powerful chairman, and it began to look like the compact would be stillborn. A compromise was eventually reached, and more U.S. grant assistance sweetened the deal; in the words of an Interior Department official, "The island governments were simply bought off."

By January of 1987, only Palau was still a part of the TTPI. Although its people had approved the compact by a majority in 1983, a court ruled that a 75 percent approval was needed to override a measure in Palau's constitution that bans nuclear materials from Palau. Since it is U.S. policy to refuse to say whether or not a military vessel carries nuclear materials, a new impasse was created. As of this writing, it had not been resolved.

Palau's constitution was the first "nuclear-free" constitution in the world. It is perhaps not surprising that this Micronesian nation should be in the forefront of the nuclear—or antinuclear—issue, for Micronesia has played a major role in the nuclear age. The atomic bombs destined for Hiroshima and Nagasaki were loaded onto B-29 bombers on Tinian, in the Northern Marianas. The first great series of nuclear testing, including the testing of the hydrogen bomb, took place in the Marshall Islands. These are dubious distinctions, but they mark important historic milestones with implications far beyond these islands.

Long a battleground for the wars of others, Micronesia is to-day increasingly an arena for a cold war face-off. Here the U.S. and Russia vie with one another for influence and a presence, while the nations of both the Pacific Basin and the Insular Pacific play one against the other. A regional fisheries agreement in which the U.S. participates competes with Soviet fishing successes in Vanuatu, Kiribati, and Fiji. The Japanese refuse to recognize the sovereignty of the Federated States of Micronesia and the Marshalls Republic for fear of antagonizing Russia. And so on. Meanwhile, the Pacific, where America fought its *last* three wars, is thick with submarines and surface ships of both superpowers, plying their way among the islands of Micronesia.

The "American lake" has both enjoyed and suffered a U.S. policy that has at best been confused and lacking in cohesiveness. In the eyes of many observers, America's benign neglect of these islands has done little to develop resources—economic or human. According to this view, the American notion of letting the islanders "do it themselves" has not worked; the massive grants-in-aid have meant that government is the only significant employer in most island nations, while politics is the only growth industry. Others see it differently. Janet McCoy, the last U.S. high commissioner, not only of the TTPI but anywhere on earth, has called Micronesia "the sleeper of the Pacific," insisting that its economic future is bright.

Of its obligations under the trusteeship, the U.S. may be said to have succeeded in fostering free public education and in encouraging respect for fundamental freedoms. Egalitarianism is in the air here, a noticeable difference from the rest of the Pacific. In many other former colonies, a New Zealander or Australian or British expat seems to sit next to and behind every islander in power—in the banks, the post offices, the ministries of government. This seems less the case in Micronesia; that cool distance between islanders and expats doesn't exist, and political life, while often Byzantine, frequently irresponsible, and occasionally corrupt, is very vital and thoroughly Micronesian.

# THE NATURAL ENVIRONMENT

In this diversity of islands is a diversity of biotic communities. Climate adds to the complexity, although in general, temperatures are warm all the time, cool northeast tradewinds blow through the winter, and rainfall is pretty well distributed—more so in Ponape, one of the wettest places on earth.

The lushness of the high islands to the west, with their rich volcanic soil, dwindles markedly as you travel east. To this day, many atoll dwellers use distant reefs and distant islands as pantries to supplement the meager resources of their own islands.

Coconut, of course, as well as pandanus, breadfruit, taro, tapioca, and yam are cultivated on both high and low islands, although on many atolls taro must be grown in deep pits. The high islands show the usual progression of vegetation from mangrove through coastal plain and on up the slopes of the hills. Ferns are common everywhere; their tiny spores can be carried far on the Pacific winds.

Flying foxes and insect-eating bats are indigenous to some of the western islands; other animal life—pigs, dogs, chickens—was introduced.

Bird life is more abundant than animal life, although here too, the number of native species is small, and what abundance there is declines from west to east. The islands are winter havens for the migrating birds from the north and serve as nesting areas for seabirds that settle near the rich food supply of reef and ocean.

Indeed, it is the marine life of Micronesia that is particularly extravagant, while the coral reefs here constitute lush gardens unto themselves. From the cradle of Indo-Pacific marine life in the triangle bounded by New Guinea, the Philippines, and Malaysia, the entire rest of the Pacific was colonized. Virtually every form of Pacific marine life can be found in the waters of Micronesia, especially in the west, closer to the cradle. Although the variety of coral is also less to the east, the traveler to these remote atolls has an unparalleled opportunity to explore reef construction. Snorkel among the swatches of color that mark the location of patch reefs in the lagoon. Head out to the reef flat at the edge of the lagoon; inside will be a sandy islet supporting few species and possibly covered with bits of debris and fragments of coral colonies. But head over the expanse of the reef flat to the outer reef face, where coral life may be so abundant it is often categorized into zones, within which there are further variations. The snorkeler or diver will have a field day in Micronesia, but exercise caution—shark, barracuda, sea urchins, stonefish, and poisonous sea snakes are all at home in these clear, warm waters.

What is particularly important about the island environments of Micronesia is their fragility. The small size of these islands (even the large ones are relatively small) renders them vulnerable to catastrophe. A typhoon, an introduced predator, thoughtless development—any or all of these have the power to radically alter, if not destroy, an island environment. With the nuclear testing of the 1940s and 50s, Micronesia's environment has already paid a steep price.

## CRAFTS

The handicrafts of Micronesia deserve special mention. Form rather than representation has long characterized traditional Micronesian art. House-building, textile design, and canoe building were highly developed pursuits, in which the scarcity of raw materials dictated simplicity and elegance of design. Some historians have theorized that skill in crafts was essential in a region where interisland links represented a mainstay of the economy; the crafted objects could be traded for food or assistance.

Woodcarving, usually in breadfruit or Calophyllum, includes canoe models found almost everywhere, the dance paddles of Ponape, and the love sticks of Truk. The carvings are often inlaid with mother-of-pearl shell designs. The Marshall Islands are the recognized leaders in weaving, mostly with pandanus and coconut fiber; look for bags, baskets, mats, and headbands. Ornaments include coral and shell jewelry and the famous combs of Yap. Palau is known for its glass money, replicas of which are made from coral. Stone and wood statuary are found only in Palau and Ponape, and the Mortlock Islands of Truk produce the only traditional masks in Micronesia—devil masks.

## THE TRAVELER IN MICRONESIA

The backbone of air travel in Micronesia is Air Continental/Air Micronesia, universally known as Air Mike. The airline runs a regular Guam-Truk-Ponape-Majuro-Honolulu flight, the famous island-hopper or puddle-jumper, the key trans-Micronesia route.

From Guam, the undisputed gateway to Micronesia, Air Mike also flies south to Palau and Yap and north to the Northern Marianas. These routes are also served by a number of other airlines—Air Guam, Air Nauru (usually), Freedom Air, Japan Airlines, and SPIA.

At most stops along the island-hopping route, internal airlines offer interisland links—Pacific Missionary Aviation in Yap and Ponape, Airline of the Marshall Islands and Air Tungaru in the Marshalls. From the Marshalls, it may also be possible to fly to Kiribati or Narau. These flights enable connections to Fiji and the South Pacific, but they have typically been on-again, off-again propositions.

In addition to Air Mike, Micronesia introduces a new element into Pacific travel—or, at least, a new variation on an old theme—the field-trip vessel. It departs the gateway island to move among the outliers, carrying passengers, freight, and officialdom and picking up copra. Supposedly, field trips are made on a regular basis, perhaps once a month or twice a month, but in fact, as one old Micronesian hand has put it, "*All* field trips are late getting off, take longer than expected, and may or may not stick to the proposed route. There is no regular schedule." Nor is there much in the way of comfort—officialdom usually gets the cabins, anyway. But if you have time, it is recommended that you try at least one field trip. Pick a short one perhaps, and pick one to an outlier where you can get a plane back to the gateway. Or, get off at an island and stay until the vessel picks you up on the way back—that is, if the captain sticks to the route and comes back that way.

Guam, one of the least charming destinations in the Pacific, is both the gateway to Micronesia and the traveler's resource center for Micronesian travel. Make as many arrangements here as you can—especially your Air Mike puddle-jumper reservation, which you must of course reconfirm at every stop. The Air Mike office, a travel agency, and/or the Micronesia Regional Tourism Council should be your homes away from home in Guam; if you don't want to be bound by hard-and-fast reservations, at least use these resources to find out all you can about the destinations you have chosen, particularly accommodations. If you are so inclined and so equipped, Micronesia is the one region of Oceania where camping is both possible and easy. Just ask. Be prepared to rent cars for travel in Micronesia.

The itinerary presented here starts in Guam (to which it unhappily returns from time to time) and ends in Majuro en route to Honolulu, Stateside. From Guam, our hypothetical Pacific traveler heads north to the Northern Marianas, then back to Guam to pick up a southbound flight for Palau and Yap. It is back to Guam again, this time to pick up the puddle-jumper and head for Truk, Ponape, and Majuro in the Marshall Islands. Kosrae, one of the Federated States of Micronesia, is off the Air Mike route and difficult and costly to get to; it is reluctantly deleted from this itinerary. Kiribati, the archipelago of the Gilbert Islands, is even more difficult and expensive to get to, which is one reason it makes such a tempting destination. It is not included in our itinerary.

## Micronesia Address

Micronesia Regional Tourism Council
P.O. Box 682
Agana, Guam 96910

(Maintains updated lists of accommodations)

## CHAPTER 16

# GUAM

*Name:* Territory of Guam
*Political status:* Unincorporated, organized territory of the United States
*Island groups:* One offshore island, Cocos, a private resort/ wildlife reserve
*Capital:* Agana
*Population:* 106,000
*Land area:* 554 square kilometers
*Language:* English, Chamorro
*Currency:* United States dollar ($US)

Guam is the undisputed gateway to Micronesia—its business and intellectual center, its travel hub. It cannot be avoided, and from the traveler's viewpoint, that's a shame. A Navy man stationed there for five years told the author his mind still freezes when he hears the word Guam. A New Jersey native stuck there for several days likened it to "Route 17—a line of home improvement stores, car lots, and drive-up banks." An expat from California who lived on Guam for several years before moving to Ponape described it quite simply but perhaps best of all. "Guam," she said, "is a K-Mart." Now there is nothing wrong with K-Mart, but it is hardly necessary for an American to travel halfway around the world to find one. To be fair, there are many people here—Guamanians, U.S. military personnel, and various alien workers and resident expats—who find life on this island thoroughly delightful. But for the traveler, unless he is a World War II buff or scuba diving fanatic, Guam is for getting through—as fast as you can.

## GEOGRAPHY, TOPOGRAPHY, CLIMATE

The westernmost territory of the United States, Guam is far closer to Manila (2400 kilometers), Tokyo (2600 kilometers), and Sydney (4800 kilometers) than to Honolulu (5900 kilometers) or the continental U.S. (9000 kilometers). It sits at 13 degrees north latitude, 145

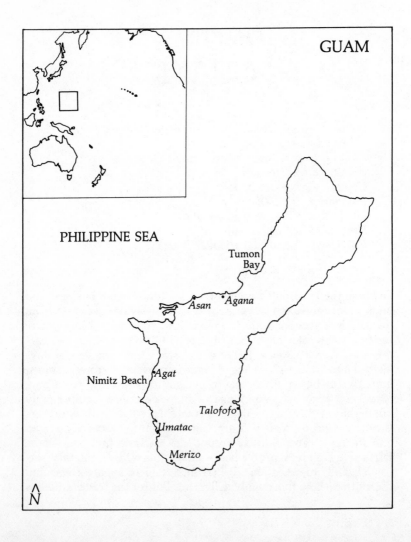

degrees east longitude at the bottom of the 685-kilometer-long Marianas Archipelago and right on the Marianas Trench, at more than 11,000 meters the deepest point of the Pacific. Guam is the largest and most populous of the 15 Marianas islands, but it is politically separate from the other 14, which now constitute the Commonwealth of the Northern Marianas. Forty-eight kilometers long, 20 kilometers across at its greatest width, and only 6 kilometers from coast to coast at the cinched midsection, Guam is the largest landmass between Hawaii and the Philippines.

The island was formed in successive undersea volcanic upheavals. The earlier upheaval formed the north, already capped with coralline limestone when the second upheaval created the south. The pinched-waist middle of Guam connects the two. The north is a plateau of rolling hills and steep (as high as 183 meters) volcanic cliffs along the coast; it completely lacks surface streams. The north is also the primary home of the heavy U.S. military installation here, making much of the area, including the island's best beach, effectively off limits. The south has low volcanic mountains—the highest point, Mount Lamlam, is 407 meters—red clay hills, savannahlike expanses punctuated by junglelike valleys and ravines. This is the sleepier part of the island—most of the population lives right around Agana, the capital on the west coast—and it offers some picturesque scenery and picturesque small towns. A coral reef surrounds the island. There is a safe harbor, Apra, and good swimming on the west; the east coast is rough, with high waves a surfer will love.

Guam is on the Pacific's Ring of Fire and has repeatedly been hit by earthquakes. It is also in the path of twice-yearly tropical storms and typhoons that gather strength as they move westward; Guam has been badly damaged by super-typhoons in the past, most terribly in 1976 and 1982.

The climate is tropical year-round. July through October is the wet season. The driest months are December through February.

# THE NATURAL ENVIRONMENT

Guam is rich in vegetation—vines, savannah, palm, coconut, breadfruit, banyan, the economically important *ifil*—ironwood, bananas, and many flowering plants. Although freshwater fish are not common, the coastal areas yield a variety of crabs, the protected reef is home to one of the most diverse fish populations in the world, and deep-water fish as well as green and hawksbill sea turtles, both endangered, are plentiful outside the reef.

There is a limited range of animal life. Two species of bats are the only native mammals, and of the species introduced by the

Spanish, the most successful has been the water buffalo, brought from the Philippines. (No, there is no fresh mozzarella produced here, strangely enough.)

But Guam's bird and reptile life, or lack of same, yields an interesting and important ecological story.

The story concerns the end of bird life on Guam. World War II destroyed much of the bird population, as did postwar insecticide spraying. But by the 1980s, it had become clear that some other force was at work. Three of Guam's six endemic bird species had become extinct—the bridled white-eye, Guam broadbill, and rufous-fronted fantail. The most famous endemic species, the flightless Guam rail or *koko (Rallus owstoni)* had disappeared from the island. Very few Micronesian kingfishers were left. The Mariana crow had been greatly reduced in number. Six other bird species, native but not endemic, were threatened, and birds were vanishing constantly. While the Guam government sought endangered species status for seven species of birds and two of bats from the U.S Fish and Wildlife Service—it took the Feds five years to grant the status—scientists tried to figure out what was killing the birds of Guam.

There was no evidence of disease. The scientists looked again. One of them, a University of Illinois graduate student named Julie Savidge, finally found the answer in 1982—the *Boiga irregularis*. Routinely misidentified as the Philippine rat snake, the *B. irregularis* is neither from the Philippines nor is it a rat snake. It is a bird-eating tree snake, and it is found in New Guinea and along the coast of Australia. How it got to Guam is unknown, but it had been here some forty years when Julie Savidge cut open a few specimens to uncover the birds and bird eggs inside.

Before the arrival of *B. irregularis*, Guam had been virtually snakeless, except for a blind, earthwormlike snake that burrowed in the soil and fed on termites. Freed from reptilian predation, the birds of Guam never developed the defenses that could protect them against *B. irregularis*. They were an easy mark for the snake, which had also escaped its own natural predators back home. The birds of Guam are almost all gone now, while *B. irregularis* pretty much runs free, a common fact of life on the island, where its population may soon suffer from overcrowding—as well as from extermination by humans.

Meanwhile, some of the species of Guam birds *have* been saved. Under a plan sponsored by the American Association of Zoological Parks and Aquariums and the Guam Division of Aquatic and Wildlife Resources, survivors of the last three endemic species have been airlifted to U.S. zoos to breed—successfully—in captivity. The point of such captive breeding programs is to produce, in a protected environment, a representative sample of a gene pool, a seed bank for ultimate reintroduction if and when a way to control *B. irregularis* is found. Nature writer David Quammen has pointed out (in "Island Getaway," *Outside Magazine*, October 1985) that, if the birds are successfully introduced, "then their likely eventual fate is exactly the same: disappearing without a trace. Their small-remote-island habitat, by its very nature, is what promises them an evolutionary dead end. . . . Small islands especially are the black holes to oblivion."

But that, Quammen goes on, is not the point. The point, in his words, is to "say no to the inevitable. . . . For mortal creatures, on a slow-dying planet, in the ocean of space, there's really no other option."

For the traveler, this is all food for thought. To see the surviving species of Guam's avian world, however, you must visit the zoos back home.

# HISTORY

As is true throughout Micronesia, the history of Guam before the 16th century is obscure, although some archaeologists believe that, given the chance, they might find here some of the richest remains in the Pacific. That humans had arrived here by 3000 B.C. is confirmed by the carbon dating of cooking pits, and archaeological evidence of permanent settlement dates to about 2300 B.C. By that time, Guam had already assumed its role as the major population and trade center for the Marianas Archipelago.

The early people were Chamorros, from whose word *guahan*, "we have," the island's name derives. They either originated on the Malay Peninsula or had prolonged contacts with people who did, and they may also be ultimately related to the ancestors of the Polynesians. In fact, cultural and linguistic analyses show resemblances to cultures of Malaysia, Indonesia, and the Philippines. The most important archaeological remains left by these early people are the latte stones, megalithic monuments that were probably used as house posts for the homes of nobles in the rigidly caste-bound Chamorro society. In Agana, there is a park filled with latte stones, although the traveler can also see these in the Northern Marianas, especially on Tinian.

The first contact with the West was the arrival of Ferdinand Magellan in 1521, during history's first circumnavigation. Magellan called Guam and the chain of islands to the north Islas de Ladrónes (Islands of Thieves) when a skiff from his ship was stolen by natives in what is today Umatac on Guam, inspiring the great explorer to destroy the offending village and to kill a number of villagers. After

Magellan, there were other infrequent European contacts—enough to provide another early name, Ilhas das Velas (Islands of Sails), after the triangular sails on the native canoes. Spain claimed Guam in 1565, and it became a useful way station on the Mexico-to-Philippines hemp route. The Jesuits arrived in 1668; it was a Jesuit who gave the island chain the name that stuck, Marianas, after Mariana of Austria, widow of Philip IV of Spain.

The Jesuits were somewhat insensitive to Chamorro society and beliefs, but they left a record of both even as they destroyed them. Society was divided into nobles, commoners, and outcasts. The nobles held such high-status occupations as navigator, village chief, canoe builder, warrior, or trader and mingled fairly freely with commoners. But between those two classes and the outcasts was a wide gap, defined by numerous taboos.

The extended family was the main social unit, living in villages of from 50 to 150 huts. Descent was matrilineal, and marriage was monogamous, but both concubinage and divorce were permitted.

In 1672, the natives openly revolted against Spanish domination, and in the intermittent hostilities over the next two decades, many were killed. The introduction by the Spanish crews of smallpox, syphilis, and other diseases further reduced the population—from an estimated one hundred thousand in the early 1600s to five thousand at the end of the century. After the Jesuits were booted out of the country, the Spaniards managed to deplete the island even further; the indigenous population was down to 1500 by 1783.

The U.S. received Guam as a prize of the Spanish-American War of 1898. The island came under the jurisdiction of the Navy, which developed it as a naval base. Its inhabitants became U.S nationals.

Guam was seized by the Japanese three days after the attack on Pearl Harbor. They proceeded to conscript Guamanians for labor and later moved them all into concentration camps. Several natives, including a highly popular priest and a highly successful businessman, were publicly mutilated and executed for their Allied sympathies. The American Marines landed on July 21, 1944, and the Japanese surrendered less than three weeks later—except for one diehard, who holed up in the interior until 1972. (Some Guamanians think there are more Japanese soldiers hiding out in caves in the interior; they will emerge, it is said, in 1994, the fiftieth anniversary of the battle. Another island legend, more of an ongoing joke, tells of an American GI, Sergeant Cletus Webb, still in hiding and afraid to come out because he believes, from the evidence he sees when he peeks out of his cave, that the Japanese have won the war and own the island.) Guam then became an armed camp, headquarters of the U.S. naval forces in the Pacific. It still is. A number of native landowners have filed suit for compensation for lands appropriated by the military during the war and still not paid for.

In 1950, the administration of Guam was transferred to the Department of the Interior, and Guam's citizens became U.S. citizens, although they cannot vote in U.S. national elections and their congressman may vote only in committee and not on the floor of the House. Guam is governed by a popularly elected governor and a unicameral legislature. Amendments are routinely sought to the Organic Act that defines Guam's administration. For example, Guam has sought exemption from the requirement that goods shipped between Guam and the U.S. travel on U.S. ships, and it asked to be exempt from environmental regulations requiring stringent emission control standards by industry; this latter exemption was granted. The Commission on Future Politcal Status will presumably resolve these and other matters.

Today, there are no "pure" Chamorros left, although the vast majority of the fast-growing population traces its ancestry to Chamarros. Twenty percent of the population is U.S. military personnel and dependents; other Americans are here at the university, with its well-known Marine Laboratory Institute and Micronesian Area Research Center, and in numerous service and support roles. Chinese, Filipinos, Japanese, Koreans, and Micronesians, for whom Guam is the big city, also live here, creating a cosmopolitan feeling.

Cosmopolitan but very Americanized. The traveler will note the completely American style of today's generation, but he should also note the more Spanish or Filipino style among older Guamanians. The long period of Spanish domination started the erosion of traditional ways here; the war speeded up the process; the Americans have probably finished it, although there is, not surprisingly, a revival of cultural interest in Chamorro culture. Nevertheless, not for nothing is this island called "Guam USA."

# THE TRAVELER TO GUAM

Most of your fellow visitors will be Japanese, and most of them will be honeymooners. For them, the trip is short, the fare reasonable, the hotels almost all owned by Japanese—and now by Chinese from the People's Republic—the water sports fine, the weather good. One of the more haunting images of a visit here is to see the hordes of Japanese tourists photographing one another at the small replica of the Statue of Liberty. Tumon Bay, with its strip of hotels, restaurants, shops, and beach activities, is often called Japan's Miami Beach—and it looks it. For the Japanese tourists who flock here, Guam is an easy way to have a holiday in the sun and shop duty free. For the English-speaking traveler, that means that finding a guided tour or tourist brochure in English will be difficult.

If you are spending time here, your best bet is to rent a car—in fact, there's really no other way to see the island or get around at all. (You can also rent bikes or mopeds. Taxis are very expensive.) Make the Guam Visitors Bureau your first stop; here you can pick up sightseeing maps and brochures.

For the war buff, Guam offers 71 points of interest, and the GVB has an excellent brochure guiding you to all of them.

War sites are a large part of any tour here. Heading south from Agana, you pass Asan and Agat—Nimitz Beach—where the U.S. landings took place, and at Umatac is the park in memory of the Guamanians who fought and died in Vietnam. Umatac is billed as one of the sleepier, more picturesque villages of Guam. (It's possible to rent a room above the hot-dog stand, if you want to stay.) The black-sand beach of the bay looks inviting, but a resident of Umatac told a visitor that her children get ear trouble when they swim there; the river brings down pollution as well as silt. The traveler might expect Guamanian resentment against the American presence, yet the opposite is usually the case. In what may be the ultimate Americanization, most people here have had their expectations raised, or at least changed; in any event, what they want is more. An Umatac woman, for example, complained that her youngest child, aged 12, declared gifted in school, was already bored with his education. "I want my children to have the opportunities I didn't have," the woman told her visitor; "I want them to have choices." If these are clichés, they are difficult to argue with.

As far as Umatac and Merizo, a pretty village boasting the oldest Spanish building—the parish house—on the island, the look of the land has been dry hills tumbling down to the Philippine Sea. But here, the coast turns to mangrove, and as you head up the east, you ride atop cliffs and through thicker vegetation. On the inland side are the lush green hills that are the spine of the island. The north, cliffbound plain, is predominantly military.

There are in fact some fine hikes on Guam—among the southern mountains, to waterfalls, along clifftops and beaches, to visit war sites. The GVB offers a brochure that is a good guide.

For divers, Guam is something of a paradise. Right on the Marianas Trench, this huge ocean's deepest point, the water is clear, and the university reports that more than 110 different families of fish swim in these waters, with some 800 different kinds of fish to be observed. There are drop-offs, crevices, caves, and wrecks; right in Apra Harbor are the scuttled World War I German cruiser *Cormoran* and the Japanese freighter *Tokai Maru*, sunk in World War II. Best of all, Guam dives are accessible—there are some twenty walk-in sites.

The suburban sprawl around Agana will be familiar—colored pennants announcing car and boat sales, McDonald's and the Colonel, U.S. banks and chain stores, and what American radio man and writer Jean Shepherd has called "the worst-looking bar in the Pacific—the *worst*." Try to guess.

Finally, the traveler should visit the Guam Museum in Agana, right in the rather Spanish-looking main plaza. The museum has an excellent collection including prehistoric implements, ancient pottery shards, a *belembautuyan*—a stringed musical instrument similar to those found in Brazil, samples of *rai* discs—the stone money of Yap, artifacts from early European sailors, and war relics.

The Chamarro language today is colored with Spanish, English, and Tagalog terms, and everybody has his own idea about proper vocabulary and spelling. *Hafa adai*—sounds like "half a day"—is the standard greeting; it means "what?" as in "what's up?" and is often shortened to *fa*. Like many other Pacific peoples, Guamanians use eyebrow talk, full of nuances; if an islander squints at you, he either has the sun in his eyes or doesn't believe a word you're saying.

## Guam Address

Guam Visitors Bureau
P.O. Box 3520
1220 Pale San Vitores Rd.
Tamuning
Guam, USA 96911
Tel. (671) 646-8516/8466, 646-5278/9

# CHAPTER 17

# THE NORTHERN MARIANAS

*Name:* Commonwealth of the Northern Marianas
*Political status:* U.S. commonwealth
*Island groups:* 14 islands, three main ones (Saipan, Tinian, Rota), four others sparsely inhabited
*Gateway island:* Saipan
*Capital:* Saipan (Capitol Hill, civic center at Susupe)
*Population:* 16,700
*Land area:* 478 square kilometers
*Language:* Chamorro, Carolinian (Trukic), English
*Currency:* U.S. dollar ($US)

Gentle western shores with calm waters and soft sand oppose rugged eastern shores pounded by ferocious surf on these islands. But what the Northern Marianas most recall for the traveler is war. Saipan holds the dubious distinction of having suffered the worst devastation of any of the islands in the Pacific. On Tinian, the traveler can see the pits from which bombs were loaded onto the B-29 Flying Fortresses that would carry them to Hiroshima and Nagasaki.

## GEOGRAPHY, TOPOGRAPHY, CLIMATE

The 14 islands of the Northern Marianas Chain run in a narrow line from 15 to 20 degrees north latitude on a slight curve along 146 degrees east longitude. Saipan, the main island and capital, is some 206 kilometers north of Guam—about a 30-minute plane ride. Tinian, the second largest of these tiny islands, is a five-minute flight from Saipan. Rota sits between Guam and Saipan and is closer to the former. The lovely islands of Anatahan, Almagan, Pagan, and Agrihan continue up the chain and are reachable by field-trip vessel. (The World War II Japanese airstrip on Pagan is occasionally visited by chartered plane.)

The Marianas are the high, volcanically formed peaks of a massive mountain range rising some 10 kilometers from the floor of the Marianas Trench. The Pacific Plate, the only one of earth's six principal plates that does not include a sizeable portion of a continent, has pushed to its northwest limit here, diving to destruction in this, the deepest part of the ocean. From depths of more than 9000 meters to the immediate east of the island chain, the Marianas Ridge begins its rise. Volcanic activity along the ridge created the island arc—a series of high, volcanic thrusts with not an atoll among them. The highest point, 965 meters, is achieved on Agrihan.

The climate is tropical and maritime. Summer runs from May to October, and July through November see storms, often typhoons. Rainfall is plentiful, averaging 1500 millimeters a year, most of it in the north.

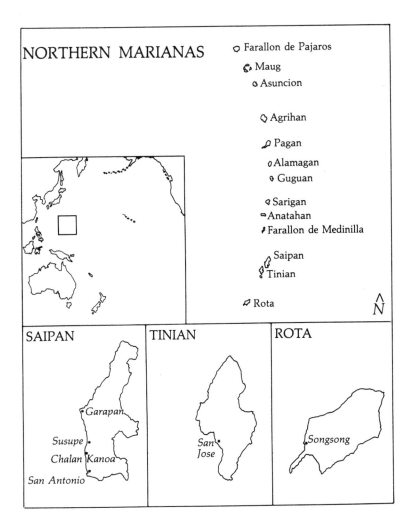

# THE NATURAL ENVIRONMENT

Vegetation is generous and diverse. Mangrove predominates in coastal flats; coconut trees abound inland but give way to scrubby growth and grassland on hills; the upper slopes yield wet, mossy scrub and ferns.

In fact, the most prevalent form of vegetation is *tangan tangan* brush. After the war, the U.S. military seeded the islands with tangan tangan as an expedient for preventing erosion and filling bomb craters. The brush succeeded all too well and now covers the ground, tenaciously rooted.

Giant African snails were brought here by the Japanese as survival food for the war; they're everywhere. Coconut crabs also abound. There are few land birds, but numerous marine and shore birds—tern, booby, tropicbird, frigate, heron. Marine life is very rich, including just about every species characteristic of Pacific waters—bonito, tuna, shark, sea bass, shrimp, and the giant tridacna clam.

# HISTORY

Earliest archaeological remains date to 2000 B.C. The archipelago's recorded history is a series of takeovers. In 1698, after a failed revolt against Spanish rule, the Chamorro populace was removed en masse to Guam. Here they adopted Catholicism and much of Spanish culture—not to mention Spanish blood. When their descendants returned in 1816, they found that communities of Carolinians had settled here; the Carolinians stayed on as fishermen, the Chamorros turned to farming. Germany purchased the Northern Marianas from Spain in 1899. They augmented the population by offering homesteads to Guamanians, ordered everyone to plant food, and built the first roads. The islands were next seized by the Japanese, who ruled between the wars, developing lively sugarcane and tuna fishing industries.

Although Rota was bypassed in World War II, Saipan and Tinian were won by the Allies in fierce and destructive battles. The main battle was fought in the skies. It is officially known as the Battle of the Philippine Sea; unofficially, it was called the "Great Marianas Turkey Shoot." The taking of Saipan cost 3000 American dead and 11,000 wounded, 24,000 Japanese casualties, and the deaths of 419 Saipanese. Tinian, taken at less cost, was turned into the biggest airbase of its time. From here, B-29s could fly the short distance to Japan nonstop to drop their bombs. In a sense, the nuclear age began here; the atomic bomb went aboard the *Enola Gay* at Tinian. The Northern Marianas remained under the jurisdiction of the U.S. Navy until 1962.

In that year, the headquarters of the Trust Territory of the Pacific Islands (TTPI) was relocated to Capitol Hill on Saipan, and U.S. aid—and Marianas dependency—began. From the beginning of the trusteeship, Marianas leaders showed an inclination for close ties with the U.S. When it seemed likely that negotiations would not result in commonwealth status for all of the TT, the Marianas delegation sought separate negotiations. In 1975, the U.S. and the Northern Marianas signed a commonwealth covenant, affirmed by plebiscite that same year. President Ford's signing of the covenant marked the first time the U.S. had acquired territory since its purchase of the Virgin Islands from Denmark in 1917. Under the agreement, the commonwealth is self-governed, but the U.S. controls defense and foreign affairs. The people of the commonwealth are U.S. citizens.

## THE NORTHERN MARIANAS TODAY

The U.S. has leases on the northern portion of Tinian, the tiny island of Farallon de Medinilla, and a tract of Saipan harbor. The land at Tinian has been used for military training, and two supply boats are based there, plying the route to Guam. The Pentagon routinely proposes further use of the area and construction on the site, but, thus far, nothing has been done.

The economy, once so promising under Japanese domination, has faltered considerably and depends heavily on U.S. aid. Although Japanese tourists flock here for the water sports and to visit the war sites, much of the tourism is prepaid in Japan and most of the tourist hotels are Japanese owned.

The Chamorro language here shows traces of German and Japanese. The descendants of the Carolinians speak a central Carolinian or Trukic.

It's possible to get good local food here—as well as the sushi and hamburgers featured in restaurants and snack bars. Try roast suckling pig, red rice, coconut crabs, chicken in a very hot *finadene* sauce, *escabeche* (fried fish with vegetables), fried noodles, fried bananas, and *tuba*, a fermented coconut drink from the sap of the palm sprout.

Saipan International Airport—very pretty—is 13 kilometers from Garapan and is a good place to rent a car; there's no public bus service, but if you get stuck, someone will give you a ride—the islanders are delightful.

## THE TRAVELER IN THE NORTHERN MARIANAS

The three islands accessible by airplane—all have pretty airports—

are the gateway islands of Saipan, Tinian, and Rota. The traveler should arrange his arrival and hotel on Saipan with Air Mike or a travel agent in Guam. Arrangements for Tinian and Rota can be made at the same time, or with the airline or an agent in Saipan.

Saipan is the tourist hub of the Northern Marianas. Although much slower paced than Guam, it too is a center for expat activity (on the wane since the compact was approved) and a mecca for Japanese tourists, who can fly here directly from either Tokyo or Nagoya. The island's war sites have a particular place in Japanese history and a particular hold on the Japanese heart.

Tinian is only 5 kilometers from Saipan—you can easily see one from the other—but regular ferry traffic doesn't exist. You may be able to take the weekly vessel that touches all three islands, but think twice about hitching a motorboat ride between Saipan and Tinian— the waters of the Saipan channel are extremely rough. By air, Tinian is an easy day trip. Its sights can be seen in a short time, and it has little, as of this writing, in the way of tourist facilities. This, of course, makes it particularly attractive to some travelers.

Rota is a tiny gem of a place—a beautiful island with a village that gives a good look at Chamorro life and with a range of accommodations.

# SAIPAN

At 122 square kilometers, Saipan is the largest of the Northern Marianas. A large reef shelters its western shore, creating a gentle lagoon and low, sandy beaches. To the east, the coast is rocky and rugged. The north, the Marpi area, is the setting for dramatic inland and coastal cliffs.

Beach Road runs along the western shore, and here are the towns—together constituting virtually one long municipal strip—of Garapan, once the Japanese capital, Gualo-Rai, Oleai/San Jose, Susupe, center of government activity, Chalan Kanoa, the commercial center, and San Antonio. This strip is the locus also of the tourist hotels, restaurants, and water sports facilities. Most airline offices and the nice little Saipan Museum are in Garapan.

In the high center of the island is Capitol Hill, once the site of the TTPI and from 1951 to 1962 a CIA base where Nationalist Chinese guerrillas were trained. From Capitol Hill, a jeep track leads three kilometers up to the top of Mount Tapotchau, highest point on the island.

On the south of the island, a jeep track leads to Obyan Beach, where small white arrows mark a path to latte stones hewn in about 1500 B.C. and to the huge bunker that guarded the Saipan Channel during the war.

Near the northern end of the island is the concrete-reinforced natural cave that was the last command post of the Japanese, and Suicide and Banzai cliffs. One of the more chilling events of the war took place here, and a visit to the cliffs, now covered with Japanese memorials, is a moving experience. The battle for Saipan had been a resounding defeat for the Japanese troops. Their commander committed ritual suicide while his troops prepared for a final banzai charge. To the thousands of Japanese civilians on the island, the commander left a message that spoke of "the disgrace of being taken alive" and reminded the people of the *oyaku-shinju*, the parents-children death pact. The civilians for years had heard tales of the atrocities committed by the American barbarians, before whose onslaught they now fled in panic to Marpi Point. There they jumped, many carrying the corpses of the children they had already killed, from what has come to be known as Banzai Cliff. In the water, Japanese-speaking islanders on American destroyers begged the people not to jump, assuring them they had nothing to fear; the destroyers steered among the bodies, saving one out of every five who jumped. Suicide Cliff was worse, however; as the traveler will see, jagged rocks lie below. It is said that families lined up here, the smallest child first. Each family member pushed the one in front. Finally, the father pushed his wife off the cliff, then turned with his back to the sea before falling backward off the cliff.

The Saipanese will tell you that before the war there were no white birds on their island. Now they ride the winds over Suicide and Banzai cliffs, vessels of the souls who died there.

# TINIAN

By prearrangement from Saipan (or Guam), your Piper Cherokee or Twin Otter will be met by a guide from Fleming's Hotel, Japanese owned and, as of this writing, the only hotel on the island. It is a flat island of layered limestone plateaus covered by tangan tangan. Pine trees, planted before the war by the Japanese, are the tallest things around, but ironwood lines the beaches, and there are flame trees and wild papaya everywhere. Once one of the world's greatest producers of sugarcane (under the Japanese), Tinian today yields only a few scattered clumps of wild cane.

There are approximately five times as many cattle on Tinian as people; they (the cattle) graze on the eastern third of the island, a huge ranch. The people themselves are relative latecomers. Only a few dozen Micronesians lived here when it was a Japanese island; the present population is mostly an expatriate Chamorro colony from Yap shifted here in the late 1940s. *The* town is San Jose, in the southwest of the island. There is excellent tuna fishing in these waters, and Tinian's spacious harbor, just south of the town, is used for transshipping—tuna for U.S. consumption is processed at Pago Pago, American Samoa. On the northeast coast of Tinian, looking across the channel to Saipan, are extraordinary blowholes through which the sea shoots up quite fiercely. From this vantage, the channel between the two islands looks very rough indeed.

The second major sight on the island is the House of Taga, a park near San Jose. Taga was Micronesia's Paul Bunyan, and the latte stones here are far bigger than those of Guam, hewn from the craggy volcanic rock that lines the coast. The exquisite but minute Taga Beach nearby has holes that may represent cuttings for the taga stones. The House of Taga itself is on the National Register of Historic Places.

North along the west coast is Chulu Beach or Hagoi Beach (the Japanese name for Tinian was Hagoi) or Invasion Beach. Having set up a diversionary landing at San Jose, the Americans were able to surprise and quickly overrun a small garrison of Japanese defenders at Chulu when they landed on July 25, 1944. The island was secured a week later, and the Americans proceeded to build it into an airbase. The Seabees, to whom there is a lovely monument on the island, engaged here in the biggest construction job of the war. They built, not just an airbase, but what amounted to a city to supply and man it. Indeed, deciding that Tinian was shaped somewhat like Manhattan (it is, too), they called the main road Broadway and laid out a Central Park, Times Square, 42nd Street, 69th Street, 72nd Street, and 96th Street.

The airbase, North Field, had four runways each 1800 meters long. In full operation, it was the largest and busiest airfield in the world for its time. On mission days, two B-29s abreast took off every 45 seconds for the seven-hour ride to Japan.

One mission day was August 6, 1945. From the bomb pits that are today Tinian's major attraction, atomic bombs were loaded onto *Enola Gay* for the trip to Hiroshima. Three days later, more bombs were loaded onto *Bock's Car*, the B-29 headed for Nagasaki. The bomb pits are simply that—holes in the pavement, filled in today and planted with plumeria and with monuments in both English and Japanese. "From this loading pit," the English sign reads, "the first atomic bomb ever used in combat was loaded aboard a B-29 aircraft and dropped on Hiroshima, Japan, August 6, 1945." It is a sobering and indelible experience for an American visitor to stand here, side by side with a Japanese guide who reads a tourism decription of the site and the events—in slightly fractured English, consistently polite. Around you is the expanse of North Field—the coral runways now cracked, weeds threatening to overtake them, the vast field itself now overgrown with tangan tangan. This seems as remote a place as the two of you can be, a tiny speck in the ocean both your countries share, an ocean now crashing against the shoreline not too far from where you stand. Near the pits is a message painted onto the runway—huge letters to be seen by Pope John Paul II during his flyover of Tinian when he toured the Pacific in 1984: WELCOME POPE. TINIAN ATOMIC BOMB PITS.

# ROTA

Tiny Rota—83 square kilometers—is very much a resort for Japanese tourists. The island is shaped like a hand with the finger pointing to Guam. The finger is Tapingot Peninsula, and on it sits the so-called wedding cake, a flat-topped mountain that looks like what its name implies.

Songsong, the island's town, is on a neck of land between two harbors—and within earshot of both the Pacific Ocean and the Philippine Sea—at the land end of the peninsula. The west and northwest of the island contain the best beaches and most of the hotels. A second village, Sinapalo, is inland near the airport. This is an island for walks, beachcombing, beach lying, and the hotel-sponsored water sports. It can be toured in half a day on the circle-island road.

For sights to see, there is the old Japanese steam locomotive at West Harbor, sitting beside the shell of the sugar mill it once served. Just a short walk from Songsong is Taga Cave, a huge cavern with stalagmites and stalactites, used by the Japanese as a hospital. The road passes the Japanese towers that once supported cable cars used to bring phosphate from the mines to the harbor. There is also a huge Japanese gun aimed seaward from a pillbox fortress. Inland are a water cave and waterfall, a Japanese cemetery, and a latte stone quarry. At the north end of the island, near Machong Beach, are remains of an ancient Chamorro Village and latte stones.

Rota was bypassed by the Allies during the war.

### Northern Marianas Address

Marianas Visitors Bureau
P.O. Box 861
Saipan, CM 96950

# CHAPTER 18

# PALAU

*Name:* Republic of Belau
*Political status:* Self-governing republic
*Island groups:* Palau cluster, five other units
*Gateway island:* Koror
*Capital:* Koror
*Population:* 15,000
*Land area:* 461 square kilometers
*Language:* Palauan, Trukic (Sonsorolese), English
*Currency:* U.S. dollar ($US)

"The coconut that contains no milk is not known until it is opened."
So runs a proverb of Palau, an island nation just now being opened
by the wider world, to whom it is showing that it contains an independent spirit, a commitment to tradition, and some of the most
perfect, travel-poster scenic beauty in the Pacific. The Rock Islands,
also called the Floating Garden Islands, are among the most photo-
graphed sights in the whole huge ocean, but no photograph does
them justice. Kayangel, accessible only by boat, is a perfect coral
atoll. Crocodiles are hunted in the sinister mangrove swamps that
fringe the thick jungle of Babeldaob Island, largest in the chain and
rich also in art and archaeology. Peleliu was the scene of one of
World War II's ugliest and perhaps most pointless battles. Angaur
is the place for a romantic island idyll. In the island nation's main
town on Koror, politicians come and go, arguing about how to
end—and follow—colonialism. In a sense, Palau is for the traveler
a microcosm of the Pacific, a short course in the Pacific journey.

## GEOGRAPHY, TOPOGRAPHY, CLIMATE

Palau—Belau to its people—comprises some 350 islands, ranged in
six clusters down a 700-kilometer northeast-to-southwest stretch from
Kayangel in the north to the islet of Tobi in the south. This is the
westernmost extreme of the Caroline Archipelago, about seven
degrees north of the equator at about 135 degrees east longitude.

Palau sits on the edge of the Palau Minitrench, in the northwestern corner of the West Caroline Basin. (The basin is formed by
Palau to the west and, to the east, the Eauripik–New Guinea rise,
continuing upward from PNG's Admiralty Islands.) How these
islands were formed is little understood, but they may be an island
arc in the making. Only the northern islands have exposed volcanic

rocks. Most of Palau is surrounded by elevated reefs. The extensive barrier reefs along the west seem to be the result of recent subsidence, while the east has the fringing reefs. The conclusion is that the region around the islands may be settling, tilting slightly to the west.

The major island group is the Palau cluster—about two hundred islands, of which eight are permanently inhabited. Kayangel to the north is Palau's only atoll; several islets encircle its interior lagoon. Kayangel may be the bottom end of the tilt that uplifted Peleliu and Angaur to the south. Between them lie Babeldaob (sometimes written Babelthuap)—at 396 square kilometers the second

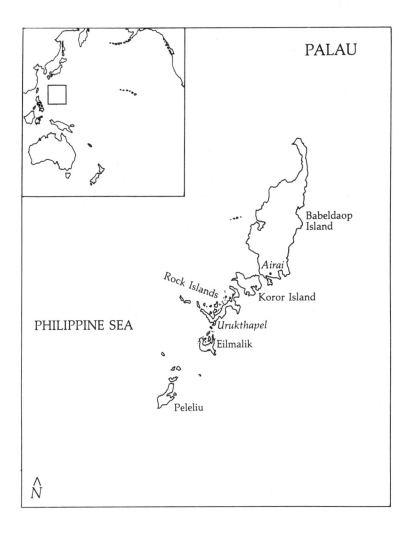

largest island in Micronesia (after Guam); Koror, the gateway island, and the nearby islets attached by causeway; Urukthapel; and Eilmalik. The Southwestern Islands—Sonsorol, Tobi, and Pulo Anna—are sparsely populated, by Trukic-speaking people.

From the Kossol Reef just south of Kayangel to Peleliu, a 105-kilometer-long barrier reef shelters a wide lagoon along the west of Palau. The five islands lying within this barrier reef—Babeldaob, Koror, Malakal, Arakabesang, and Peleliu—historically linked by ease of travel and communication, share a cultural homogeneity. The barrier reef also shelters the Rock Islands—Chalbacheb in Palauan—dotted down the lagoon south of Babeldaob for some 37 kilometers. At one time coral limestone reefs, the Rock Islands were uplifted by seismic activity and undercut by waves. From the air, the undulating line of the Rock Islands creates a maze of interior marine lakes of the clearest aquamarine color. The mind strains for analogies—mushrooms, green pin cushions, emeralds. The dark-green, thickly vegetated tops overhang gray stone arches and caves, and to at least one visitor, there is an almost northern look about these islands with their forest-green and gray colors and their fjordlike jutting—except that they are set in the most unnorthern lagoon. Among them are perhaps thousands of isolated beaches giving onto the protected waters, beaches washed by two-meter tides, that are the setting for an extremely rich coral and marine life. Indeed, Palau is in the center of what has been called the world's richest and most diverse marine biogeographic region.

February to April and October to December are the driest, sunniest months. Westerlies bring the southwest monsoon from July to October, and northeast trades blow from November to April. Typhoons have been rare here, but the heaviest rainfall, mostly in the morning, comes between May and September.

# THE NATURAL ENVIRONMENT

Land wildlife is limited. Fruit bats have flown in, and dogs, pigs, cattle, goats, rats, and monkeys (on Angaur) have been brought in. There are plenty of geckos, two species of nonvenomous snakes, monitor lizards, toads, centipedes, and two species of seawater crocodiles. In the rivers and mangrove swamps of Babeldaob, the crocs grow to five meters; they are hunted, at night, and there have been unpleasant (that is to say, fatal) incidents. The advanced technology for croc hunts uses a motor boat, spotlights, and high-powered rifles. But a number of locals still hunt the crocodiles in dugout canoes or rafts, using flashlight and spear. The salted skin of the croc sells for some $10 a foot, and the hunter also gets the meat of the tail for food, a decorative skull, and prestige in his village.

Dense jungle here includes bamboo, tree ferns, vines, rattan, and numerous poison plants. Tropical hardwoods are present in small supply—used for the very important carvings of Palau and for lumber. Nipa palm is used for thatching, pandanus makes the mats, and coconut fiber ties everything together. Figs, bamboo shoots, and the Malay apple are gathered wild for food, and cultivated plants include taro, sweet potato, tapioca, coconut, breadfruit, the lime to accompany the Areca palm's betel nut, sugarcane, and a variety of tropical fruits.

The total number of native bird species recorded on Palau is 32, but numerous Japanese and Asiatic birds are carried here in the autumn. As elsewhere in Micronesia, bird fauna mix genera from Asia, PNG, and Polynesia. Honeyeaters and parrots are said to be completely absent, but white parrots have been brought in to add a sense of the tropics to the grounds of the luxury resort hotel on Arakabesang, and colored parrots have been seen among the Rock Islands.

The richest arena of Palau's environment is underwater. The islands' proximity to the Indo-Malay faunal region is one reason— as with bird and plant life, marine life becomes less abundant and varied as you move east. Another reason is the variety of habitats created by a complex system of barrier, fringing, and patch reefs. There are more than fifteen hundred different types of fish and seven hundred corals and anemones in the lagoons and on the reefs. The rare dugong, a sea mammal, grazes underwater here. Sea turtles are numerous and are hunted for food. Sharks, barracuda, crustaceans, and all the luminescent fish of the tropics are easily visible in these unbelievably clear waters.

# HISTORY

It is not known for sure where the Palauans originated, although present-day Palauans are an admixture of Polynesian, Malayan, and Melanesian—with sizeable recent dollops of German, American, and Japanese. The language is derived from the Austronesian family. Mostly Malay, it is of the same origin as Filipino and Chamorro, but while Palauans and Chamorros can sometimes understand one another, Palauans and Filipinos cannot.

Legend, of course, does explain Palau's origin. It tells of Uab, who, even as a young boy, wanted only to eat huge amounts of food and to sleep. He grew to be enormous, eating all the food his family could produce, then all the food his neighbors could produce. His house became too small for his body, and he had to move out, yet he still continued to eat until the whole community was facing starvation because of the need to feed Uab. The people decided to burn the giant and end their misery. They built a large fire around him, and though it raged, Uab remained upright. Finally, he began to topple over. As he hit the ground, he kicked out violently with his outsized foot; this succeeded in hurling Peleliu and Angaur apart. His legs were Koror, which has the most activity, and the great bulk of his body became Babeldaob: his penis became Aimeliik, which is why it has the most rain in Palau; his stomach formed Ngiwal, which is rich in food and where the islanders eat seven times a day; and Uab's head rested in Ngerchelong, which has the smartest and most talkative people in Palau.

Abandoned village sites on the Rock Islands have been carbondated to 1000 B.C. Terracing on Babeldaob, at its peak by around 1000, seems to have been abandoned by 1600—no one knows why. At the time of European contact, Palauan society was a thriving network of villages, most situated away from the coast, where the men hunted and fished while the women grew taro. Villages typically consisted of clans organized matrilineally. Councils of male chiefs from the ten ranking clans governed the village, and parallel councils of ten titled female elders held a significant advisory role, especially when it came to the control of land and money—the two most significant factors of Palauan society, holding central importance as the symbols of wealth and conceived to be the property of the clan. The ancient system of bead money was extremely intricate; *udoud,* as it is called today, was then (as it is now, augmented by U.S. currency) the essential accompaniment to all important events. The famous stone money of Yap, meanwhile, was quarried from the Rock Islands and transported to Yap by outriggers—part of a history of interchanges between Palauans and other early Pacific peoples that is but sketchily understood.

The men of Palau built and decorated the *bai,* men's house, and war canoes. Numerous other groupings of both males and females had social, defensive, and economic purposes. The war canoes were used when various regional alliances required fighting—or when they fell apart. In the bai on Babeldaob, the intricate artwork shows women "manning" war canoes.

In 1783, the East India Company's ship *Antelope,* Captain Henry Wilson in command, was wrecked on the Rock Islands. Spanish and Portuguese navigators had passed through in the past, but Wilson stayed to rebuild his boat and befriend the High Chief Ibedul of Koror. When Wilson returned to England, he brought Ibedul's son, Lebbu, with him. Lebbu died of smallpox in England, but the story of Wilson's experiences were told by George Keate in *An Account of the Pelew Islands,* a book that caused a brief sensation in Europe and helped open the islands to further European trade. Of course, firearms were among the items traded, inspiring internecine battles and increased hostilities toward the Europeans themselves. Diseases against which the islanders had few immunities were also imported— from 1783 to 1900, the population went from forty thousand to four thousand.

The British were dominant until 1885, when Pope Leo XIII acknowledged Spain's claim to the Carolines. In their short regnum— 1885-1899—the Spaniards concentrated on the introduction of Christianity and the alphabet. Palau was sold to the Germans in 1899 with the rest of the Carolines. The Germans coerced the natives to plant coconut and established a phosphate mining operation on Angaur, but they also instituted important sanitary and disease control measures, stopping the flood tide of depopulation.

Under Japan, Koror became the administrative center for all Japanese possessions in the South Pacific. Economic development was the goal, and to pursue and profit from it, the population became five times as Japanese as Palauan. For Japanese residents, roads were paved, electricity brought in, shops opened, and a streetcar started. In the 1930s, the Japanese began to fortify Palau; in 1938, it became a closed military area. One way or the other, it would remain such until 1962.

With hindsight, students of the Pacific war say that Peleliu should have been bypassed. Fearing that Japanese aircraft launched from there would endanger the invasion of the Philippines, U.S. commanders decided that Peleliu should be stormed. They believed it flat and easy to take; they were criminally unaware that a thickly forested limestone ridge was riddled with caves heavily fortified by the Japanese. Moreover, the new Japanese military policy, in the face of inevitable defeat, was one of attrition. Already neutralized by bombardment, the Japanese garrison on Peleliu was ordered to wage a costly and extended defense. They knew the Americans were coming because U.S. planes had showered leaflets onto the island, warning the civilian population to flee, which they did. The Japanese dug in and waited.

William Manchester has written of the Battle of Bloody Nose Ridge, the taking of Peleliu, that it was "a bad battle, fought at a bad place and a bad time, with an enemy garrison that could have been left to wither on the vine without altering the course of the Pacific war in any way" (*Goodbye, Darkness: A Memoir of the Pacific*, Little, Brown & Co., Boston, 1979). It is indeed likely that, had the island been bypassed, the only result would have been that the Japanese garrison there, like those on Koror and Babeldaob, would have been cut off, impotent, ready to surrender after the fall of Japan in 1945. Instead, after two and a half months of fighting, eleven thousand Japanese had been killed, two thousand Americans had died, and eight thousand more were wounded.

U.S. forces in fact did not enter Koror until the war was over. It had been devastated, and 526 Palauans had perished. Medical care, education, trade, and even the food supply were virtually destroyed. Antiforeign feeling ran deep and strong. Even in the 1980s, a canvass of Palauans' attitudes toward the compact with the U.S. showed that the main opposition came from older people. They had lived through the Japanese era, knew of the wartime plans, never carried out, to execute the entire population, had felt the brunt of being a target in a war of someone else's making. They feared becoming a target again.

Palau today combines a *very* democratic government with the traditional system of hereditary chiefs. The constitution stipulates that the chiefs shall be an advisory body only, but it doesn't always work out that way, and the tension between tradition and contemporary democracy is often intense. Indeed, for many reasons, Palau's politics have long been troubled. The first president of Palau, Haruo Remeliik, was assassinated in June 1985. Controversy has continued to surround the convictions of the three men quickly charged and tried for the crime. Charges and countercharges of corruption and extremism still shadow this event, which deeply scarred the new republic's beginning.

Palau is divided into 16 separate states, each with its own governor, lieutenant governor, and legislature. Some state governors are popularly elected, and a few are hereditary chiefs. There are also a president, vice president, cabinet of five ministries, a judiciary, and a bicameral national legislature. One long-time Micronesian observer has dubbed Palau "the most overgoverned place on earth." There is a joke about the man who walks into a bar in Koror and calls out "Hey, Governor"—half the people in the bar stand up.

## THE TRAVELER IN PALAU

Koror is the tourist hub of Palau—site of hotels, restaurants, a lively nightlife, commercial and government activity. Palauans will tell you that Koror is not really Palau, just as Americans often say that New York is not America. Both are wrong, although Koror is a far cry from New York.

Babeldaob is connected to Koror by the K-B Bridge, once billed as the longest single-span, box-girder, concrete-reinforced bridge in the world. No longer; another has since come along to claim that title, and yet another will soon undoubtedly destroy *that* claim. The southern part of Babeldaob, mostly coastal plain, is easily seen by road. The center of the island, however, is thick jungle, lined with waterways and fringed by mangrove swamp. To hike here, secure a guide. The north of Babeldaob, rich in archaeology and containing beautiful beaches, is best reached by boat or by plane to Melekeok on the internal airline, Aero Belau.

Aero Belau also runs a twice-daily, reasonably priced commuter service from Koror to Peleliu and Angaur; you can thus see both islands in one visit. Peleliu is also reachable by boat, and there are frequent tours. Kayangel, an idyllic spot, is reachable only by field-trip vessel. It has one village, no tourist facilities, untouched beaches, and a perfect lagoon. Arrangements can be made; if the not-very-lively tourist office in Koror cannot help you, try a travel agent, folks on the street, or just get there and ask for lodgings—no problem.

The sights of Palau are the sparse but interesting relics of its past—native, Japanese, and war related—and the very exciting art being created today. The major attraction here, however, is underwater. Palau is on every diver's list of the top five, most divers' list of the top three, and it is to a great many divers the finest dive site in the world. One diver said of it that "what is so fantastic is that you almost don't need to dive at all. Virtually everything is visible from the surface—you can look right down 75, 80, 100 feet. But *underwater*, your visibility is even greater—200 horizontal feet. Really."

There are 28 known and marked sites covering both coasts and numerous islands. Among the blue holes and drop-offs along the barrier reef, Ngemelis Drop-Off is consistently rated the world's best. Coral and shell collecting are prohibited, so the reefs and bottom do not have the picked-clean look. The variety of marine life in these waters is too staggering to enumerate, and there are ship and aircraft wrecks as well. Divers flock to Palau from all over the world, and even the Sunday snorkeler and glass-bottomed boat passenger will easily see why. Dive operators meet the plane; they will set up arrangements on the spot or give you a card at the very least. There is also a dive shop at the Palau Pacific Resort Hotel, the luxurious, Japanese-owned hostelry on Arakabesang.

# KOROR

As with the Northern Marianas, or any other destination in Micronesia, it is possible to make arrangements in Guam for at least your initial hotel in Palau. The traveler arrives at Airai Airport—actually on Babeldaob, 16 kilometers west of Koror. A hotel bus meets the flight, as do all those dive operators and numerous agents for numerous hostelries.

For travel around Koror and its "affiliated" islands—connected by causeway and so linked to Koror that you're hardly aware of passing from one island to the next—the traveler may rent a car, join a tour, or ride in taxis. The latter are not metered, and while fares are not controlled, you can usually strike a fair deal with a driver. For scheduled boat excursions, check with a travel agent or tour operator. To hitch an unscheduled boat ride to Babeldaob, or further afield to Peleliu or Kayangel, check at the various docks around town.

The best place to start a visit to Palau is at the Belau National Museum. Once a Japanese weather station, the building today houses exhibits of local artifacts and crafts, models of bai and dugout canoes, and war relics. Palau is a vital center of Pacific art, known particularly for its story boards. These developed in a most interesting fashion from the traditional bai. As the center of village life, each bai was decorated—its gables and interior beams adorned with paintings and carvings telling stories or displaying decorative motifs. (The traveler will see this on the only authentic extant bai in Palau, on Babeldaob.) During the German and Japanese occupations, however, bai building came to a virtual halt. Then, in the early 1930s, a Japanese folklorist named Hisataku Hijikata almost single-handedly revived the tradition of Palauan art while setting it on a fresh course.

The original painted story boards of the bai tell tales from legend and the local religion, *Modekngei*, still widely practiced in Palau. The story boards, which read in long, continuous panels—like comic books—were originally painted in earthy red, black, and yellow tones over a background of lime white. The style is flat, with no overlapping figures—just profiles or outlines. Hijikata, himself a painter, taught his Palauan students the form, but since they were no longer working on long beams and gables, their story boards of necessity showed only one or two events—symbols of the larger story. Eventually, carving outstripped painting as a medium. Today's artists mostly produce relief work, with much overlapping and detailed pattern. The wood grain is often enriched with brown shoe polish. Approximately thirty different stories are drawn from—the stone money being transported to Yap, the coming of the breadfruit tree—along with variants and reinterpretations. The carving can be extremely complex, and the shapes of the boards vary widely. The prison in Koror is a center for the carving of story boards.

Weaving is another Palauan art that is seeing a major revival. Palm is used for ordinary utilitarian baskets, while pandanus is woven into purses, hats, and mats for sale to consumers.

Replicas of traditional money made from red and black coral are also created for sale. The real money, on exhibit at the museum or on the people, is made of glass and ceramic beads, and often from the vertebra of the dugong. *Iek*, necklaces, are assembled from these pieces of money and worn by high-ranking women on special occasions. Single pieces are worn at other times. The crescent-shaped pieces are of the highest value. History, size, and perfection of quality determine the value of any single type of money.

One major Palauan art form not frozen in a museum is traditional dance, often performed at local fairs, events, celebrations. In the women's dance, the *ngloik*, the performers face one another in two lines. In rhythmic, unified movements, accompanied by chanting that is often antiphonal, the message of the legend or story is conveyed. The *ruk*, a men's dance, was often a victory dance or performed in celebration of the completion of a new bai.

East of town are numerous Japanese relics and, en route to the Palau Nikko Hotel, the remains of a huge Shinto shrine. From the hotel grounds, there are superb views of the Rock Islands of Iwayama Bay.

Further east is Malakal Island, Koror's industrial center. The park here, just opposite the Marine Culture building—a research facility, whose outdoor tanks may be visited—is called Ice Box Park. Jutting into the sea, it catches every breeze, although the name will seem excessive to the traveler from a northern clime. There is a tower atop Malakal that can be reached on foot; once a Japanese lighthouse, it offers splendid views of the harbor, embraced by the long green arms of these irregular islands—so much water, so little land.

Arakabesang Island rises to a height of 100 meters and seems to lord it over the harbor and Koror. Once a major Japanese base (the islanders were all evicted) it is the site of the Palau Pacific Resort Hotel.

# BABELDAOB

Babeldaob contains ten separate states, in case you wanted to dispute Palau's being "the most overgoverned place on earth." The road goes along the east through Airai and along the west through Aimeliik. Another piece of road goes across Ngarard State. Going along the east, through several pleasant villages, you come to the new bai. Continue on the road, passing numerous wrecks and memorials of war, to the site of the old bai, built in 1882. If you are traveling independently, you should proceed first to the headman's house at the top of the path—it's obvious, or ask—to say that you would like to pay admission and visit the bai.

It is quite a wonderful structure. With its steeply pitched roof and sharp triangular metopes thrusting forward at either end, it is reminiscent of the haus tamburans of Papua New Guinea. The building is on a platform, and the roof is matted from *tewel*, a mangrove plant. The place is painted all over. Cross beams, gradually narrower and shorter as they go up the ceiling, show scenes with sailing canoes and dugouts, fishing with baskets and spears, and fighting with shields and spears. Among the warriors depicted are women, sitting high in their war canoe brandishing their spears. It is very exuberant stuff, and artfully done.

In Aimeliik State, the traveler can see vestiges of the ancient terraces near Ngechemiangel Village; old bai platforms at Medorm Village; and some scenic waterfalls.

To visit the north of Babeldaob, hitch a ride from one of the several docks of Koror to one of the several docks along the west coast of Babeldaob. You can hitch from dock to dock or hike around the coast or across the island at the north end. Or, hop the air taxi to Melekeok and start up the east coast and around to the west to catch a boat back to Koror.

Starting a Melekeok, your first stop should be at the so-called Stone Faces. These are five stone monoliths, about one to three meters high. Odalmelech, the god of Ngermelech Village here, wanted to lay stonework over the village ground. Workers starting bringing in reef stones that night, but when dawn came, they had not finished. For the shame of being caught working in the morning sun, Odalmelech ordered his crew to carve their own faces on the monoliths and place them where they would always be in the eye of the rising sun.

Melekeok was once the seat of the high chief of Babeldaob, and ruins of an old village and bai platform can also be seen.

Good trails lead to Ngchesar Village, where there is a war canoe named *Bisebusech*, "lightning." *Bisebusech* was lashed together and painted in the traditional manner. When completed, it was housed in a traditional thatched canoe house, called a *diangel*, which now guards the dock entrance. Painted carvings of the sting ray and shearwater, the hook-billed bird that skims the ocean's surface, adorn the canoe; the sting ray and shearwater represent the gods of Ngchesar.

Along the coast of Ngchesar State, near the mouth of the Ngersuul River, is the site of some of the best pottery clay in Palau. You can ride the river to wander through tropical rain forests and to visit Shimizu, the nation's agricultural salad bowl.

Moving north, the traveler comes to Ngiwal State, with the long, sandy strand known as Honeymoon Beach. A trail arched by orange trees leads from beach to village. Ngiwal is the site of a famous storyboard story—easily recognized by the image of a breadfruit tree with a fish emerging from its broken limb. The story tells of the female demigod, Dirrachedebsungel. Having taught Palauans how to grow taro, she settled down on the island of Ngibtal off the Ngiwal Coast. The gods gave her a magical breadfruit tree with hollow trunk and broken limb. Each tide brought numerous fish up through the tree to Dirrachedebsungel's front yard. The other islanders grew jealous and cut the tree down. The next wave that came drowned them all— except Dirrachedebsungel, who gave birth to the four village-founding children, Melekeok, Koror, Ngeremlengui, and Aimeliik. Divers have found a sunken village off the coast here.

Ngarard State gives the traveler access to docks on either coast, with a road connecting them. The east coast here has stupendous beaches.

Ngerchelong, at the very top of Babeldaob, contains Badrulchau, one of the most impressive archaeological sites in Palau. On about five acres of prehistoric terraces, between the villages of Ollei and Mengellang, are 37 monoliths in two rows. Radiocarbon tests have dated these to the period 90–1665, and some say they were built by Portuguese craftsmen. Legend has it that the gods constructed the columns as a support for a bai, never finished, to hold thousands of people. Off the coast at the village of Ngerbau is a piece of stone said to be another piece of the unfinished bai.

Coming around to the west of Babeldaob, in Ngardmau State, are Palau's largest waterfall and its highest peak—217 meters. There are numerous old stone platforms and bai foundations in the vicinity.

Ngeremlengui State also contains prehistoric terraces and the remains of numerous old villages.

Hilly Ngatpang State is the site of the country's forestry station and cattle project. Also here is the Ibobang School of the Pacific, founded in 1974 as a joint project of the Janss Foundation of California and practitioners of the local Modekngei faith to foster Palauan culture and traditional ways.

# KAYANGEL

From the northern tip of Babeldaob, it is only some 32 kilometers to Kayangel. The traveler who seeks a respite from snorkeling or doing nothing at all should read the stories carved on the beams of Kayangel's bai.

# PELELIU

A platform island just within the southern tip of the barrier reef,

Peleliu is primarily visited for its war story—the beaches where the Americans landed and the deep natural caves and crevices of Umerbrogol Mountain, where the Japanese constructed a labyrinth of defenses. There are also outstanding beaches here and an inland cave with saltwater swimming.

The traveler will see war relics everywhere—it is a punishable offense to remove any—and both Japanese and American memorials at Bloody Nose Ridge, scene of the battle.

The inhabitants of Peleliu live in three villages all at the northern edge of the island, which is less than 100 kilometers long in any case, and you may be able to lodge with them; there are no hotels or restaurants.

# ANGAUR

War buffs come here as well, but Angaur, outside the barrier reef, is best known now for its seasonal blowholes (on the north coast), for its monkeys, and for the remains of the phosphate mining industry started here by the Germans. A pleasant road circles the island, and you can "do" the whole island in a day.

## Language

| | |
|---|---|
| Alii (a-LEE) | Hello/look out! |
| Ke ua ngerang? (ka-wannga-RAHNG) | How are you? |
| Sulang (soo-LAHNG) | Thanks |
| O'oi (OH-OY)/Choi | Yes |
| Ng diak (in-dee-AHK) | No |

## Palau Address

Palau Tourist Commission
P.O. Box 256
Koror
Republic of Palau 96940

# CHAPTER 19

# THE FEDERATED STATES OF MICRONESIA: YAP, TRUK, PONAPE

*Name:* Federated States of Micronesia
*Political status:* Independent, in free association with the U.S.
*Island groups:* Four states of Yap, Truk, Ponape (Pohnpei),
    Kosrae (Kusaie)
*Gateway islands:* Yap Proper, Moen, Ponape, Kosrae
*Capital:* Kolonia, Ponape
*Population:* 90,000
*Land area:* 723 square kilometers
*Language:* English, Carolinian
*Currency:* U.S. dollar ($US)

The three states the Pacific traveler will visit in the Federated States of Micronesia are effectively three different island nations. In Yap, the traveler visits one of the Pacific's most evident traditional societies. To be in Truk is to be in on a transient moment of Pacific geology, an atoll in the making, while the resting wrecks in Truk lagoon hold, for the diver, a frozen moment of Pacific history. Ponape is one of the world's wettest places—and one of the most beautiful.

## GEOGRAPHY, TOPOGRAPHY, CLIMATE

The four Federated States of Micronesia comprise the largest and most populous nation of the former Trust Territory of the Pacific Islands. These are the islands of the Caroline Archipelago, along with Palau—indeed, the westernmost islets of the Yap Group are politically part of the Republic of Palau. The FSM contains 607 islands, of which some 65 are inhabited. The islands range from about 137 to 162 degrees east longitude and between about 5 and 10 degrees north latitude; closer to the equator are the Ponapean atolls of Kapingamarangi and Nukuoro, Polynesian fringe outliers. The distance from Yap in the west to Kosrae in the east is more than 2500 kilometers, yet the total landmass of the FSM is just a smidgin above 700 square kilometers.

Almost every type of Pacific topography is here: the high volcanic islands of Ponape and Kosrae; the sedimentary rock of Yap;

an atoll-to-be in Truk; elevated atolls like Fais, part of Yap State; and a thousand flat atolls, coral islands, and reefs.

Rainfall is heavy, heaviest from April through December, and increasingly heavy as you move east. Ponape is one of the wettest places in the Pacific, often called "the garden spot of Micronesia" for the extreme lushness of its vegetation.

# THE NATURAL ENVIRONMENT

Vegetation and animal life follow topography and climate. On the low islands are coconut palms, breadfruit, casuarina, pandanus, creeping vines, sedges, and strand growth. The coastal flats of the high islands grow mangrove plants, nipa palm, and other salt-resistant vegetation. Inland, the high islands yield coconut on the flats, rain forest or grassland on the lower slopes, scrub forest and fern on the upper slopes.

Fruit- and insect-eating bats are prevalent on both high and low islands, and there are the usual introduced animals—dogs, pigs, rats, horses, cattle, water buffalo, goats, cats, deer.

There are relatively few land birds but abundant marine birds and shorebirds. Almost every form of fish and marine life capable of living in these waters does so in abundance.

# HISTORY

From the time of contact with Europeans, the histories of the four states of the FSM are pretty much shared (corresponding also to the history of the Marshall Islands). There were the usual chance visits by the 16th-century Portuguese and Spanish navigators, but it was the 19th-century traders, whalers, and missionaries who put these islands on the world map. Toward the end of the century, Spain and Germany vied with each other for influence, until Pope Leo XIII decided the issue, giving sovereignty of the Carolines to Spain but allowing Germany to trade, fish, and establish settlements in the archipelago. Spain sold the Carolines to Germany, along with the Marianas, in 1899.

German rule didn't last long. Japan seized the islands at the start of World War I and efficiently integrated them into the growing Japanese empire. The Carolines were important bases for Nippon's World War II thrust into Southeast Asia and the South Pacific. They were mandated to the U.S. after the war as a strategic trust.

Almost all of the population today is Micronesian—Carolinian, to be more exact—speaking eight distinct Carolinian languages and a number of dialects. Fewer than a thousand Polynesians live on

Ponape's outliers, and several hundred more have established themselves in Ponape's capital, Kolonia. Except for the Roman Catholic Yapese, the Carolinians are predominantly Protestant; in Kosrae, Congregational missionary influences created a virtual theocracy in the mid-1800s. Today, the airline that flies to Kosrae is called Pacific Missionary Aviation. On Yap, there is a Baha'i Center. The Mormons have recently begun making inroads in the FSM, particularly in Yap and Truk.

The FSM is a constitutional democracy with three branches of government—executive, legislative, and judicial. The constitution has a bill of rights and provisions for traditional rights. It organizes the FSM on the principle of federalism and state governments, ensuring the primacy of the national government over the four component states.

## THE TRAVELER IN THE FSM

Only the gateway islands of each of the four states have tourist facilities—hotels, restaurants, organized excursions. The traveler who makes arrangements to spend time on one or more of the FSM outliers thereby has a wonderful opportunity to see Micronesian life as it has been traditionally—more or less—lived.

Yap in particular remains a corner of traditional Micronesia and affords the visitor a pretty thorough immersion into that environment, even without going to the outliers.

Truk is known above all for its lagoon, which is a scuba diving shrine. Divers come from all over the world to explore the staggering number of wrecks here—the very heavy shipping losses suffered by the Japanese in Operation Hailstone of February 1944.

Ponape is a lush island that offers the visitor one of the most extraordinary archaeological sites in the Pacific, if not the world—Nan Madol.

Kosrae, particularly difficult to get to because of the paucity of seats available to travelers—especially to those who have not booked well in advance—will not be covered in this itinerary.

## YAP

What a pleasure it is, after the sterilized inefficiency of Guam's airport, to land at the down-home shed that is Yap Airport, six kilometers southwest of Colonia, the capital (not to be confused with Kolonia, capital of Ponape *and* of the FSM). A crowd is there to meet the plane, which disgorges islanders, officials, Seabees who work at the nearby installation, the omnipresent Japanese businessmen, aid workers, and the occasional traveler. Among the meeters are many men in *thus*, the traditional loincloths. You can spot the outislanders because their thus are one-piece cloths of a single color, any they choose. The men of Yap Proper, as it is called, wear multilayered, multicolored thus of red, blue, and white, often adorned with strands of dried hibiscus. The women, a number of whom may be topless, wear lavalavas of woven banana fiber or hibiscus or cloth in a lined pattern. Almost everyone is either chewing betel or preparing it for chewing: wrap a fresh green nut in a mint leaf, sprinkle with lime powder, pop in the mouth, chew, and every now and

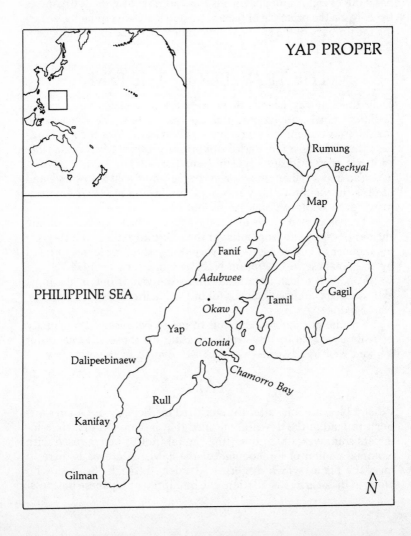

again, spit. The broad smiles are outlined in the telltale red of betel chewing, which produces a high. Yapese say this is what they miss most when they go off-island.

Yap State comprises Yap Proper, itself a compact group of four major islands, and 134 outlying islands and atoll islets. Rumung, Map, Gagil-Tomil, and Yap Island are the four islands of Yap Proper; Rumung is reached by boat, while the others are connected by causeways. Yap is formed of exposed metamorphic basement rocks, part of a 1400-kilometer submarine ridge along the Yap Minitrench. These four islands were once one, and it is only recently (geologically speaking) that subsidence has separated them. The limestone reef around the island shelters a lagoon that is really many enclosed and isolated remnant lagoons—left over from a once-extensive lagoon system and now filled by sedimentation and reef building.

Of the outliers, Ulithi, with 49 islets, claims the fourth largest lagoon in the world. It's easy to understand why it became a staging area for the Allied invasion of the Philippines during World War II. Fais and Satawal are raised atolls, without lagoons. Eauripik has a closed lagoon. The highest point in Yap State is on Yap Island in Yap Proper: Mount Matade at 167 meters.

# HISTORY

Archaeology confirms that Yap has long had links with Palau, evident even today, when both island nations share an air route. Even earlier links with the Marianas can be shown; carbon-dated remains from 1500 B.C. in both island groups show definite similarities.

The Yapese name for the island is Waqab, pronounced something like "ew-op." It means paddle. The story is that when an exploring ship arrived here, the Yapese went out to greet it in their canoes, raising their paddles out of the water as they pulled up. The ship's captain asked the name of the island, and the Yapese thought he was asking the word for paddle, so they answered *waqab*.

The Portuguese Diego DeRocha is credited as the first European to land here, "discovering" Ulithi in 1526. Of the Spanish influence, apart from Roman Catholicism, the only significant remains are pieces of a wall and foundation, on top of which the present cluster of government offices in Colonia is located.

One of the more colorful characters of the colonial period was the Irish-American David O'Keefe. Shipwrecked here in 1871, O'Keefe stayed on and developed a lucrative trade, bringing in the highly valued stone money from Palau in exchange for copra and sea slugs. On a small island in the middle of Tamil Harbor, called Tarang or O'Keefe's, he built his residence and headquarters, a few remains of which still exist. He came to be called His Majesty O'Keefe, and to a generation of moviegoers, he looked exactly like Burt Lancaster.

During Japanese rule, but well before Pearl Harbor, the U.S. and Japan were at odds over the radio communications station left by the Germans. The U.S. had used the station as a backup for its Guam-Manila-Shanghai line; the line allowed communications to China and the Philippines through Guam. In fact, the first telegraph message to go around the world passed through the station. Before the U.S. would recognize Japan's claim to Micronesia under the 1922 League of Nations mandate, they insisted on access to Yap and the station. In 1941, of course, that ended quickly. Yap had been heavily fortified by the Japanese, and although it was never invaded by the Allies, American bombardment was heavy. Numerous Japanese planes caught on the ground during the bombing remain today— ruined aircraft on a ruined airfield.

# THE TRAVELER IN YAP

The main attraction of Yap is the opportunity it affords the traveler to explore traditional island culture. Ancient Yap culture was a rigidly caste-bound hierarchy (of nine distinct castes), linked through a complex kinship system and organized around villages and village districts. Significant vestiges of all of these remain, although contemporary politics, with its insistence on civil rights, has taken the master-serf relationship out of the caste system.

The importance of land cannot be overstated. Every parcel of land in a Yapese village has a name and rank. The land of the highest-ranking man is the chief, not the man himself; land is thus power. Inheritance of land, status, and valuables is patrilineal. Land ownership also defines caste, and all villages are inhabited by members of the same caste. Clan attachment, however, is matrilineal; the clan is not a landholding group but a regulator of marriages and mutual aid.

## Villages

The villages of Yap today are unique for their paved-stone footpaths and above all for the *rai*, the famous stone money of Yap. The rai are large, doughnutlike disks of crystalline calcite or aragonite. Their value consists in the difficulties encountered—and the loss of life suffered—in quarrying these stones (in Palau) and transporting them home. There may have been 13,000 rai in Yap at one time; today, there are less than half that number, many having been destroyed during the Japanese occupation. Rai are found only in Yap, in villages and in village-owned stone-money "banks," and in a number of museums and private collections in some 12 foreign countries.

But here is where they come from, and it is here that they are still valued as objects of prestige, heredity, and tradition.

The traveler may also see *pebai*, village meeting houses, *faluw*, men's houses, and *dapal* or *ipul*, houses where women must remain during menstruation—when sexual activity and association with the day-to-day tasks of cooking and gardening are taboo. There are also boys' houses, *fang*, where youths today store their fishing gear. These

*Pebai*, a village meeting house, Yap, Federated States of Micronesia. *Photo by Susanna Margolis.*

structures all wear the traditional look—on platforms, made of wood and thatch, with steep roofs that thrust forward at either end. In front of the pebai or faluw is the *malal*, the dancing area, where Yap's most highly developed art form may occasionally be seen by the traveler. What you are unlikely to see is the *mitmit*, a form of ceremonial exchange between villages or between people within a village, the most traditional of Yap festivals.

For the traveler, the important thing to remember about exploring Yap's villages is to *ask permission*. Before walking past a village, even if it's obviously on a public road, before using a beach, before approaching a faluw or pebai, ask the nearest person; if he's not the official permission giver, ask who is. Women should *not* wear shorts, bathing suits, or short skirts—the Yapese are offended by the sight of thigh. Don't point at people; don't step over an outstretched leg; don't just shoot pictures. Yapese carry a piece of green vegetation in one hand when walking through a village; it shows peaceful intentions.

## Seeing Yap

Yap has two hotels, both in Colonia, on opposite sides of Chamorro Bay, both utilitarian and friendly, both with restaurants, one with a bar. The personnel at both can help you with any arrangements; indeed, perhaps the best way to get oriented is to take a tour with a driver-guide.

Colonia itself—Donguch in Yapese—is centered around the government offices, which actually sit on a small island connected by causeway. There are several stores, including the Women's Association Handicraft Shop—excellent for lavalavas, hair ornaments, combs, *yar* currency (mother-of-pearl shell tied with sennit), spoons, belts, necklaces, and carvings, and the Family Chain Store and Yap Cooperative Association—excellent for everything else. The open-air market is called the Bambu Market. There are several snack bars and restaurants and O'Keefe's Oasis, the local watering hole. A small tourism office sits just opposite the state legislature building, and there is a small but interesting museum. The post office and Bank of Hawaii branch just about complete downtown Colonia.

North of Colonia, you will see stone-money banks—and stone money lining the roads—and a number of faluw. You travel upland over red-clay terrain, past the former Coast Guard station called Loran, and then downhill through more tropical terrain into the 19 hamlets that constitute Gagil, one of the loveliest of traditional settlements. Further on, over rough and rutted road, you are in Map, overlooking the exquisite northeast coast. Azure water, curling reef, white sand beach—the best in Yap Proper, whose jagged coastline is mostly mangrove and rock. At Bechyal near the northern tip of

Map is what is being called a cultural center—several traditional buildings, a few of them reconstructed. To get to Rumung, you'll need government permission; the main sight there is the largest extant rai, nearly four meters in diameter.

To the northwest of Colonia at Okaw is a superb pebai, and there is another at Adubwee, right on the water, up an impressive stone path. A U-shaped ridge strides across the island near here, and a kind of cross-island road follows it. This offers great views to the west—it's a favorite sunset-watching spot—and, on the eastern loop of the ridge, great views down to the harbor of Colonia and the east coast.

South of Colonia, the traveler sees the remnants of the German communications station just behind the Seabee camp, and the ruined Japanese airport with its skeletons of planes and guns. Where the road's paving ends, dirt track continues, and this southern part of Yap makes for a lovely walk—ask *permission*. At the village of Ngof, head west and then loopingly south. Stay on the road—don't go off onto side roads to hamlets unless asked to. Here is the lovely traditional village of Gilman, with numerous remains of stone money, stone platforms, and pebai and faluw that are often a mix of materials with tin roof, some concrete, and some thatch. Here you walk or drive through a beautiful rain forest of unbelievably outsized taro, coconut palms, nipa palms, and, closer to shore, dark mangrove inhabited by brightly colored crabs. You can walk or drive to the southern tip of the island this way and return via the old Japanese airstrip.

## The Outliers

The traveler must ask the permission of the government to visit outliers; government officials may also be able to help with arrangements. Check with tourism. Pacific Missionary Aviation flies to Ulithi twice a week; most people stop here, but with the right prearrangements, you may be able to get over to Mogmog, the chiefly island. A field-service trip also goes to Ulithi and usually one other island fairly regularly. The longer field-service trip will take you to some of the most remote islands on earth—Woleai, where isolated Japanese starved to death; Satawal, still the center of navigational and canoe-building skill; the lively atoll of Fais. But schedules of course bend with the wind and every other possible eventuality, so you need plenty of time and an easygoing nature.

## Diving

There is good diving off Yap's east coast, and there is an on-again, off-again dive shop in Colonia. Your best bet is to be well equipped when you arrive—everything but air tanks. Ask at the tourism office or at your hotel about arranging trips.

## Hiking

Any of the roads of Yap make good walking, and most of the tracks make excellent walking—if the traveler remembers the rules of conduct. Here are a few marked hiking trails:

• From Colonia, follow road and track to the summit of Mount Matade, about three-quarters of a mile uphill.
• In the northeast, follow the track opposite Fanif (Rumu) School going westward.
• At the northern tip of Yap Island, walk in from the road to Ruun'uw Village at Fitbileeyamol Hill.

In addition, almost all of the northern and central hills, to which tracks lead, offer fine views.


## Yap's Tourism Plan

"We want controlled tourism," a Yapese tourism official told a visitor; "we don't want to turn into Guam and Saipan."

The people at Yap's Office of Tourism and Commerce value their island traditions not only for their own sake, but also because they understand that the preservation of those traditions is the nation's primary attraction for the traveler. They seem determined not to turn Yap into yet another playground of sun, sand, and surf with drinks served poolside. Rather, they plan a noninstitutionalized tourism, out in the villages, involving the villagers, stressing outdoor activities; a controlled tourism that will be spread slowly and carefully to the out-islands.

Yap has already said no to the kind of tourism that pervades much—perhaps too much—of the rest of the Pacific. When Nanyo Boeki Kaisha (NBK), the Japanese multinational, sought to develop a major tourist complex in Map—air-conditioned blockhouses and a swimming area dredged from the inner reef—the chiefs of Yap drafted a protest petition. Here is the preamble to that petition:

> Whereas we love our lands and the ways in which we live together there in peace, and yet live humbly and still cherish them above all other ways, and are not discontent to be the children of our fathers, it has become apparent to us that we have been persuaded to subscribe to processes that will quickly extinguish all that we hold dear. . . .

And here is the petition's conclusion:

Micronesians cannot defend themselves against the great powers who now seek to make the islands of Micronesia something else and something less. It is the powers themselves who must learn what the unique island beauty means to the eye and ear, and to the conscience.

# TRUK

NOTE: Cholera has been an issue in Truk in the past; check with your airline about prevention and clearance.

TRUK LAGOON

Almost everyone getting off the plane here carries a net bag with regulator, buoyancy control device, mask, and fins. Truk Lagoon, with more than seventy findable, divable wrecks, is a scuba diver's dream, a magnet for underwater explorers from all over the world. The lagoon's area is 2129 square kilometers, encircled by a reef that is some 200 kilometers around and as much as 64 kilometers in diameter. Several passages through the reef allow entry by large ships, which find excellent anchorage in the lagoon itself. The Japanese Combined Fleet was here, its staff headquartered on the island of Dublon, in 1944. Most of the warships had left when the U.S. unleashed Operation Hailstone in February, but the ships and planes sunk here at that time today form the largest man-made reef in the world.

The landmass of the state of Truk comes to 127 square kilometers—15 island groups containing some 300 individual islands. Only about 40 islands are regularly inhabited, but many others are used by nearby islanders as farmland. The island group of Truk Proper, which accounts for more than 75 percent of the total landmass, consists of 11 high, volcanic islands set in the midst of the azure lagoon and enclosed by a necklace of 87 tiny low coral islets. The outlying island groups are the Halls, north of Truk Proper; the Westerns, to the west; and to the southeast, the Upper and Lower Mortlocks—all low, palm-and-sand atolls.

Truk Proper and the Halls and Mortlocks show the greatest similarities of culture and language; communications along this north-to-south route has long been facilitated by northeasterly tradewinds. The Western Islands, however, have had infrequent interaction with the other islands and remain remote in feeling as well as distance; one of the Westerns, Puluwat, is particularly renowned for canoe building.

In general, Trukese society continues to look to matrilineal descent groups as collective economic and land-holding units. On the outliers in particular, the senior male of the lineage that first settled the particular island exercises significant authority in local decision making.

Truk has one of the world's highest suicide rates for young men aged 15 to 24. Altogether too common an occurrence among young Micronesians, suicide is seen by some as the ultimate explosion of temper in a culture that spoils its young people but demands from them a heavy burden of guilt if they "shame" their families. Add to this the pressures of rapid and confusing social change, and the response, too often, is this desperately conclusive act.

# HISTORY

Truk shares with the other Federated States of Micronesia the progression of Spanish, German, and Japanese influence. Before World War II, it was Japan's major naval base in the region, the so-called Gibraltar of the Pacific. By 1942, the center of naval operations had shifted to Rabaul, but the Truk installation was still substantial. The Japanese had built two airstrips on Moen, the gateway island, and one each on Eten and Param in the lagoon. Dublon, one of the four "big" islands in the lagoon (the others are Moen, Fefan, and Uman), housed a large Japanese population and had as well piers, hospital, railway, seaplane base, schools, Shinto shrines, houses, government buildings. The capital area, between the present Municipal Building and Catholic mission on Dublon, was called Tokyo.

In early February 1944, an American reconnaissance plane was spotted over the lagoon, and the Japanese command shrewdly ordered all warships present to remove to Palau. A week later, throughout February 16 and 17, U.S. Task Force 50, a carrier-based air fleet, carried out its three-goal mission, a rearguard action designed to protect the Allied convoy heading for the Marianas and Guam: to destroy Japanese air opposition and establish air supremacy over the atoll; to render the Japanese airfields unusable; to destroy Japanese shipping. Only the latter goal was not completely met; with the major warships gone, most of the ships sunk here, amounting to 210,000 total tonnage, were merchantmen converted to war use. More than 60 vessels were sunk, however, and from 250 to 275 Japanese planes were destroyed or damaged. The U.S. lost 29 planes.

U.S. forces then proceeded to Saipan, bypassing Truk and the 45,000 Japanese virtually marooned here. The Japanese, along with numerous Trukese, suffered from the serious food shortage for the rest of the war, and many died of starvation.

# THE TRAVELER IN TRUK

It is difficult for the traveler to find much charm on Moen, the gateway island. Still, some 12,000 Trukese inhabit the island, and many of the nearly 19,000 who inhabit the lagoon islands come here to work (another 7000 inhabit the outliers, for a total state population of some 38,000). A ride around the island takes very little time; in essence, you're circling a basalt central hump, although the south of the island is vegetated plain. At Mwan, you pass the tomb of Chief Petrus, still the most respected man in Truk. In the opposite direction, at the end of the paved road, you come to Xavier High School, once a Japanese communications center. From just behind the school, a path leads quickly and steeply upward to the old Japanese lighthouse and a splendid view of the barrier reef and Northeast Pass.

Nearer the harbor and the funky "downtown," the houses are

cheek by jowl, and the villages are strung together. This produces a kind of urban street life, enhanced by the bright colors the Trukese wear and the slapdash, slumlike appearance of the houses that mix tin, concrete, thatch, and bright paint, the separate pieces of each house going in separate directions. Over-the-water outhouses, the *benjos* of Truk, happily are disappearing, but much squalor remains, and a cholera outbreak in the early 1980s still gives many travelers pause. Be cautious about tap water and raw fish, and keep clean. In this regard, all of the (very few) hotels of Moen are perfectly fine places to stay.

Moen also offers numerous places to eat—Japanese, Chinese, Korean, and basic hamburger—in addition to the hotel dining rooms. The island is officially "dry," but since all imported beverages meant for the out-islands are off-loaded at Moen, the occasional case of beer or liquor does make its way ashore. If you're at the dock when a boat pulls in, you can buy it directly; otherwise, ask someone of a less than official nature where you might find a six-pack.

Moen is the traveler's resource center, from laundromat to post office to shopping. The Truk Trading Center is the major emporium— T-shirts and a light smattering of the usual Pacific trade-store books (romances, trash, and Michener). Here and at the Small Industries Center, look for crafts, especially the famous love sticks of Truk. At one time, every man of Truk designed and carved his own love stick. Often as much as four meters long, these could easily be thrust through the thatched wall of a hut to reach the desired woman. The man would turn the stick, entangling it in the woman's hair till she woke. By the feel of the stick, she would know who the man was. If she wanted him, she would pull the stick inside the hut; if she wanted to go outside to join him, she would shake the stick; if she thrust the stick back out, the message was equally clear. Love sticks are not easily forced through corrugated tin or concrete walls, so they have gone out of fashion, except as objects for travelers to buy. In addition, *tapuanu*, the only masks made in Micronesia, are still fashioned in the Mortlocks where they once were worn at dances or ornamented the gables of men's houses or intimidated enemies while hiding a warrior's true identity. In this respect, the mask was closely tied to the Trukese reverence for magical or supernatural powers; even today, it is said, Trukese hide their inner feelings because knowledge of such feelings by others makes the person vulnerable to magical powers. Masks were originally made from the wood of the breadfruit tree so that they could protect the fruit during storms; today, they are made of hibiscus. War clubs, baskets, trays, lavalavas, hangings, and stools are other handicrafts made by the out-islanders for sale in Moen.

Moen is also the jumping-off place for exploring the lagoon, either on the surface or underwater. For boat trips to islands in the lagoon, ask. Ask at the Office of Tourism and Commerce; ask at your hotel; ask at the waterfront; ask around. To travel like a commuter, go down to the harbor opposite the post office, or to the landing across from Truk Trading Company. Village boats, *yamas*, bring workers over to Moen in the morning and then hang around to take them home in the afternoon; this means the traveler will likely have to spend the night on the island, and arrangements should be made. There are also larger boats making day trips on some business or other, and there are often private outboards heading back and forth between Moen and the nearby islands. If you do hitch a ride, offer to split the cost of fuel. If you do ask for accommodation in a private home, you should offer payment there as well. Check with the tourism office as to an appropriate amount.

## Islands of the Lagoon

Truk proper is the largest island group in the Carolines. Forty-one of Truk's islands and numerous islets make up the encircling barrier reef, through which five major passes allow access and egress. The passes are North Pass at 12 o'clock, Northeast Pass at 2 o'clock, Uligar at 5 o'clock, Otta at 6 o'clock, and Piaanu at 8 o'clock. The volcanic islands are lushly beautiful and offer spectacular views; a few beaches punctuate the mangrove fringes of these islands: Dublon, Fefan, Uman, Tol, Param, others. The ring of encircling islands offers white sand and thick palm.

Dublon, only 12 kilometers away, has the most to see—at least, in terms of the Japanese installation. Find a guide—again by asking—or walk around on your own to see the remains. Most are not far from the wharf. Two Japanese guns are up a track off the road at Enin. Eten, visible from here, was turned into a stationary aircraft carrier by the Japanese; two hundred planes were based at the airstrip before it was destroyed in Hailstone. The hospital is on the other peninsular arm at Sapou. Another gun sits in a cave up a track from Nukuno. Perhaps the most impressive site is right off the road at Roro—a network of tunnels still used as a storm shelter; bring a flashlight.

Fefan Island is a center for cultivation and for handicrafts. At the top and along the sides of the mountains that are Fefan's center are numerous caves with numerous Japanese guns. An around-the-island walk takes perhaps four hours.

Also near Moen are Tsis and Romanum, small humpbacked islands with excellent beaches and a good sense of Trukese island life. Osakura, *on* the barrier reef, also has an excellent beach—it is uninhabited.

The Faichuk Islands are the tallest of the inner lagoon. The 40-kilometer-or-so boat ride takes about an hour from Moen, depending on which island you're aiming for. Udot, lush and picturesque, is inhabited only to the south; the rocks of the north are seen to be the abode of supernatural powers, and no humans live there. The Tol complex consists of three islands—Tol, Polle, and Patta—gently isolated from one another by narrow channels and mangrove-swamp fringe. Boats go pretty regularly from Moen to Fason, the administrative center, on Tol. (There are daily boats to Polle as well.) Here are giant Japanese cannons still guarding Piaanu Pass, mangrove swamps and channels, villages rarely visited by outsiders, and a challenging peak, Mount Winipot (443 meters). A guide is certainly recommended for exploring the islands of Tol, especially if you are a solo woman traveler.

There was once a chief magistrate of Tol (also its leading shopkeeper) who pitched professionally in the Japanese leagues. It is said that he hurled against both DiMaggio and Mantle in exhibition games.

## Diving Truk Lagoon

Scuba experts say the best months for diving here are September, October, February, and March; this doesn't stop people from coming during the other eight months of the year. June through September offers the calmest lagoon waters, and visibility improves after that.

There are numerous scuba operators on Moen; if you somehow manage to miss them, ask at your hotel or tourism. You can go out for a dive, come back for lunch, and head out again, or you can go out and stay out—doing two or three dives a day. Even in several weeks, you won't come to the end of sites here. The dive operators of Truk vie with one another to find the wrecks not yet located; as of this writing, there were eight still awaiting discovery *within* the lagoon, a goodly number more without.

This is the greatest assortment of Japanese war wreckage in the Pacific, and it is almost all easily accessible—most wrecks are off Dublon and Fefan just a short ride from Moen. (The diver may also want to explore aircraft wrecks, concentrated off Eten.) The wrecks lie as they sank, upright or on their sides, with guns poking up and artifacts still lurking within—the whole now overgrown with marine life. When the first scuba pioneers started taking off with souvenirs, the Truk government declared the lagoon and all its ships a state monument; that means, happily, that the "pickings," which may not be picked, are lush.

A number of the wrecks are at snorkel depth—the important

*Shinokoku Maru,* the *Dai Na Hino Maru,* and the listing patrol boat, *Susuku Maru,* among others. The *San Francisco Maru,* at 75 meters, requires one of the deepest dives. The *Amagisan Maru,* lying 45 degrees to port on an incline, offers superb photography opportunities. The *Fujikawa Maru* is said to be one of the most beautiful wrecks, covered by marine growth, with a cargo that includes several aircraft and various other instruments of war, and with artifacts scattered throughout. Such "artifacts"—someone's tin cup, a water tank marked "Kobe, 1938"—are sudden, poignant reminders that the lagoon, now swarming with marine life, was also the grave of thousands of people, not so very long ago.

# PONAPE

Although not nearly as famous as Bora Bora, Ponape vies with it for the title of world's most beautiful island. Ponape partisans contend that, despite the lack of beaches, the island's exceptional lushness and dramatic terrain meet anyone's standards of paradise. Sokehs Rock, a soaring promontory on Sokehs Island near the capital, is often called the Diamond Head of Ponape. The sun sets into the lagoon beside the promontory, spreading its red-gold over the water, washing the horizon with progressively more burnished hues. From a distance, Ponape's looming central spire, clothed in mossy green, seems suspended from the clouds that perpetually surround it—Bali Ha'i perhaps, calling from the rim of the sea.

Ponape State consists of Ponape Island, at 334 square kilometers one of the largest in Micronesia and the second largest in the Carolines (after Palau's Babeldaob), plus eight outlying atolls and Minto Reef. Six of the outlying atolls are permanently inhabited: Mokil, Pingelap, Ngatik, Oroluk, and the Polynesian outliers of Nukuoro and Kapingamarangi. The combined land area of these atolls is just a tad over five square kilometers—not nearly enough to support their population, more of whom live on Ponape proper rather than on their native out-islands.

Ponape Island is the slightly submerged remnant of a chevron-shaped volcano, encircled by a barrier reef of more than 25 islets, some of them volcanic. Its towering interior, rock thickly carpeted with rain forest, rises to 772 meters and is riven by more than 40 streams and rivers that have carved wide valleys down from the ridge; they sometimes hurtle down in waterfalls, ending in freshwater pools excellent for swimming. Everything grows in profusion, nurtured by rainfall averaging 5000 millimeters in the plain and twice that in the interior. The traveler can expect *some* rain at *some* point. When it ends, the sun returns to shine on foliage weighted down to eye level by the moisture; banana leaves and coconut fronds and hibiscus and every bit of green and colored lushness shine brilliantly, the extravagant colors of the tropical flowers glinting like faceted jewels against the limpid turquoise sea in the distance and the dark green hills above.

The state is the most populated in the FSM—some 24,000 inhabitants, 22,000 of whom live on Ponape proper, 5000 of them in the capital, Kolonia, which is also the capital of the FSM. Sokehs Island, connected to the mainland by causeway, is also heavily

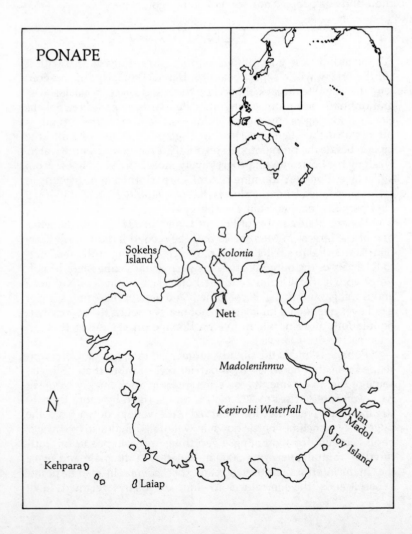

populated, as is Madolenihmw (Mad-o-len-*ee*-um), on the south-eastern side of the island. Ponape Island was the Spanish and German capital of Micronesia before coming under Japanese and then American domination. It retains ruins from every period of its history; among them is the most intriguing archaeological site in the Pacific—Nan Madol, which no traveler should miss.

# HISTORY

Throughout its history, Ponape has been closely linked with Kosrae to the southeast. Legend has it that a group of people "from the east" sailed west and found a small piece of land jutting from the sea, only enough land to fit between canoe and outrigger. They added mountains and valleys to it, planted mangroves to break the waves, and circled the whole with a reef to keep the sea at bay. They also built a stone altar *(pehi), on* which *(pohn)* they could worship their gods—hence the name Pohnpehi, or Pohnpei.

A dynasty of chieftains, the Saudeleurs, eventually took control, dividing the island into three kingdoms. A uniform culture developed, and a common language evolved. The construction of Nan Madol was probably begun in the 13th century. The Saudeleurs were overthrown by the legendary warrior Isokelekel, and his band of 333, also from Kosrae. Isokelekel established himself at Madolenihmw and founded the Nahnmwarki dynasty, still the traditional chiefly rank, in about 1628.

The first European sighting was by Quirós sailing under the Spanish flag in 1595; although he did not land, the island he charted, called Quirosa for some time, was almost certainly Ponape. Over the next two centuries no contact was recorded, although there were undoubtedly intermittent and transient contacts between the islanders and passing ships.

Ponape saw some of the more colorful Pacific characters during the 19th-century era of traders and whalers. James F. O'Connell, the so-called Tattooed Irishman, was on the island for five years after having been shipwrecked in the vessel *John Bull* in 1827. O'Connell's book, *A Residence of Eleven Years in New Holland and the Caroline Islands*, is filled with fanciful exaggeration and a certain amount of valuable information about the terrain and culture. Bully Hayes also spent time on Ponape, although he was better known for the mischief he got into in Kosrae, where his ship, the *Leonora*, was sunk in the harbor. It was between Ponape and Kosrae that Bully himself was finally done in, possibly killed by his cook, certainly coming to his final rest in this part of the deep.

In O'Connell's day, there were an estimated fifteen thousand

Ponapeans. But, in 1854, the American whaler *Delta* landed six men infected with smallpox that spread and killed half the population. The presence of whaling ships also turned Ponape into what must have been the most remote battlefield in the U.S. Civil War. The Confederate raider *Shenandoah* arrived here in April 1865 and proceeded to burn four Yankee whalers and to strand their crews ashore before heading back out to sea in pursuit of more of the whaling fleet. Had the Rebels and Yankees but known it, the *Shenandoah's* arrival at Ponape had coincided with the signing of the peace at Appomattox, so the "Battle of Ponape" was altogether nugatory.

The Spaniards and Germans vied with each other for influence here as elsewhere in Micronesia, and while the Spaniards won the papal blessing, they found, in Ponape, that they were involved in a cold war with the natives that occasionally turned into armed conflict. The Germans, purchasing the Carolines in 1899, suffered the last armed rebellion of Ponapeans against foreign rule—the Sokehs rebellion of January 1911. For this Ponapean response to rather oppressive German rule—forced labor, corporal punishment, and the like—17 Ponapean "miscreants" were killed by firing squad, and nearly the entire population of Sokehs was exiled to Palau, their lands confiscated by the government.

Under Japanese rule, the local economy was developed, and Ponape became entirely self-supporting in produce. Preparing for war, the Japanese fortified the island but lightly; its terrain made it a natural defensive position. In the end, the Allies decided to bypass Ponape—it had too much rainfall for an airbase and didn't seem worth the price of an amphibious landing—but they took the trouble to bomb it heavily during 1944, when the Japanese showed that Ponape could be an effective link in their offensive chain.

Today, Ponapeans are mostly subsistence farmers, except for the Polynesians on the southern atolls of Kapingamarangi and Nukuoro, who are excellent fishermen and navigators. An American Jesuit who has lived on Ponape for years explained to a visitor why the Ponapeans were not particularly "keen" on larger-scale agriculture. "They are disinclined to make commitments on the theory that it would be terrible if circumstances made it necessary to break the commitment. If I commit to harvest at a certain time, someone might die on that day, and I would be obliged to violate the commitment." Violating a commitment is unthinkable, and it is equally unthinkable not to leave time for the Ponapean pattern of living—a funeral, for example, lasts four days. At The Village, one of the loveliest resort hotels in the Pacific, the American owners have accommodated this pattern of living in the hiring and management of the Ponapean staff.

While in numbers the total staff often outnumbers the guests, all work part time to ensure time for tradition and for leisure.

The Micronesians on Ponape have the distinction of living in scattered hamlets or even in isolated single-family homes, rather than in villages as almost everywhere else in the Pacific. Today's municipalities coincide with former kingdoms, each divided into some twenty or thirty sections headed by traditionally appointed leaders. Each municipality also has three social ranks. At the top is titled royalty or nobility; they are either Nahnmwarki or Nahnken, the ruling chiefs. To qualify, both parents must belong to these ruling clans. The second rank includes those who have at least one parent who belongs to a ruling clan. The third tier, the largest, comprises the commoners, neither of whose parents claim membership in a ruling clan. Traditional leaders continue to wield considerable sway in political and social matters, and they are typically treated with great deference.

One of the most enduring Ponapean traditions is the drinking— and preparation—of *sakau*, similar to the kava of Polynesia. Although the traditional ceremony is wrapped in formality and proceeds strictly according to rank, sakau houses, *nahs*, are now prevalent and have become centers of Ponapean nightlife. F. W. Christian, who traveled these islands and wrote about them in the 19th century, said of sakau drinking that "the head remains perfectly clear, but the legs sometime suffer a temporary paralysis." After three cups of it, Christian went on, when the drinker tries to rise, "one leg struggles south while the other is marching due north." The 20th century has not dimmed the potency of this drink. Be warned.

# THE TRAVELER IN PONAPE

If Nan Madol is the cultural and historical apex of a visit to Ponape, it is by no means all there is to see. The island can be explored on foot and with wheels. The lagoon should be explored—underwater, by divers. Two monthly field trips head either east to Mokil and Pingelap or south to Ngatik, Nukuoro, and Kapingamarangi. You'll need to make your own arrangements for accommodations.

The Ponape Tourist Commission office is right on Kolonia's main street, and various government agencies, of both the state and the FSM, are not far away. Check with the tourist office for the schedules of presentations at the Micronesia Cultural Center at Nett— authentic dancing, foods, handicraft making, and sakau drinking.

Most of Ponape's hotels are in Kolonia, an endearing Pacific capital; the most frequented hotels stand side by side up the hill in the area known a Porakiet, a community of Polynesians from the fringe outliers. It is also possible to stay in cottages on islands in the lagoon. To stay at Joy Island, near Nan Madol, you must make arrangements at the Joy Restaurant in Kolonia. The island is a laid-back paradise—you must bring your own bedding and food, although islanders say it is possible to just walk out on the reef at low tide and pick up lobsters. You can find similar experiences on Kehpara and Laiap islands off the south of Ponape. The Village, about half an hour from "downtown" Kolonia, is also special—up a hill overlooking islets and passages of the lagoon, locked in a forest of coconut and gum, offering private thatched cottages through whose screened walls the Pacific breezes blow, an open-sided bar-restaurant, and tropical garden.

There is a variety of means for getting around Ponape. Pickup truck taxis head out from Kolonia in either direction and effectively circle the island, although the road, due to the heavy rainfall, often makes for a rugged ride. The same is true if you rent a car, although this provides the traveler the most mobility; Kolonia has numerous car rental agencies. You can circle the island by outboard canoe and ply the lagoon in speedboats heading for the islands; check at the docks down the hill from Kolonia. Finally, there are numerous tour operators who can tailor excursions to your design.

## Kolonia

At the top of Main Street sits the remnant of the Spanish Wall. Built in 1887, the wall once marked the boundary of the Spanish settlement. Today it fronts a park where kids may be playing baseball; across the park is the Catholic mission bell tower, built in 1907 by the Germans. The German cemetery, with the graves of those who died putting down the Sokehs rebellion, is up the hill near Porakiet, not far from "hotel row." The cemetery of the islanders who died in the rebellion—a mass grave site—is at Piedra Point, at the northernmost tip of Kolonia, in a residential area where its location is somewhat obscured.

Wander funky Main Street, with its weathered wood and tin buildings housing shops and offices. One of Ponape's most famous products is black pepper—delicious. A line of cosmetics—coconut-based soap, shampoo, and skin creams—is also prepared for export and for the tourist trade. These come nicely packaged in pandanus-weave baskets.

When you ask about crafts in Kolonia, most people refer you to Porakiet, where the Polynesian community from Kapingamarangi and Nukuoro offer wood carvings, wall hangings, and baskets, Polynesian style. Among the most distinctly Ponapean artifacts are coconut-grating stools, intricately detailed model canoes, and dance paddles. Look for these crafts in the shops of downtown Kolonia.

Shopping for needed supplies is best accomplished in the dock area below the town, where there are boatyards, the government dock, restaurants, and a number of large supermarketlike stores.

## Nan Madol

Tour operators and hotel managements offer tours to Nan Madol, but these are often combined with snorkeling and picnics. If you want a longer look at this intriguing and baffling archaeological site, try to make your own arrangements. If you go by road to Madolenihmw, proceed to PATS, the Ponape Agricultural and Trade School. At this experimental farm and school, or at the nearby shops and homes, you may be able to find a guide with outrigger. At high tide, canoes paddle to Nan Madol; at low tide, it is possible to wade over, but be careful you don't get stuck there.

Nan Madol suffered some two centuries of neglect from its abandonment sometime in the 18th century to the present. In 1985, however, the ruins were designated a National Historical Landmark by the U.S. Department of the Interior; Nan Madol is the only site

Nan Madol, for five centuries the headquarters of Ponapean royalty, now one of the Pacific's major archaeological sites, Federated States of Micronesia. *Photo by Susanna Margolis.*

in the FSM with this distinction. This status guaranteed protection of the site and served as a further spur to archaeological investigation. One thing you don't have to be an archaeologist to figure out is that the construction and maintenance of this extraordinary place had to have been effected by a highly advanced, tightly disciplined, extremely well-organized civilization.

Nan Madol is 93 man-made basalt islets, mostly rectangular in shape, ranging in size from about 350 square meters to 8400 square meters. Radiocarbon dating of the material shows that the structures were built in about 1200, but excavations below the tidal level indicate occupation in the area dating back to 200 B.C. Where the slabs came from is not known, although the most common guess is Sokehs, the island off Kolonia. It is believed that they were brought here on bamboo rafts, then raised into place on inclined palm tree trunks. This is astonishing when you consider that one-ton slabs are commonplace, while a two-ton sakau-pounding stone has been located, and one corner stone (on the islet called Nandauwas) is estimated to weigh 50 tons!

The shape of the slabs is natural, not man-made. The walls are crisscross formations of slabs and blocks, the courses interlined with local coral rubble, and the corners fitted together in tongue-and-groove construction. Each islet seemed to have had its own purpose in what archaeologists believe was a center for the residences of elite royalty and their retainers: a cooking island, a coconut-processing island, another devoted to the kingly tomb-cum-dungeon. The western half of the 93 islets was presumably an administrative center, Madol Pah; the eastern town, Madol Powe, was the ritual and religious center. The whole was originally called Soun Nan-leng, the reef of heaven. *Madol* is Ponapean for the spaces between structures—in this case, canals. No wonder Nan Madol is sometimes called the Venice of the Pacific.

You might think so yourself as you pole or paddle your way among these extraordinary structures. What on earth ever possesed the Ponapeans of the 13th century to build this place? And what made them abandon it? Oral history tells that Isokelekel's victory was here, and that it was here that he established the Nahnmwarki dynasty in 1628. Five succeeding Nahnmwarkis occupied Nan Madol, the last in about 1725, after which it was occupied only intermittently.

## Freshwater Pools

En route back to Kolonia from Nan Madol, stop at Kepirohi. A short walk along the well-worn path beside the stream brings you to this crashing cascade with its wide, welcoming pool. After a long day among the saltwater canals of Nan Madol and under a fierce sun, nothing is nicer than to loll here, occasionally turning your face up to meet the rushing wall of water.

Another striking waterfall is at Liduduhniap, in the Nett District, not far inland from Kolonia. In fact, these are twin waterfalls, surrounded by thatched huts where you can rest or picnic.

## Hiking

A two-day cross-island trek should only be undertaken with a guide. A guide will also be useful for two more accessible hikes: up Sokehs Mountain, or Pohndolap, and up Sokehs Rock, Paipalap. The latter is less forbidding than it looks, although the rock can be slippery. The climb up Pohndolap, on the other hand, may be hard to follow.

## The Lagoon

Pakin and Ant, two usually uninhabited atolls west of Ponape, are each a short—under two hours—boat ride away. Scuba operators often arrange day trips that include dives in the channels between islets, with a picnic lunch on the perfect white beaches of these perfect Pacific islands. Even if you don't dive, see if you can hitch a ride on one of these trips, or arrange something similar on your own. Coconut palms lean over the soft white sand, and the water spreads outward in bands of color: crystal clear at the shoreline over the white sand, aquamarine further out, royal blue in the distance. Paradise may be subjective, but a day at Ant Atoll would meet anyone's standards.

### FSM Addresses

Office of Tourism and Commerce
Yap State Government
Yap 96943

Office of Tourism and Commerce
Truk State Government
Truk 96942

Ponape Tourist Commission
P.O. Box 66, Kolonia
Ponape 96941

# CHAPTER 20

# THE MARSHALL ISLANDS

*Name:* Republic of the Marshall Islands
*Political status:* Independent, in free association with the
   U.S.
*Island groups:* Ratak Chain, Ralik Chain
*Gateway island:* Majuro
*Capital:* D.U.D. Municipality (Darrit-Uliga-Dalap), Majuro
*Population:* 31,000
*Land area:* 181 square kilometers
*Language:* Marshallese, English
*Currency:* U.S. dollars ($US)

Majuro may be as close to a slum as you can find on the main travel route of the Pacific, while the outlying Marshalls may be as close as you can come to paradise. Perhaps the best known of the Marshall Islands are those you cannot get to—nor would you want to: Bikini and Eniwetok, sites for U.S. nuclear testing from 1946 to 1958, and Kwajalein, the world's largest atoll. "Kwaj," the site of fierce fighting in World War II, is now a target and tracking center for missiles test-fired from Vandenberg Air Force Base in Santa Barbara County, California, 6900 kilometers away. (The Guam-Honolulu island-hopping flight lands there, but only authorized personnel get on or off, unless you obtain special permission from Washington or Majuro.)

## GEOGRAPHY, TOPOGRAPHY, CLIMATE

The Marshalls consist of 34 major island units—29 atolls and 5 low islands comprising a total of some 1225 individual islands or islets and 870 reefs. Twenty-five of these 34 atolls and islands are inhabited. The archipelago is located in the easternmost part of Micronesia between 161 and 173 degrees east longitude and between 4 and 12 degrees north latitude. The total land area of all the islands—181 square kilometers—spreads itself over two million square kilometers of ocean.

   The islands range in two chains running northwest to southeast for some 1300 kilometers at a separating width of 240 kilometers. The northeastern chain, Ratak (Sunrise), includes the large atolls of Mili, Majuro, Maloelap, Wotje, Likiep, and 10 more; the Ralik

(Sunset) Chain to the southwest includes Jaluit, Ailinglapalap, Kwajalein, Rongelap, Bikini, and 12 others. Farther west are the two isolated atolls of Eniwetok and Ujelang. Within an atoll, there may be other, smaller atolls; the islands that make them up are like stepping stones—literally so at low tide, when the traveler can wade from islet to islet along an atoll chain.

The 29 atolls have large lagoons encircled by rings of coral reefs resting on submerged mountaintops. Kwajalein has the world's largest lagoon—145 kilometers long at its extreme and 32 kilometers across—ringed by 96 islets. The five single coral islands—Jabwot, Jemo, Kili, Lib, Mejit—are formations of coral limestone and sand.

The climate is tropical but not uniform. The northern islands stay cooler and drier, and, in general, January through March sees lower temperatures and less rainfall. Hurricanes are rare.

## THE NATURAL ENVIRONMENT

These tiny specks of islands are too small and too far east along the migration route of flora and fauna to sustain any great diversity of plant or animal life. Colonial administrations made cash crops of

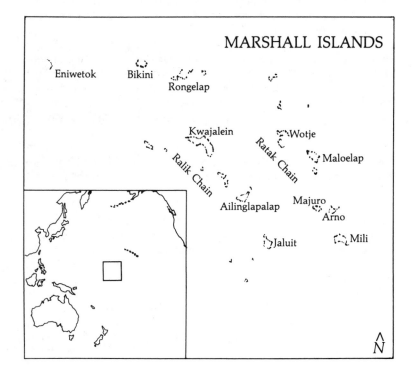

MARSHALL ISLANDS

copra and some fishing, while the islanders themselves often navigated their way to nearby garden islands when their own land failed to grow enough, or when they had fished out their own waters.

The real environmental story here is the nuclear testing that began shortly after World War II. The war had ended in an atomic explosion that even the bomb's inventors did not fully understand, so the U.S. decided to carry out further tests. The remote island of Bikini was selected as a test site because it was well away from sea and air routes, and because winds tended to blow across the atoll in predictable directions. Aware of the islanders' piety, the Navy representative met with them after church services, suggesting that their island was needed for a project that would benefit mankind. The islanders agreed to remove temporarily to another island—first Rongerik, then Kwajalein, finally Kili, where most now remain, with others scattered among the other islands of the archipelago.

The first test was off Bikini on July 1, 1946. In 1947, Eniwetok Atoll was declared a closed military area for testing. In all, there were more than sixty explosions in these waters over the 12 years of testing. One of them, on March 1, 1954, was Bravo, the 15-megaton blast that was the first U.S. test of a hydrogen bomb. Bravo, exploded over the 242 square miles of the Bikini lagoon, held more destructive strength than the combined power of all the weapons fired in all the wars of history up to that time.

It would be an understatement to say that the U.S. military didn't know what it was doing at the time the tests were planned. A few hours after the first blast, sailors boarded the radioactive target ship to swab down the decks. Monitoring devices were inadequate, and the men wielding them often took off their gloves in contaminated areas—many had to be treated with acid to remove the outer layer of skin.

The great miscalculation was about the effect of the blast on the islands—and about how long the effect would last. What continues to make it impossible for Bikinians to return to their island is cesium 137. Established in the soil, it has contaminated the groundwater and the food crops; a steady diet of such crops can cause serious problems. This happened in the 1970s, when a number of Bikinians returned home, only to become ill a few years later. With a half-life of 30 years, cesium 137 presents the islanders with the dismal prospect of not being able to return to their island before about 2076.

There may, however, be faster ways of cleaning the island. The Bikini Atoll Rehabilitation Committee (BARC), a group of U.S. scientists appointed by Congress to make Bikini livable again, has come up with several remedial possibilities. One is to fertilize the soil with a substance rich in potassium. Another possible solution would require scraping the top 12 inches of soil off Bikini's acreage. Whatever the answer, as one scientist on BARC has put it, "The U.S. owes it to Bikini's people to return their atoll as close as possible to its original condition."

In a horribly ironic twist, the sacrifice of the Bikinians may indeed have benefited mankind, as the islanders were promised it would. The nuclear testing carried out in the Pacific, demonstrating all too hideously the destructive power available at the touch of a button, has surely helped to alert the world's people to the danger they face and the responsibility they must assume. The fallout from Bravo, when "the sun rose in the west and there was a rain of white dust," caught a group of Japanese fishermen aboard the boat *Lucky Dragon*. All the men were hurt; one died. The event dramatically caught the attention of the American public. In *Harper's* magazine, the atomic physicist Ralph E. Lapp wrote an article documenting the grim developments of the testing program. The article was illustrated by a famous series of drawings and paintings, The Saga of the Lucky Dragon, by the American artist Ben Shahn. The images Shahn created, at times tormented, at times lyrical, remain a searing commentary on the destructiveness of nuclear weapons and on the dispassionate attitude of military powers toward human experience and human suffering. The U.S. eventually called a halt to the testing.

It may be little consolation to the Bikinians on Kili—deprived, on this lagoonless island, of their traditional way of life—but the name of their forlorn soil continues to be a potent symbol in the campaign for control of nuclear weapons.

# HISTORY

Little is known of the prehistory of these islands. Legend says they were formed when grains of soil drained slowly from a hole in the basket carried through the air by Etau, son of the first human, who had fled from home to find his own place to live. Recent studies show historical and cultural links between the Marshallese and the mariner peoples of Kiribati, Nauru, the Poneapean atolls of Mokil and Pingelap, the Mortlock Islands of Truk, and Wake Island.

The Spaniard Alvaro de Saavedra was the first European to "discover" the islands, in 1529. They then virtually disappeared from Western consciousness until 1767, when Samuel Wallis landed on Rongerik. In 1788, the British captains John Marshall and Thomas Gilbert charted more islands in the group, but it was the Russian explorer Otto von Kotzebue, in two trips here, who put together the first clear picture of this archipelago of atolls. It was Kotzebue who named the islands after Marshall.

The early 19th century saw the usual whalers, missionaries, traders, buccaneers, and blackbirders, although the Marshallese were often successful in resisting European incursions. In 1861, however, the first German trader established himself on Ebon (said by many, including Somerset Maugham, to be one of the loveliest islands on earth). In 1878, Chief Kabua of Rongelap concluded a treaty giving the Germans exclusive use of the harbor at Jaluit and special trading privileges in the Ralik Chain. The Marshalls became a German protectorate in 1885.

German rule was mostly indirect; as long as copra could be successfully produced, the Germans were content to let traditional chieftains maintain authority. Japan, which took the islands in 1914, assumed a much more direct role. Here as elsewhere in Micronesia, their aims were economic development, colonization for Japanese emigrants, integration with Japan, and militarization. The Marshalls came under heavy Allied bombardment during World War II, and Kwajalein and Eniwetok were captured by the U.S. in fierce land battles during February 1944.

The Marshallese split with the Caroline islanders in 1978, when they became the first Trust Territory district to draft and approve their own constitution. The Republic of the Marshall Islands declared self-government on May 1, 1979. In the 1983 vote on the Compact of Free Association, two-thirds of the Marshallese voted in favor of the compact, but 89 percent of Bikinians voted against it, fearful of the end of the welfare that sustains them in their exile.

Forty percent of the population lives on Majuro—the word means "place where many people will come to stay"—and another 20 percent are crowded onto Ebeye, routinely called the "slum of the Pacific"—a squalid bedroom community for islanders who commute to jobs on Kwaj. Jaluit, Arno, and Ailinglapalap are also heavily populated.

A complex class system still prevails in the Marshalls. At the bottom of the ladder are the *kajur*, commoners. Everyone belongs to the clan, *bwij*, of his mother; land tenure and land use are determined by clan. An *alab* or headman directs each clan and represents clan interests at the higher levels—to the *iroij*, chiefs of the aristocratic families, and the *iroij laplap*, paramount chief.

The Marshallese language is closely related to the Gilbertese of Kiribati and to the Carolinian languages. Differences in intonation and inflection divide Marshallese speakers into two separate although mutually comprehensible dialects for the Ratak and Ralik chains.

# THE TRAVELER IN THE MARSHALL ISLANDS

Once called "the pearl of the Pacific"—by no less an observer than Robert Louis Stevenson—Majuro today is a busy melting pot of islanders from all over the archipelago and something of a garbage dump. Its minimal sights are easily seen; its more potent interest is the vitality of its political life, closely linked to its nightlife. Majuro is the traveler's resource center, and it is the place to make arrangements for visiting one or more outliers.

As of this writing, the Airline of the Marshall Islands (A.M.I.) flies to twenty outliers, as well as to Kosrae and Tarawa. (The Tarawa connection is key, for there the traveler can connect with Air Nauru; this thus provides a route south from the eastern Pacific.) The availability of seats on the Dornier plane will be a prime factor in determining where you go, and the schedule of flights will dictate how long you stay. Check with the airline, your hotel, Peace Corps volunteers, or anyone you meet about families to stay with on the outliers. This is easily done; as an official of A.M.I. put it, "The people out there are real mellow."

Four field-trip vessels ply the archipelago, going north, south, east, and west. The northern and western trips are quite long; the trips to the south and east are relatively short. The Government Transportation Office is right next to A.M.I. on the waterfront at the old dock, so the traveler can conceivably make air, boat, or combined arrangements all at once. *Conceivably.*

## Majuro

Majuro is several islands joined by loads of coral rubble welded into place by Navy muscle. The result is a long—56 kilometers— curling finger of island. To the southeast, where the finger curls back on itself, is the D.U.D. Municipality, Majuro's "downtown," formed by the three joined islands of Dalap, Uliga, and Darrit. D.U.D. is only 200 meters wide, but its administrative buildings, offices, shops, and restaurants are strung along either side of the road for five kilometers—none of it pretty, much of it resulting from a 1979 tidal wave that destroyed just about everything.

The hotels of the Marshall Islands are in or near the D.U.D. The biggest of these, Robert Reimers, run by the same entrepreneurs who have the biggest store in town, the biggest car rental agency, etc., is right in the center of everything in a modern office-store complex that only lacks a bar and restaurant. Bars and restaurants abound, however, as do fast-food and take-out places.

The airport is 15 kilometers west of D.U.D. At the far western tip of Majuro is Laura, a lovely community and beach, while at the far eastern tip is Rita, the least attractive kind of Pacific urban sprawl. At low tide, it is possible to walk from Rita to the next islet, Ejit, home of numerous relocated Bikinians. It is also said to be possible to reef-walk from Laura the three or four miles over to Rongrong, but if your timing isn't right, this long walk could turn into a long swim.

Rent a car or—better—hire a taxi and driver to take you the length of Majuro. Start at the less appealing Rita end of the island, then work your way through the D.U.D. traffic until the ramshackle urban blight finally thins out. When it does, you are riding a ribbon of highway down the center of the island, cutting in half groves of coconut, banana, and brush, with the ocean roaring on one side of you and the limpid lagoon on the other. At some points, the stretch of land between the two can be crossed in seconds. The few houses are hodgepodges of plasterboard, plywood, tin, and concrete, often patched by coconut frond or pandanus thatch. A Taiwanese agricultural station not far from Laura provides locally grown fresh vegetables. It's the only farm on the island to do so, although islanders often keep gardens beside their homes. Laura itself is a quiet settlement of a few stores and houses.. Where the paved road ends, the traveler is at Majuro's highest point—six meters above sea level.

Pacific islet, part of the fringing reef of the Majuro Lagoon, Marshall Islands. *Photo by Susanna Margolis.*

A monument was erected here by the Japanese in memory of the people lost during a typhoon in 1918. Laura's beach is beautiful, and the offshore snorkeling is splendid.

The Alele Museum at Uliga is the main tourist's sight in D.U.D.; it has an interesting collection of artifacts and photographs. Although war remnants on Majuro are few, there are some old pillbox fortifications near the high school on the ocean side of Rita. Most stores and offices are near the old dock in Uliga. Eateries and watering holes stretch out from Uliga to Dalap. Perhaps *the* place to hang out in the evening—at least at the start of the evening—is Charlie's Bar in Uliga. Owned by a prominent Marshallese family, Charlie's is named after the bar in Honolulu where many of the republic's leadership—as well as leaders of other Micronesian countries—used to hang out in the 1960s when all were students together. In the U.S. Charlie's, Marshallese, Palauans, Ponapeans, Trukese, and others talked about how things would be when the compact was signed and they were in charge of their young nations. Now many of them *are* in charge, and at Charlie's the traveler can meet political leaders, journalists, aid workers, contract expats, and the few other travelers who pass through here.

Majuro is a center for the sale of the very excellent crafts produced in the Marshall atolls—known especially for weaving. The Marshalls Handicraft Co-op behind the museum is a good source, and there are shops and concessions around town that also offer a selection. Here can be found the best baskets in Micronesia as well as mats, belts, headbands, wall hangings, fans, and jewelry. One of the most uniquely Marshallese of the items for sale are stick charts, navigational aids that record the wave patterns of the sea and were used to train young people in navigation. Thin strips of wood describe the swells, and shells represent the islands that interrupt the ocean's currents to produce the swells.

Other shopping in Majuro reminds the traveler just how close to the U.S. he is: lots of clothing from California (although most island women wear Mother Hubbards) and lots of recent books—Majuro looks to be one of the most literate places in the Pacific. The traveler will also see a great deal of junk food for sale. Malnutrition is in fact a serious health problem here; parents keep fresh vegetables to sell to market and find it easy to assuage their kids' hunger with potato chips and candy. Blindness and brain damage often result—an unconscionable state of affairs. And the garbage piles up; candy wrappers, soda cans, and beer bottles join the detritus floating among the ships in the busy harbor.

But then there is the lagoon. Hop a boat and in no time you have left the squalor of D.U.D. and are riding the calm surface of this wide body of water ringed by islets. Some of these appear to be in the making or unmaking, just white sand and green clump rising up from a reef in water so clear you can see a hundred feet down through it even from the surface. Scuba diving can be arranged in Majuro—ask at your hotel—and is well worth it. Snorkeling, sailing, fishing, and of course swimming are all splendid here.

## The Outliers

If the Majuro Lagoon is a taste of everyone's Pacific fantasy, time spent on an outlier may well be its ultimate realization. Men are particularly keen to visit Arno, where a school teaches the local girls the domestic arts and skills in lovemaking in preparation for marriage. But pick almost any of these islands—go wherever the plane or field-trip vessel is heading. Step off, find a home or stretch of beach to sleep on, and enter into island life. You don't need a book for this.

### Marshall Islands Address

Tourism Office
Republic of the Marshall Islands
Majuro, Marshall Islands 96960

# APPENDICES

# QUICK REFERENCE GUIDE

| Country | Airport | Entry Requirements | Departure Tax |
|---------|---------|--------------------|---------------|
| French Polynesia | Faaa International, 7 km from Papeete | Passport, onward ticket | ----- |
| Cook Islands | Rarotonga International, 2 km from Avarua | Passport, onward ticket, hotel reservations | ----- |
| Western Samoa | Faleolo, 35 km from Apia | Passport, onward ticket | $WS20 |
| American Samoa | Pago Pago International, 11 km from Fagotogo | ----- | ----- |
| Tonga | Fua'amotu, 22 km from Nuku'alofa | Passport, onward ticket | $5 |
| Fiji | Nausori, 25 km from Suva | Passport, onward ticket | $10 |
| | Nadi International | | |
| New Caledonia | Tontouta, 45 km from Nouméa | Passport, onward ticket | ----- |
| Vanuatu | Bauerfeld, 3 km from Port Vila | Passport, onward ticket | 1000 VT |
| Solomon Islands | Henderson, 11 km from Honiara | Passport, onward ticket | $10 |

# TO PACIFIC DESTINATIONS

| Health Requirements | Arrival Procedures | Currency |
|---|---|---|
| Cholera, yellow fever immunization if coming from affected area | If arriving from Fiji or American Samoa, luggage is fumigated<br><br>Plane sprayed on arrival | CFP (Cours du franc pacifique)<br>Notes: 500, 1000, 5000<br>Coins: 1, 2, 5, 10, 20, 50, 100 |
| Smallpox immunization if coming from affected area | If arriving from Fiji, Western Samoa, or Hawaii, luggage is fumigated<br><br>Plane sprayed on arrival | New Zealand dollar<br>Notes: 1, 5, 10, 20, 100<br>Coins: 1, 2, 5, 10, 20, 50 |
| ----- | Plane sprayed on arrival | $WS (tala), divided into 100 senes (cents/¢)<br>Notes: 2, 5, 10, 20 tala<br>Coins: 1, 2, 5, 10, 20, 50 sene, 1 tala |
| ----- | ----- | $US |
| ----- | Plane sprayed on arrival | $ (pa'anga), divided into 100 seniti<br>Notes: 50 seniti; 1, 2, 5, 10 pa'anga<br>Coins: 1 pa'anga; 1, 2, 5, 10, 20, 50 seniti |
| ----- | Plane sprayed on arrival | $ (Fijian dollar)<br>Notes: 50¢; 1, 2, 10, 20 dollars<br>Coins: 1, 2, 5, 10, 20 cents |
| ----- | Plane sprayed on arrival | CFP |
| Start malaria prophylaxis 1 week before arrival | ----- | VT (Vanuatu vatu)<br>Notes: VT 10, 500, 1000<br>Coins: VT 5, 10, 20, 50 |
| Start malaria prophylaxis 1 week before arrival<br><br>Note: Chloraquin-resistant mosquito present | Plane sprayed on arrival | $SI (dollars)<br>Notes: 2, 5, 10, 20<br>Coins: 1, 2, 5, 10, 20 cents, $1 |

## Pacific Destinations

| Country | Airport | Entry Requirements | Departure Tax |
|---------|---------|--------------------|---------------|
| Papua New Guinea | Jackson, 11 km from Port Moresby | Visa (costs K5), passport, onward ticket | K10 |
| Guam | Tamuning, 6 km from Agana | (For non-U.S. citizens: passport, U.S. visa) Passport for U.S. citizens not arriving from U.S., onward ticket | ----- |
| Northern Marianas | Saipan International, 13 km from Garapan | Passport (except U.S. citizens), onward ticket | ----- |
| Palau | Airai, 16 km from Koror | Passport (except U.S. citizens), onward ticket | ----- |
| FSM: Federated States of Micronesia | | | |
| Yap | Yap, 6 km from Colonia | Passport (except U.S. citizens), onward ticket | ----- |
| Truk | Truk | | ----- |
| Ponape | Ponape, 3 km from Kolonia | | |
| Marshall Islands | Majuro, 15 km from D.U.D. | Passport (except U.S. citizens), onward ticket | ----- |

# TIME

| TOMORROW | | | | TODAY |
|----------|--|--|--|-------|
| Papua New Guinea | New Caledonia Vanuatu Solomon Islands New Britain Bougainville | Fiji | Tonga | Cook Islands |
| 10 AM | 11 AM | Noon | 1 PM | 1:30 PM |

## *Continued*

| Health<br>Requirements | Arrival<br>Procedures | Currency |
|---|---|---|
| Start malaria prophylaxis 1 week before arrival. In the west, potential typhoid, tetanus, cholera | Plane sprayed on arrival | Kina (=100 toea)<br>Notes: 2, 5, 10, 20 kina<br>Coins: 1, 2, 5, 10, 20 toea |
| ----- | ----- | $US |
| ----- | ----- | $US |
| ----- | ----- | $US |
| ----- | ----- | $US |
| Check re cholera | ----- | $US |
| ----- | ----- | $US |

# CHART

| French Polynesia<br>Hawaii | San Francisco | Denver | Chicago | New York | London |
|---|---|---|---|---|---|
| 2 PM | 4 PM | 5 PM | 6 PM | 7 PM | Midnight |

# AIRLINES SERVING THE PACIFIC

The following airlines fly to Pacific island destinations from North America. The routes listed are flown with varying frequency; the schedules for continuing service also vary. All routes and schedules are of course subject to change.

*Air France:*

Los Angeles–Papeete

*Air New Zealand:*

Los Angeles nonstop to Papeete, connections to Rarotonga and Fiji
Los Angeles–Honolulu–Fiji
Vancouver–Honolulu–Fiji
Vancouver–Los Angeles–Papeete

*Canadian Pacific:*

Vancouver–Honolulu–Nadi

*Continental:*

Honolulu–Johnston Island (only authorized personnel may disembark)–Kwajalein (only authorized personnel may disembark)–Majuro–Ponape–Truk–Guam
Los Angeles–Papeete
Honolulu–Nadi

*Hawaiian Airlines:*

Honolulu–Pago Pago–Apia–Tonga

*Qantas:*

Los Angeles or San Francisco–Honolulu–Nadi

*South Pacific Island Airways (SPIA):*

Honolulu–Pago Pago–Apia
Honolulu–Rarotonga–Papeete
Honolulu–Majuro–Guam–Koror

*UTA:*

Los Angeles or San Francisco–Papeete–Noumea

# REGIONAL AIRLINES

The following regional airlines provide internation service as well as, in some cases, interisland service within an island nation. Check about routes between specific destinations with a travel agent or, if none is available, by means of the addresses and telephone numbers in the appropriate area's chapter. Below are the major destinations each airline serves.

*Air Nauru:*

Nauru, Fiji, Guam, New Caledonia, Vanuatu, Kiribati, Solomon Islands

*Air Niugini:*

Papua New Guinea, Solomon Islands

*Air Pacific:*

Fiji, Western Samoa, Tonga, Solomon Islands, Vanuatu

*Air Tahiti:*

French Polynesia, American Samoa, Cook Islands, Tonga, Fiji, New Caledonia

*SPIA:*

American Samoa, Western Samoa, Cook Islands, French Polynesia, Marshall Islands, Guam, Palau

In addition, several of the above regional airlines serve New Zealand and Australia, where further "feeder" connections can be made.

# STOPOVERS

The so-called circle-Pacific airfare, which goes under a number of labels depending on the airline, is a deal allowing from four stopovers to unlimited stopovers *within a geographic progression and on the same airline.* Typically, the circle-Pacific route is offered by an international carrier flying from North America to New Zealand, Australia, or destinations in Southeast Asia, Japan, the Philippines. In some cases, depending on your desired route, it may be more economical to purchase this ticket than to fly directly to specific island destinations; check with a reliable, knowledgeable travel agent.

# LIMITED-TIME TRAVELERS: RECOMMENDED ITINERARIES

Travelers with limited time will, it is hoped, be able to use this book to choose those destinations most suited to their interests or curiosity. For most short-term trips to the Pacific, close and careful planning will be required to strike the right balance between airline schedules and personal inclination. Here are some suggested itineraries, aimed at showing you the best or most typical of the Pacific:

## THE TWO-WEEK WHIRLWIND

Two suggestions here. The first gives the traveler a taste of all three Pacific regions—Polynesia, Melanesia, Micronesia; the second focuses on Papua New Guinea, one of the most fascinating of Pacific destinations.

1. Fly via American Samoa to Apia, Western Samoa, for three days offering an excellent look at traditional Polynesia; fly on to Fiji for another three days, straddling Polynesia and Melanesia; head for the Solomon Islands for three days in the heart of Melanesia; then fly to Ponape, possibly via Nauru, for two to three final days in Micronesia. On this itinerary, flight times between destinations are reasonable—except for the international passages and the transit from Honiara to Ponape.

2. Fly the north Pacific puddle-jumper route to Ponape, spend two days; fly to Port Moresby to spend five days in Papua New Guinea; fly to Fiji for a three-day stay on Viti Levu; head for home. Each transit effectively takes about a day, if, indeed, the right connections can be scheduled.

## THE FOUR-WEEK TOUR

A month provides a reasonable amount of time for seeing numerous Pacific islands in all three regions, although you may be limited to the gateway islands much of the time. This itinerary touches most of the more famous Pacific island destinations, as well as a few of the more obscure.

Fly from the U.S. west coast directly to Papeete, Tahiti, for three days in French Polynesia; connect to Apia, Western Samoa, for four days, and on to Tonga for another four. This somewhat covers Polynesia.

Fly to Suva, and either work your way across Viti Levu to Nadi or try to see some outliers before departing Nadi for Port Vila, Vanuatu, for two days. Fly directly, or via Espiritu Santo, to Honiara in the Solomons for a three-day stay, finishing Melanesia.

Connect via Nauru to Ponape for three days; then jump, via Guam, to Saipan and Tinian over a two- to three-day period before reconnecting at Guam with the island-hopper plane back to Honolulu.

## AROUND OCEANIA IN EIGHTY DAYS

The summer traveler, the person who can vacation from mid-June to Labor Day, has an excellent opportunity to roam widely and probe deeply among the islands of Oceania. Remember that the time period typically includes abundant rainfall north of the equator, with the possibility of typhoon or hurricane—travel plans *may* be disrupted. (If your two-and-a-half-month summer occurs in the northern winter, that caution goes for travel south of the equator.)

Fly directly to Tahiti for a week in French Polynesia, concentrating on Huahine and Rangiroa. Head for Western Samoa—five days—then for Tonga, spending ten days on the gateway island and among the Vava'u and Ha'apai groups. Depart Polynesia for Fiji.

Spend ten days in Fiji, concentrating on outliers. Give Vanuatu another ten days, again concentrating on outliers. And spend ten again in the Solomons, working your way across the outliers to Papua New Guinea.

Give PNG at least two weeks, to cover Sepik, highlands, bush, and coast.

Connect via Guam to Palau for four days, to Yap for another four, to Ponape for another four en route back to the U.S.

# FIELD
# RESEARCH TRIPS

The increasingly popular form of travel known as the field research trip, in which the traveler donates his expenses (tax deductible) and labor to a research project in any one of a range of disciplines, reaches several Pacific islands, offers an opportunity to make a contribution to the region, learn something, and enjoy an unusual travel experience.

Three nonprofit organizations are preeminent in this field, and all run projects in the Pacific. The range of disciplines covers the earth, life, and marine sciences, anthropology, archaeology, palaeontology, geography, conservation, and more. Projects range in length from one week to six. Those who participate work as a team, live—typically—in comfortable but less than luxurious accommodations, and spend their days serving as field workers under the direction of the project's author and director. Participants pay their fare and a "contribution"; these costs are tax deductible provided expenses are itemized.

1. Earthwatch
   680 Mt. Auburn Street
   Box 403
   Watertown, MA 02272
   617/926-8200

A powerful presence in the Pacific, with a branch office in Sydney, Earthwatch runs projects in everything from archaeology, botany, and climatology to vulcanology and zoology. The average project lasts two to three weeks, but the range is from ten days to six weeks. A membership organization, Earthwatch costs $25 per year; members receive the organization's quarterly magazine and the quarterly *News*, both providing notices of upcoming projects and reports on past projects. A list of upcoming projects is available free on request.

2. Foundation for Field Research
   787 South Grade Road
   Alpine, CA 92001-0380
   619/445-9264

Private, nonprofit, not a membership organization. Projects last from one week to one month. Inquire by mail or phone for news about upcoming projects.

3. University Research Expedition Program
   University of California
   Berkeley, CA 94720
   415/642-6586

Participants assist university faculty in field research projects covering numerous disciplines in the natural and social sciences.

Other field trips, run by museums and nature organizations (the Cousteau Society, for example), typically are not work trips but rather organized tours with a particular focus on the natural history, or an aspect of the natural history, of Pacific destinations—another good travel alternative for those with these specific interests.

# ALERT
# TO BIRDERS

Species-counters will want to concentrate on the larger islands if they are looking to lengthen their life lists; the smaller the island, the fewer the number of species. *The* bird-watcher's mecca in the Pacific is Papua New Guinea; other good spots are the more mountainous areas of Fiji, New Caledonia, and French Polynesia.

There is no one birding guide to Oceania. Here are some titles recommended by Mary LeCroy, senior scientific assistant in the Bird Department of the American Museum of Natural History and an authority on bird life of the Pacific region:

*Birds of the Fiji Bush,* by Fergus Clunie and Pamela Morse. Published in Suva by the Fiji Museum and featuring Clunie's paintings, 1984.

*Birds of Fiji, Tonga, and Samoa,* by Dick Watling. Published by Millwood Press, Wellington, New Zealand, but often available through bird-book catalogues. *Not* a field guide.

*Birds of New Guinea,* by Bruce McP. Beehler. Princeton: Princeton University Press, 1986.

*Birds of the Southwest Pacific: A Field Guide to the Birds of the Area Between Samoa, New Caledonia, and Micronesia,* by Ernst Mayr. First published in 1945, reissued in a paperback edition by Charles E. Tuttle Company, Rutland, Vermont, 1978. Though pictorially meager, the book lists all the birds of the region.

*A Field Guide to the Birds of Hawaii and the Tropical Pacific,* by Douglas Pratt. Princeton: Princeton University Press, 1986. Good for Micronesia.

*South Pacific Birds,* by John Dupont. Published by the Delaware Museum of Natural History in Wilmington and reportedly difficult to obtain. Valuable for its pictures.

In addition, local field guide books and pamphlets are available throughout the Pacific.

# NOTES ON YACHTING

## THE PASSAGE ACROSS

The most common yachting route westward across the Pacific catches the tradewinds from California or Mexico to Tahiti via the Marquesas or Hawaii. Heading eastward, the route typically rides north from Tahiti or Samoa along the Line Islands, then catches the strong tradewinds to strike out east from Hawaii to California. The passage takes some three to four weeks, and most yachtsmen avoid the months June through October, hurricane season across the passage route.

## PREPARING TO GO

Two books in particular serve as "bibles" for the Pacific yachtsman: *Landfalls of Paradise: The Guide to Pacific Islands*, by Earl R. Hinz (published by Western Marine Enterprises, Inc., Box Q, Ventura, CA 93002), covering 33 islands and 66 ports of entry and including a hundred and fifty charts; and *Cruising Guide to French Polynesia*, by Fred Boehme, privately printed in the U.S. and updated as of 1985.

U.S. charts for the region are listed in the U.S. Government Printing Office catalogue and are available from the Printing Office. In addition, you can order any of these charts as well as British charts to the region from the New York Nautical Instrument and Service Corporation, 140 West Broadway, New York, NY 10013, tel. 212/962-4522. New York Nautical Instrument is reputed to have the nation's largest supply of nautical charts.

Other information about cruising the Pacific may be obtained from the nation's major yacht clubs; a good tip is to chat with the club librarian to find out what is current or has been newly published about the region.

## CREWING

Yachting magazines—the classified listings—and the bulletin boards of major west coast yacht clubs are good sources for placing or finding notices about crewing positions for the passage out to the Pacific. Many crew members work the passage out, then fly home, so French Polynesia is a good place to look for skippers who need replacement crews. Wander the Papeete yacht basin, or check at the Hotel Oa Oa in Bora Bora, a major yachtie hangout.

Yachts needing crew members may be found on any island in the Pacific, but major ports include, in addition to Tahiti: Pago Pago, Vava'u, Suva, and the ports of New Zealand and Australia, where many yachts wait out the southern Pacific hurricane season from November to March-April. Yachts in the northern Pacific must wait out the months July to December, so the ports there may be fertile ground for hustling crew slots during those months.

# THE VOCABULARY OF PACIFIC TRAVEL

(*Italicized words* within a definition are cross-referenced.)

**atoll** Ring of *coral* reefs and/or islands built over a subsided volcanic base and enclosing—nearly or completely—a *lagoon.*

**balolo** See *palolo.*

**barrier reef** A reef adjacent to an island or continental landmass, separated from the land by a *lagoon* too deep for *coral* growth.

**bêche de mer** Trepang, sea cucumber, sea slug, the edible marine animal highly prized in Oriental cuisine; also used as a term for *pidgin.*

**betel nut** The seed of the fruit of the betel palm *(Areca catechu)* chewed, together with betel leaves and lime, by many populations of Melanesia and Micronesia.

**bislama** See *pidgin.*

**blackbirding** Recruitment, often forced, of island labor in the 19th century. The recruited labor force was primarily Melanesian; the plantations to which they were transported were mostly in Fiji and in Queensland, Australia.

**caldera** A large crater formed from a volcano's exploding or collapsing.

**cargo cult** Melanesian religious (and sometimes quasi-political) movement or movements promising salvation through Western-style goods—the cargo—often to be brought by returning ancestors.

**cassava** Large, starchy root plant; manioc; used to make tapioca.

**coastwatchers** Volunteer intelligence agents, often civilian and mostly Australian, who operated behind Japanese lines during World War II, spotting approaching planes and ships.

**coir** The fiber from the husk of a coconut, used in making rope, matting.

**copra** Dried coconut meat from which coconut oil is extracted.

**coral** Marine coelenterates characterized by calcareous skeletons in a wide variety of shapes and forming reefs or islands.

**custom** Common tradition or usage with the force or validity of law, as in custom (or customary) land, title, owner, etc. *Kastom* in Bislama.

**cyclone** A violent windstorm characterized by masses of air rotating around a center of low atmospheric pressure; the rotation is clockwise in the southern hemisphere, counterclockwise in the northern hemisphere. Also known as a hurricane or typhoon, the storm, typically accompanied by heavy precipitation, is potentially highly destructive.

**endemic** Native to a particular region.

**fa'afafine** Samoan term for a man brought up as a woman; *manu* in French Polynesia; *fakaleiti* in Tonga.

**fakaleiti** See *fa'afafine*.

**fringing reef** A reef along the shores of an island but not enclosing a lagoon.

**hurricane** See *cyclone*.

**kapu** See *tabu*.

**kastom** See *custom*.

**kava** Traditional beverage made from the dried root of the pepper shrub, *Piper methysticum*; *yagona* in Fiji; *sakau* on Ponape.

**lagoon** Body of water enclosed by a reef.

**lavalava** Samoan word for the saronglike wraparound skirt worn virtually throughout the Pacific; *pareu* in Tahiti; *sulu* in Fiji.

**leeward** The side sheltered from the wind and toward which the wind is moving; vs. *windward*.

**malae** See *marae*.

**mana** A supernatural force endowing its possessor with authority and virtue.

**mangrove** Tropical evergreen trees or shrubs (genus *Rhizophora*) forming dense thickets along tidal shores.

**manioc** See *cassava*.

**manu** See *fa'afafine*.

**marae** An enclosure, often a sacred precinct as in French Polynesia, a village green or meeting place in Samoa *(malae)* and Fiji *(rara)*.

**masi** See *tapa*.

**motu** An islet held together by vegetation.

**off-island** Anywhere else; a place to go when island fever has set in, as in "His problem is that he hasn't been off-island for months."

**on-island** Right here, as in "Did you find this on-island?" or "I'm staying on-island this weekend."

**out-island** Not the main or gateway island; *outlier*.

**outlier** See *out-island*.

**palolo** In Samoan, the reef worm *Eunice viridis; balolo* in Fijian.

**palusami** A baked concoction of coconut cream wrapped in taro leaves, Samoan specialty.

**pareu** See *lavalava*.

**pidgin** Simplified form of speech, with limited vocabulary and rudimentary grammar, often a mixture of two or more languages, used for communication between groups who are otherwise mutually unintelligible. *Bislama* in Vanuatu; pidgin in the Solomon Islands; *Tok Pisin* in Papua New Guinea.

**pisupo** Canned corned beef in Tonga, Samoa.

**plate** Geologically, a discrete section of the earth's crust, bounded by trenches, volcanic ridges, or faults.

**rain shadow** The dry area downwind of a topographical obstacle so high that water vapor, in ascending to pass over the obstacle, is condensed and precipitated over the windward slope of the obstacle, thus leaving the downwind area in the rain's "shadow," dry.

**rara** See *marae*.

**reef** A ridgelike structure formed from the conglomerated skeletal remains of *coral* colonies and covered by living coral. The structure may rise to or near the surface of the water; see *barrier reef, fringing reef*.

**sakau** *Kava* on Ponape.

**scuba** Self-contained underwater breathing apparatus.

**sea cucumber** See *bêche de mer*.

**sea slug** See *bêche de mer*.

**sennit** Braided cordage made from *coir*.

**shoal** Shallow area or bank.

**siapo** See *tapa*.

**subduction** Geologically, the movement of one crustal *plate* sliding under another, usually creating a *trench.*

**subsidence** The action of sinking or settling, as an island does because of crustal weight or a *plate*'s shifting.

**sulu** See *lavalava.*

**tabu** Set apart, sacred; the prohibition excluding something from use because of this sacred and inviolate nature. Also *tapu, kapu, tambu.*

**ta'ovalu** The Tongan mat worn by both sexes.

**tapa** The paperlike cloth made by pounding the inner bark of the paper mulberry tree *(Broussonetia papyrifera). Siapo* in Samoa; *masi* in Fijian.

**tapioca** See *cassava.*

**taro** The starchy tuber *(Colocasia esculenta)* that is a staple food throughout the Pacific.

**tradewinds** The strong surface winds through most of the tropics, the major component of the general circulation of the atmosphere, blowing northeasterly in the northern hemisphere and southeasterly in the southern hemisphere.

**trench** Geologically, a depth formed by the *subduction* of oceanic *plate* materials.

**trepang** See *bêche de mer.*

**typhoon** See *cyclone.*

**umu** Underground, earthen oven; *lomo* in Fiji; *mumu* in PNG.

**windward** On the side exposed to the prevailing winds, the direction from which the wind blows; vs. *leeward.*

**yagona** See *kava.*

# IF YOU NEED ASSISTANCE

Official U.S. representation is meager in Polynesia and Melanesia, abundant throughout Micronesia. Should you lose your passport, or have it stolen, you must report it to U.S. authorities who will arrange issuance of a new passport—often after a bit of a delay for processing time in order to ensure against passport fraud. Should you be arrested, you have a worldwide right to contact a representative of your government. In addition, U.S. representatives can provide assistance and advice in case of medical emergencies, financial difficulties, sudden political turmoil, or in the event that you need to be located by people from home—for this, you'll have to register beforehand with the local U.S. authorities.

Here are the relevant points of contact for U.S. citizens traveling in the Pacific:

For French Polynesia, Tonga, Fiji, and New Caledonia, contact

U.S. Embassy, Suva, Fiji
31 Loftus Street
Telephone 314-466

For Cook Islands and Western Samoa, contact

U.S. Embassy, Wellington, New Zealand
29 Fitzherbert Terrace
Telephone 722-068

For Vanuatu and Papua New Guinea, contact

U.S. Embassy, Port Moresby, PNG
Armit Street
Telephone 211-455

For Solomon Islands, contact the U.S. representative in Honiara.

For American Samoa, Guam, and the Northern Marianas, all American territories in one way or another, the authorities *are* U.S. officials; apply to the relevant agency or go directly to the lieutenant-governor's office.

For Palau, contact

Status Liaison Office
U.S. Department of State
P.O. Box 6028
Koror, Palau
Western Caroline Islands 96940

For the Federated States of Micronesia, contact

> Office of the U.S. Representative
> U.S. Department of State
> P.O. Box 1286
> Kolonia, FSM 96941

For the Marshall Islands, contact

> Office of the U.S. Representative
> U.S. Department of State
> P.O. Box 680
> Majuro, Republic of the Marshall Islands 96960

# BIBLIOGRAPHY

As befits a vast area, Oceania claims a vast literature. Here is a partial listing.

## Literature

Becke, Louis. *South Sea Supercargo.* Edited with an introduction by A. Grove Day. Honolulu: University of Hawaii Press, 1967.

Hau'ofa, Epeli. *Tales of the Tikongs.* Auckland, New Zealand: Longman Paul Ltd., 1983.

London, Jack. *The Cruise of the Snark.*

Maugham, W. Somerset. *The Trembling of a Leaf.*

Melville, Herman. *Typee: A Peep at Polynesian Life,* and *Omoo: A Narrative of Adventures in the South Seas.*

Michener, James A. *Tales of the South Pacific.* New York: Ballantine Books, 1984.

_____. *Return to Paradise.* New York: Ballantine Books, 1982.

_____ and A. Grove Day. *Rascals in Paradise.* London: Corgi Books, 1960.

Stevenson, Robert Louis. *Island Nights' Entertainment.* Honolulu: University of Hawaii Press, 1975.

_____. *In the South Seas.* Honolulu: University of Hawaii Press, 1971.

Subramani. *South Pacific Literature.* Suva: University of the South Pacific, 1985.

## Environment

Celhay, Jean-Claude (with M. Guerin, J. M. Maclet, J. Rentier). *Plants and Flowers of Tahiti.* Papeete: Société Nouvelle des éditions du Pacifique, 1974.

Clunie, Fergus, and Morse, Pauline. *Birds of the Fiji Bush.* Suva: Fiji Museum, 1984.

DeLuca, Charles J., and MacIntyre, Diana. *Pacific Marine Life.* Rutland, Vermont: Charles E. Tuttle Company, 1976.

Graindorge, Maurice. *Le Ciel de Tahiti et des Mers du Sud.* Papeete: Editions Haere Po No, 1986.

Hargreaves, Dorothy and Bob. *Tropical Blossoms of the Pacific.* Kailua, Hawaii: Hargreaves Company, Inc., 1970.

_____. *Tropical Trees of the Pacific.* Kailua, Hawaii: Hargreaves Company, Inc., 1970.

Kay, E. Alison. *Little Worlds of the Pacific: An Essay on Pacific Basin Biogeography.* Honolulu: Lyon Arboretum, University of Hawaii, 1980.

Laboute, P., and Magnier, Y. *Underwater Guide to New Caledonia.* Papeete: Les Editions du Pacifique, 1979.

Martini, Frederic. *Exploring Tropical Isles and Seas.* Englewood Cliffs, New Jersey: Prentice-Hall, 1984.

Mayr, Ernst. *Birds of the Southwest Pacific.* Rutland, Vermont: Charles E. Tuttle Company, 1978.

Merrill, Elmer D. *Plant Life of the Pacific World.* Rutland, Vermont: Charles E. Tuttle Company, 1981.

Robin, B., Petron, C., and Rives, C. *Living Corals.* Papeete: Les Editions du Pacifique, 1980.

Thibault, J. Cl., and Rives, Cl. *Oiseaux de Tahiti.* Papeete: Les Editions du Pacifique, 1975.

Whistler, W. Arthur. *Coastal Flowers of the Tropical Pacific.* Honolulu: Pacific Tropical Botanical Garden, 1980.

## Histories

Calvert, James. *Fiji and the Fijians: Mission History.* Suva: Fiji Museum, 1985.

Crocombe, Marjorie. *They Came for Sandalwood.* New Zealand: Dept. of Island Territories, 1964.

D'Eaubonne, Françoise. *Louise Michel: La Canaque.* Evreux, France: Encre, 1985.

Eustis, Nelson. *Aggie Grey of Samoa.* Adelaide, Australia: Hobby Investments Ptd. Ltd., 1979.

Firth, Stewart. *New Guinea Under the Germans.* Port Moresby: Web Books, 1986.

Gauguin, Paul. *Intimate Journals.* Translated by Van Wyck Brooks. New York: Liveright, 1921.

Howarth, David. *Tahiti: A Paradise Lost.* New York: Penguin Books, 1985.

Howe, K. R. *Where the Waves Fall.* Sydney: George Allen & Unwin, 1984.

Ledyard, Patricia. *The Tongan Past.* Privately published, 1982.

Manchester, William. *Goodbye, Darkness.* London: Panther Books, 1982.

Martin, John. *Tonga Islands: William Mariner's Account.* Tonga: Vava'u Press, 1981.

Moorehead, Alan. *The Fatal Impact.* New York: Penguin Books, 1968.

Osifelo, Sir Frederick. *Kanaka Boy.* Suva: Institute of Pacific Studies, University of the South Pacific, 1985.

Robson, R. W. *Queen Emma.* Sydney, Australia: Pacific Publications, 1979.

Scarr, Deryck. *Fiji: A Short History.* Provo, Utah: Institute for Polynesian Studies, Brigham Young University, 1984.

Turner, George. *Samoa, A Hundred Years Ago.* Suva: Institute of Pacific Studies, University of the South Pacific, 1984.

Williams, Thomas. *Fiji and the Fijians: The Islands and Their Inhabitants.* Suva: Fiji Museum, 1982.

## Anthropology, Folklore

Community College of Micronesia. *Micronesian Customs and Beliefs.* Compiled and edited by Gene Ashby. Eugene, Oregon: Rainy Day Press, 1985.

Lavondes, Anne. *Traditional Art of Tahiti.* Paris: Société des Océanistes, 1979.

Losche, Diane. *The Abelam: A People of Papua New Guinea.* Sydney, Australia: Australian Museum, 1982.

Mead, Margaret. *Coming of Age in Samoa.* New York: Morrow Quill Paperbacks, 1928.

_____. *Growing Up in New Guinea.* New York: Morrow, 1930.

Oliver, Douglas L. *The Pacific Islands.* Garden City, New York: Doubleday & Company, Inc., Natural History Library, 1961.

Ravuvu, Asesela. *The Fijian Way of Life.* Suva: Institute of Pacific Studies, University of the South Pacific, 1983.

Stokes, Donald S., and Wilson, Barbara Ker. *The Turtle and the Island: Folk Tales from Papua New Guinea.* Lone Cove, NSW, Australia: Hodder and Stoughton, 1978.

Thompson, Judi, and Taylor, Alan. *Polynesian Canoes and Navigation.* Provo, Utah: Institute for Polynesian Studies, Brigham Young University, 1980.

Wright, Glen. *Salamasina, Queen of Love.* Honolulu: Conch Press.

## Language

Mihalic, Father F., SVD. *Introduction to New Guinea Pidgin.* Milton, Qld, Australia: Jacaranda Press, 1969.

Schultz, Dr. E. *Samoan Proverbial Expressions.* Auckland: Polynesian Press, in association with the Institute of Pacific Studies, University of the South Pacific, 1980.

Schutz, A. J. *Say It in Fijian.* Sydney: Pacific Publications, 1979.

Tryon, Darrell. *Evri samting yu wantem save long Bislama be yu fraet tumas blong askem.* Media Masters Publications.

## Memoirs, Observations

Brower, Kenneth. *A Song for Satawal.* New York: Penguin Books, 1984.

Calkins, Fay G. *My Samoan Chief.* Honolulu: University of Hawaii Press, 1971.

Cross, Gwen. *Aloha Solomons.* Suva: University of the South Pacific.

Dodwell, Christina. *In Papua New Guinea.* Oxford Illustrated Press, 1983.

Ledyard, Patricia. *Friendly Isles: A Tale of Tonga.* Tonga: Vava'u Press, 1974.

Nakano, Ann. *Broken Canoe.* St. Lucia, Qld, Australia: University of Queensland Press, 1983.

## Guides

Ashby, Gene. *A Guide to Ponape.* Eugene, Oregon: Rainy Day Press, 1983.

Gravelle, Kim. *The Fiji Explorer's Handbook.* Suva: Graphics (Pacific) Limited, 1985.

Kay, Robert F. *Tahiti and French Polynesia.* Berkeley: Lonely Planet Publications, 1985.

Lightbody, Mark and Wheeler, Tony. *Papua New Guinea.* Berkeley: Lonely Planet Publications, 1985.

Nolan, Riall W. *Bushwalking in Papua New Guinea.* Berkeley: Lonely Planet Publications, 1983.

Roucheux, Nicole. *Practical Guide to the South Pacific.* Papeete: Nicole Roucheux.

Stanley, David. *Finding Fiji.* Chico, CA: Moon Publications, 1985.

_____. *Micronesia Handbook.* Chico, CA: Moon Publications, 1985.

_____. *South Pacific Handbook.* Chico, CA: Moon Publications, 1986.

## Politics, General Reference

The American University. *Oceania: A Regional Study.* Washington, D.C.: U.S. Government Printing Office, 1985.

Crocombe, Ron. *The South Pacific.* Auckland, New Zealand: Longman Paul, 1983.

Institute of Pacific Studies. *Foreign Forces in Pacific Politics.* Suva: University of the South Pacific, 1983.

_____. *Politics in Melanesia.* Suva: University of the South Pacific, 1982.

# INDEX